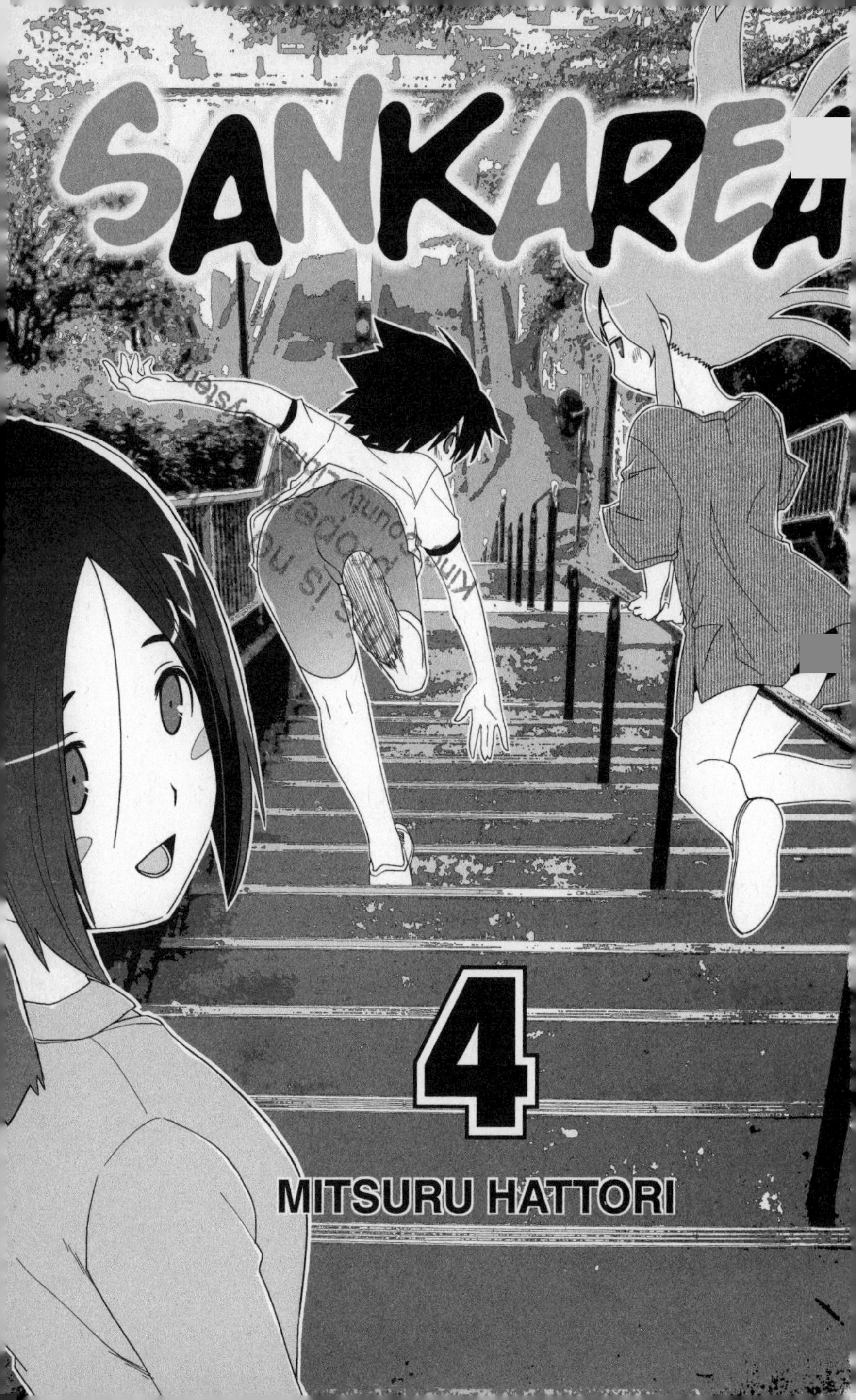
SANKAREA
4
MITSURU HATTORI

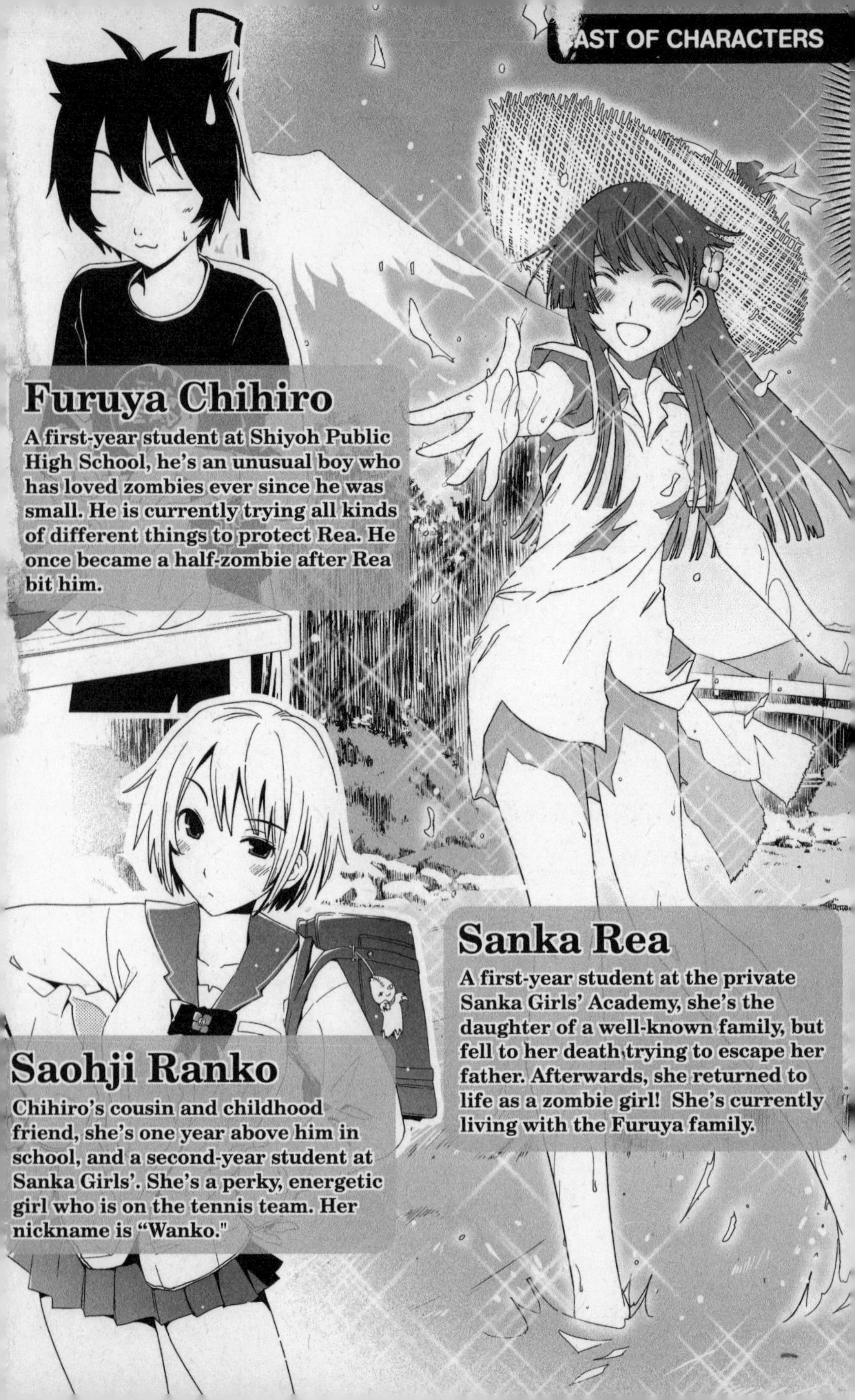

AST OF CHARACTERS

Furuya Chihiro

A first-year student at Shiyoh Public High School, he's an unusual boy who has loved zombies ever since he was small. He is currently trying all kinds of different things to protect Rea. He once became a half-zombie after Rea bit him.

Sanka Rea

A first-year student at the private Sanka Girls' Academy, she's the daughter of a well-known family, but fell to her death trying to escape her father. Afterwards, she returned to life as a zombie girl! She's currently living with the Furuya family.

Saohji Ranko

Chihiro's cousin and childhood friend, she's one year above him in school, and a second-year student at Sanka Girls'. She's a perky, energetic girl who is on the tennis team. Her nickname is "Wanko."

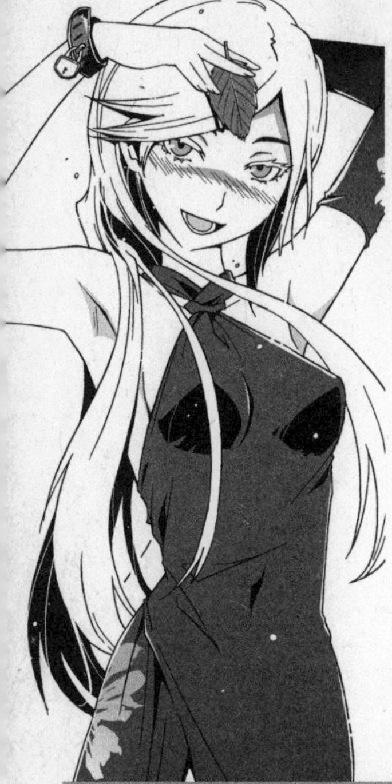

Kurumiya Darin Arciento

An expert in zombie research who came to Japan from the southern islands to visit "Professor Boyle" (Grandpa). She has a strange passion for her research. Despite her looks, she's younger than Rea.

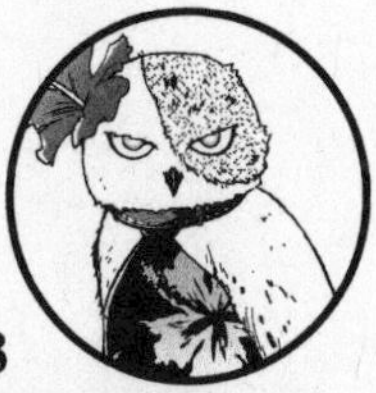

18

Darin's faithful pet. It's been zombified.

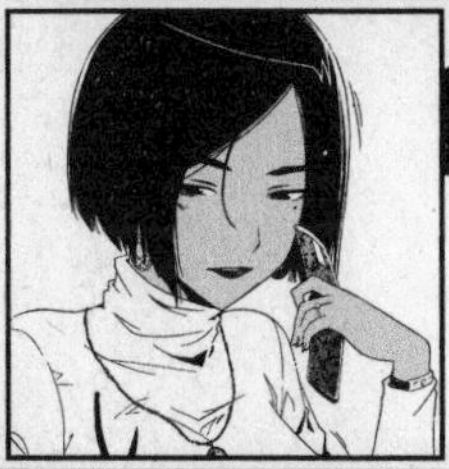

Sanka Aria

Rea's mother, indifferent to her daughter. She's also the director of the private Sanka Girls' Academy.

STORY

Rea's finally grown used to a life as a "normal girl." With Chihiro and Ranko's relationship bothering her just a little bit, Rea was enjoying her school life until a strange foreign girl named Darin began observing her as a "specimen." Rea grew friendly with Darin, who then told her, "Eventually, when they enter the 'turbid period,' zombies lose their reason and begin to eat what they love."

THE FURUYA FAMILY

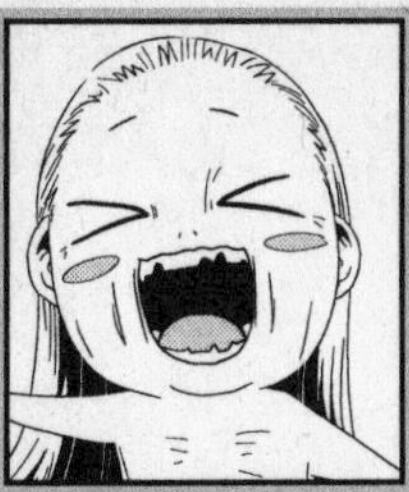

Grandpa

The most mysterious organism (?) of all in "Sankarea." Apparently he has studied zombies at an overseas research facility in the past...

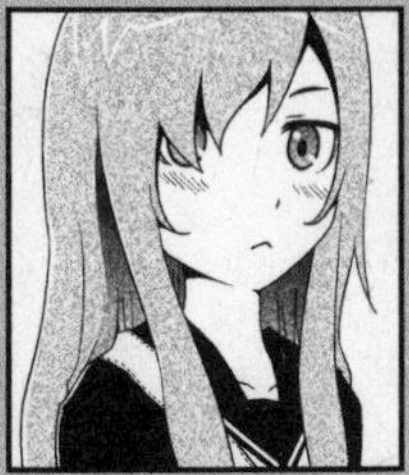

Furuya Mero

A calm and collected first-year middle school student, she presides over the chores in the mostly male Furuya household. A real Japanese-style girl, she reads the Heart Sutra for fun and is able to wear both traditional cook's clothing and the white robes of the dead in a stylish manner.

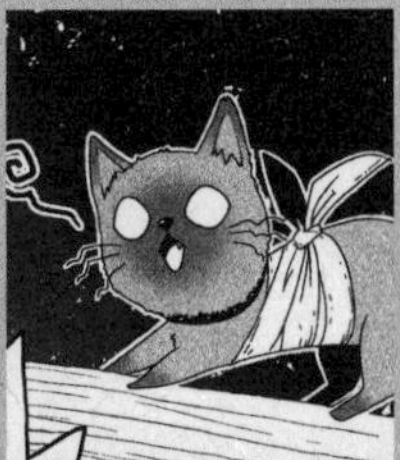

Bub

He was hit by a car and died, but came back to life thanks to the elixir Chihiro and Rea made.

MITSURU HATTORI presents

I THINK I... MIGHT WANT TO TRY EATING SOMETHING OTHER THAN HYDRANGEA SOON.

CONTENTS

SANKAREA
ANECDOTES

PAGE 90

SERIALIZED IN BESSATSU
SHONEN MAGAZINE,
MARCH-MAY, JULY AND
AUGUST 2011, AND IN
WEEKLY SHONEN
MAGAZINE ISSUE
15, 2011.

SANKAREA 4

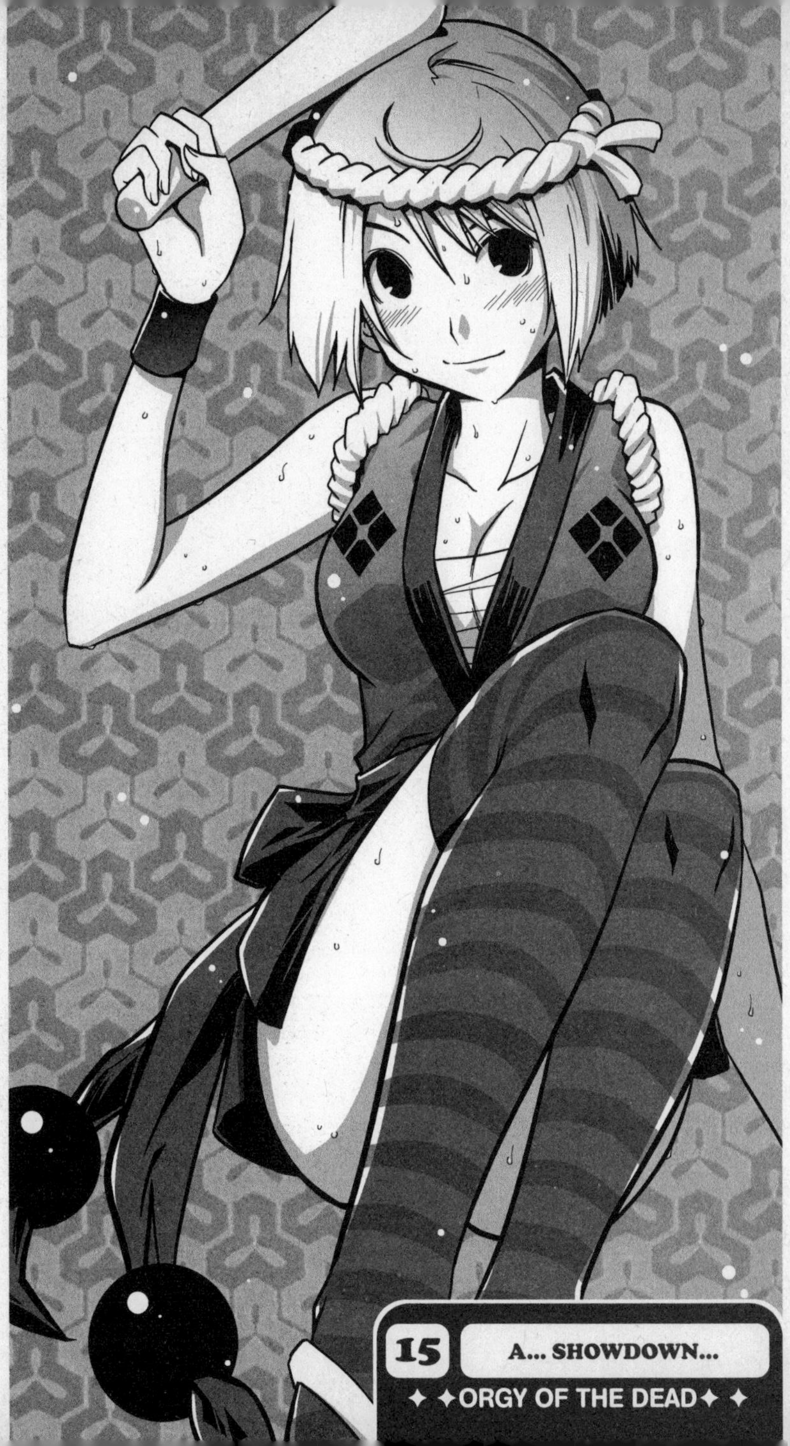
15
A... SHOWDOWN...
ORGY OF THE DEAD

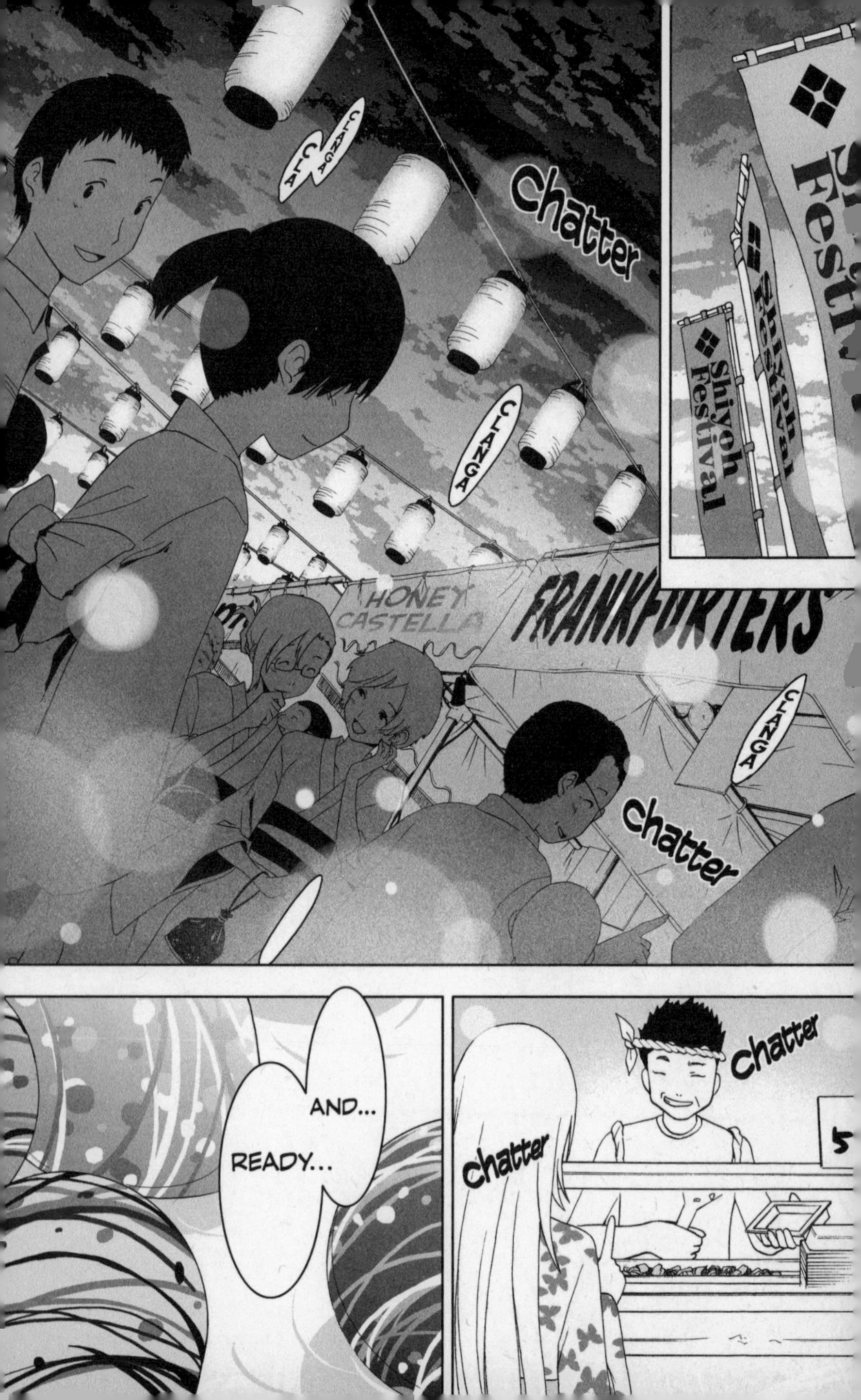
Shiyoh Festival
Shiyoh Festival
CLANGA CLA
Chatter
CLANGA
HONEY CASTELLA
FRANKFURTERS
CLANGA
chatter
chatter
chatter
5
AND...
READY...

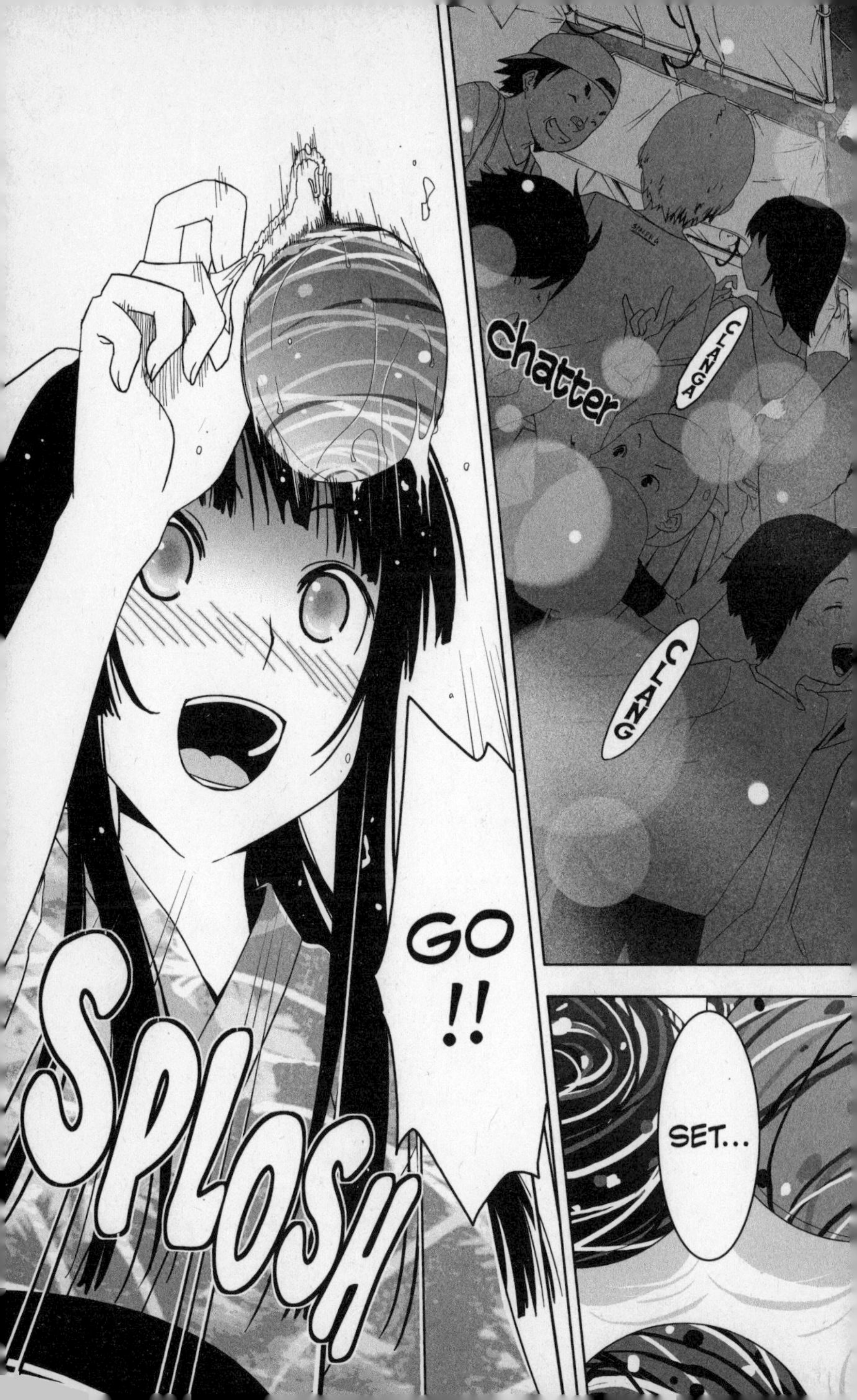
CLANGA
Chatter
CLANG
SET...
GO!!
SPLOSH

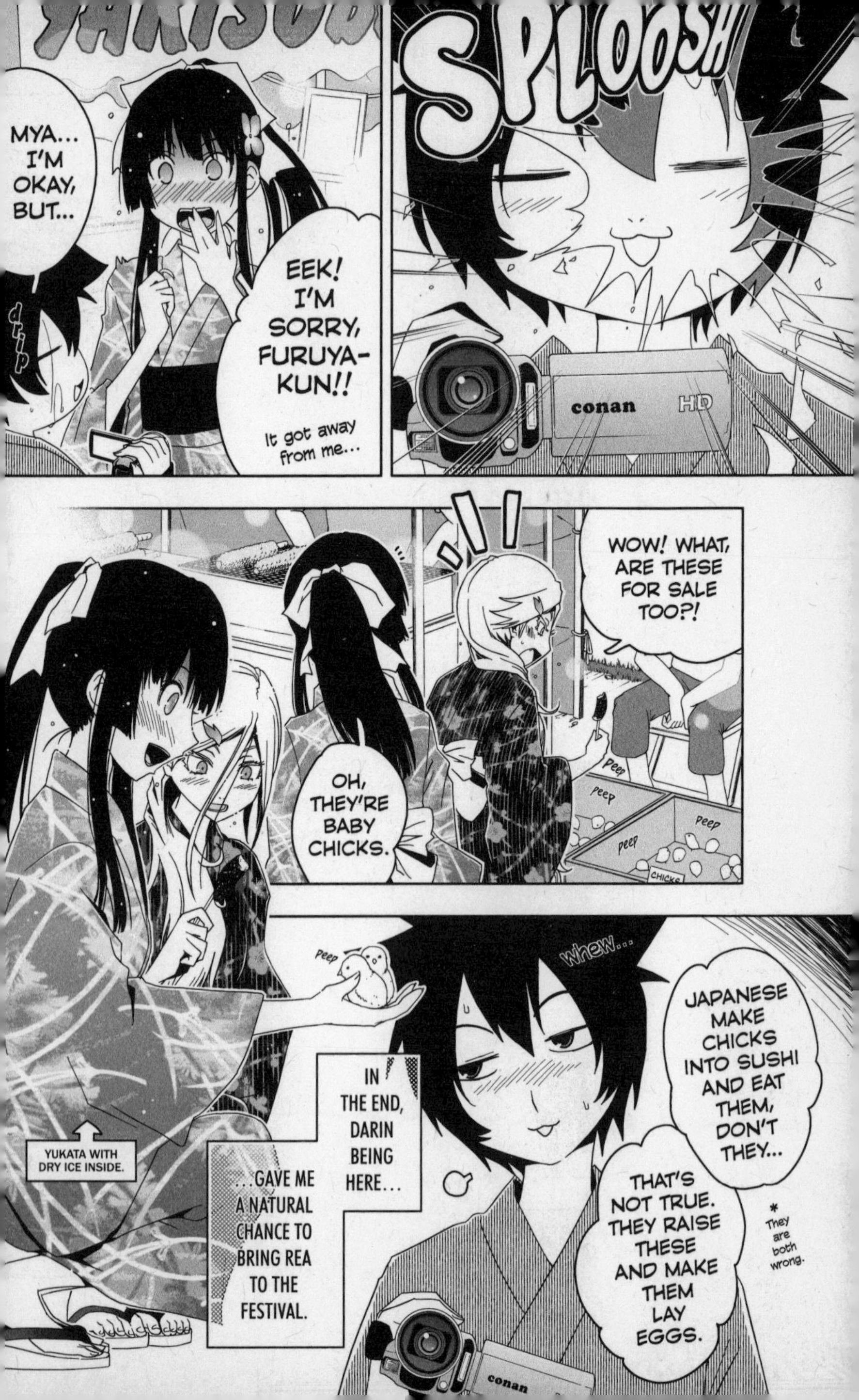
SPLOOSH
conan HD
EEK! I'M SORRY, FURUYA-KUN!!
It got away from me...
MYA... I'M OKAY, BUT...
drip
WOW! WHAT, ARE THESE FOR SALE TOO?!
peep
peep
peep
peep
CHICKS
OH, THEY'RE BABY CHICKS.
whew...
JAPANESE MAKE CHICKS INTO SUSHI AND EAT THEM, DON'T THEY...
THAT'S NOT TRUE. THEY RAISE THESE AND MAKE THEM LAY EGGS.
* They are both wrong.
IN THE END, DARIN BEING HERE...
...GAVE ME A NATURAL CHANCE TO BRING REA TO THE FESTIVAL.
peep
YUKATA WITH DRY ICE INSIDE.
conan

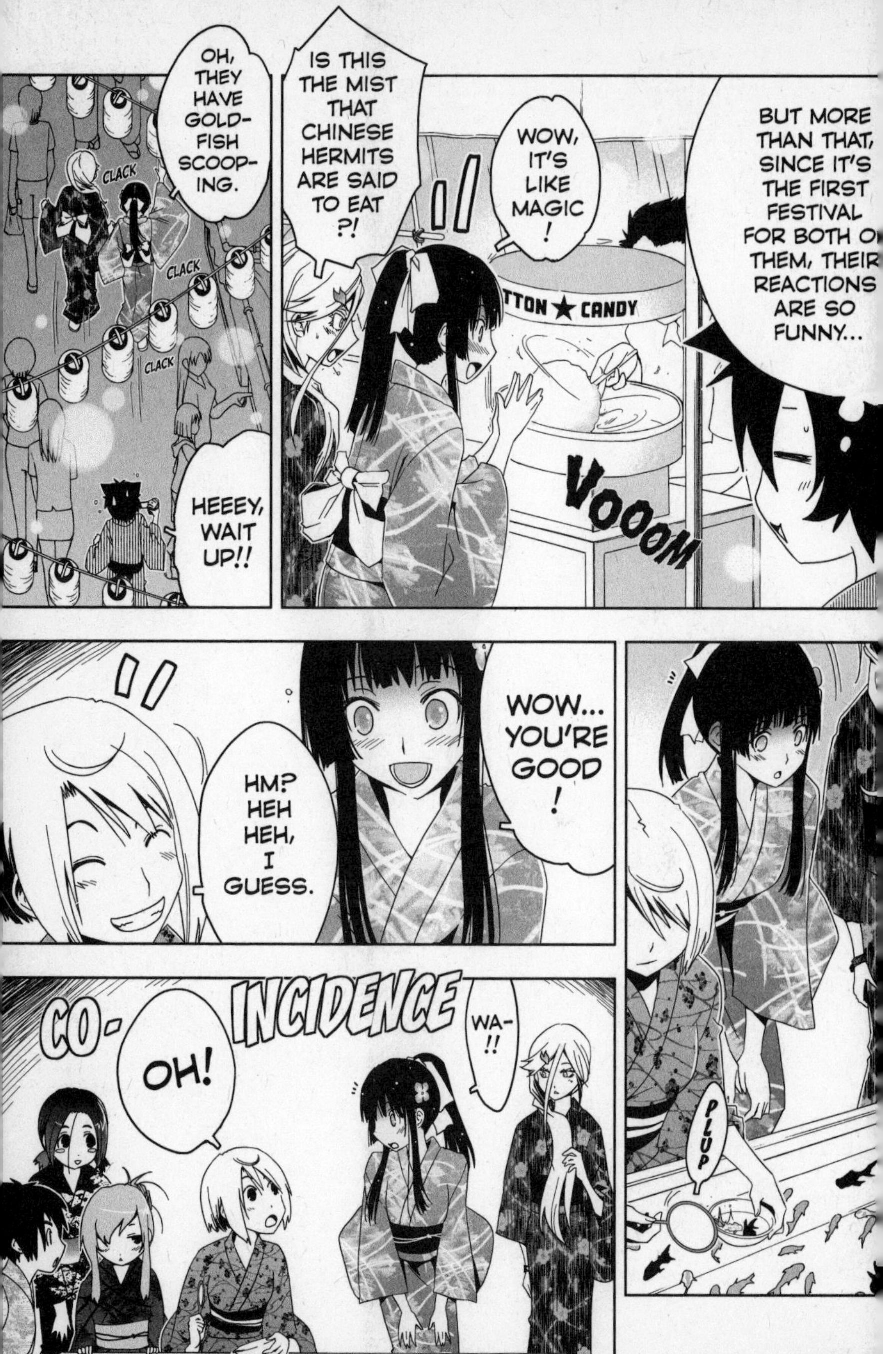
BUT MORE THAN THAT, SINCE IT'S THE FIRST FESTIVAL FOR BOTH O THEM, THEIR REACTIONS ARE SO FUNNY...
WOW, IT'S LIKE MAGIC!
IS THIS THE MIST THAT CHINESE HERMITS ARE SAID TO EAT?!
TTON ★ CANDY
VOOOM
OH, THEY HAVE GOLD-FISH SCOOP-ING.
CLACK
CLACK
CLACK
HEEEY, WAIT UP!!
PLUP
WOW... YOU'RE GOOD!
HM? HEH HEH, I GUESS.
WA-!!
CO-INCIDENCE
OH!

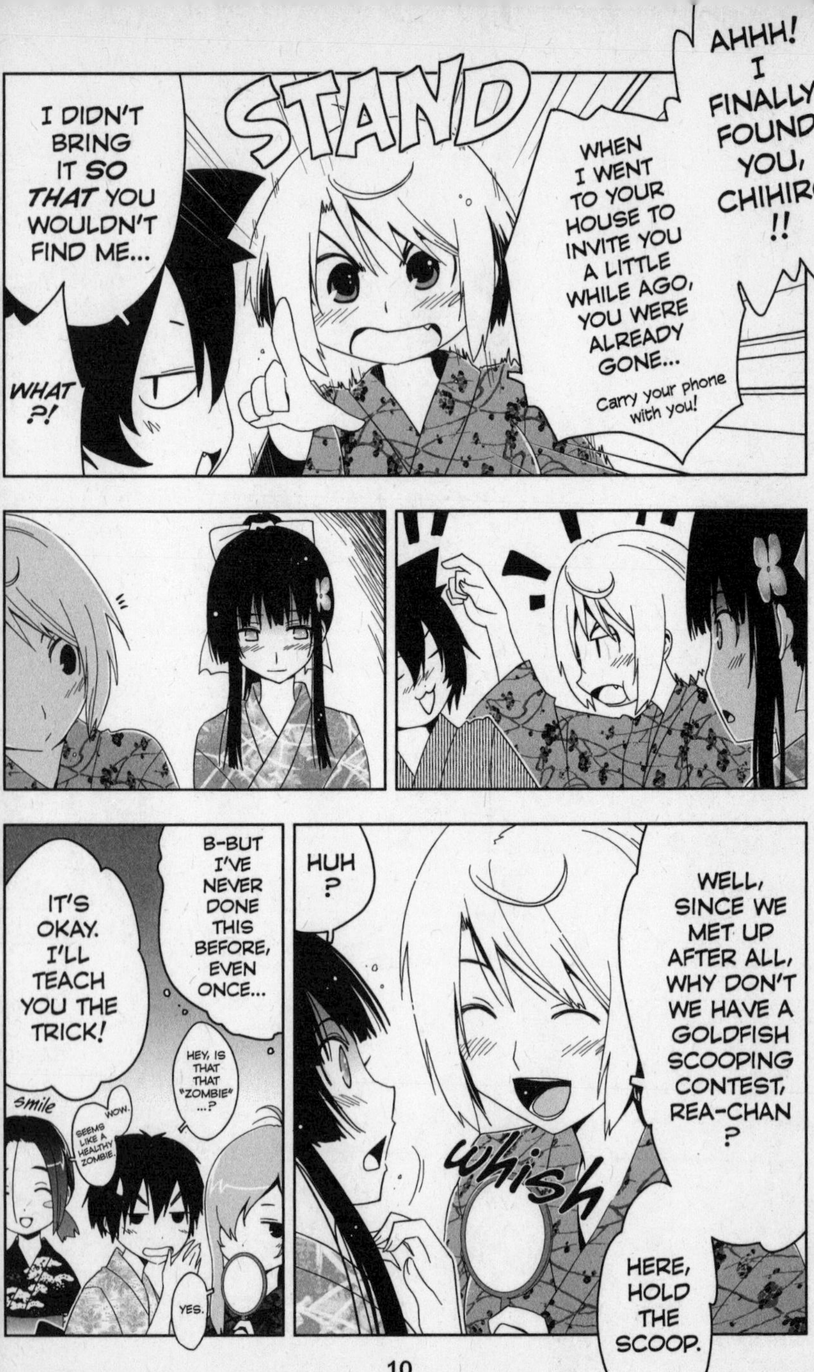
AHHH! I FINALLY FOUND YOU, CHIHIRO!!
STAND
WHEN I WENT TO YOUR HOUSE TO INVITE YOU A LITTLE WHILE AGO, YOU WERE ALREADY GONE...
Carry your phone with you!
I DIDN'T BRING IT SO THAT YOU WOULDN'T FIND ME...
WHAT?!
WELL, SINCE WE MET UP AFTER ALL, WHY DON'T WE HAVE A GOLDFISH SCOOPING CONTEST, REA-CHAN?
HUH?
whish
HERE, HOLD THE SCOOP.
B-BUT I'VE NEVER DONE THIS BEFORE, EVEN ONCE...
IT'S OKAY. I'LL TEACH YOU THE TRICK!
HEY, IS THAT THAT "ZOMBIE"...?
WOW. SEEMS LIKE A HEALTHY ZOMBIE.
smile
YES.

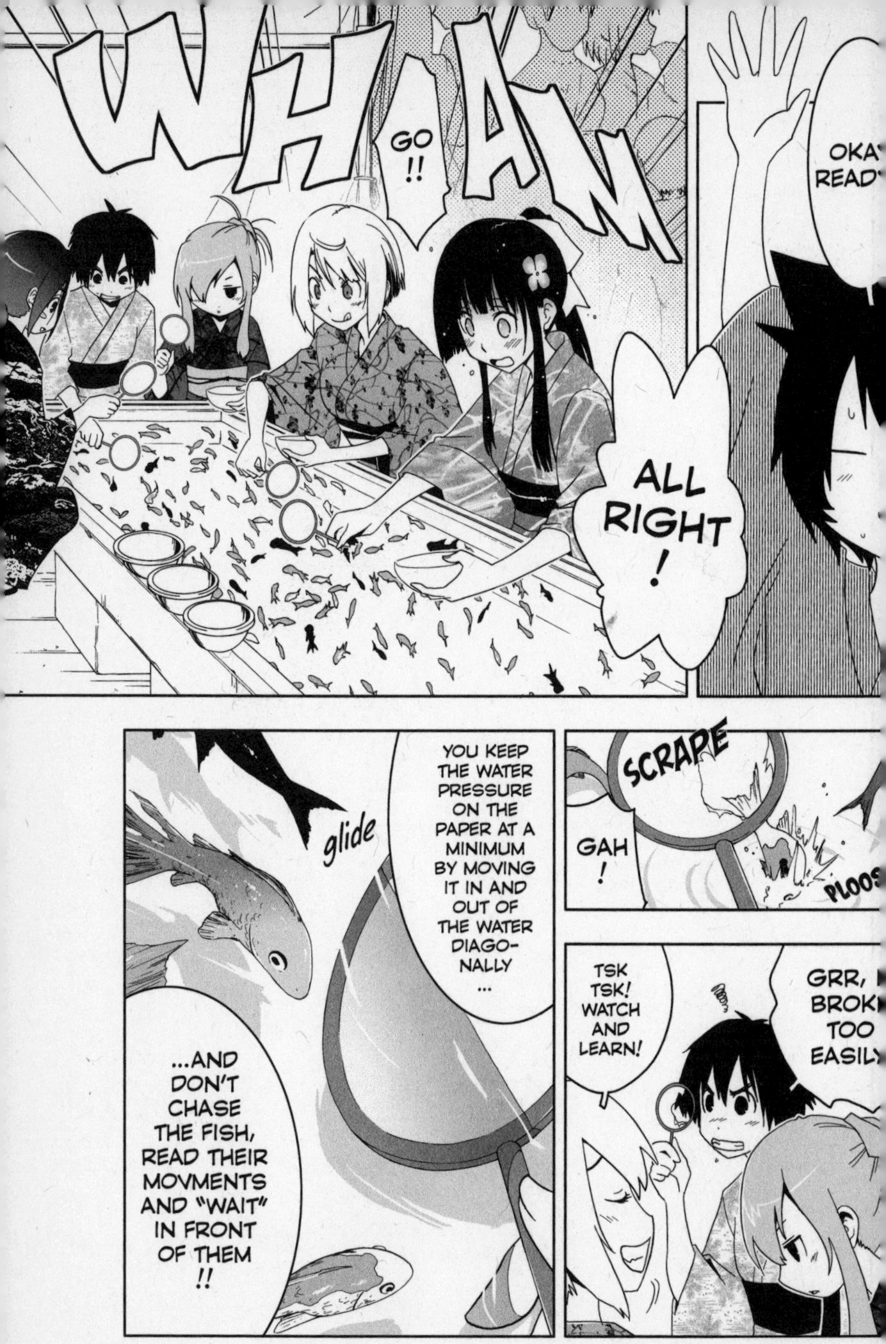
OKA READ
ALL RIGHT!
WHAM
GO!!
SCRAPE
GAH!
PLOOS
GRR, BROK TOO EASIL
TSK TSK! WATCH AND LEARN!
YOU KEEP THE WATER PRESSURE ON THE PAPER AT A MINIMUM BY MOVING IT IN AND OUT OF THE WATER DIAGO-NALLY...
glide
...AND DON'T CHASE THE FISH, READ THEIR MOVMENTS AND "WAIT" IN FRONT OF THEM!!

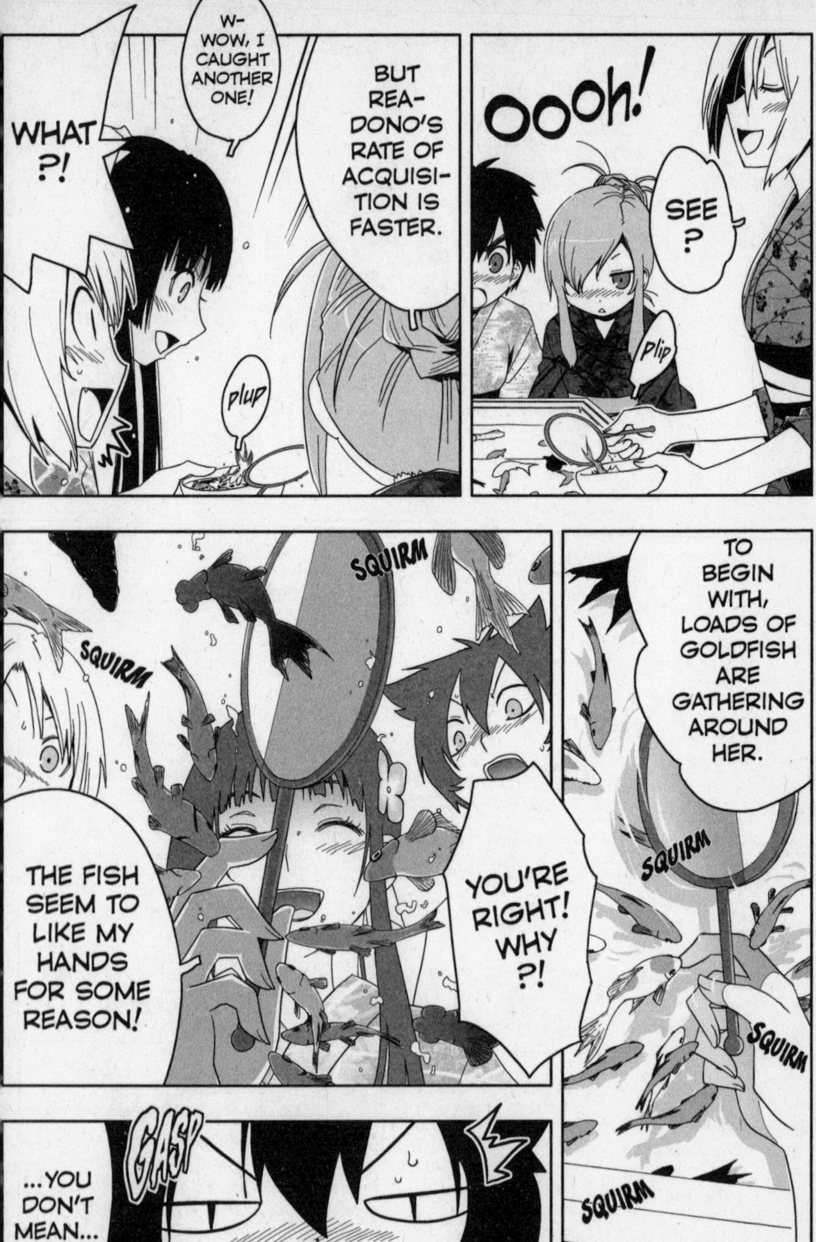

Oooh!
SEE?
plip
BUT REA-DONO'S RATE OF ACQUISITION IS FASTER.
W-WOW, I CAUGHT ANOTHER ONE!
WHAT?!
plup
TO BEGIN WITH, LOADS OF GOLDFISH ARE GATHERING AROUND HER.
SQUIRM
SQUIRM
SQUIRM
SQUIRM
SQUIRM
YOU'RE RIGHT! WHY?!
THE FISH SEEM TO LIKE MY HANDS FOR SOME REASON!
GASP
...YOU DON'T MEAN...

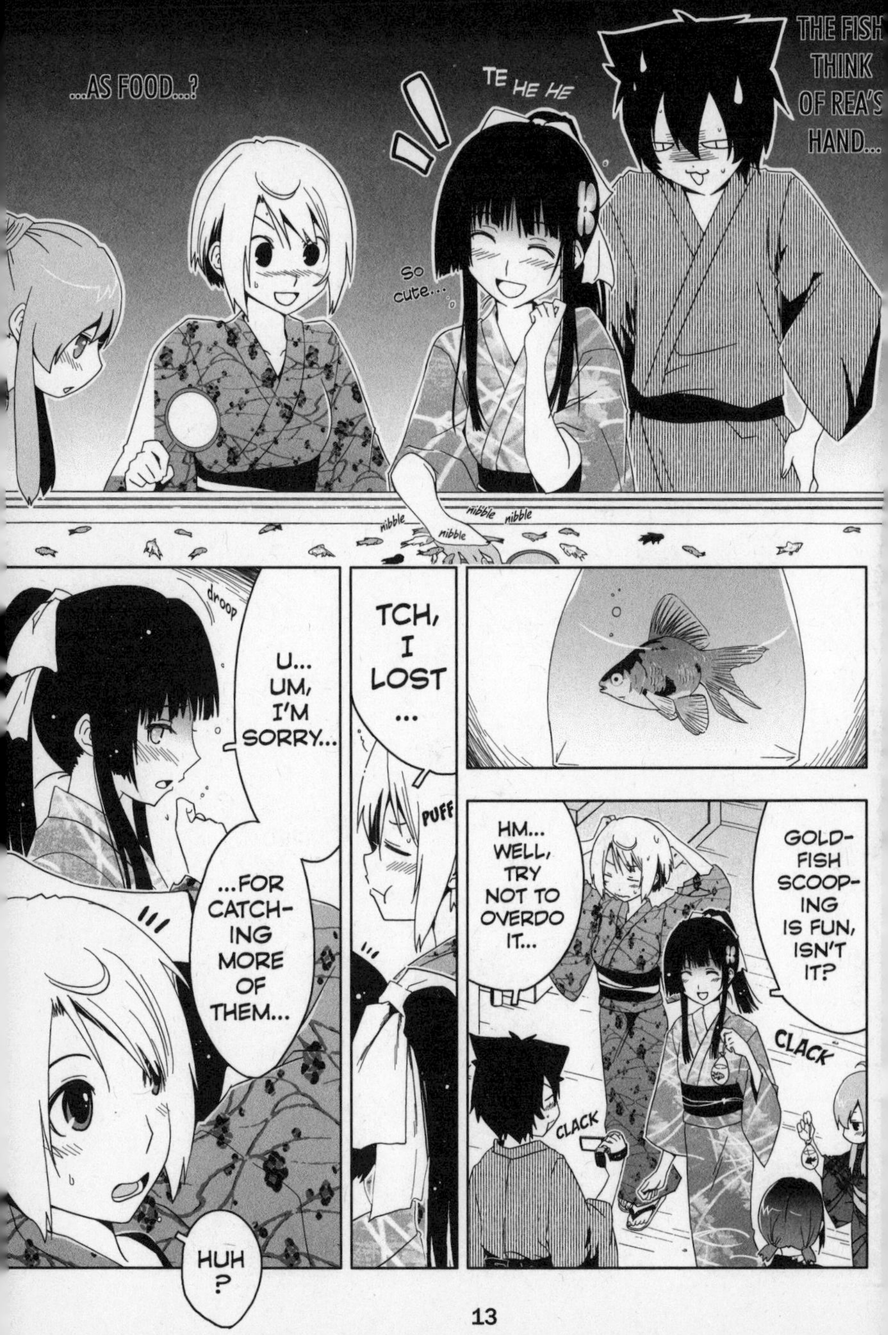
THE FISH THINK OF REA'S HAND...
TE HE HE
!
...AS FOOD...?
So cute...
nibble nibble nibble nibble
GOLD-FISH SCOOP-ING IS FUN, ISN'T IT?
CLACK
HM... WELL, TRY NOT TO OVERDO IT...
CLACK
TCH, I LOST ...
PUFF
droop
U... UM, I'M SORRY...
...FOR CATCH-ING MORE OF THEM...
HUH ?

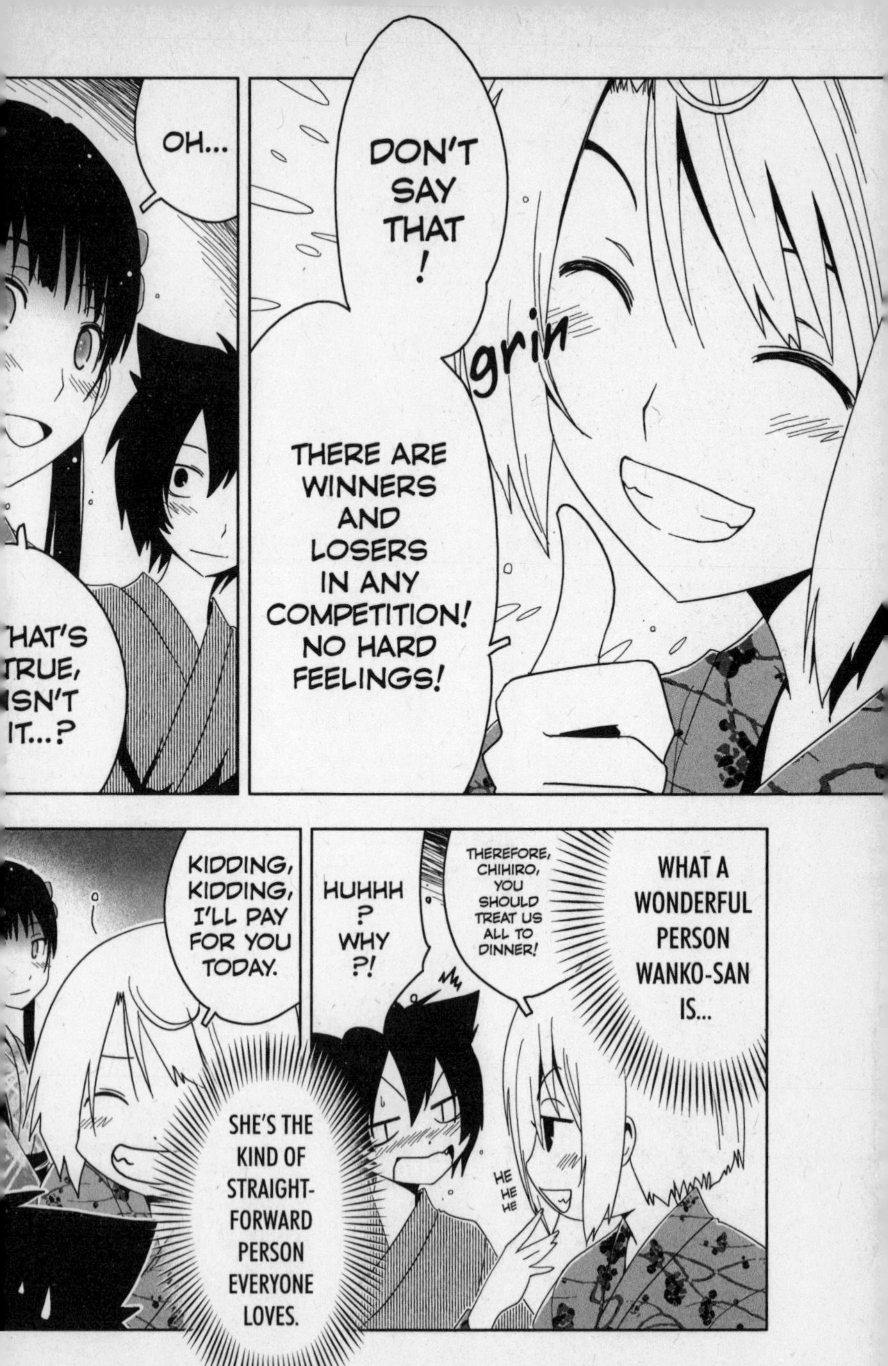
DON'T SAY THAT!
grin
THERE ARE WINNERS AND LOSERS IN ANY COMPETITION! NO HARD FEELINGS!
OH...
THAT'S TRUE, ISN'T IT...?
WHAT A WONDERFUL PERSON WANKO-SAN IS...
THEREFORE, CHIHIRO, YOU SHOULD TREAT US ALL TO DINNER!
HUHHH? WHY?!
HE HE HE
KIDDING, KIDDING, I'LL PAY FOR YOU TODAY.
SHE'S THE KIND OF STRAIGHT-FORWARD PERSON EVERYONE LOVES.

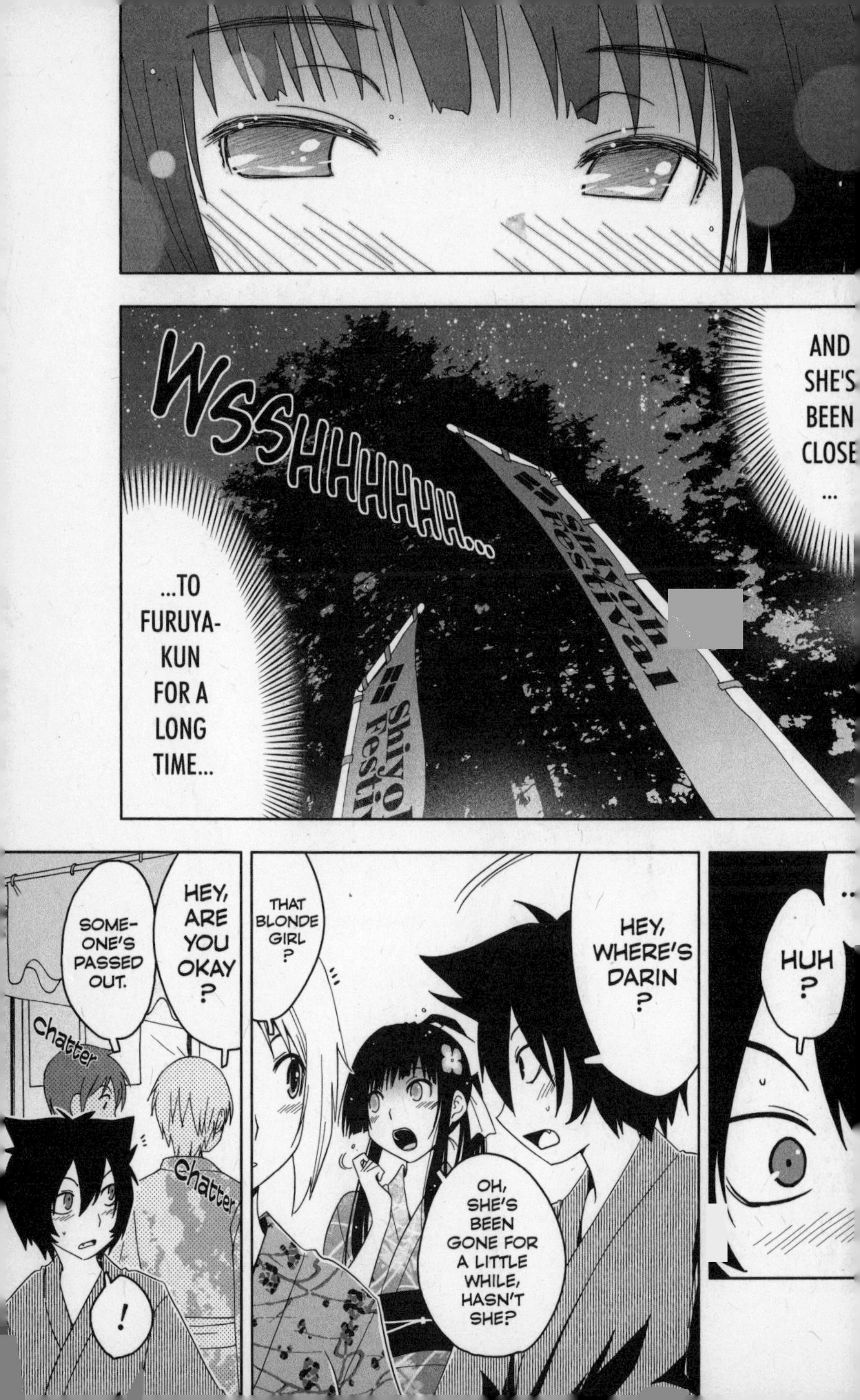
AND SHE'S BEEN CLOSE ...
WSSHHHHHH...
...TO FURUYA-KUN FOR A LONG TIME...
...HUH?
HEY, WHERE'S DARIN?
THAT BLONDE GIRL?
OH, SHE'S BEEN GONE FOR A LITTLE WHILE, HASN'T SHE?
HEY, ARE YOU OKAY?
SOMEONE'S PASSED OUT.
chatter
chatter
!

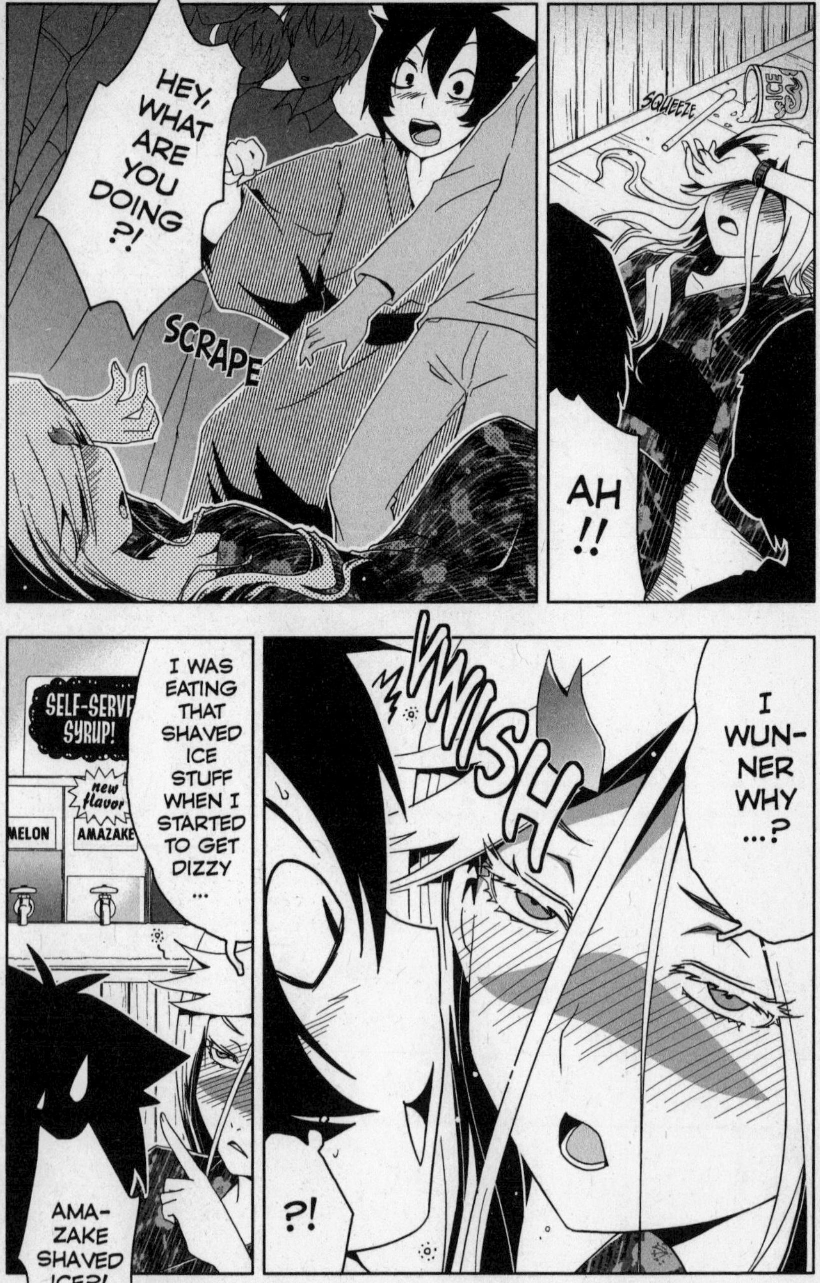
SQUEEZE
ICE
AH!!
HEY, WHAT ARE YOU DOING?!
SCRAPE
WHISH
I WUNNER WHY...?
?!
I WAS EATING THAT SHAVED ICE STUFF WHEN I STARTED TO GET DIZZY...
SELF-SERVE SYRUP!
new flavor
MELON
AMAZAKE
AMA-ZAKE SHAVED ICE?!

*Literally "sweet sake." With almost no alcohol in it, it's very hard to get drunk on this stuff.

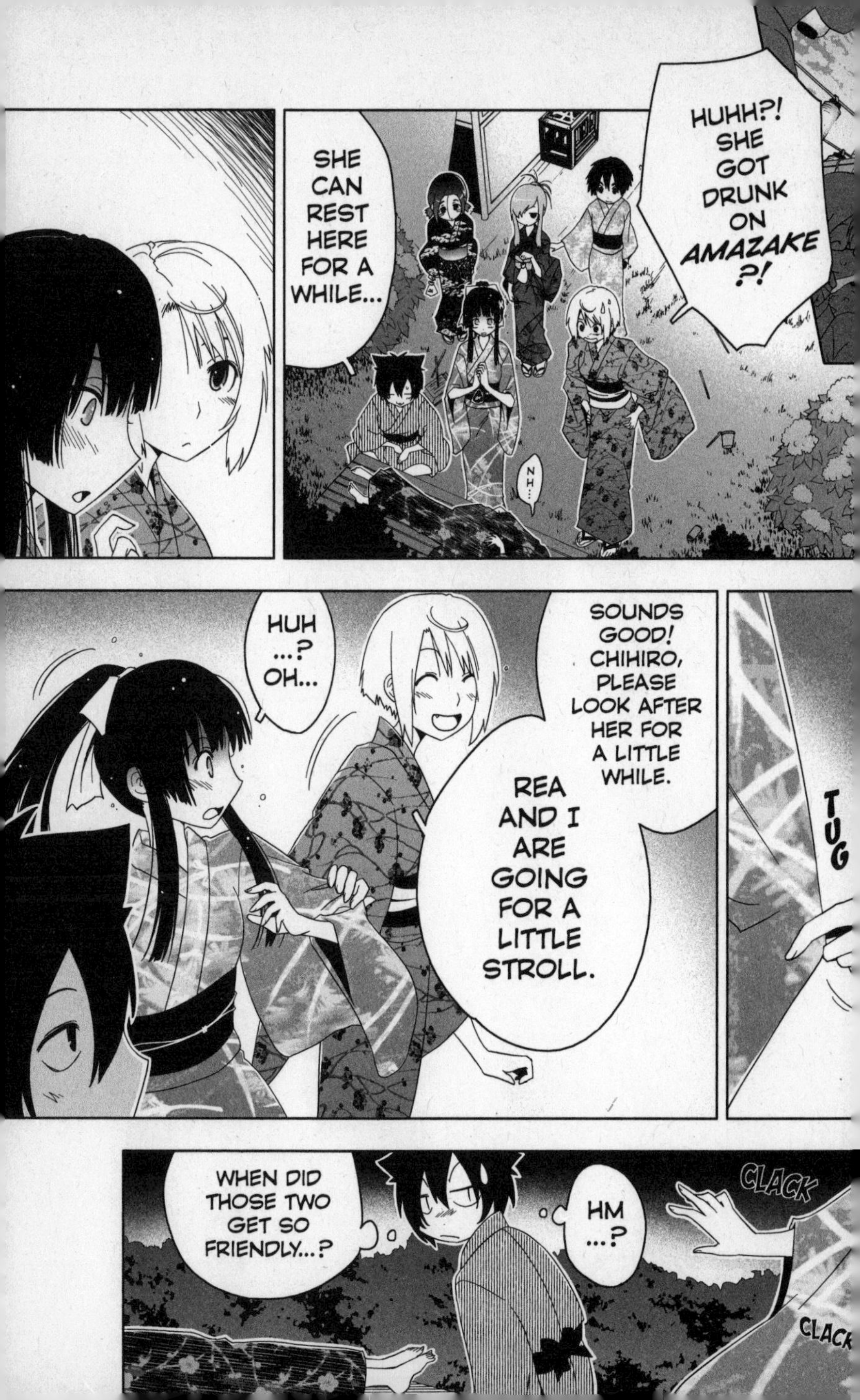
HUHH?! SHE GOT DRUNK ON AMAZAKE?!
SHE CAN REST HERE FOR A WHILE...
NH...
TUG
SOUNDS GOOD! CHIHIRO, PLEASE LOOK AFTER HER FOR A LITTLE WHILE.
REA AND I ARE GOING FOR A LITTLE STROLL.
HUH...? OH...
CLACK
CLACK
HM...?
WHEN DID THOSE TWO GET SO FRIENDLY...?

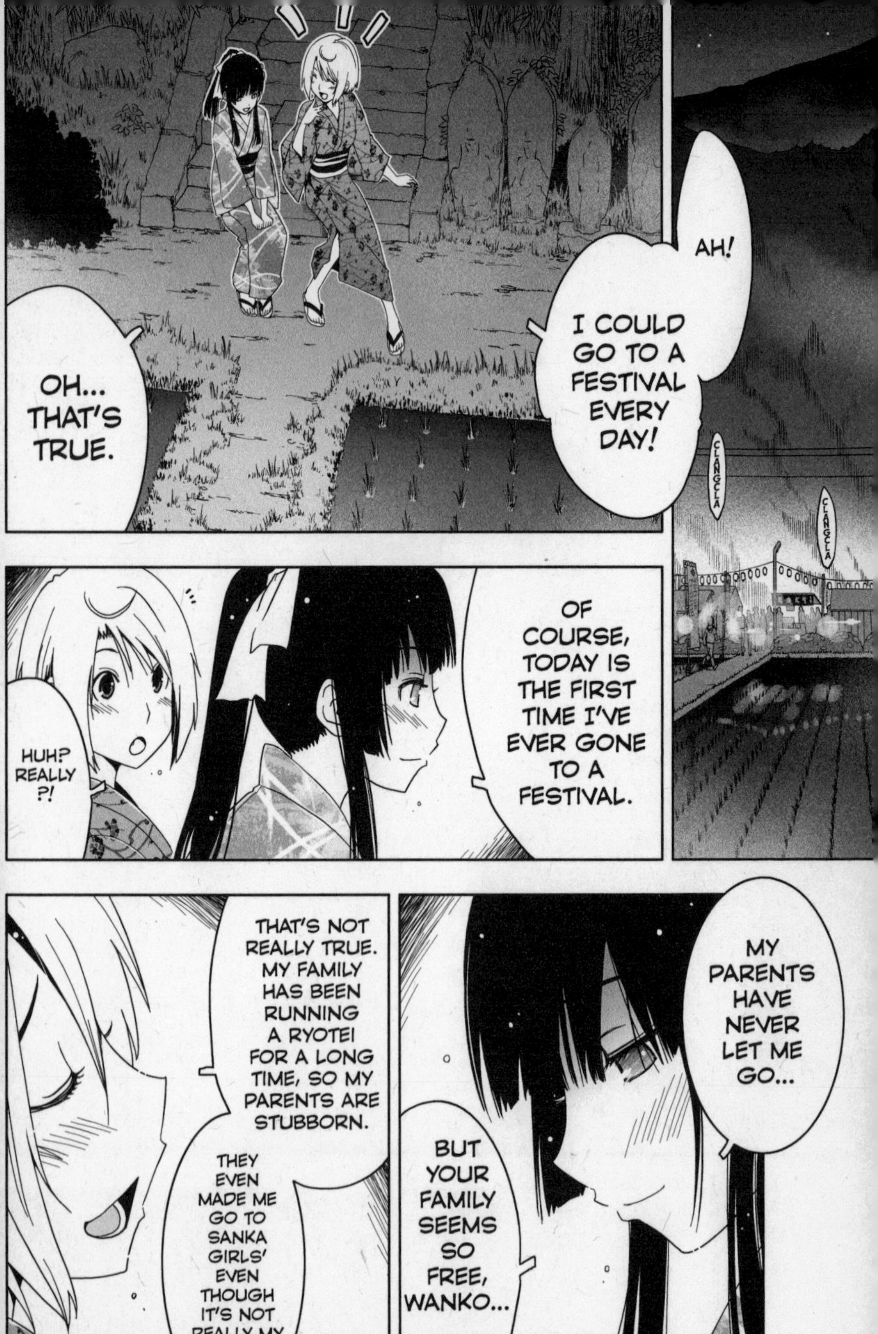
CLANGCLA
CLANGCLA
AH!
I COULD GO TO A FESTIVAL EVERY DAY!
OH... THAT'S TRUE.
OF COURSE, TODAY IS THE FIRST TIME I'VE EVER GONE TO A FESTIVAL.
HUH? REALLY ?!
MY PARENTS HAVE NEVER LET ME GO...
BUT YOUR FAMILY SEEMS SO FREE, WANKO...
THAT'S NOT REALLY TRUE. MY FAMILY HAS BEEN RUNNING A RYOTEI FOR A LONG TIME, SO MY PARENTS ARE STUBBORN.
THEY EVEN MADE ME GO TO SANKA GIRLS' EVEN THOUGH IT'S NOT REALLY MY STYLE.

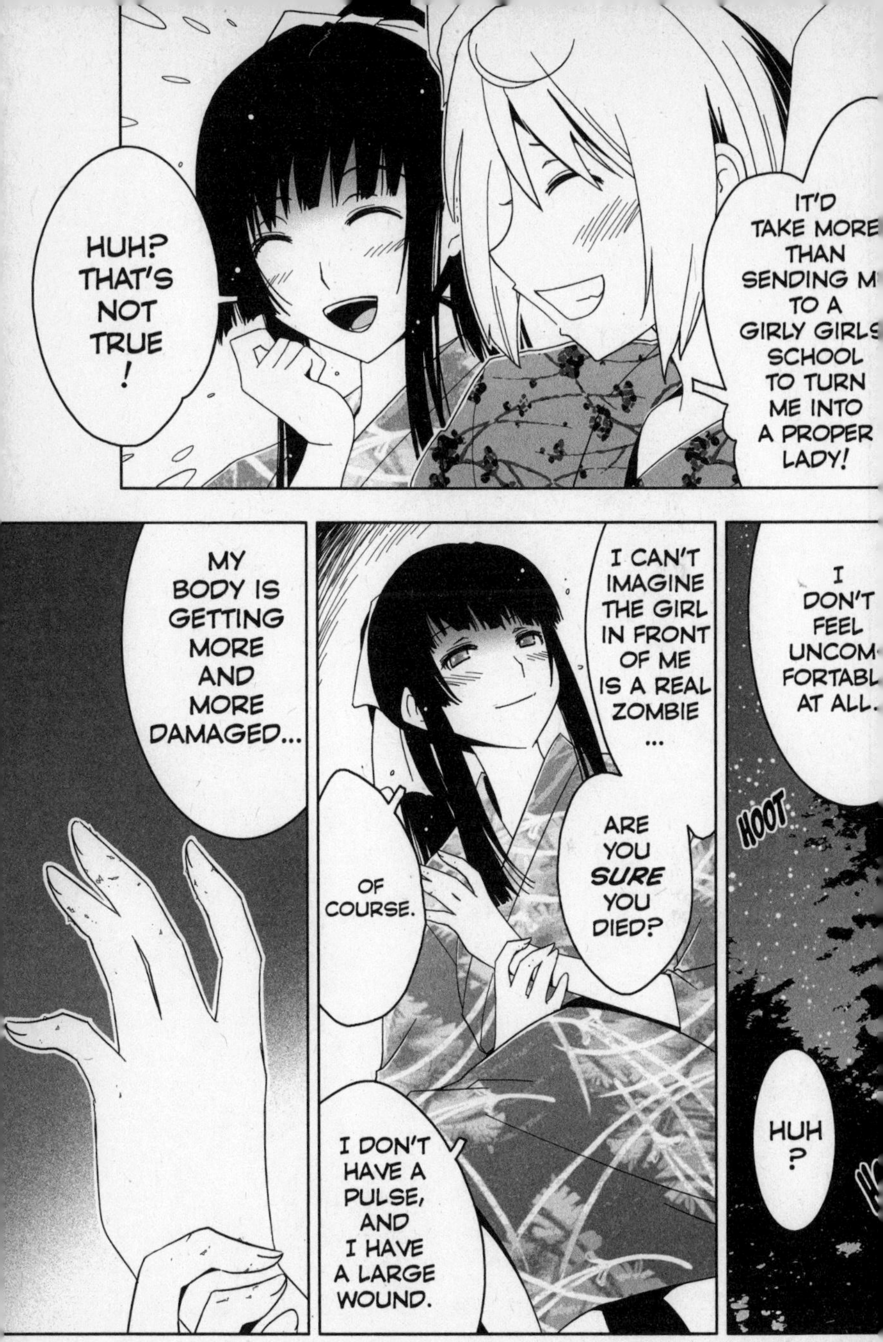
IT'D TAKE MORE THAN SENDING M TO A GIRLY GIRLS SCHOOL TO TURN ME INTO A PROPER LADY!
HUH? THAT'S NOT TRUE!
I DON'T FEEL UNCOM- FORTABL AT ALL...
HOOT
HUH?
I CAN'T IMAGINE THE GIRL IN FRONT OF ME IS A REAL ZOMBIE...
ARE YOU *SURE* YOU DIED?
OF COURSE.
I DON'T HAVE A PULSE, AND I HAVE A LARGE WOUND.
MY BODY IS GETTING MORE AND MORE DAMAGED...

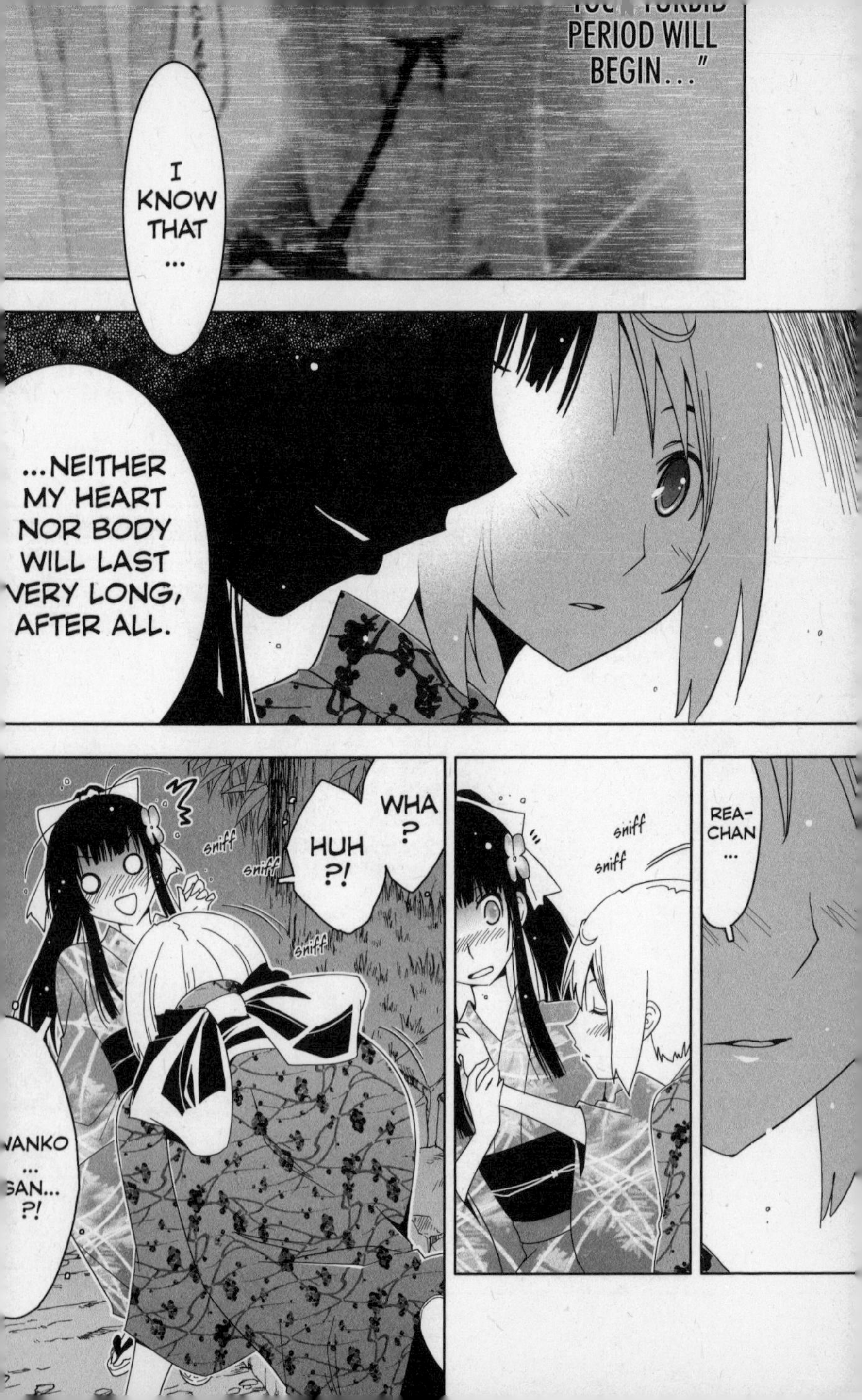
PERIOD WILL BEGIN...”
I KNOW THAT ...
...NEITHER MY HEART NOR BODY WILL LAST VERY LONG, AFTER ALL.
REA-CHAN ...
sniff
sniff
WHA? HUH?!
sniff
sniff
sniff
WANKO ... SAN... ?!

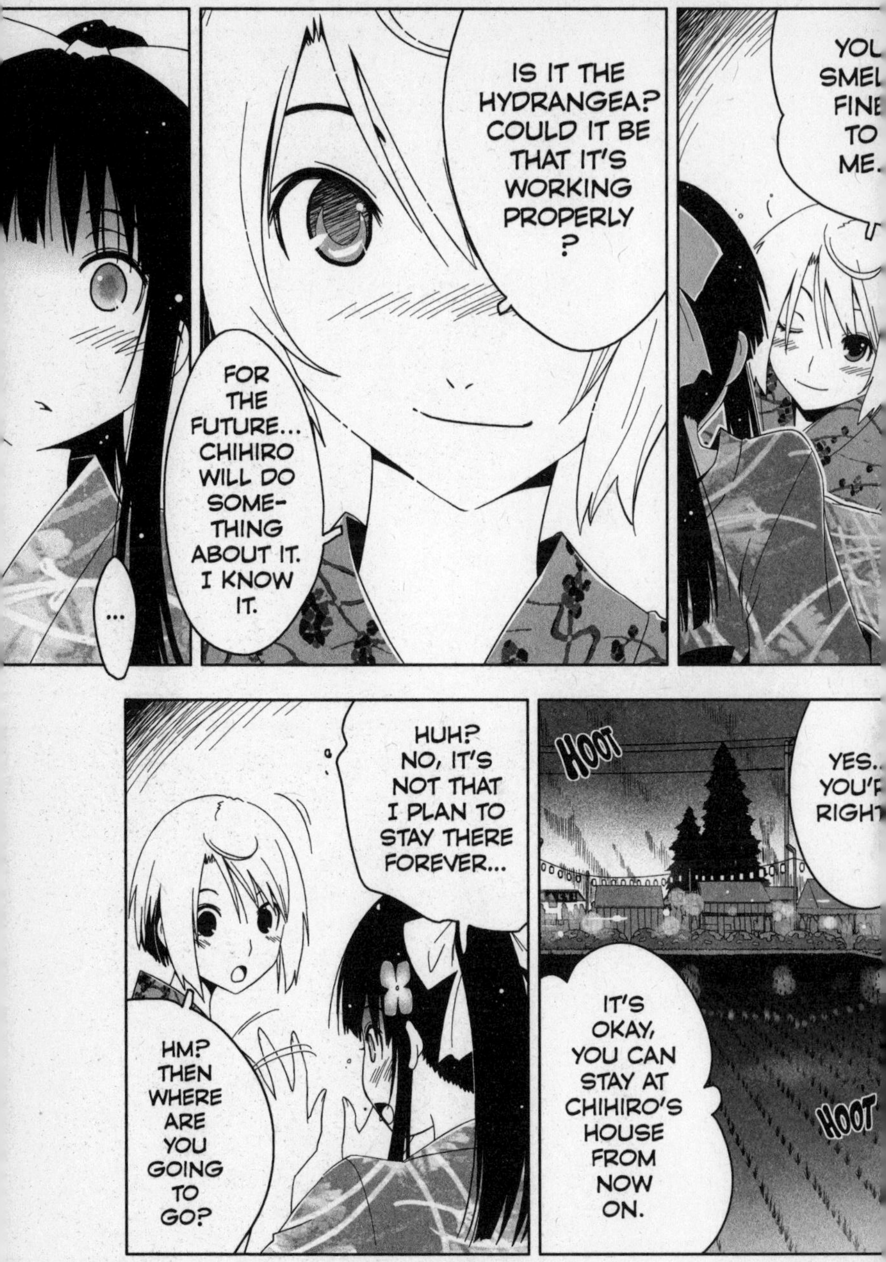
YOU SMEL FINE TO ME.
IS IT THE HYDRANGEA? COULD IT BE THAT IT'S WORKING PROPERLY?
FOR THE FUTURE... CHIHIRO WILL DO SOME-THING ABOUT IT. I KNOW IT.
...
YES... YOU'R RIGHT
HOOT
IT'S OKAY, YOU CAN STAY AT CHIHIRO'S HOUSE FROM NOW ON.
HOOT
HUH? NO, IT'S NOT THAT I PLAN TO STAY THERE FOREVER...
HM? THEN WHERE ARE YOU GOING TO GO?

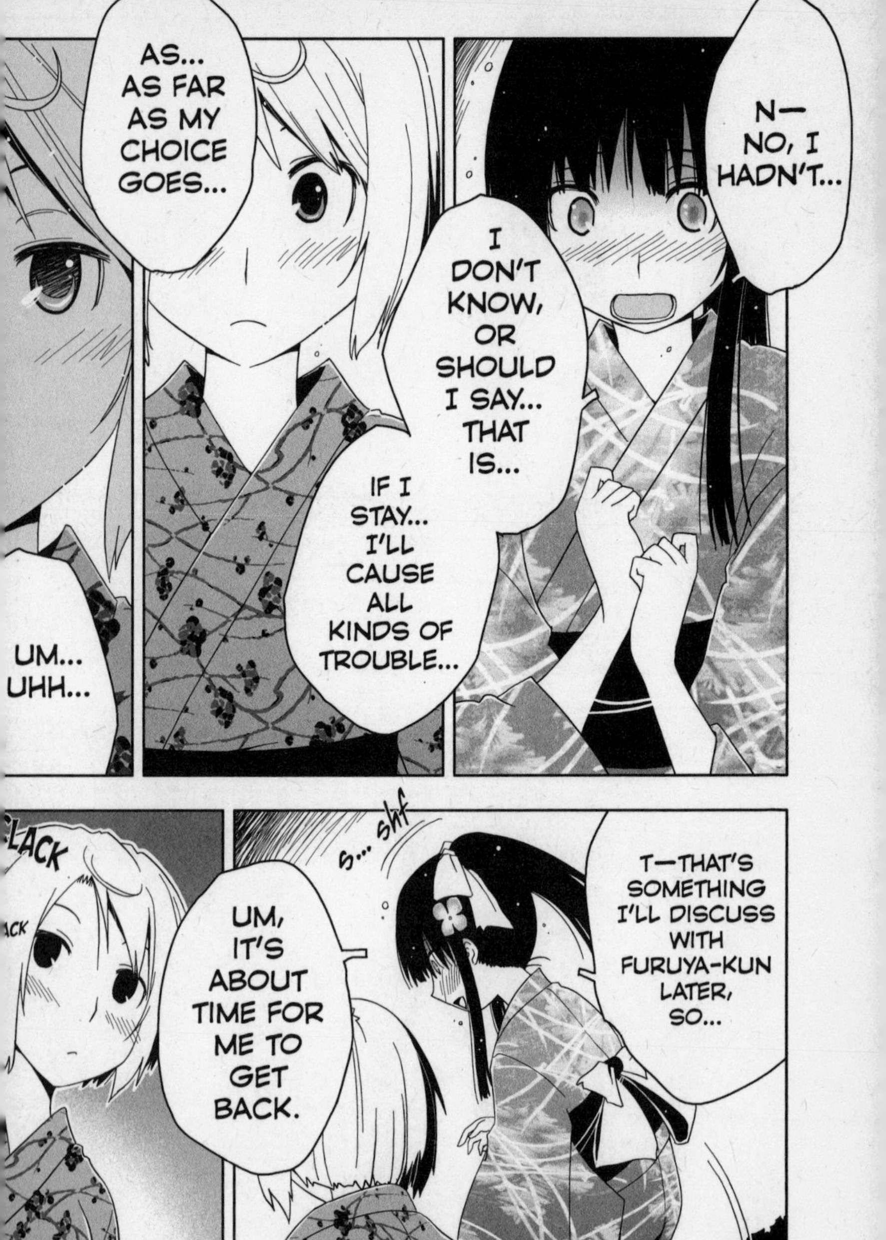
N— NO, I HADN'T...
I DON'T KNOW, OR SHOULD I SAY... THAT IS...
IF I STAY... I'LL CAUSE ALL KINDS OF TROUBLE...
AS... AS FAR AS MY CHOICE GOES...
UM... UHH...
S... SHF
T—THAT'S SOMETHING I'LL DISCUSS WITH FURUYA-KUN LATER, SO...
UM, IT'S ABOUT TIME FOR ME TO GET BACK.

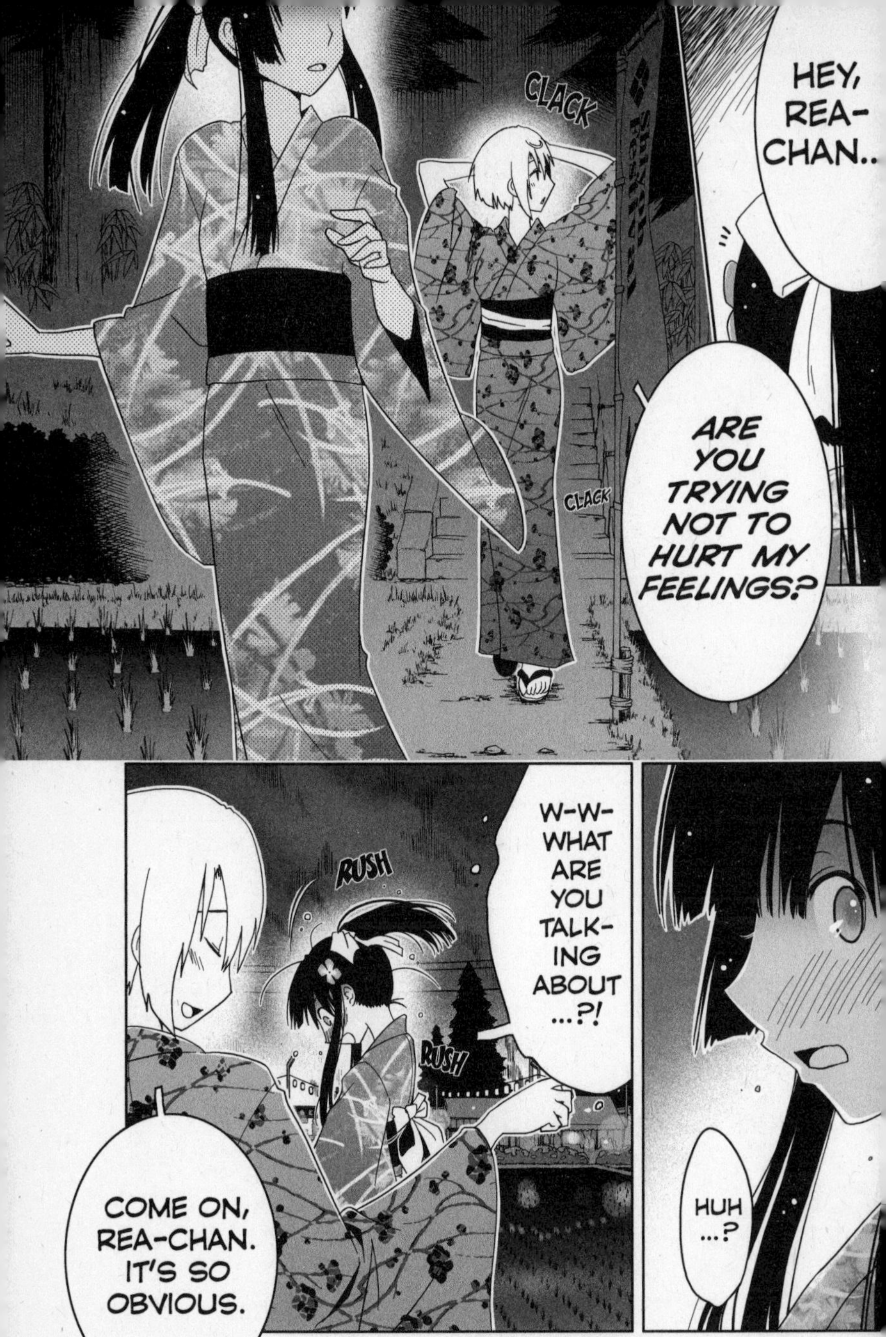
HEY, REA-CHAN..
ARE YOU TRYING NOT TO HURT MY FEELINGS?
CLACK
CLACK
HUH ...?
W-W-WHAT ARE YOU TALKING ABOUT ...?!
RUSH
RUSH
COME ON, REA-CHAN. IT'S SO OBVIOUS.

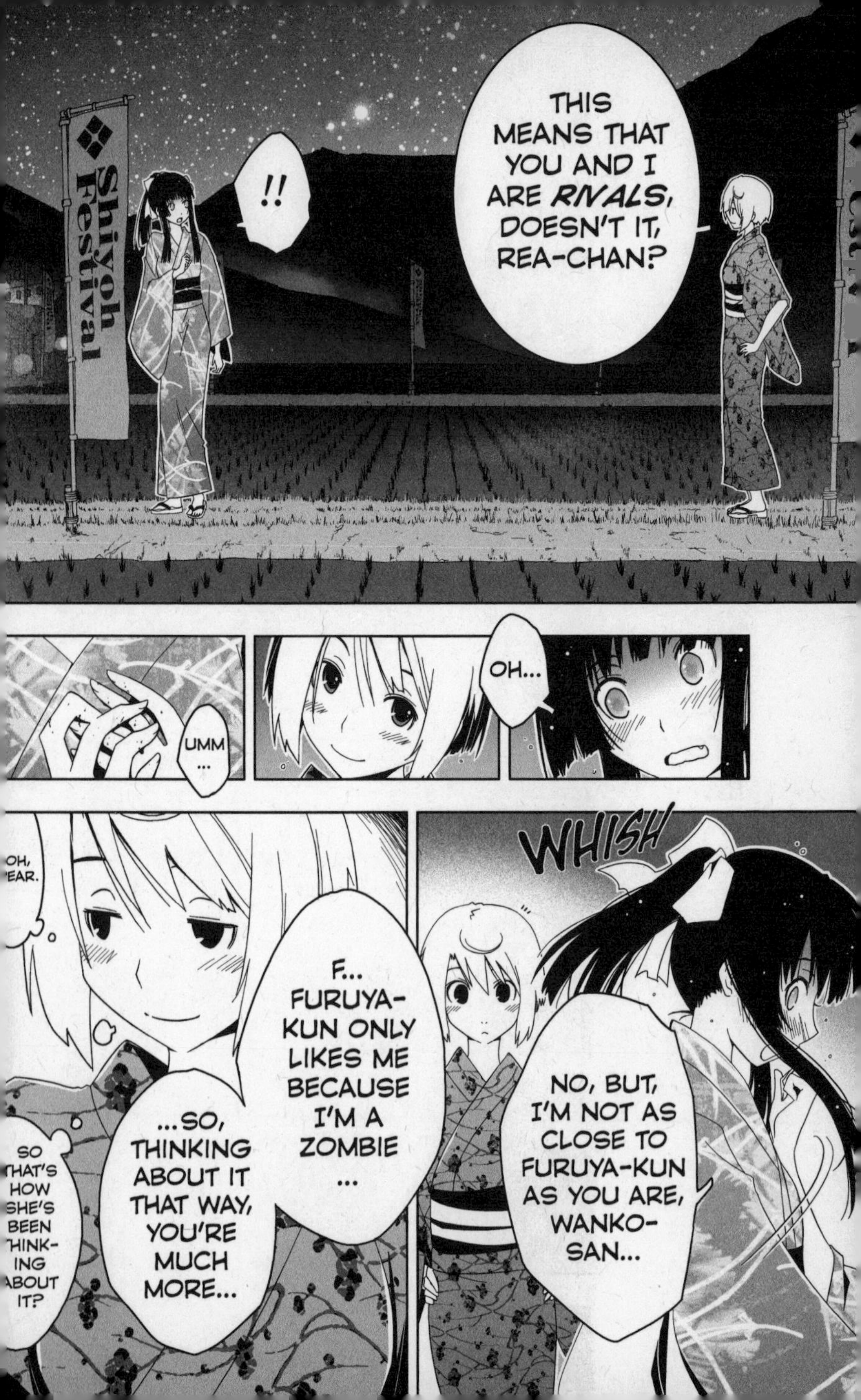
Shiyoh Festival
THIS MEANS THAT YOU AND I ARE *RIVALS*, DOESN'T IT, REA-CHAN?
!!
OH...
UMM ...
WHISH
NO, BUT, I'M NOT AS CLOSE TO FURUYA-KUN AS YOU ARE, WANKO-SAN...
F... FURUYA-KUN ONLY LIKES ME BECAUSE I'M A ZOMBIE ...
...SO, THINKING ABOUT IT THAT WAY, YOU'RE MUCH MORE...
OH, DEAR.
SO THAT'S HOW SHE'S BEEN THINK-ING ABOUT IT?

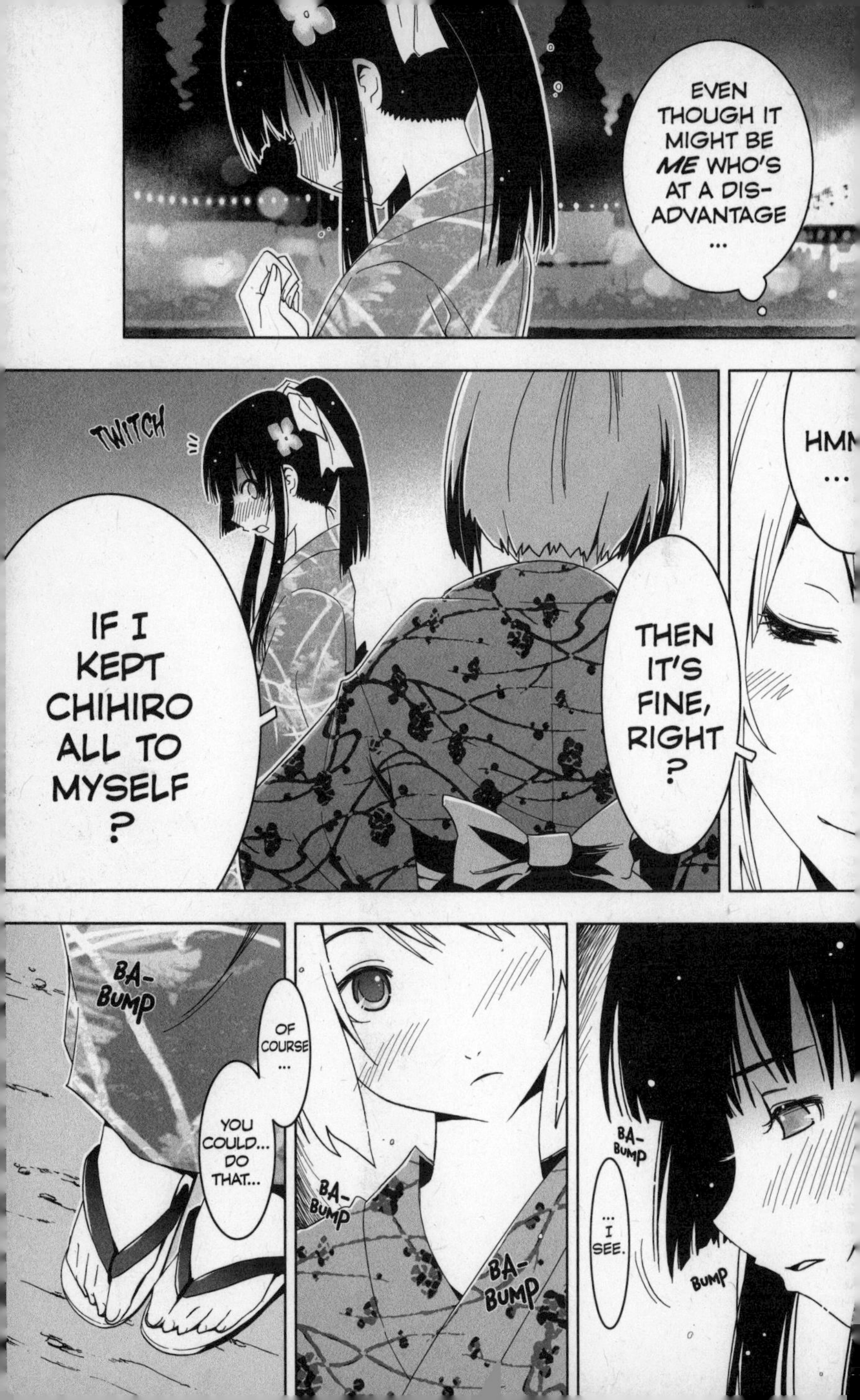
EVEN THOUGH IT MIGHT BE *ME* WHO'S AT A DIS-ADVANTAGE ...
HM ...
THEN IT'S FINE, RIGHT?
TWITCH
IF I KEPT CHIHIRO ALL TO MYSELF?
BA-BUMP
... I SEE.
BUMP
OF COURSE ...
YOU COULD... DO THAT...
BA-BUMP
BA-BUMP
BA-BUMP

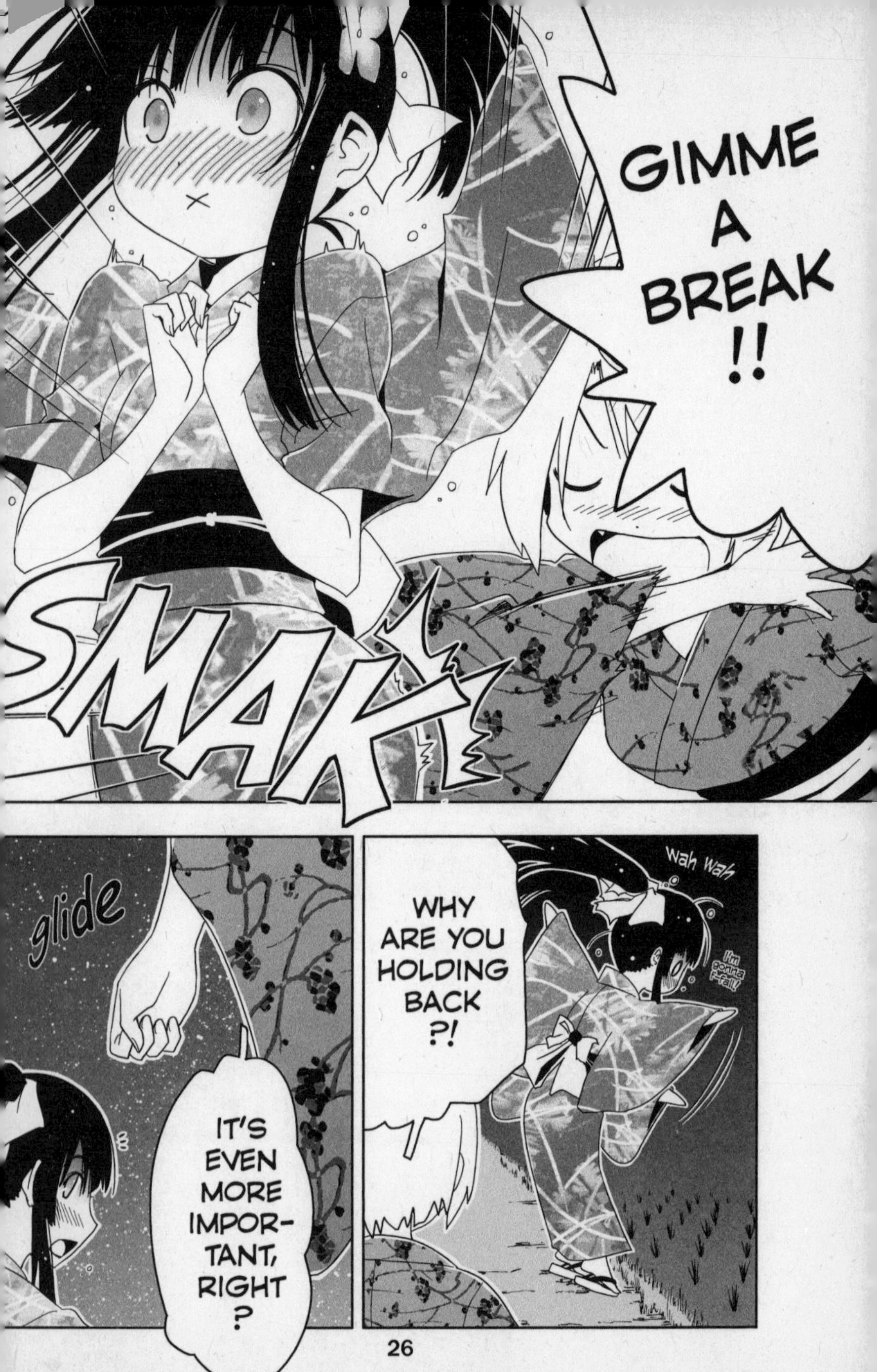
GIMME A BREAK!!
SMAK
WHY ARE YOU HOLDING BACK?!
wah wah
I'm gonna f-fall!
glide
IT'S EVEN MORE IMPOR-TANT, RIGHT?

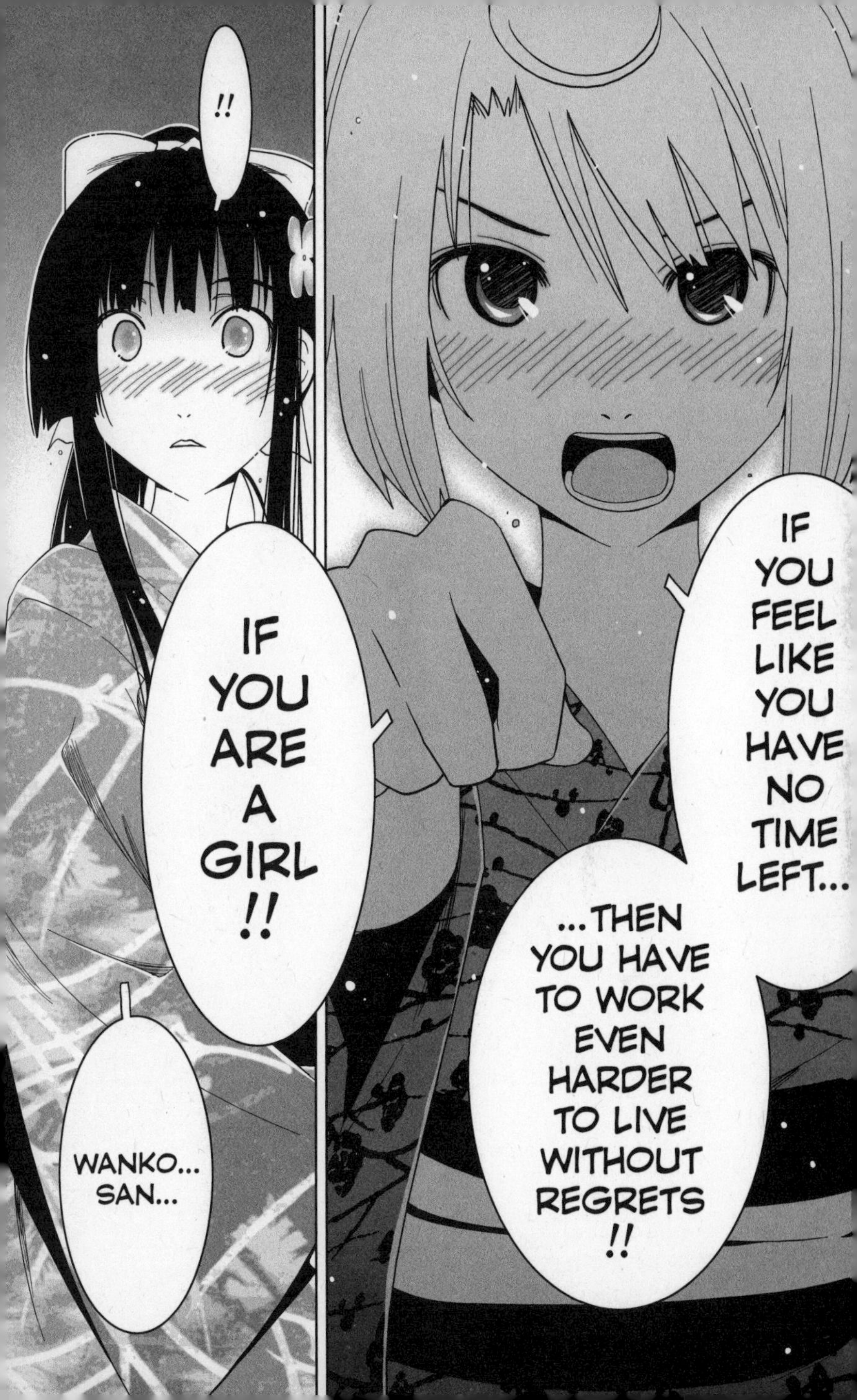
IF YOU FEEL LIKE YOU HAVE NO TIME LEFT...
...THEN YOU HAVE TO WORK EVEN HARDER TO LIVE WITHOUT REGRETS!!
IF YOU ARE A GIRL!!
!!
WANKO... SAN...

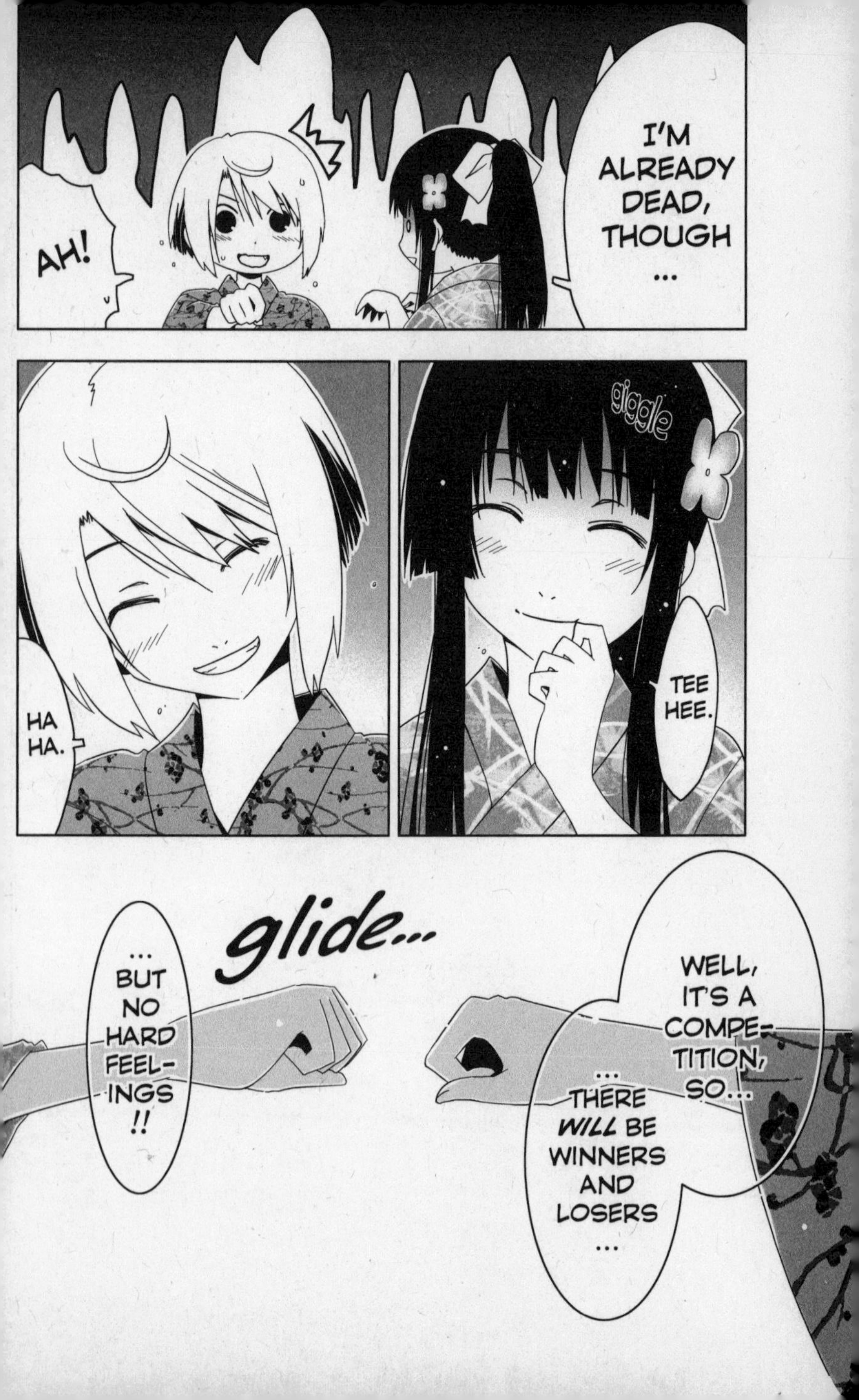
I'M ALREADY DEAD, THOUGH ...
AH!
giggle
TEE HEE.
HA HA.
WELL, IT'S A COMPETITION, SO...
... THERE *WILL* BE WINNERS AND LOSERS ...
glide...
... BUT NO HARD FEELINGS!!

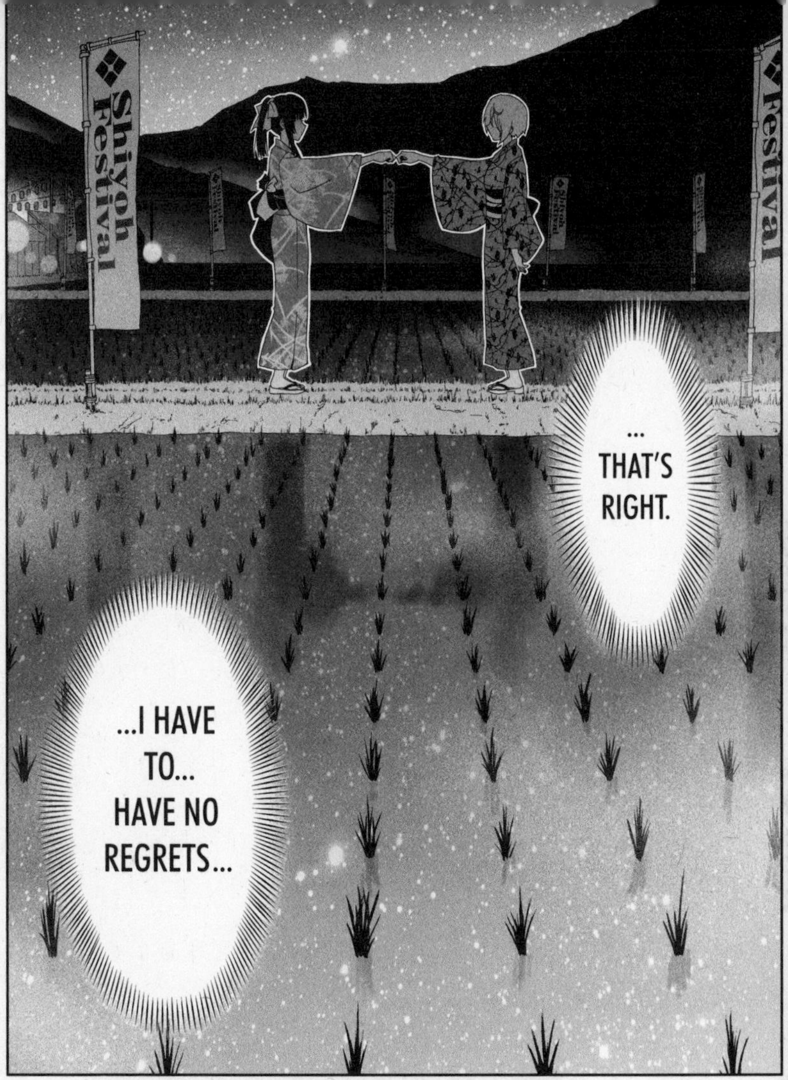
Shiyoh Festival
Festival
... THAT'S RIGHT.
...I HAVE TO... HAVE NO REGRETS...
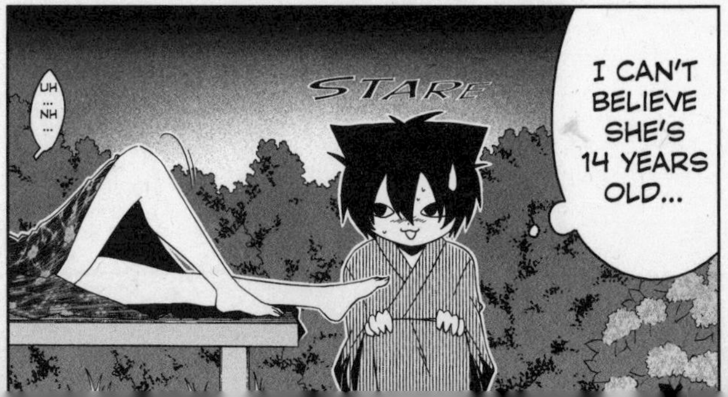
I CAN'T BELIEVE SHE'S 14 YEARS OLD...
STARE
UH... NH...

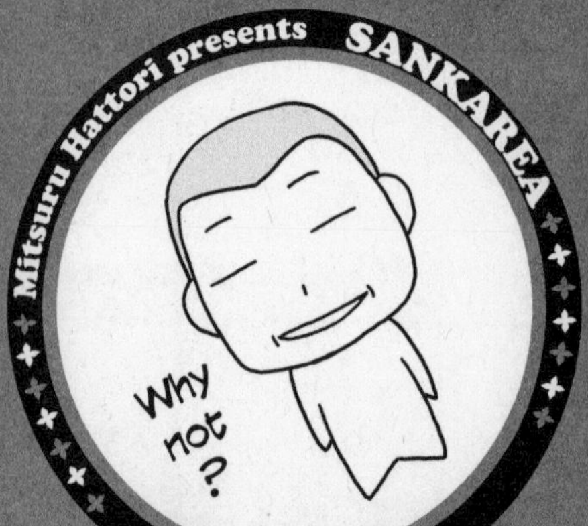
Mitsuru Hattori presents SANKAREA
Why not?

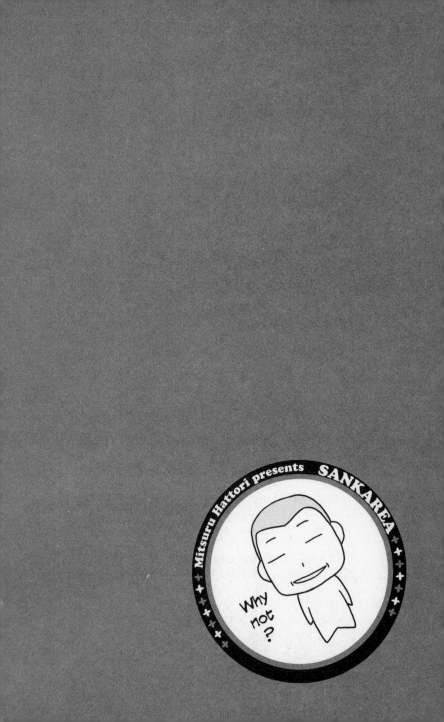

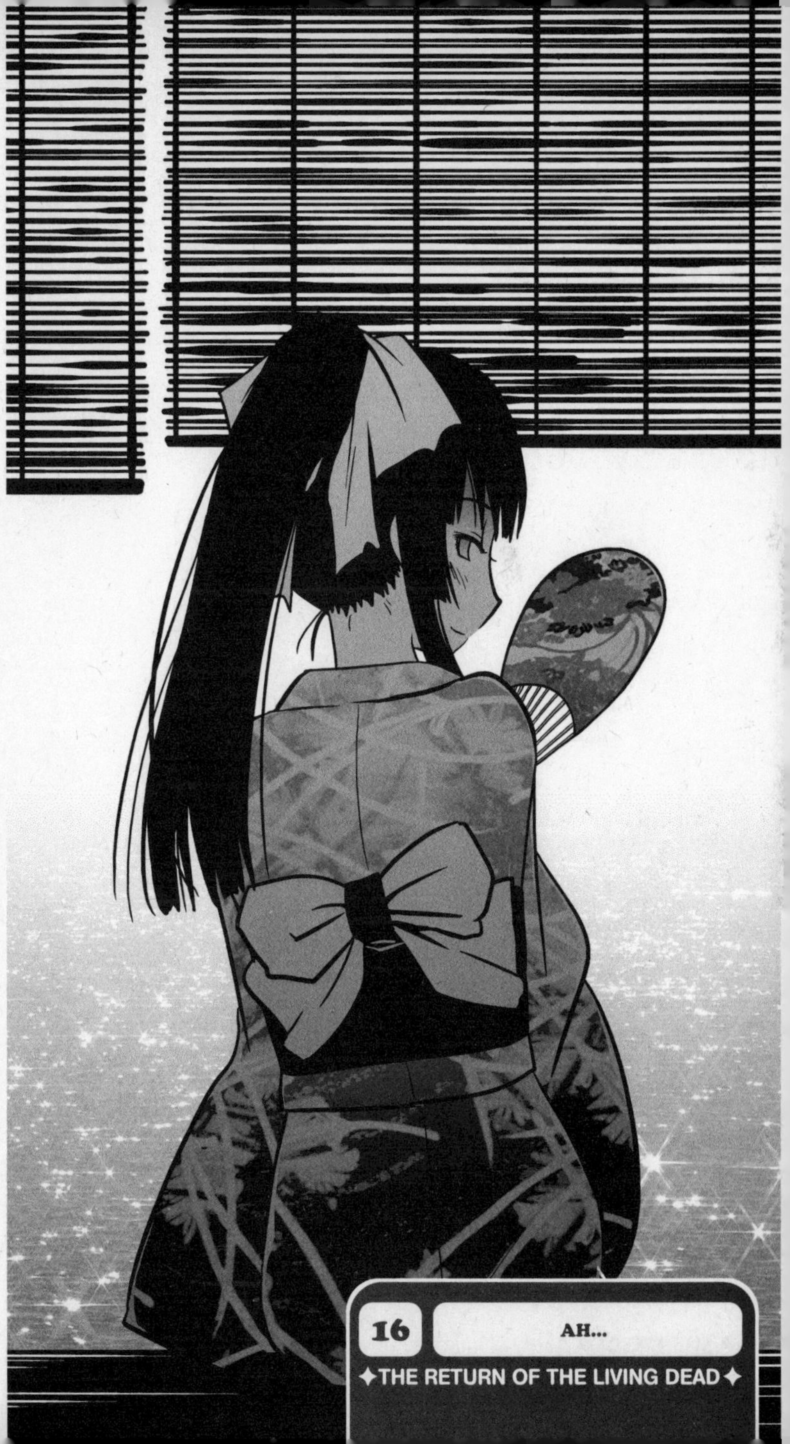
16
AH...
✦THE RETURN OF THE LIVING DEAD✦

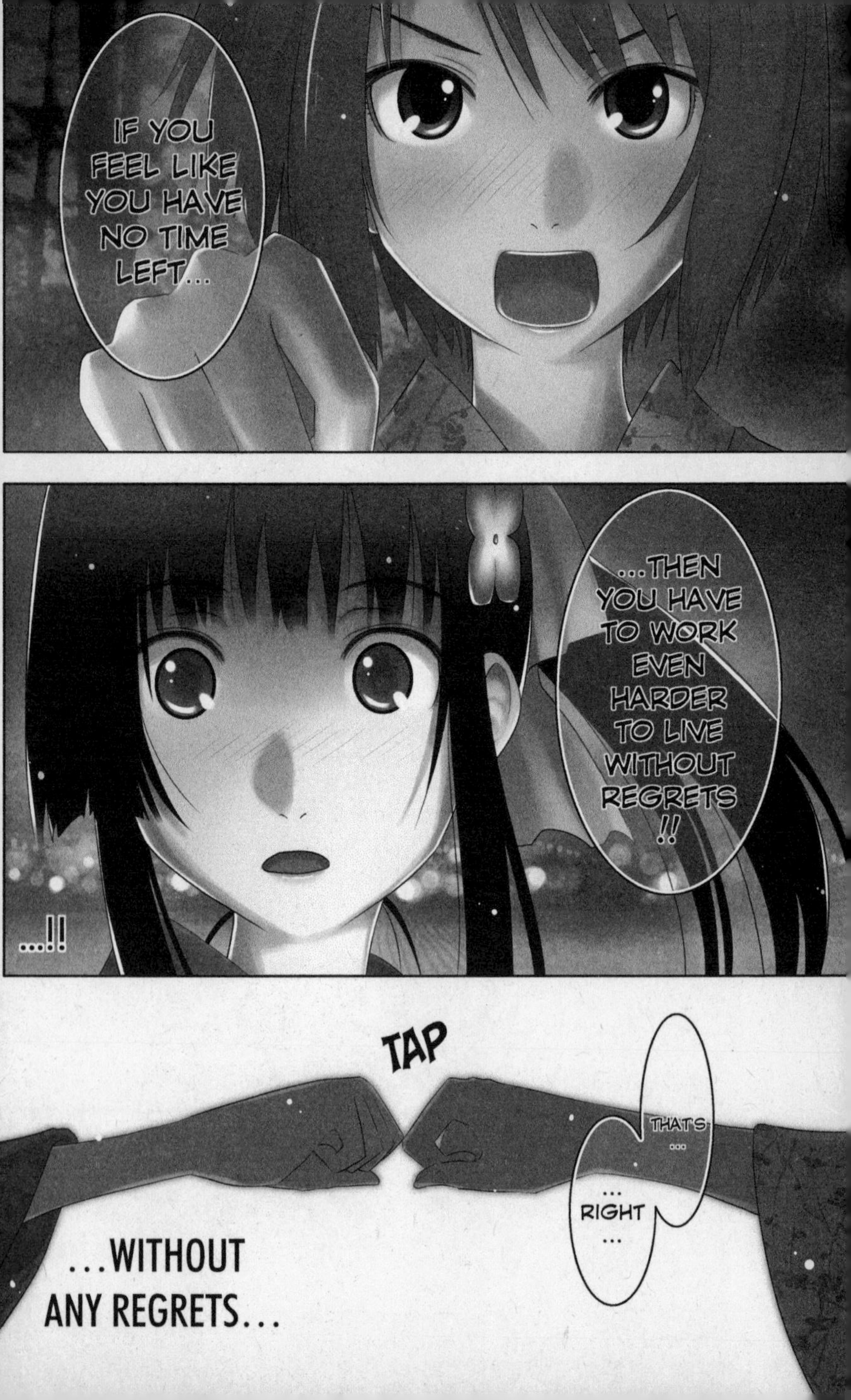
IF YOU FEEL LIKE YOU HAVE NO TIME LEFT...
...THEN YOU HAVE TO WORK EVEN HARDER TO LIVE WITHOUT REGRETS!!
...!!
THAT'S... ...RIGHT...
TAP
...WITHOUT ANY REGRETS...

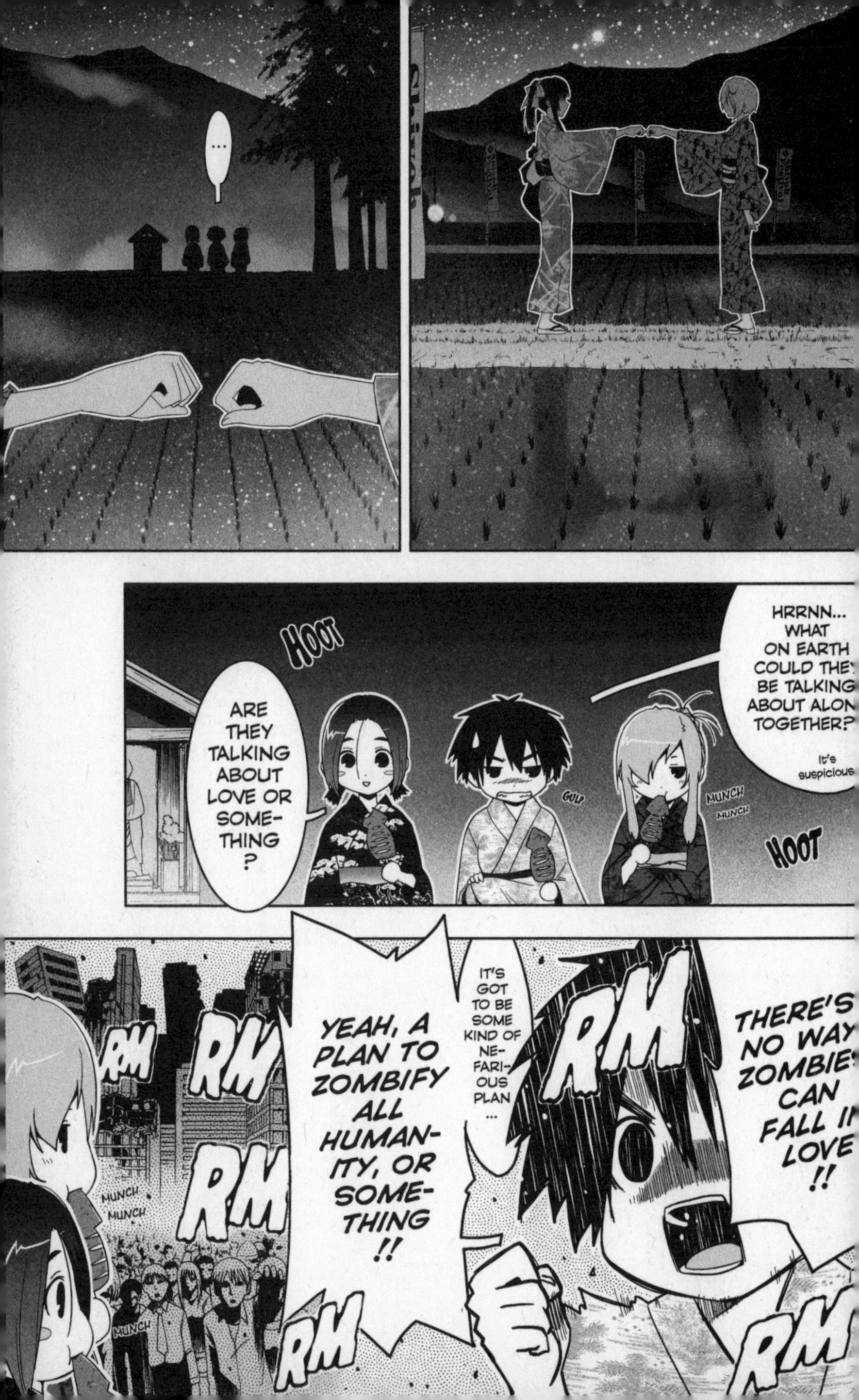
...
HRRNN... WHAT ON EARTH COULD THEY BE TALKING ABOUT ALONE TOGETHER?
It's suspicious
HOOT
MUNCH MUNCH
GULP
ARE THEY TALKING ABOUT LOVE OR SOME-THING?
HOOT
THERE'S NO WAY ZOMBIES CAN FALL IN LOVE!!
RM
IT'S GOT TO BE SOME KIND OF NE-FARI-OUS PLAN...
YEAH, A PLAN TO ZOMBIFY ALL HUMAN-ITY, OR SOME-THING!!
RM
RM
RM
MUNCH MUNCH
MUNCH
RM
RM

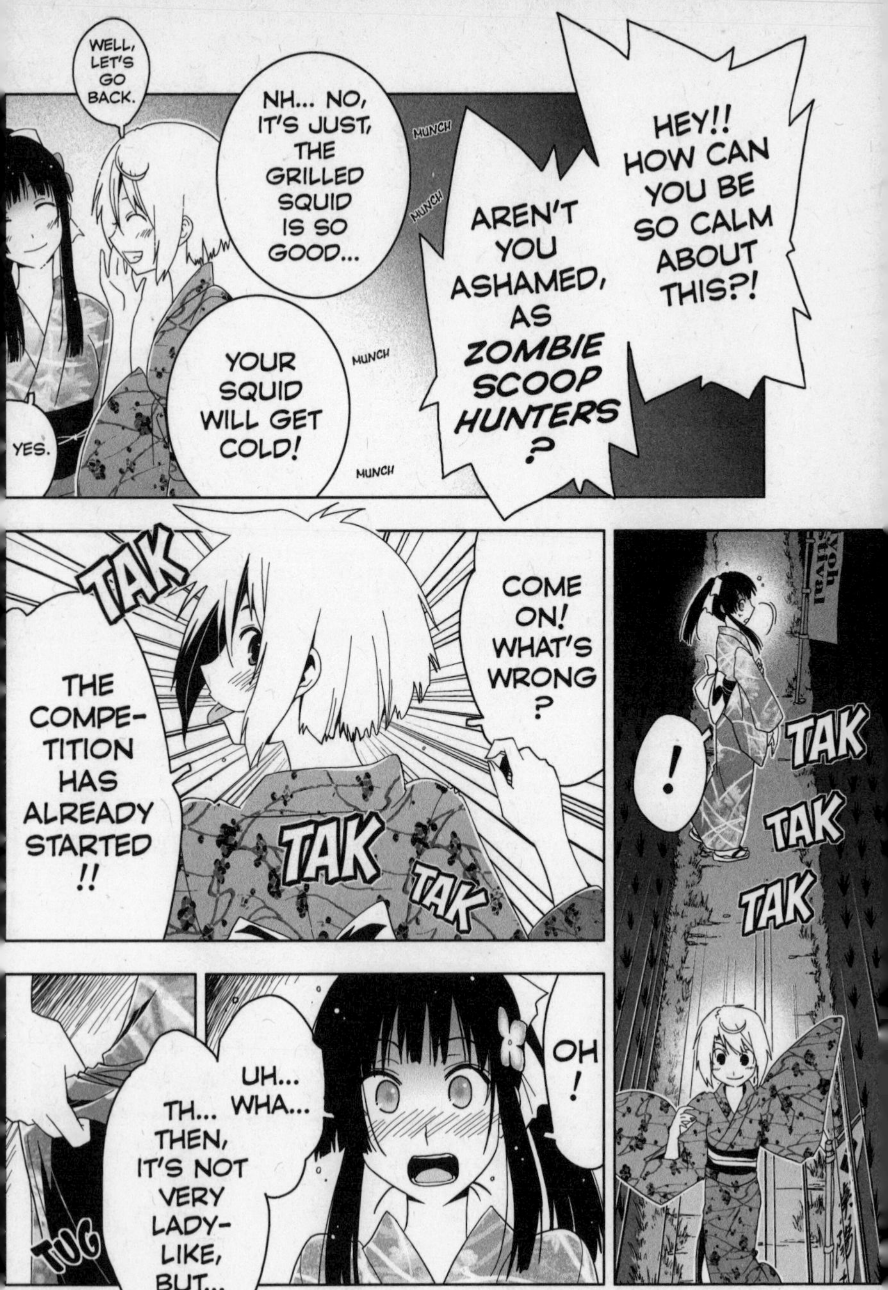
HEY!! HOW CAN YOU BE SO CALM ABOUT THIS?!
AREN'T YOU ASHAMED, AS ZOMBIE SCOOP HUNTERS?
MUNCH
MUNCH
NH... NO, IT'S JUST, THE GRILLED SQUID IS SO GOOD...
WELL, LET'S GO BACK.
MUNCH
MUNCH
YOUR SQUID WILL GET COLD!
YES.
!
TAK
TAK
TAK
TAK
COME ON! WHAT'S WRONG?
TAK
TAK
TAK
THE COMPETITION HAS ALREADY STARTED!!
OH!
UH... WHA...
TH... THEN, IT'S NOT VERY LADY-LIKE, BUT...
TUG

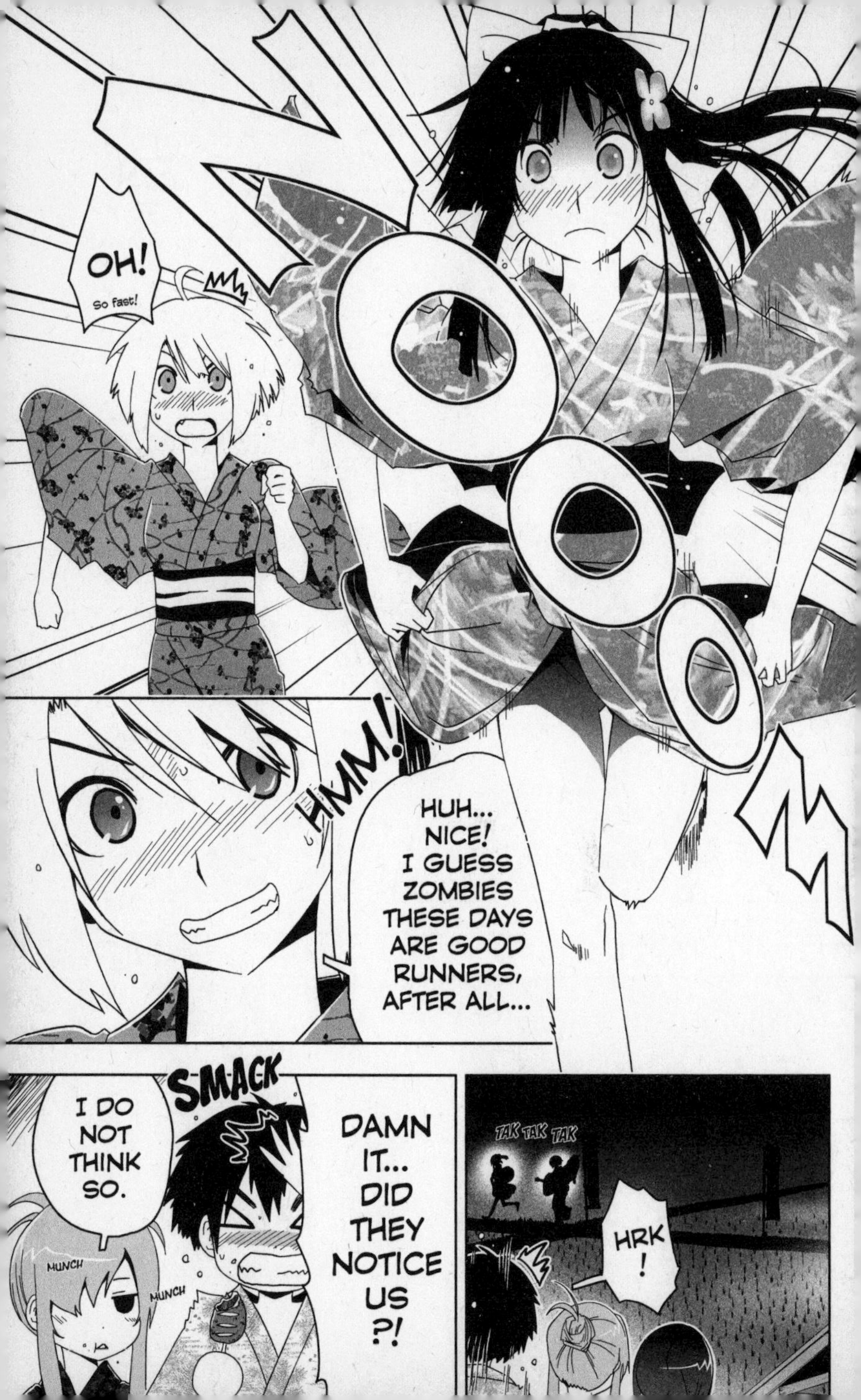
OH!
So fast!
HMM!
HUH... NICE! I GUESS ZOMBIES THESE DAYS ARE GOOD RUNNERS, AFTER ALL...
TAK TAK TAK
HRK!
DAMN IT... DID THEY NOTICE US?!
SMACK
I DO NOT THINK SO.
MUNCH
MUNCH

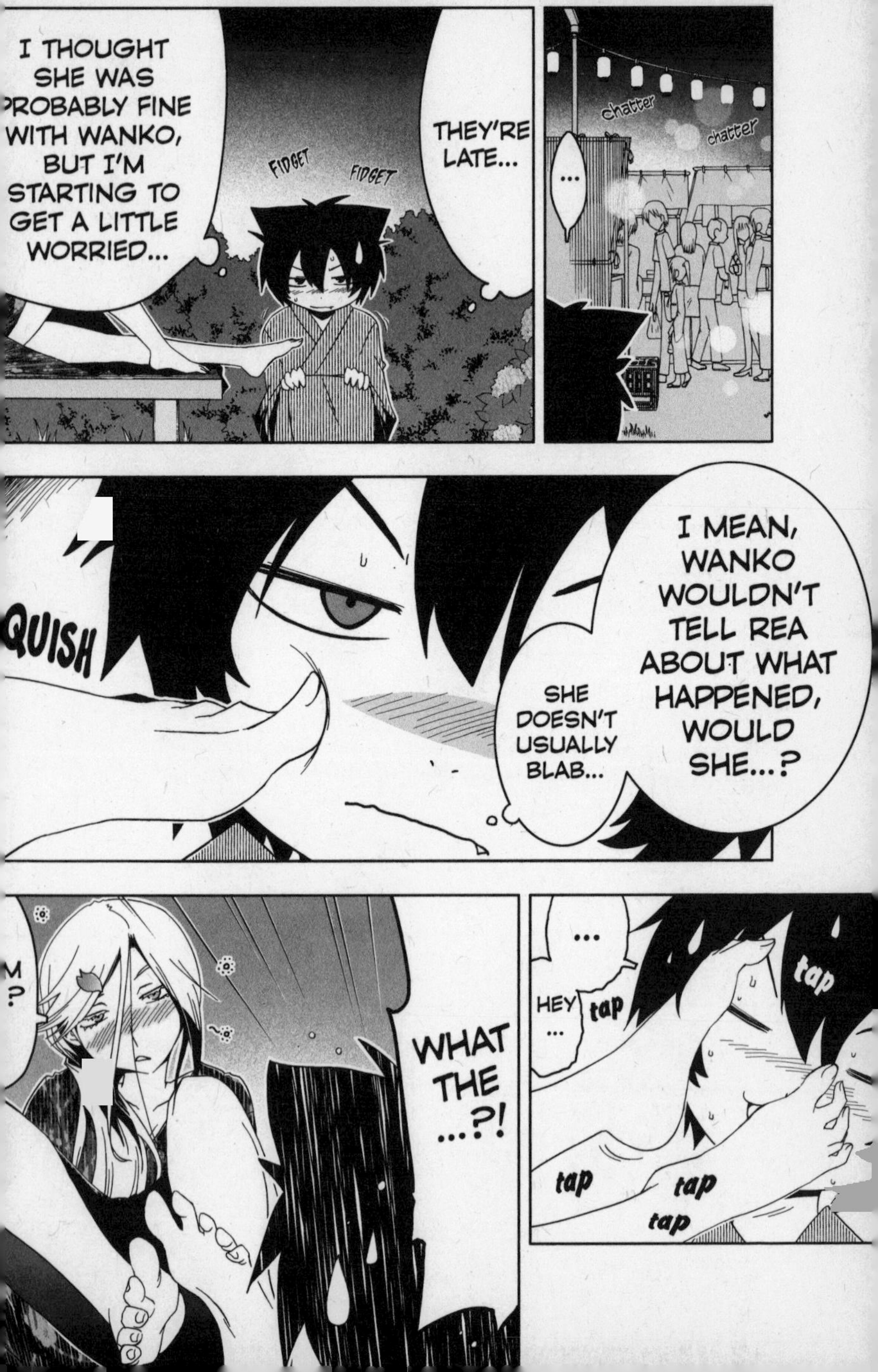
chatter
chatter
...
THEY'RE LATE...
FIDGET
FIDGET
I THOUGHT SHE WAS PROBABLY FINE WITH WANKO, BUT I'M STARTING TO GET A LITTLE WORRIED...
I MEAN, WANKO WOULDN'T TELL REA ABOUT WHAT HAPPENED, WOULD SHE...?
SHE DOESN'T USUALLY BLAB...
QUISH
...
HEY...
tap
tap
tap
tap
tap
WHAT THE ...?!
M?

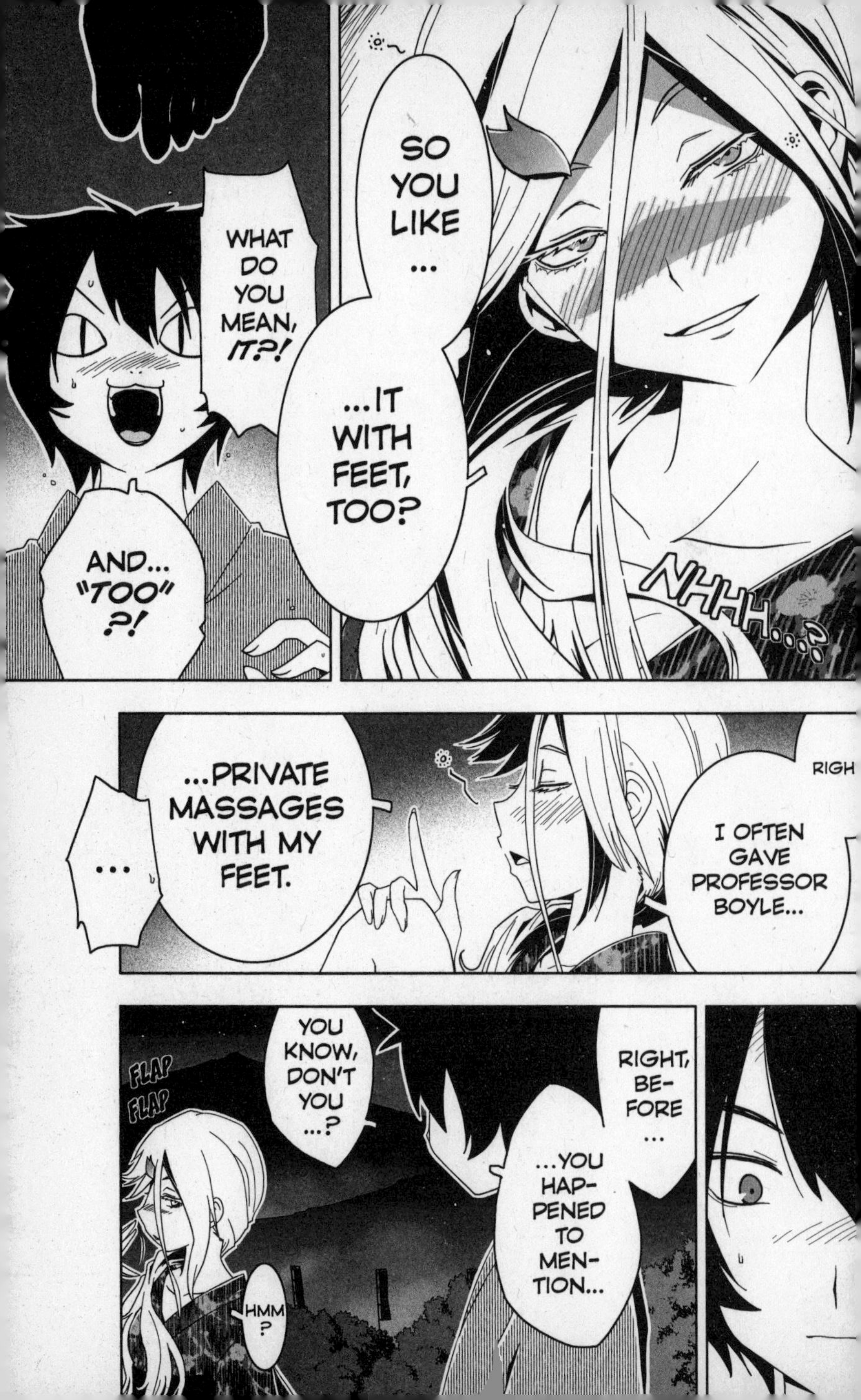
SO YOU LIKE ...
...IT WITH FEET, TOO?
NHHH...?
WHAT DO YOU MEAN, IT?!
AND... "TOO"?!
RIGH
I OFTEN GAVE PROFESSOR BOYLE...
...PRIVATE MASSAGES WITH MY FEET.
...
RIGHT, BE-FORE ...
...YOU HAP-PENED TO MEN-TION...
YOU KNOW, DON'T YOU ...?
FLAP FLAP
HMM ?

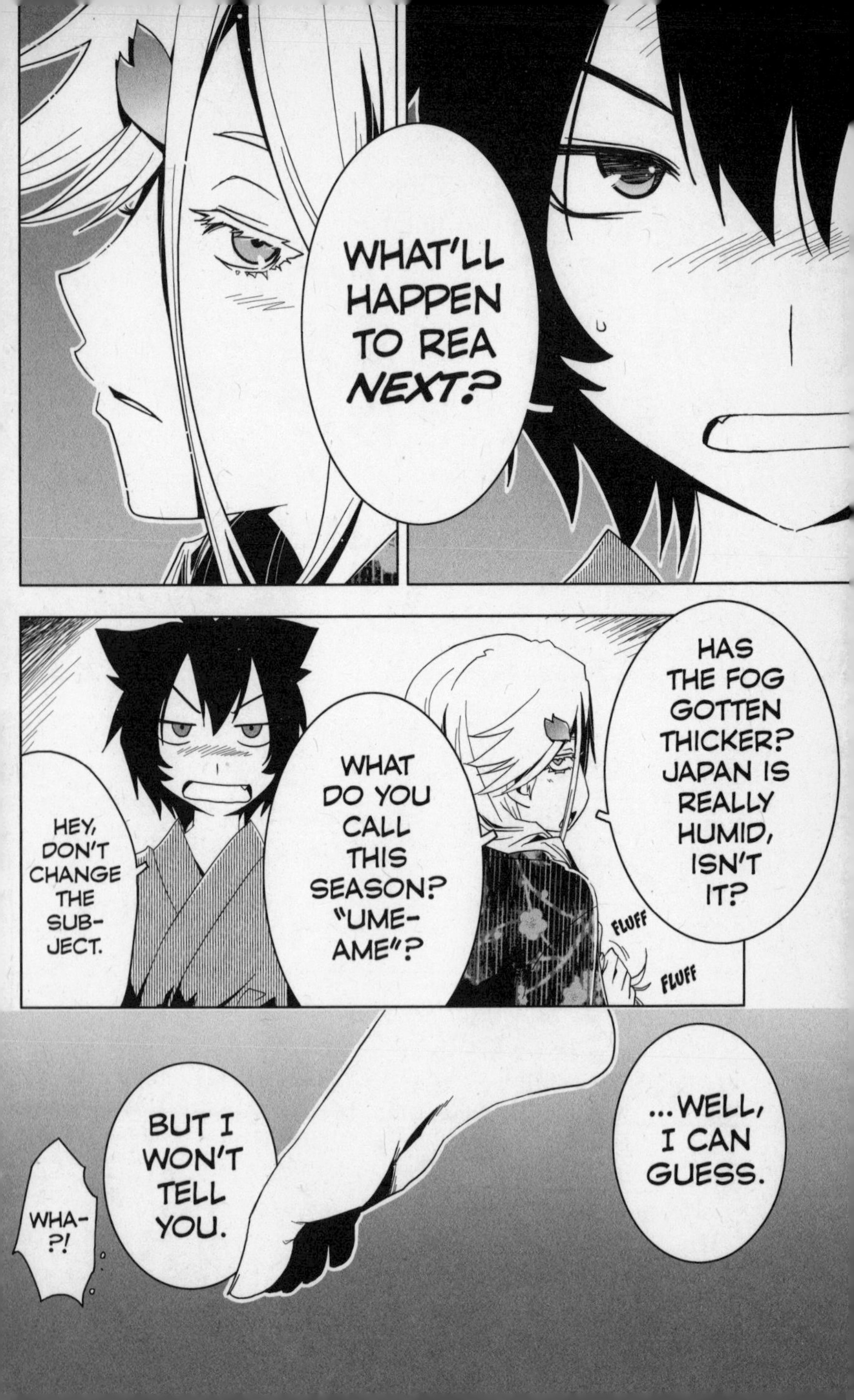
WHAT'LL HAPPEN TO REA NEXT?
HAS THE FOG GOTTEN THICKER? JAPAN IS REALLY HUMID, ISN'T IT?
FLUFF
FLUFF
WHAT DO YOU CALL THIS SEASON? "UME-AME"?
HEY, DON'T CHANGE THE SUB-JECT.
...WELL, I CAN GUESS.
BUT I WON'T TELL YOU.
WHA-?!

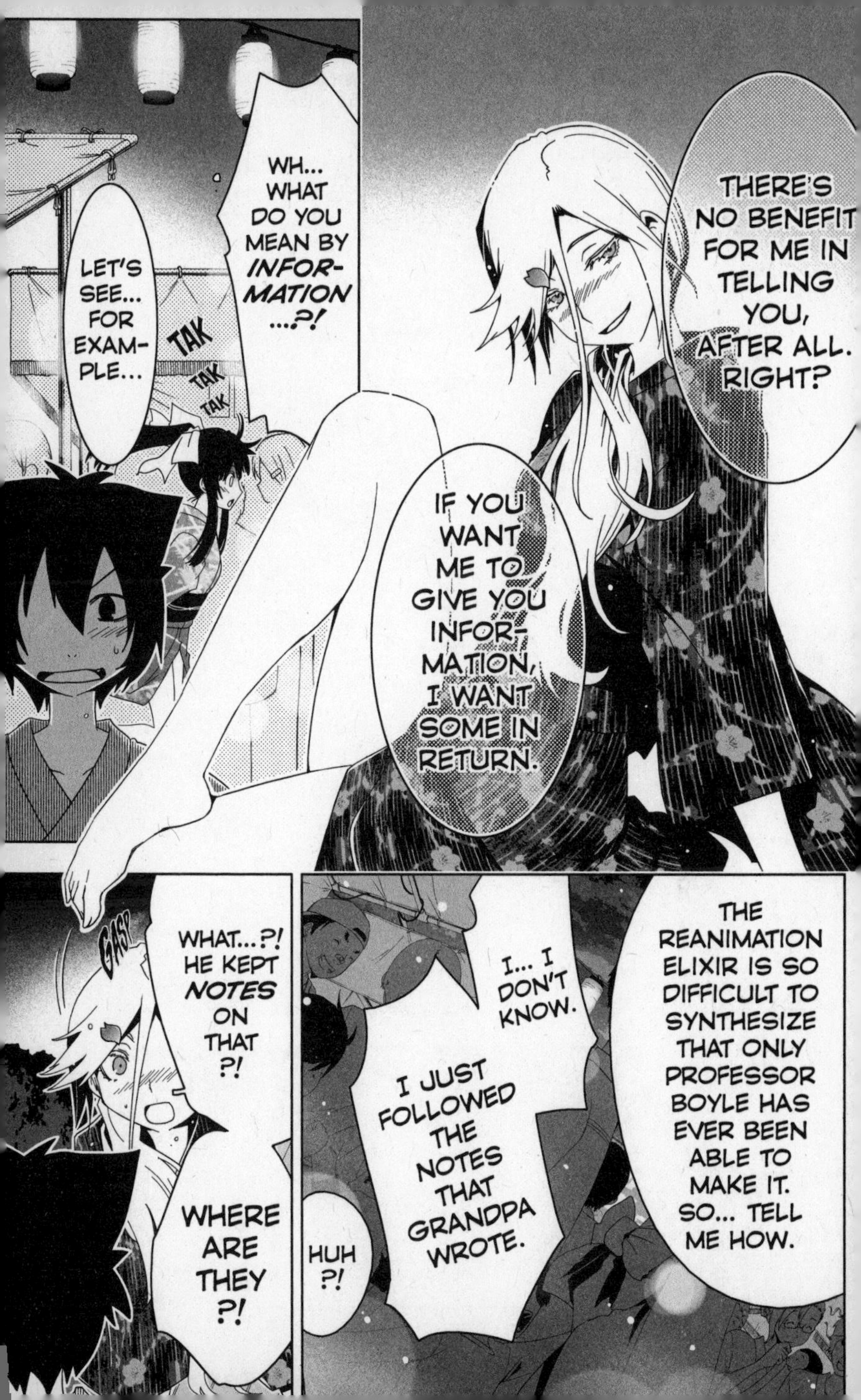
THERE'S NO BENEFIT FOR ME IN TELLING YOU, AFTER ALL. RIGHT?
IF YOU WANT ME TO GIVE YOU INFORMATION, I WANT SOME IN RETURN.
WH... WHAT DO YOU MEAN BY *INFORMATION*...?!
LET'S SEE... FOR EXAMPLE...
TAK
TAK
TAK
THE REANIMATION ELIXIR IS SO DIFFICULT TO SYNTHESIZE THAT ONLY PROFESSOR BOYLE HAS EVER BEEN ABLE TO MAKE IT. SO... TELL ME HOW.
I... I DON'T KNOW.
I JUST FOLLOWED THE NOTES THAT GRANDPA WROTE.
HUH?!
GASP
WHAT...?! HE KEPT *NOTES* ON THAT?!
WHERE ARE THEY?!

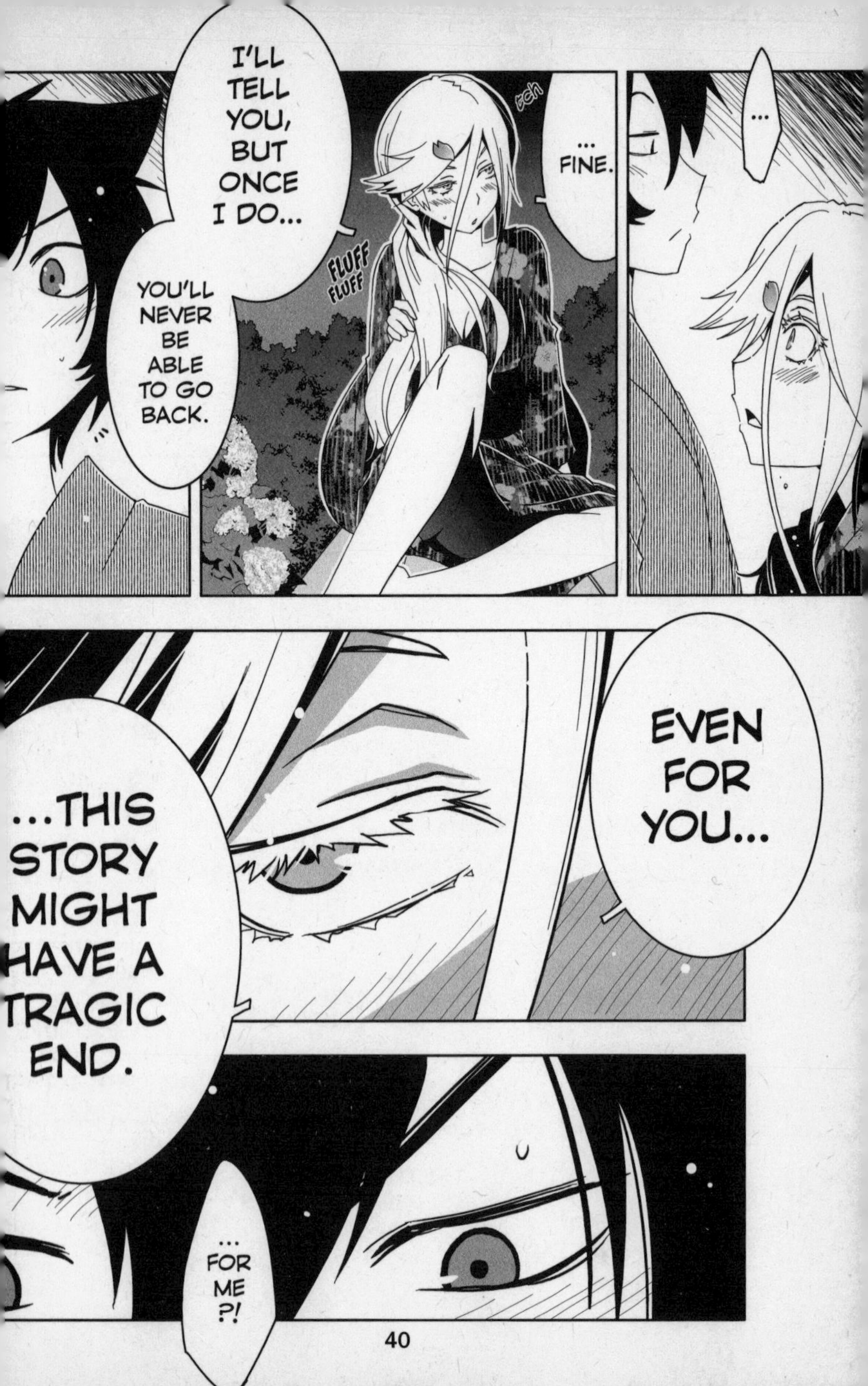
...
... FINE.
FLUFF FLUFF
I'LL TELL YOU, BUT ONCE I DO...
YOU'LL NEVER BE ABLE TO GO BACK.
EVEN FOR YOU...
...THIS STORY MIGHT HAVE A TRAGIC END.
... FOR ME ?!

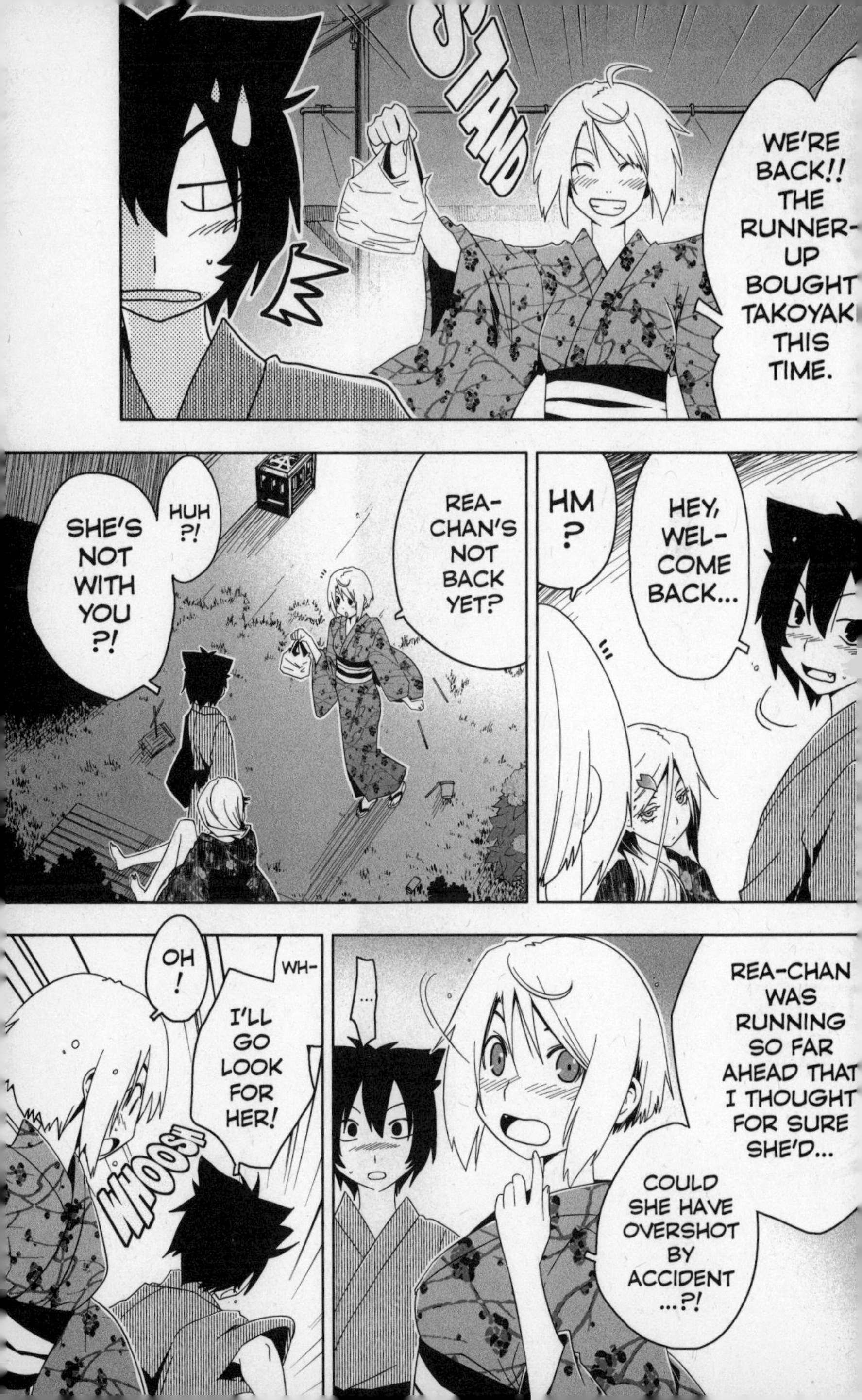
STAND
WE'RE BACK!! THE RUNNER-UP BOUGHT TAKOYAK THIS TIME.
HEY, WEL-COME BACK...
HM?
REA-CHAN'S NOT BACK YET?
HUH?!
SHE'S NOT WITH YOU?!
REA-CHAN WAS RUNNING SO FAR AHEAD THAT I THOUGHT FOR SURE SHE'D...
...
COULD SHE HAVE OVERSHOT BY ACCIDENT...?!
WH-
I'LL GO LOOK FOR HER!
OH!
WHOOSH

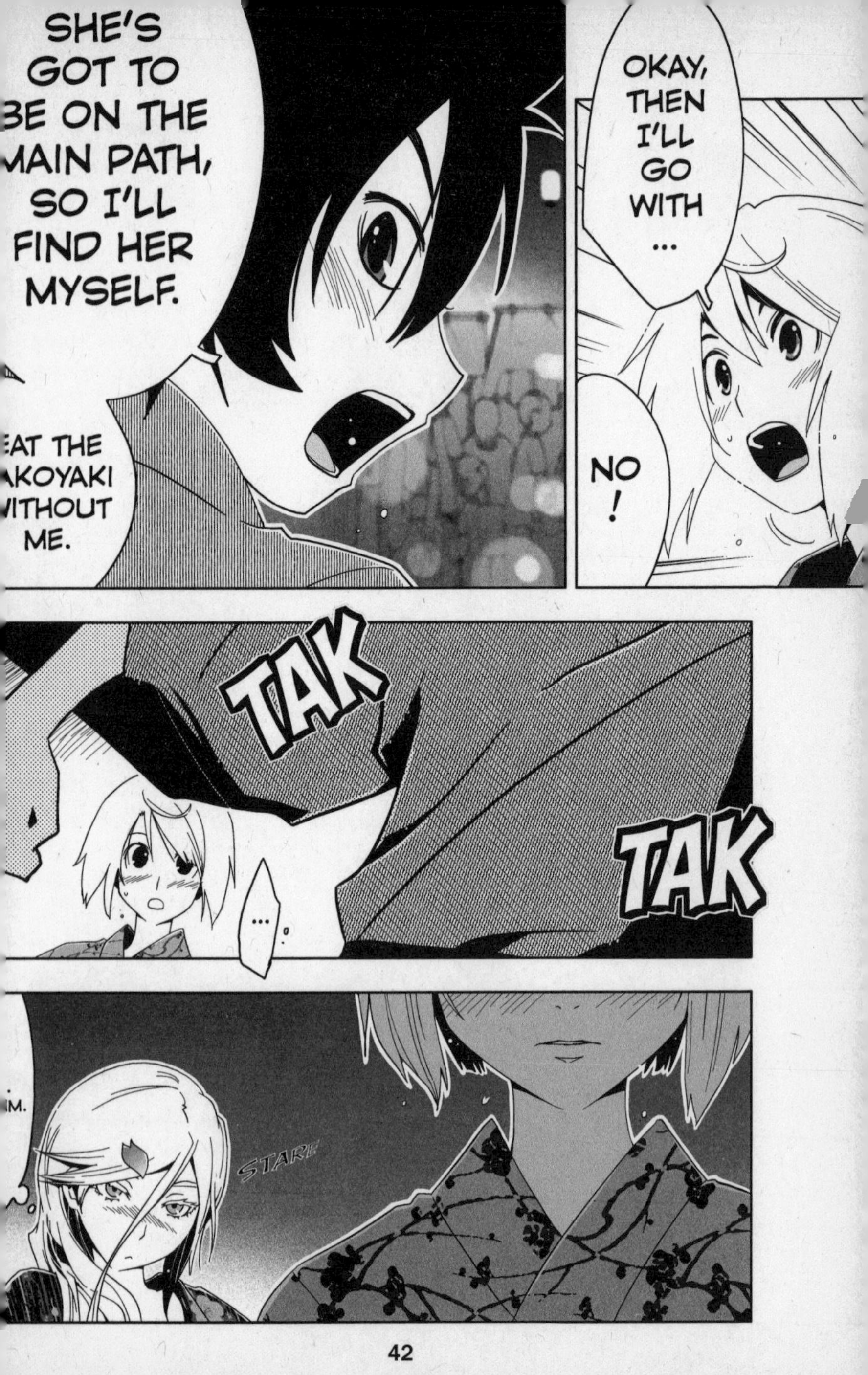
OKAY, THEN I'LL GO WITH ...
NO!
SHE'S GOT TO BE ON THE MAIN PATH, SO I'LL FIND HER MYSELF.
EAT THE AKOYAKI WITHOUT ME.
TAK
TAK
...
M.
STARE

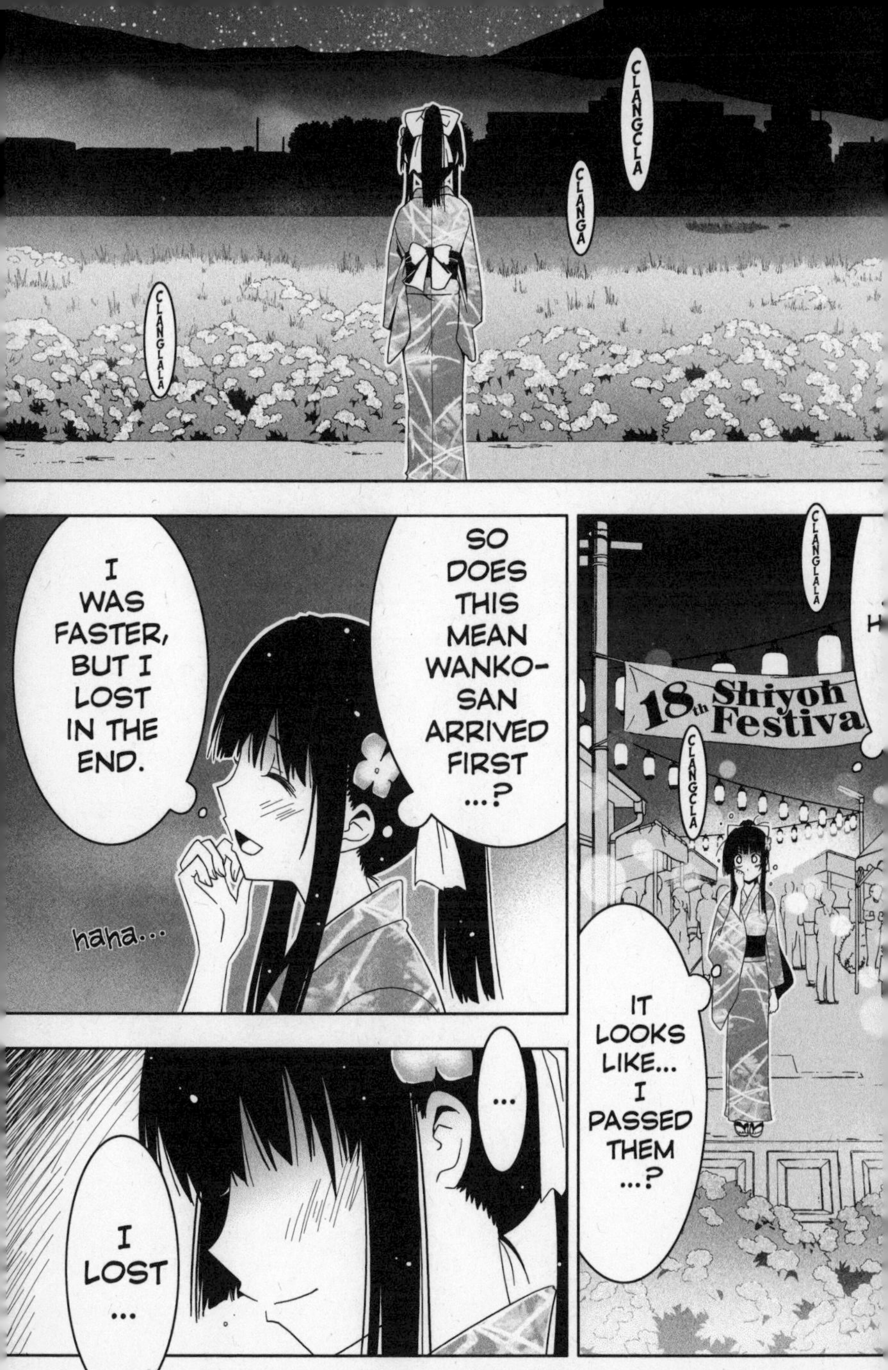
CLANGCLA
CLANGA
CLANGLALA
CLANGLALA
18th Shiyoh Festiva
CLANGCLA
IT LOOKS LIKE... I PASSED THEM ...?
SO DOES THIS MEAN WANKO-SAN ARRIVED FIRST ...?
I WAS FASTER, BUT I LOST IN THE END.
haha...
...
I LOST ...

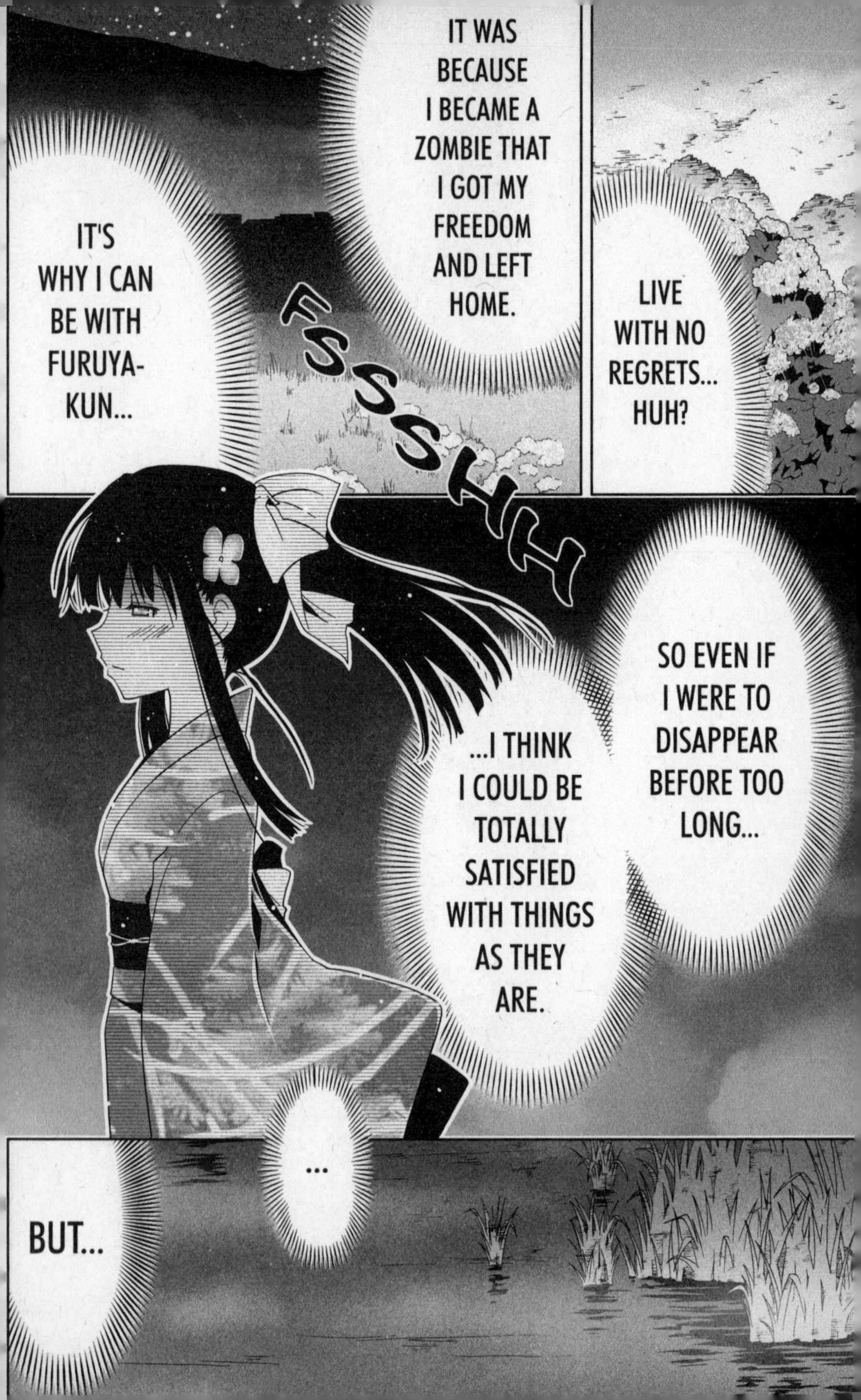

LIVE WITH NO REGRETS... HUH?
IT WAS BECAUSE I BECAME A ZOMBIE THAT I GOT MY FREEDOM AND LEFT HOME.
IT'S WHY I CAN BE WITH FURUYA-KUN...
FSSHH
SO EVEN IF I WERE TO DISAPPEAR BEFORE TOO LONG...
...I THINK I COULD BE TOTALLY SATISFIED WITH THINGS AS THEY ARE.
...
BUT...

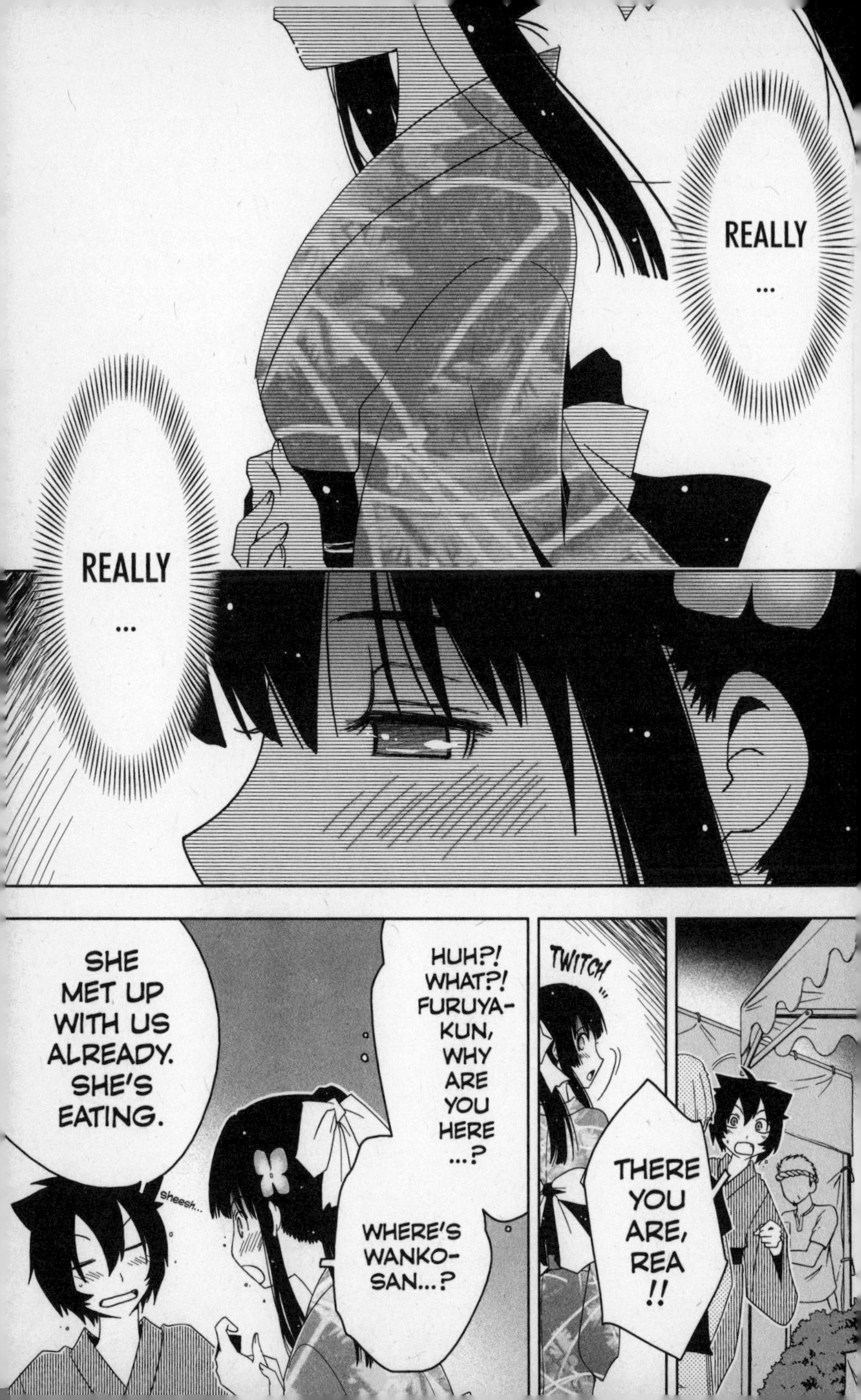
REALLY ...
REALLY ...
THERE YOU ARE, REA!!
TWITCH
HUH?! WHAT?! FURUYA-KUN, WHY ARE YOU HERE ...?
WHERE'S WANKO-SAN...?
SHE MET UP WITH US ALREADY. SHE'S EATING.
Sheesh...

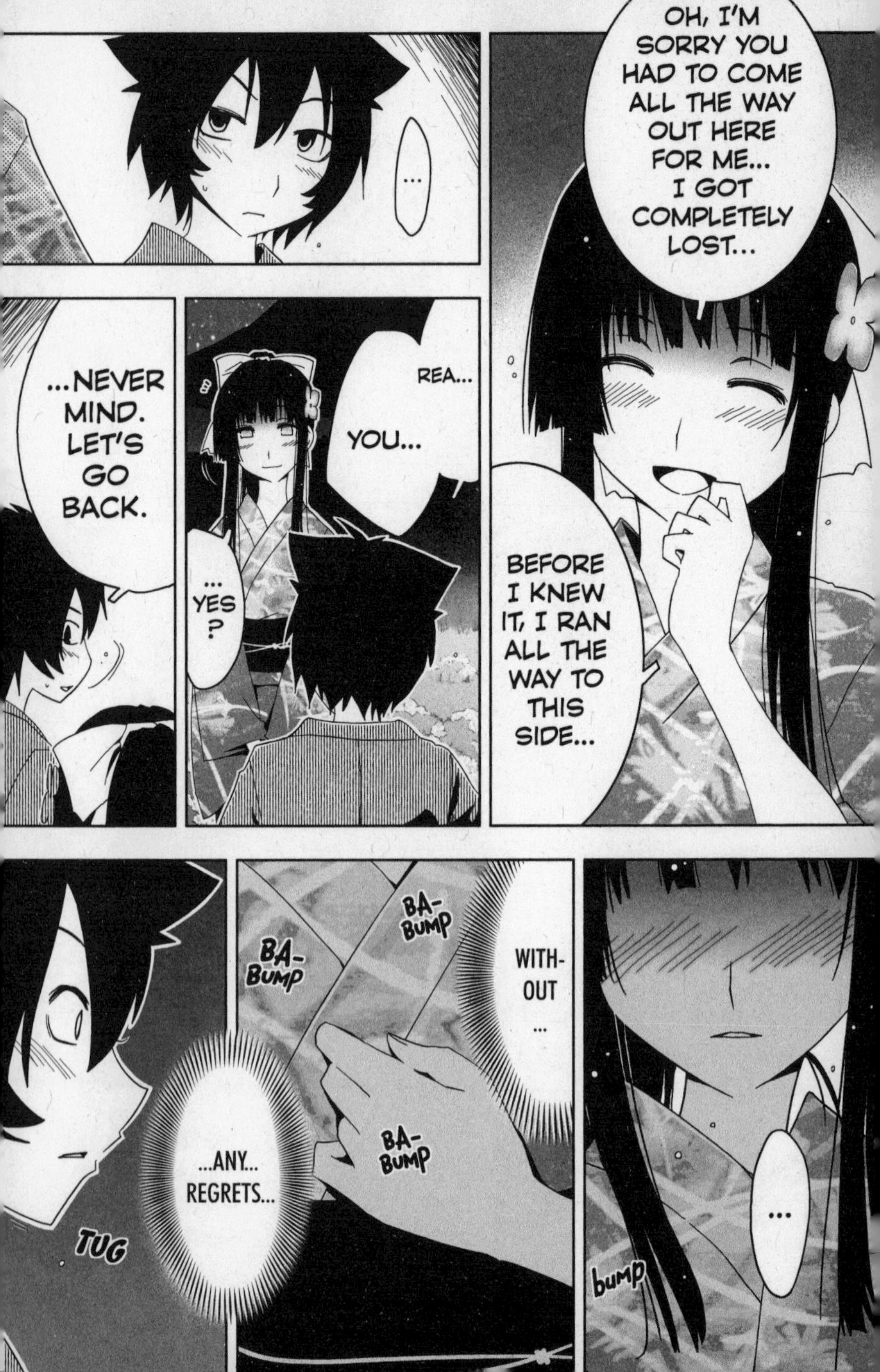
OH, I'M SORRY YOU HAD TO COME ALL THE WAY OUT HERE FOR ME... I GOT COMPLETELY LOST...
BEFORE I KNEW IT, I RAN ALL THE WAY TO THIS SIDE...
...
REA...
YOU...
...YES?
...NEVER MIND. LET'S GO BACK.
bump
...
BA-BUMP
BA-BUMP
WITH-OUT...
BA-BUMP
...ANY... REGRETS...
TUG

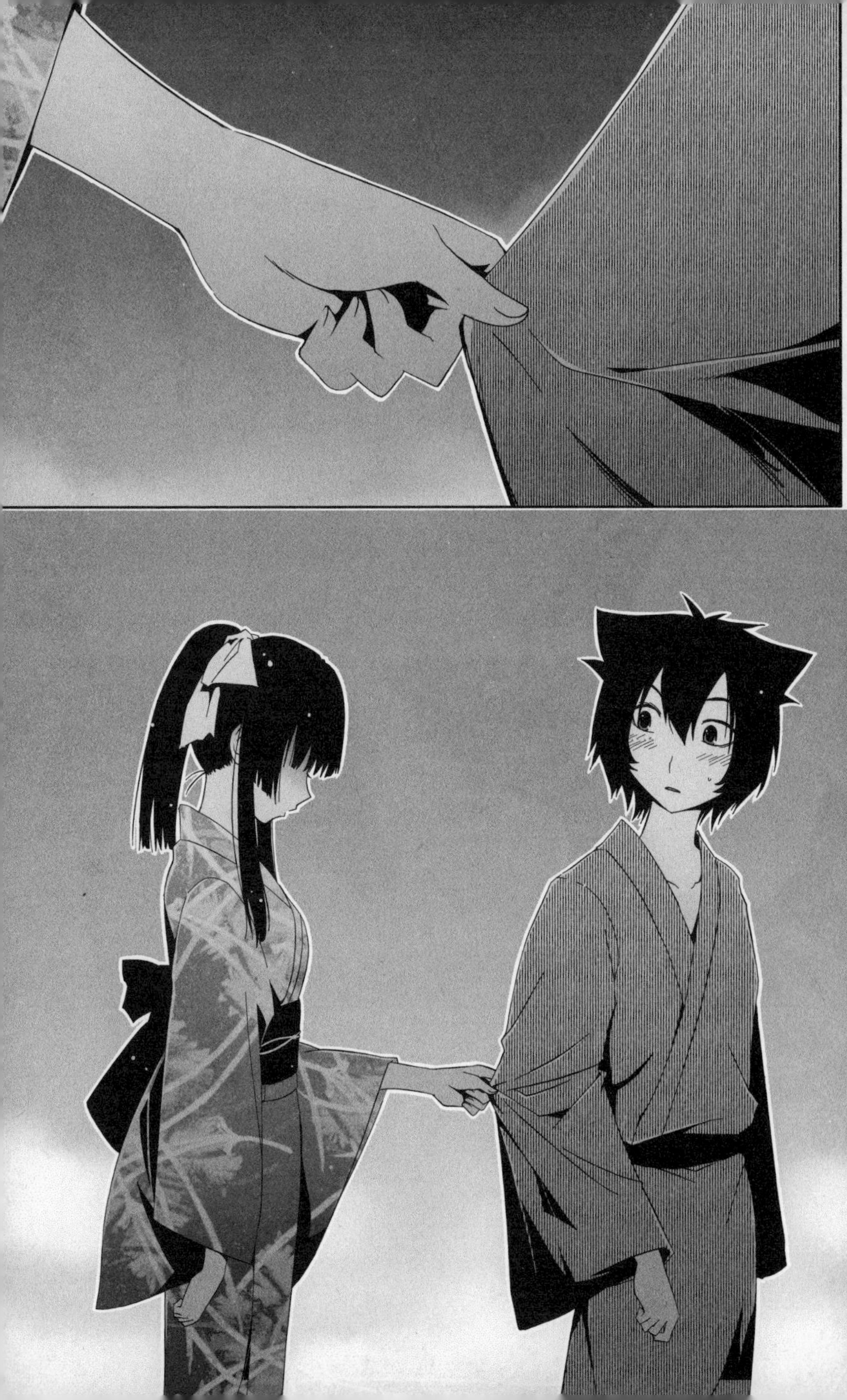

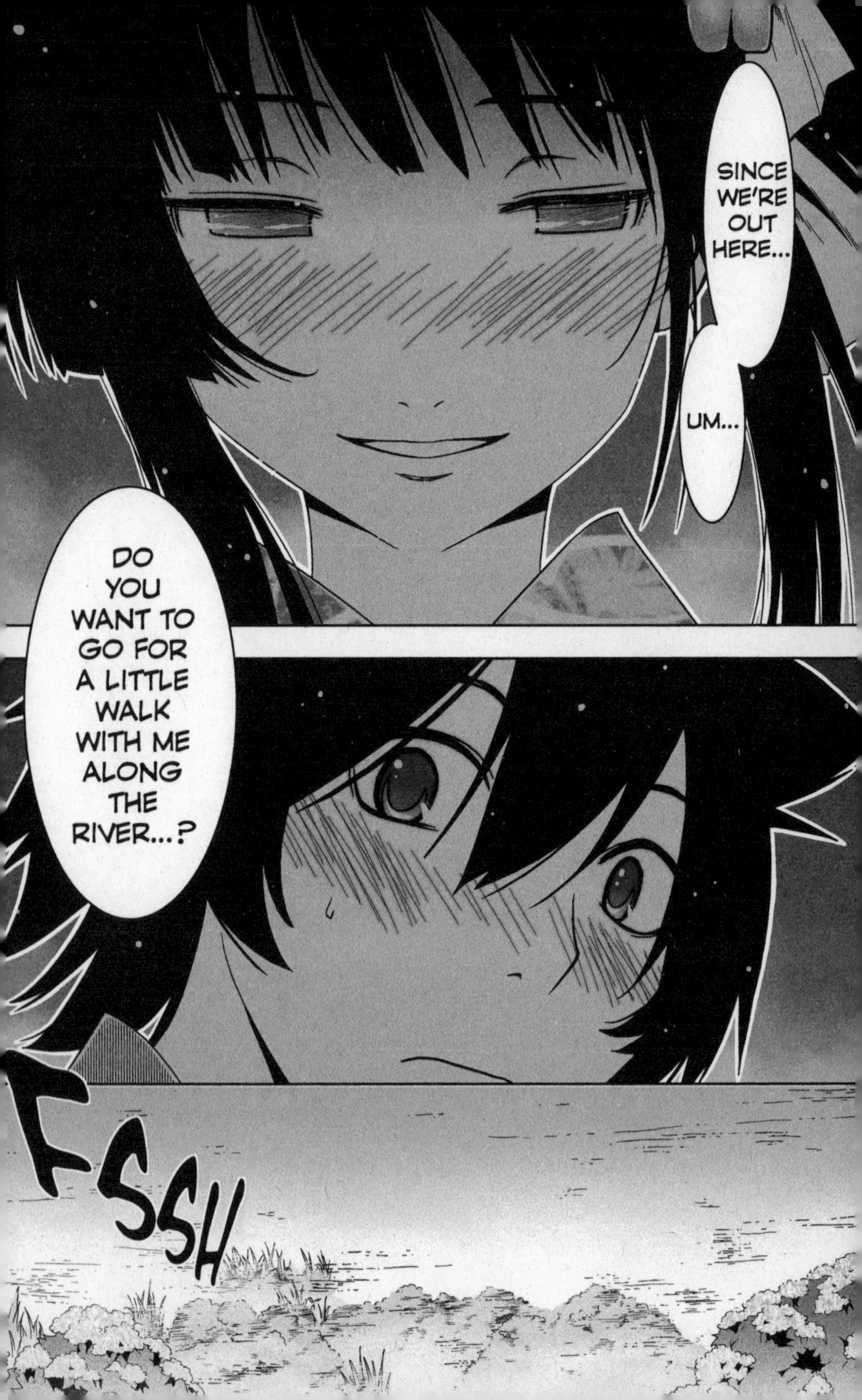
SINCE WE'RE OUT HERE...
UM...
DO YOU WANT TO GO FOR A LITTLE WALK WITH ME ALONG THE RIVER...?
FSSH

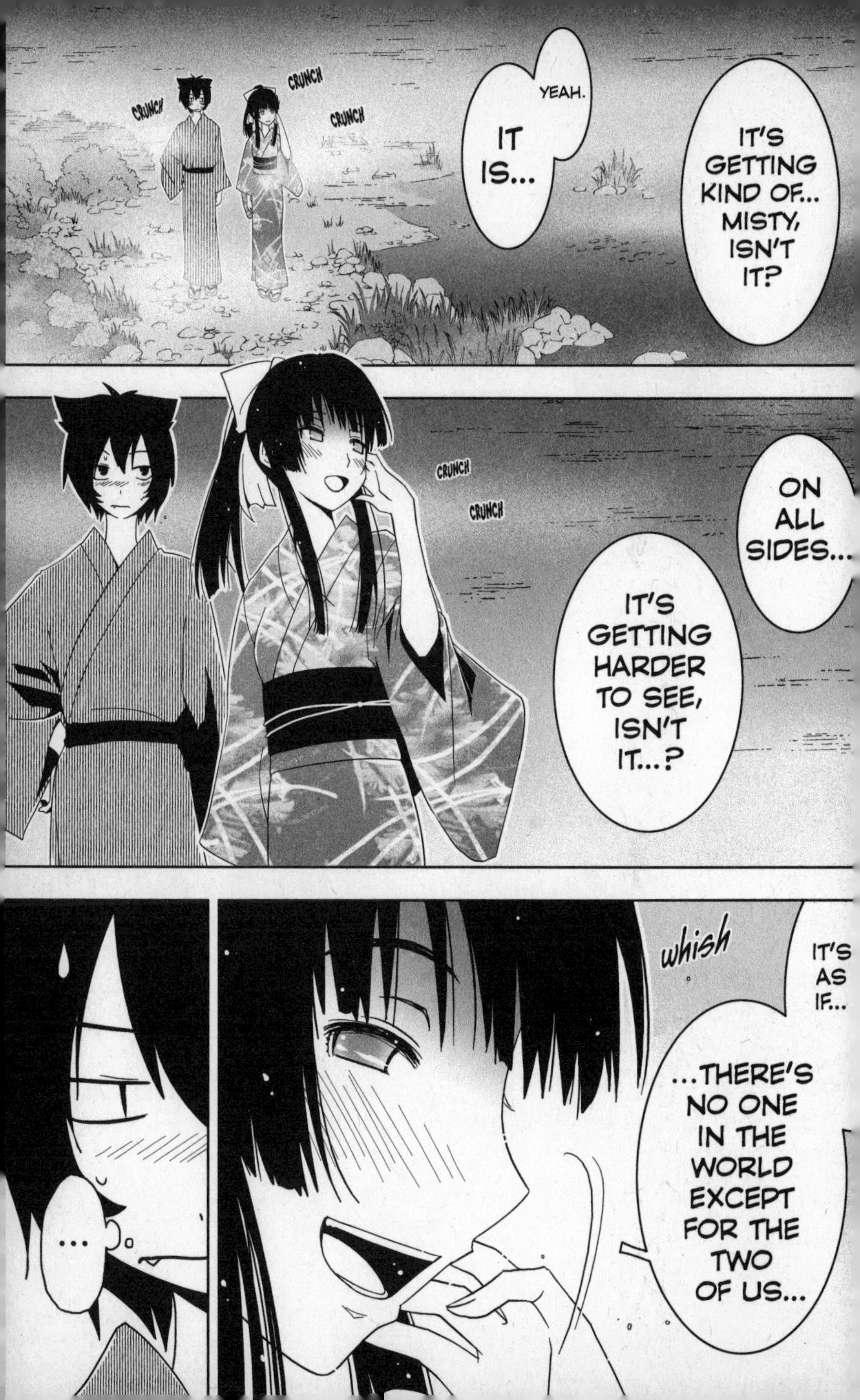
IT'S GETTING KIND OF... MISTY, ISN'T IT?
YEAH.
IT IS...
CRUNCH
CRUNCH
CRUNCH
ON ALL SIDES...
IT'S GETTING HARDER TO SEE, ISN'T IT...?
CRUNCH
CRUNCH
IT'S AS IF...
...THERE'S NO ONE IN THE WORLD EXCEPT FOR THE TWO OF US...
whish
...

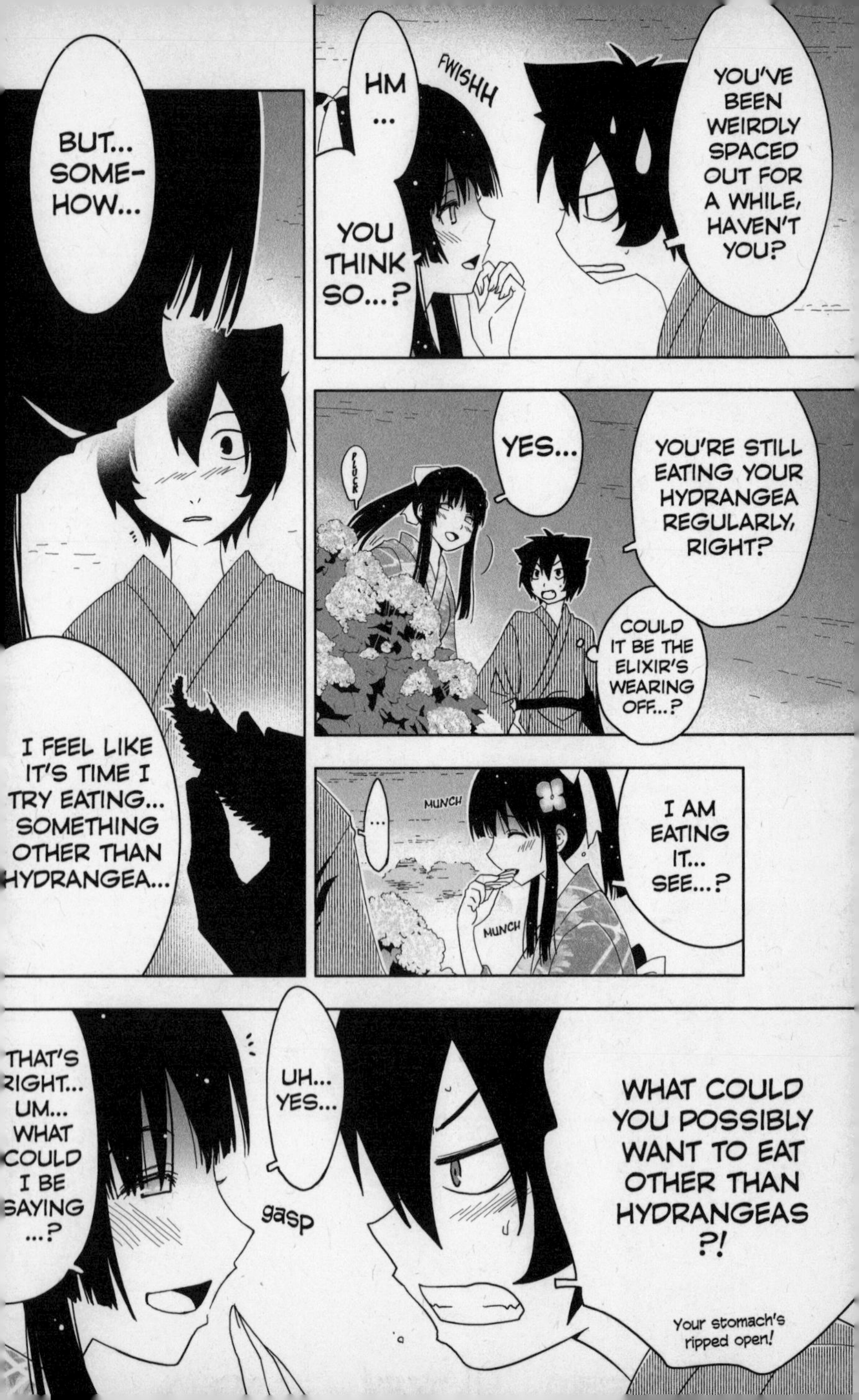
YOU'VE BEEN WEIRDLY SPACED OUT FOR A WHILE, HAVEN'T YOU?
FWISHH
HM...
YOU THINK SO...?
YOU'RE STILL EATING YOUR HYDRANGEA REGULARLY, RIGHT?
YES...
PLUCK
COULD IT BE THE ELIXIR'S WEARING OFF...?
I AM EATING IT... SEE...?
MUNCH
...
MUNCH
BUT... SOMEHOW...
I FEEL LIKE IT'S TIME I TRY EATING... SOMETHING OTHER THAN HYDRANGEA...
WHAT COULD YOU POSSIBLY WANT TO EAT OTHER THAN HYDRANGEAS?!
Your stomach's ripped open!
UH... YES...
gasp
THAT'S RIGHT... UM... WHAT COULD I BE SAYING...?

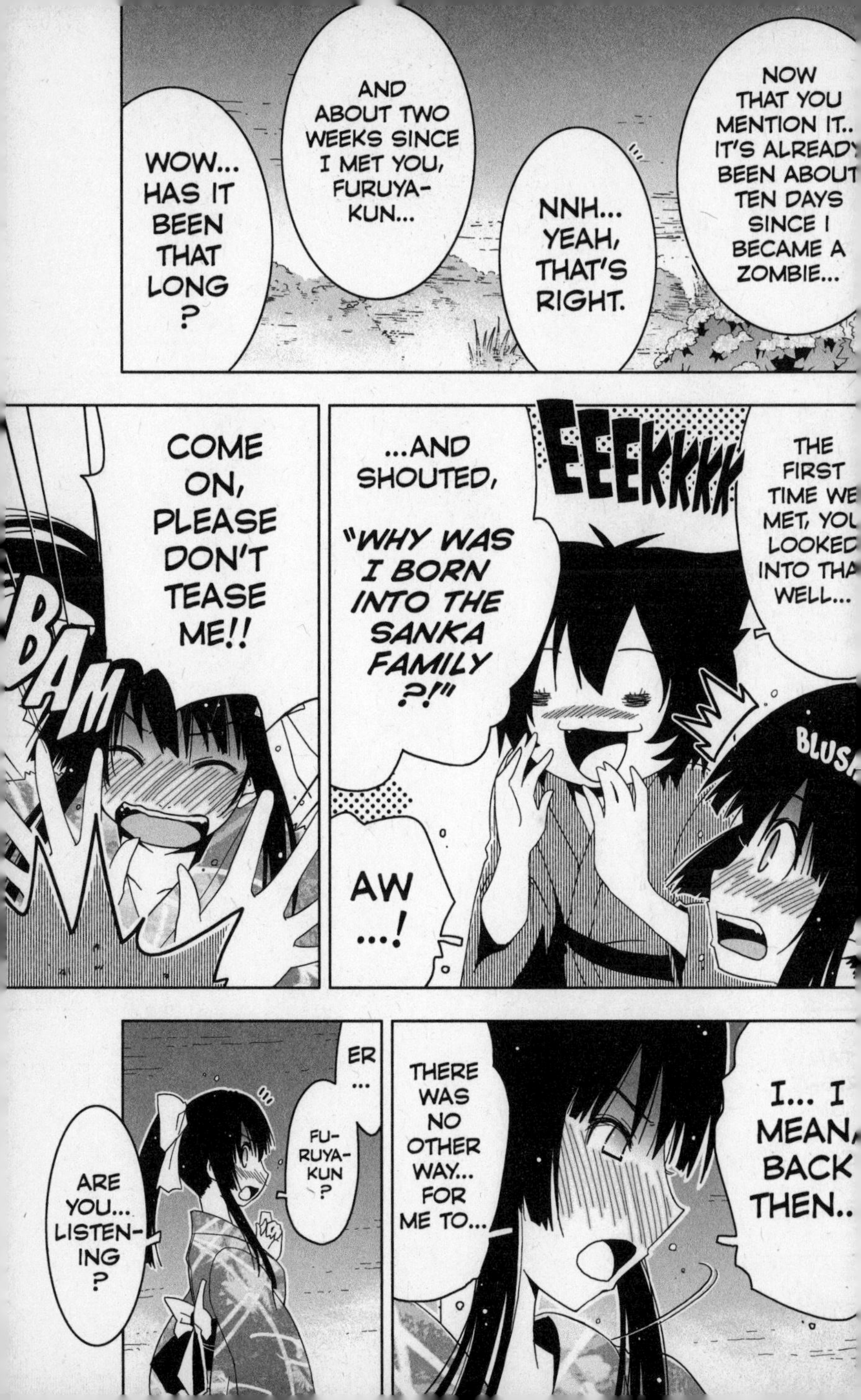
NOW THAT YOU MENTION IT.. IT'S ALREADY BEEN ABOUT TEN DAYS SINCE I BECAME A ZOMBIE...
NNH... YEAH, THAT'S RIGHT.
AND ABOUT TWO WEEKS SINCE I MET YOU, FURUYA-KUN...
WOW... HAS IT BEEN THAT LONG ?
THE FIRST TIME WE MET, YOU LOOKED INTO THAT WELL...
BLUSH
EEEKKKK
...AND SHOUTED, "WHY WAS I BORN INTO THE SANKA FAMILY ?!"
AW ...!
COME ON, PLEASE DON'T TEASE ME!!
BAM
I... I MEAN, BACK THEN...
THERE WAS NO OTHER WAY... FOR ME TO...
ER ...
FU-RUYA-KUN ?
ARE YOU... LISTEN-ING ?

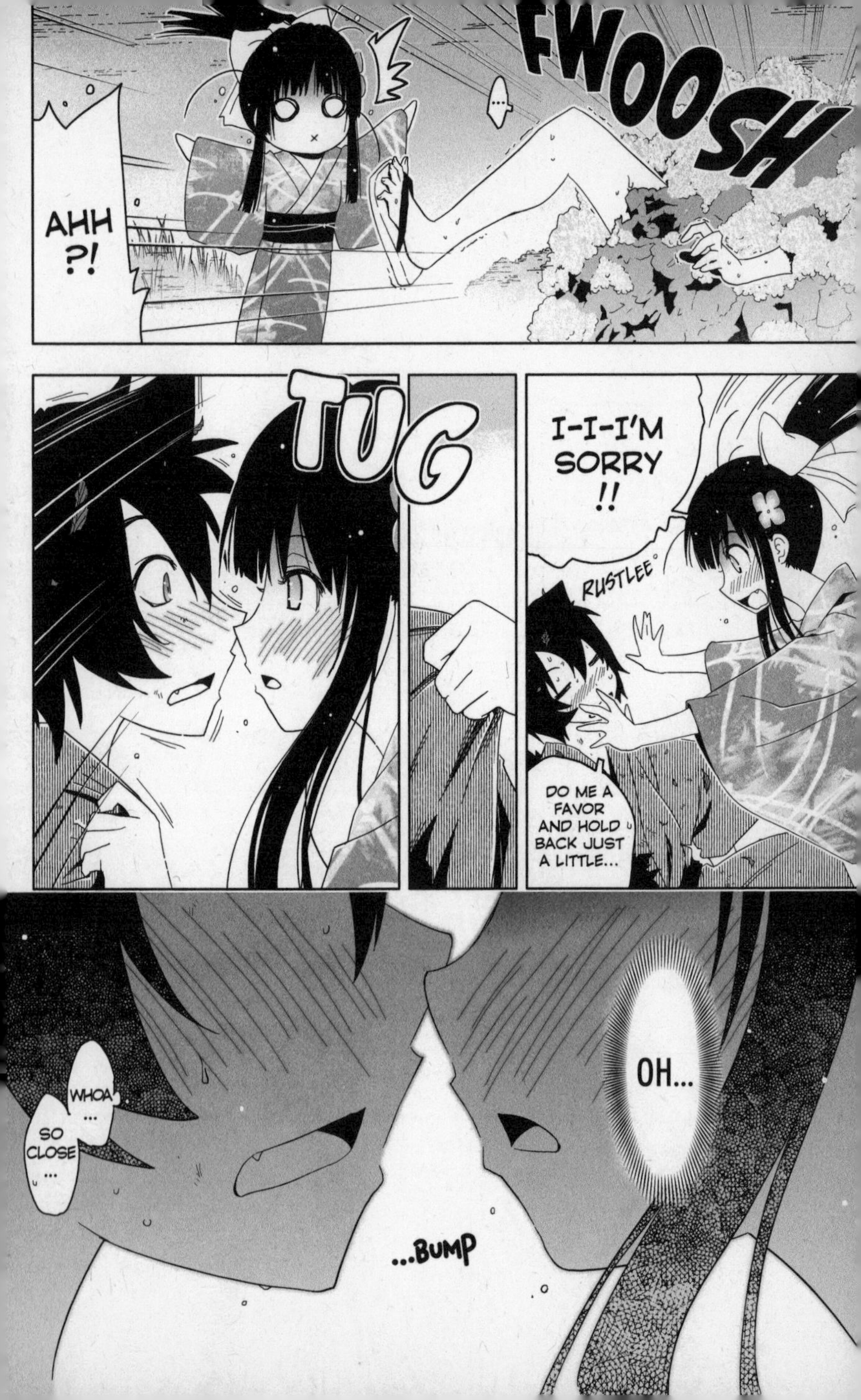
FWOOSH
...
AHH ?!
I-I-I'M SORRY !!
RUSTLEE
DO ME A FAVOR AND HOLD BACK JUST A LITTLE...
TUG
OH...
WHOA... SO CLOSE...
...BUMP

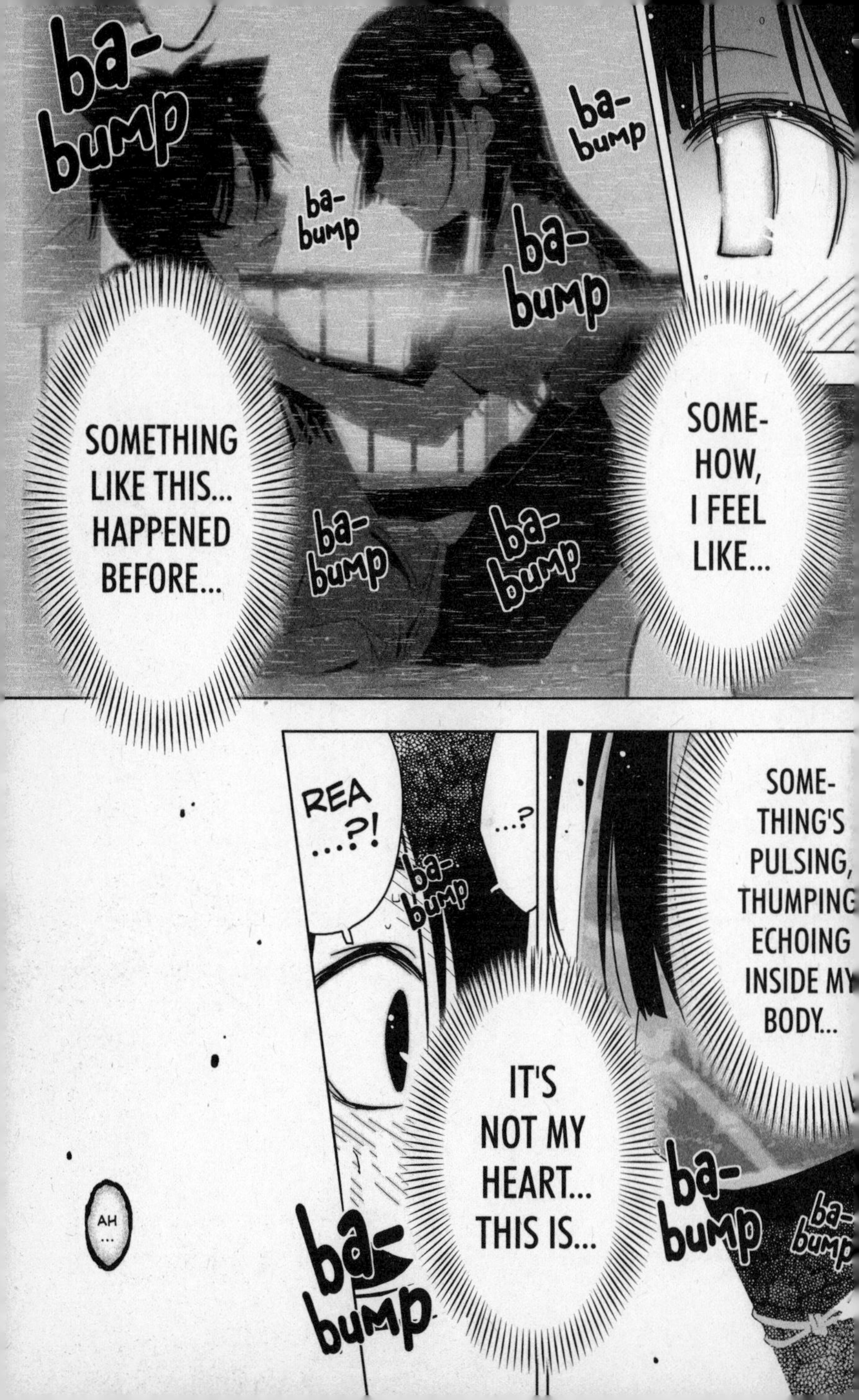
ba-bump
SOME-HOW, I FEEL LIKE...
ba-bump
ba-bump
ba-bump
ba-bump
ba-bump
SOMETHING LIKE THIS... HAPPENED BEFORE...
SOME-THING'S PULSING, THUMPING ECHOING INSIDE MY BODY...
...?
ba-bump
REA ...?!
ba-bump
ba-bump
IT'S NOT MY HEART... THIS IS...
ba-bump
AH ...

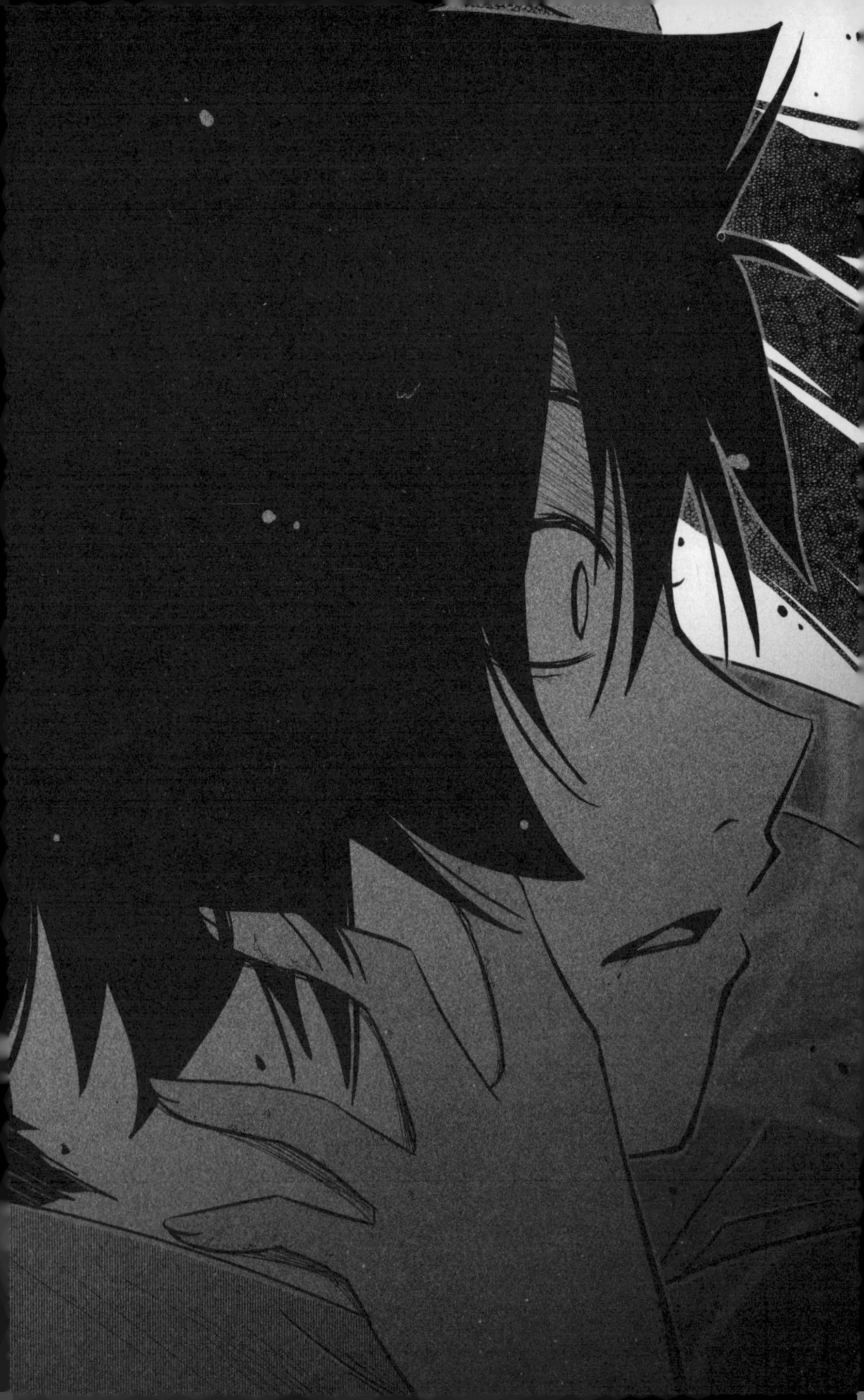

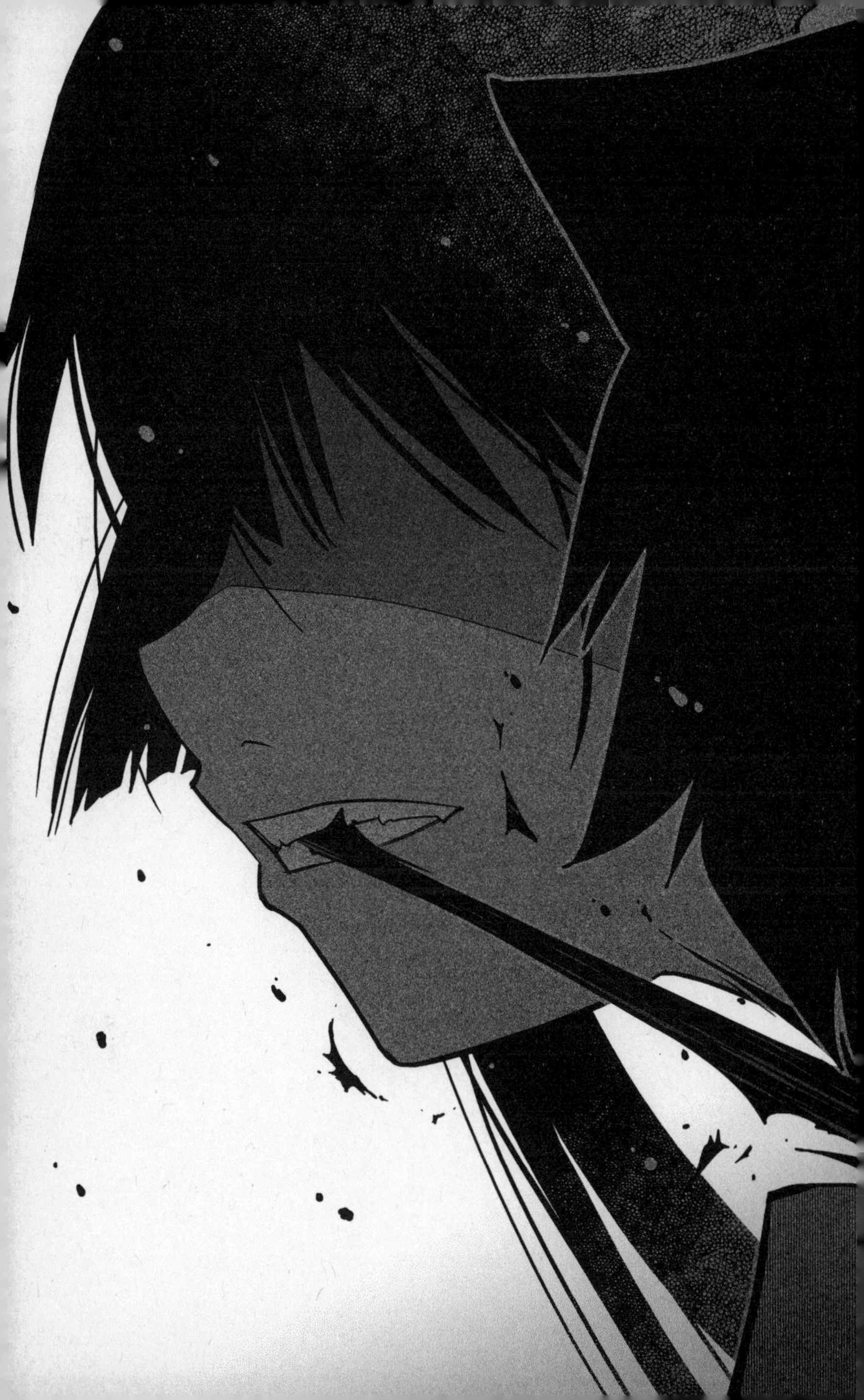

SANKAREA

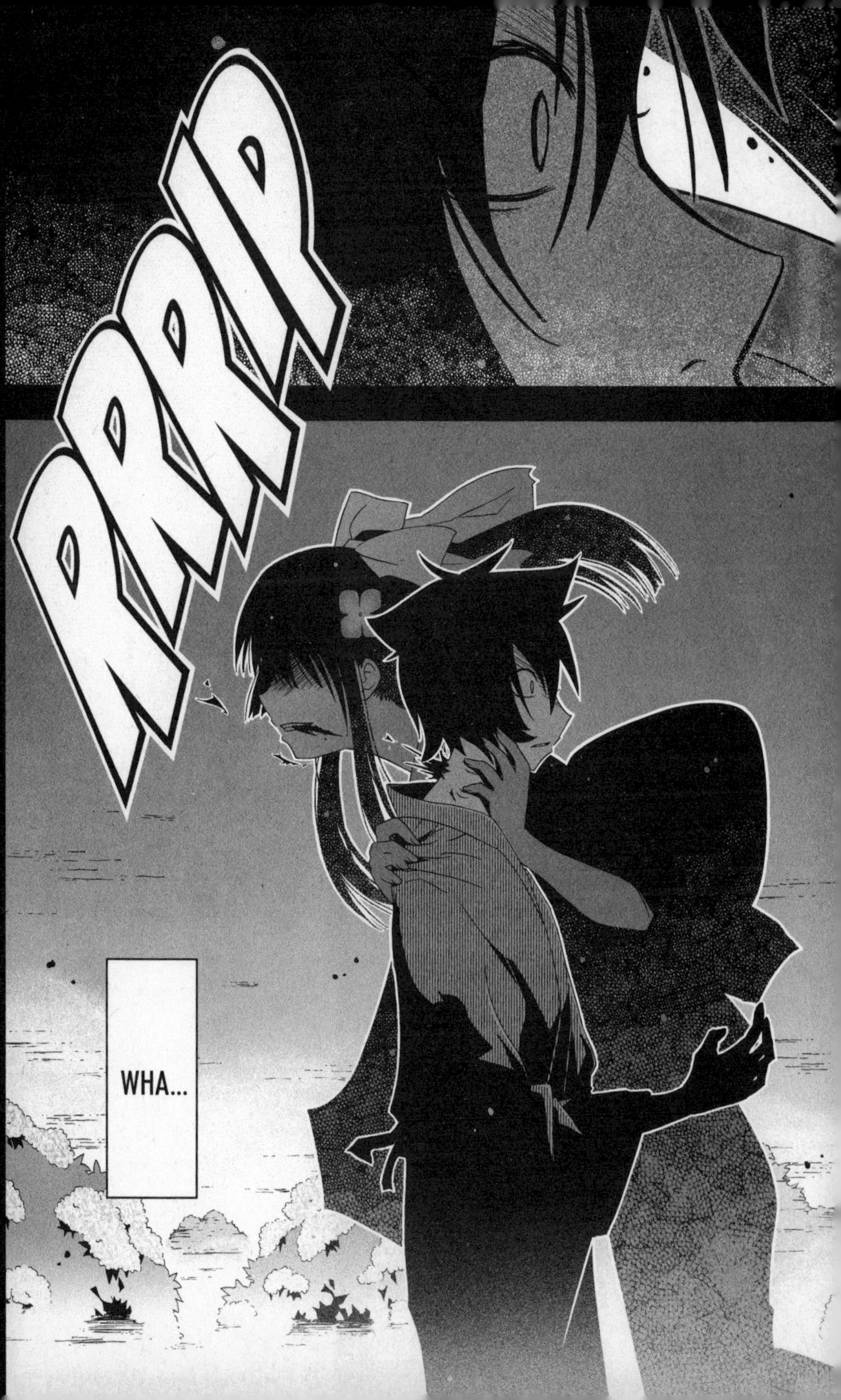
RRRIP
WHA...

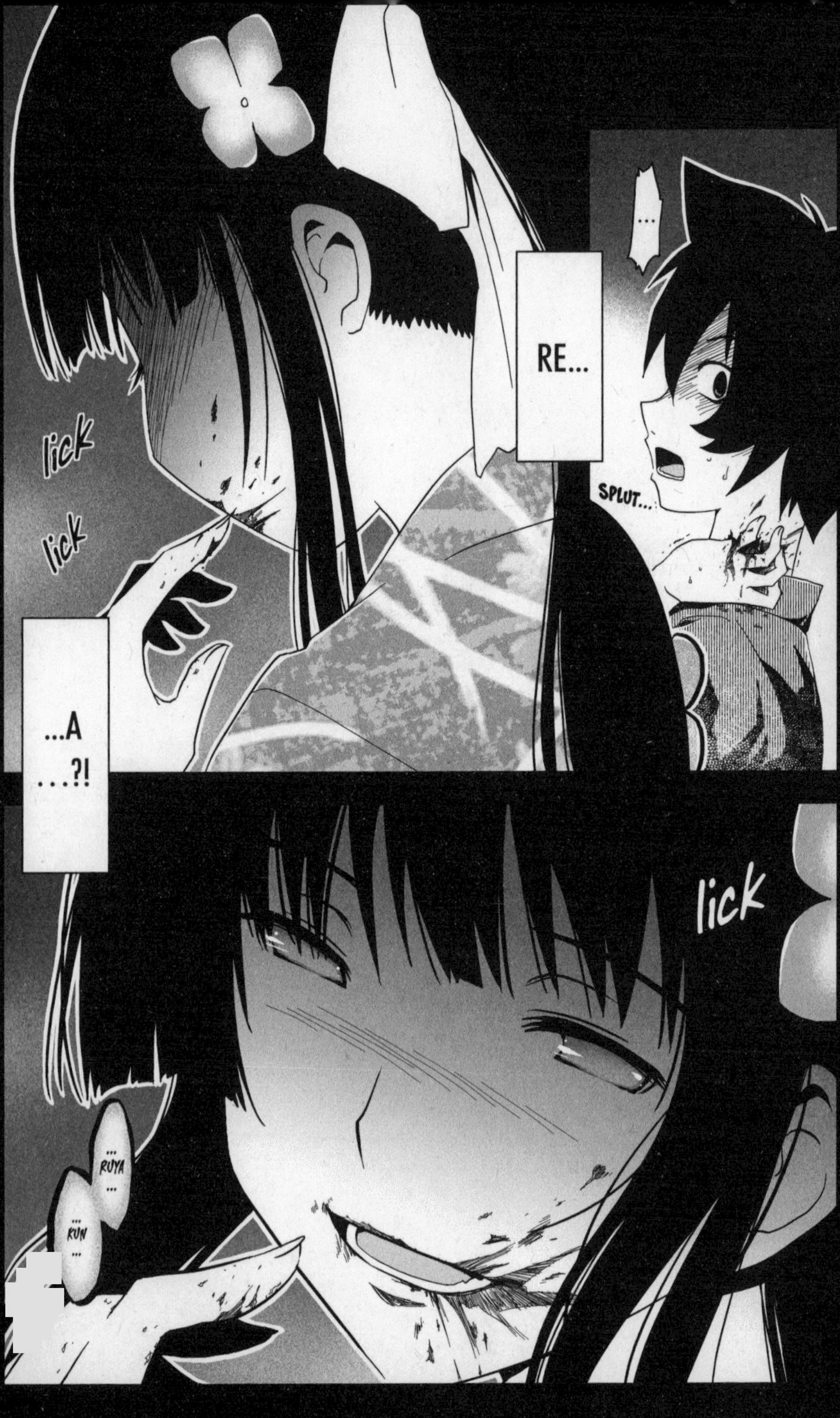
...
RE...
SPLUT...
lick
lick
...A
...?!
lick
...RUYA...
...KUN...

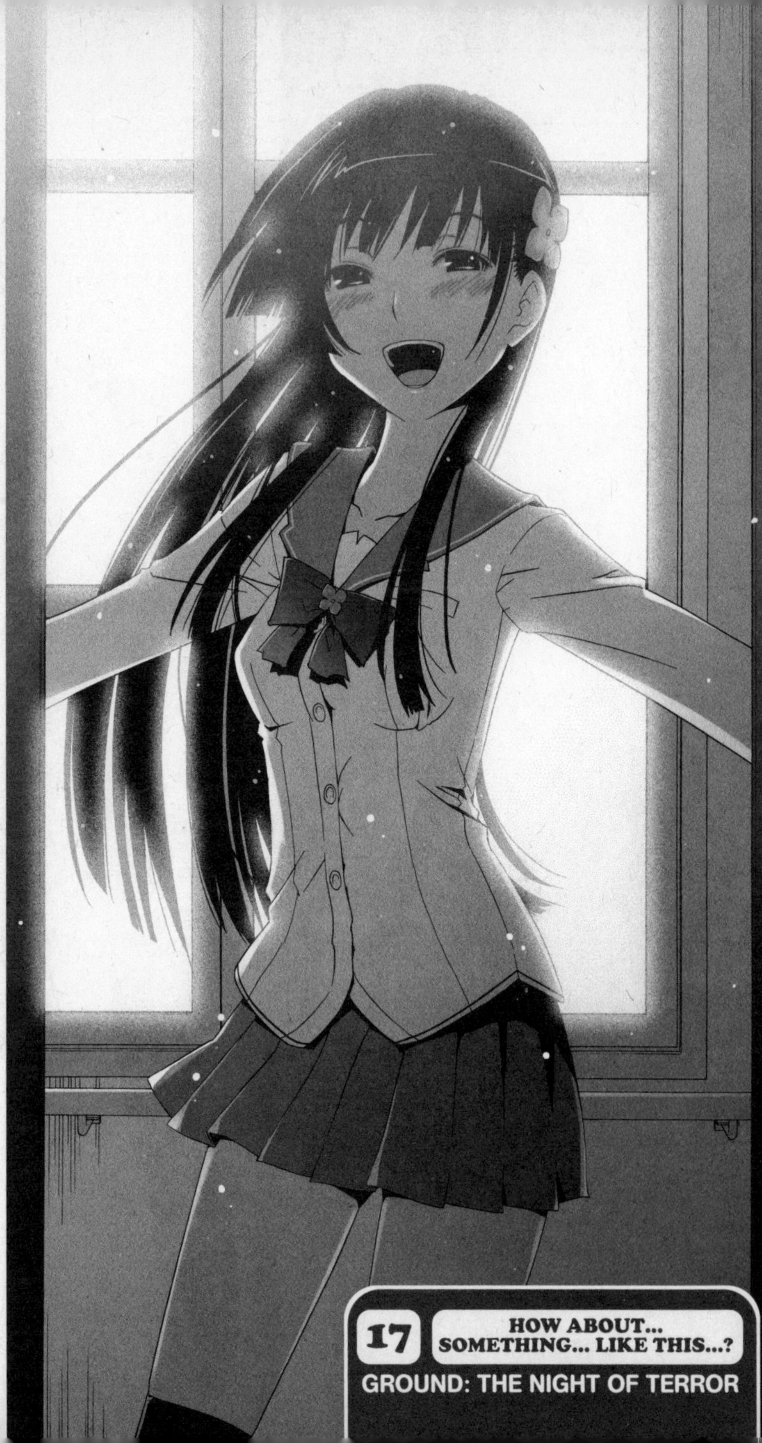

17 HOW ABOUT... SOMETHING... LIKE THIS...?

GROUND: THE NIGHT OF TERROR

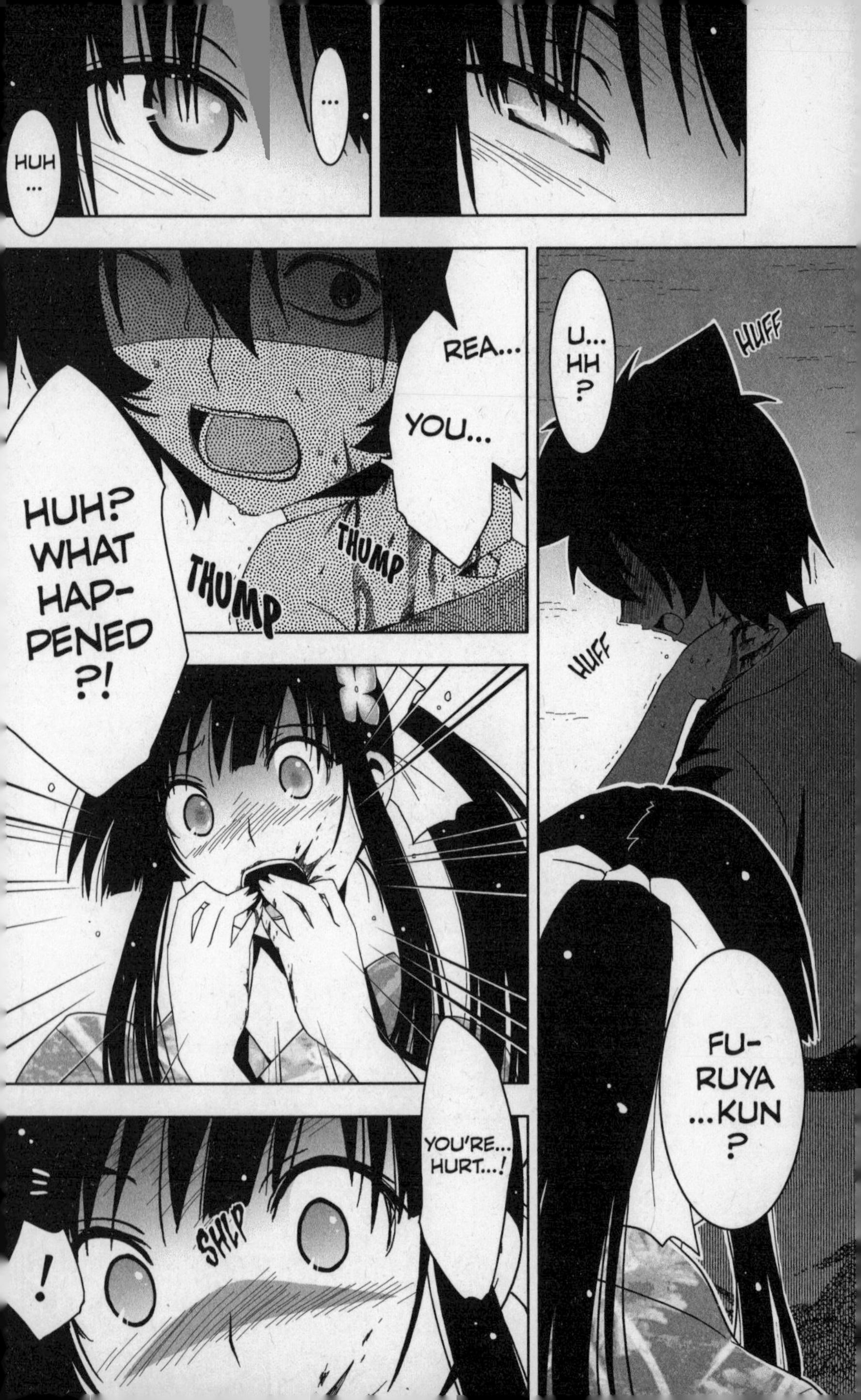
...
HUH ...
U... HH?
HUFF
HUFF
FU-RUYA ...KUN?
REA...
YOU...
HUH? WHAT HAP-PENED ?!
THUMP
THUMP
YOU'RE... HURT...!
SHLP
!

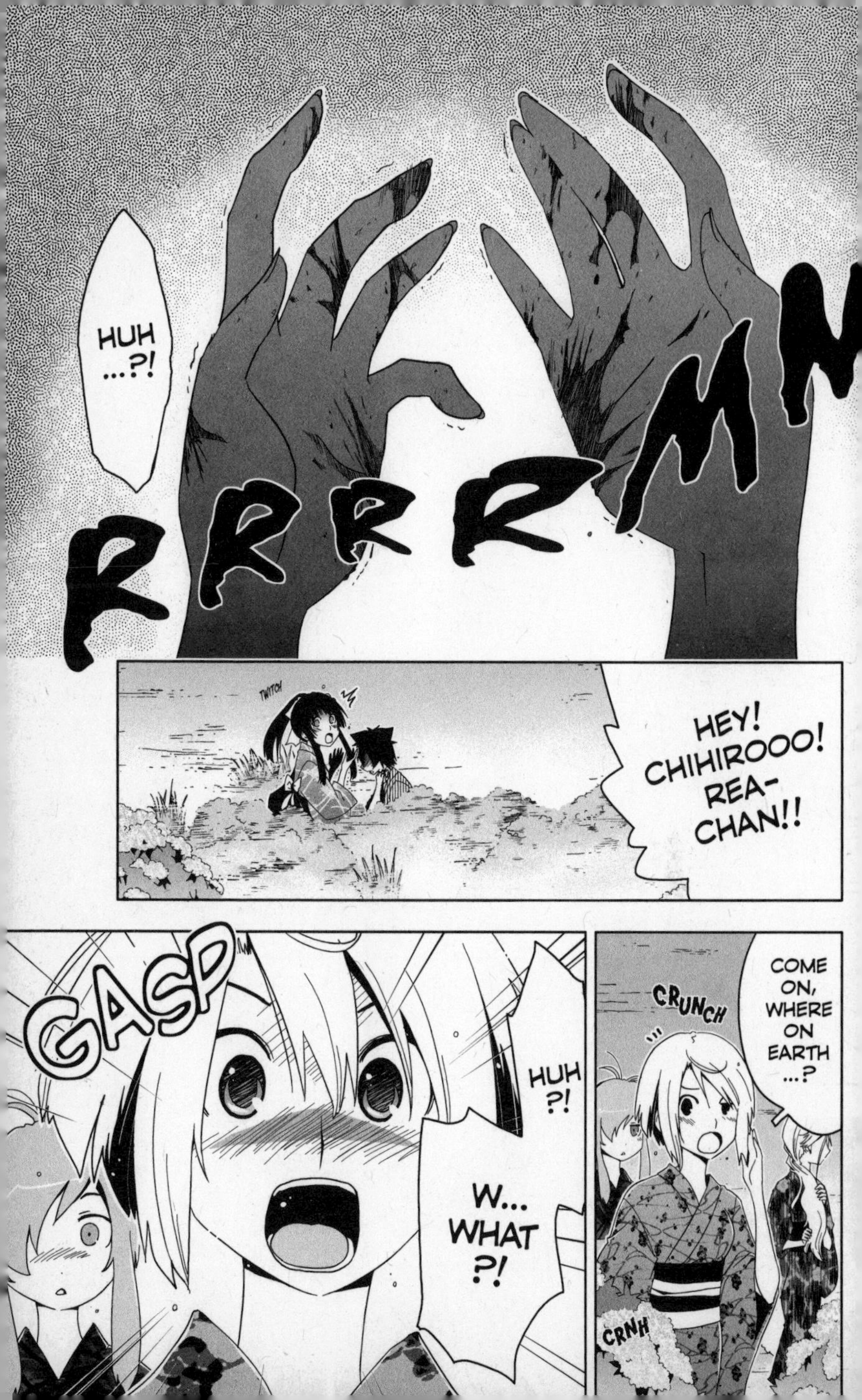
RRRRMM
HUH ...?!
TWITCH
HEY! CHIHIROOO! REA-CHAN!!
COME ON, WHERE ON EARTH ...?
CRUNCH
CRNH
GASP
HUH ?!
W... WHAT ?!

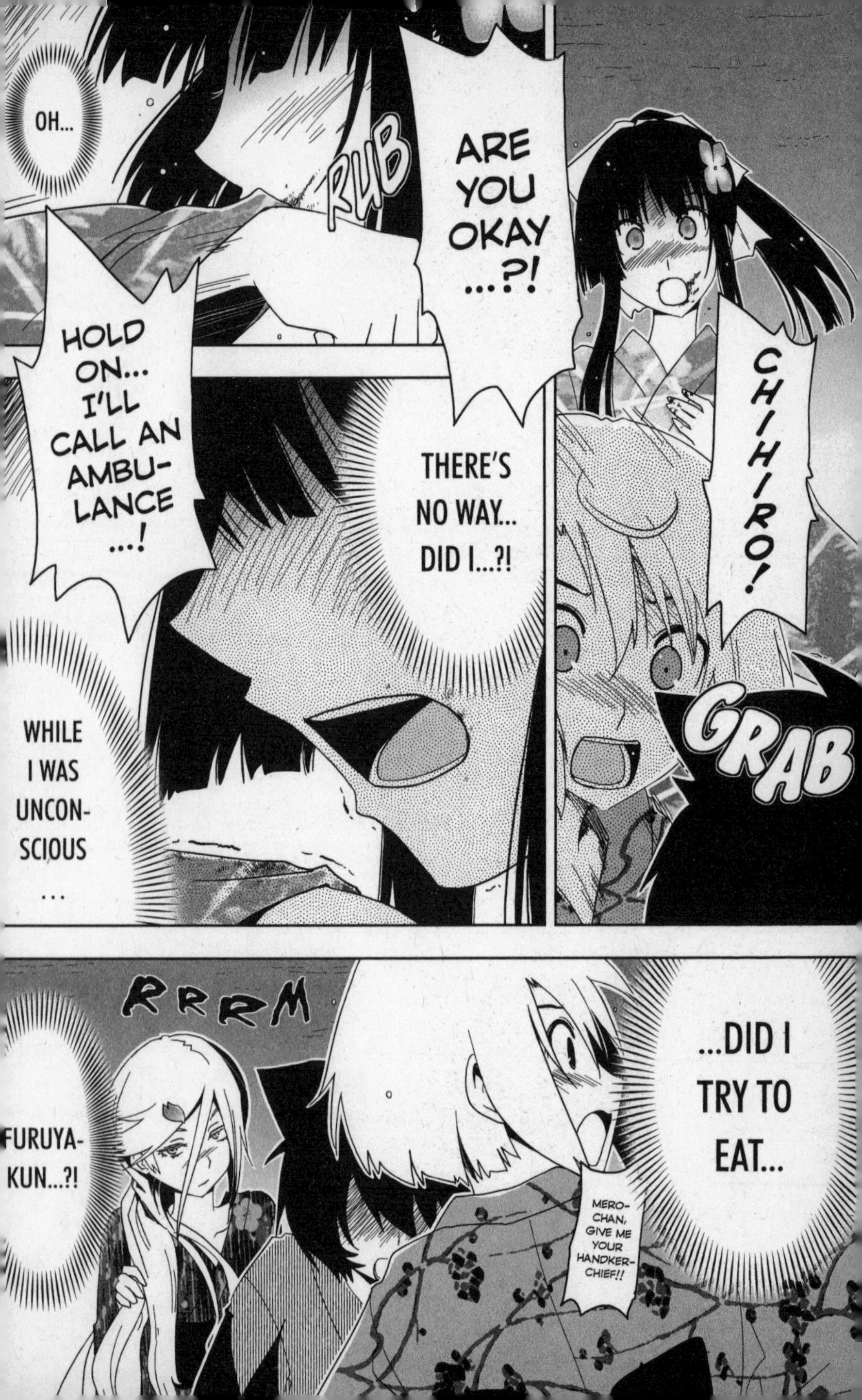
CHIHIRO!
GRAB
ARE YOU OKAY ...?!
RUB
OH...
HOLD ON... I'LL CALL AN AMBU-LANCE ...!
THERE'S NO WAY... DID I...?!
WHILE I WAS UNCON-SCIOUS ...
...DID I TRY TO EAT...
MERO-CHAN, GIVE ME YOUR HANDKER-CHIEF!!
RRRM
FURUYA-KUN...?!

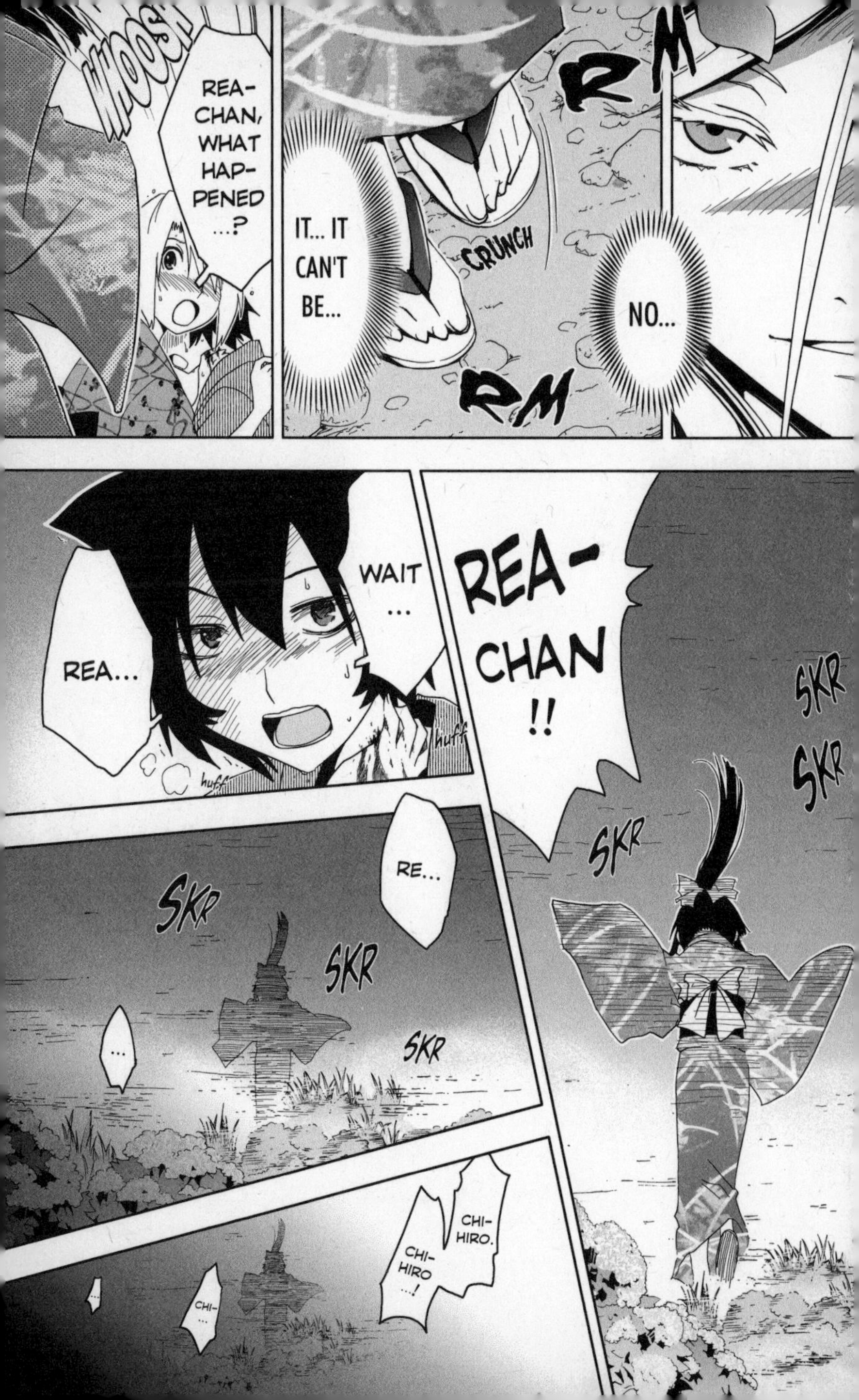
RM
NO...
CRUNCH
IT... IT CAN'T BE...
RM
WHOOSH
REA-CHAN, WHAT HAP-PENED ...?
REA-CHAN!!
SKR
SKR
SKR
WAIT ...
REA...
huff
huff
RE...
SKR
SKR
SKR
...
CHI-HIRO.
CHI-HIRO ...!
CHI- ...
.

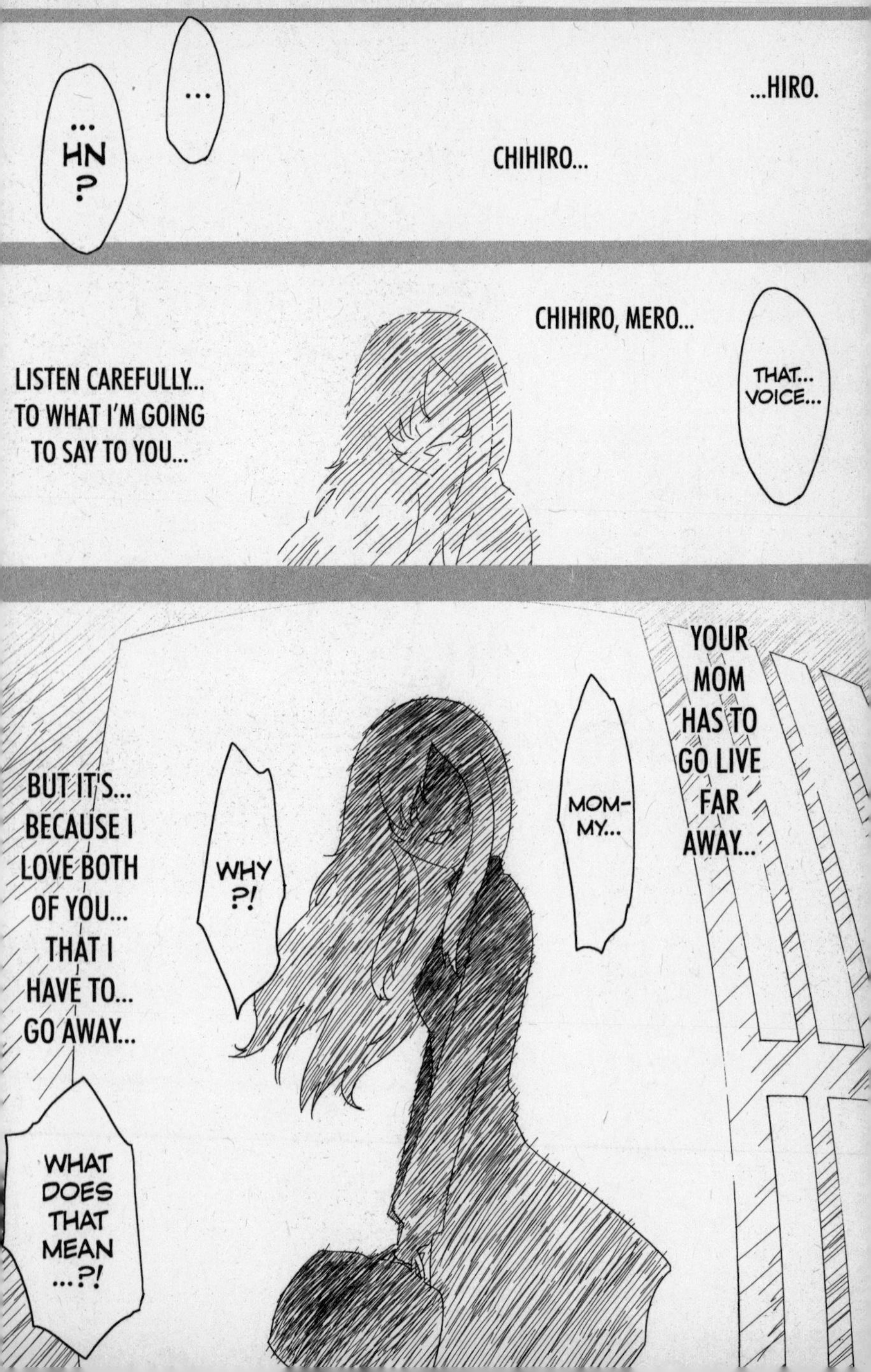
...HIRO.
CHIHIRO...
...
...HN?
THAT... VOICE...
CHIHIRO, MERO...
LISTEN CAREFULLY... TO WHAT I'M GOING TO SAY TO YOU...
YOUR MOM HAS TO GO LIVE FAR AWAY...
MOM-MY...
WHY?!
BUT IT'S... BECAUSE I LOVE BOTH OF YOU... THAT I HAVE TO... GO AWAY...
WHAT DOES THAT MEAN...?!

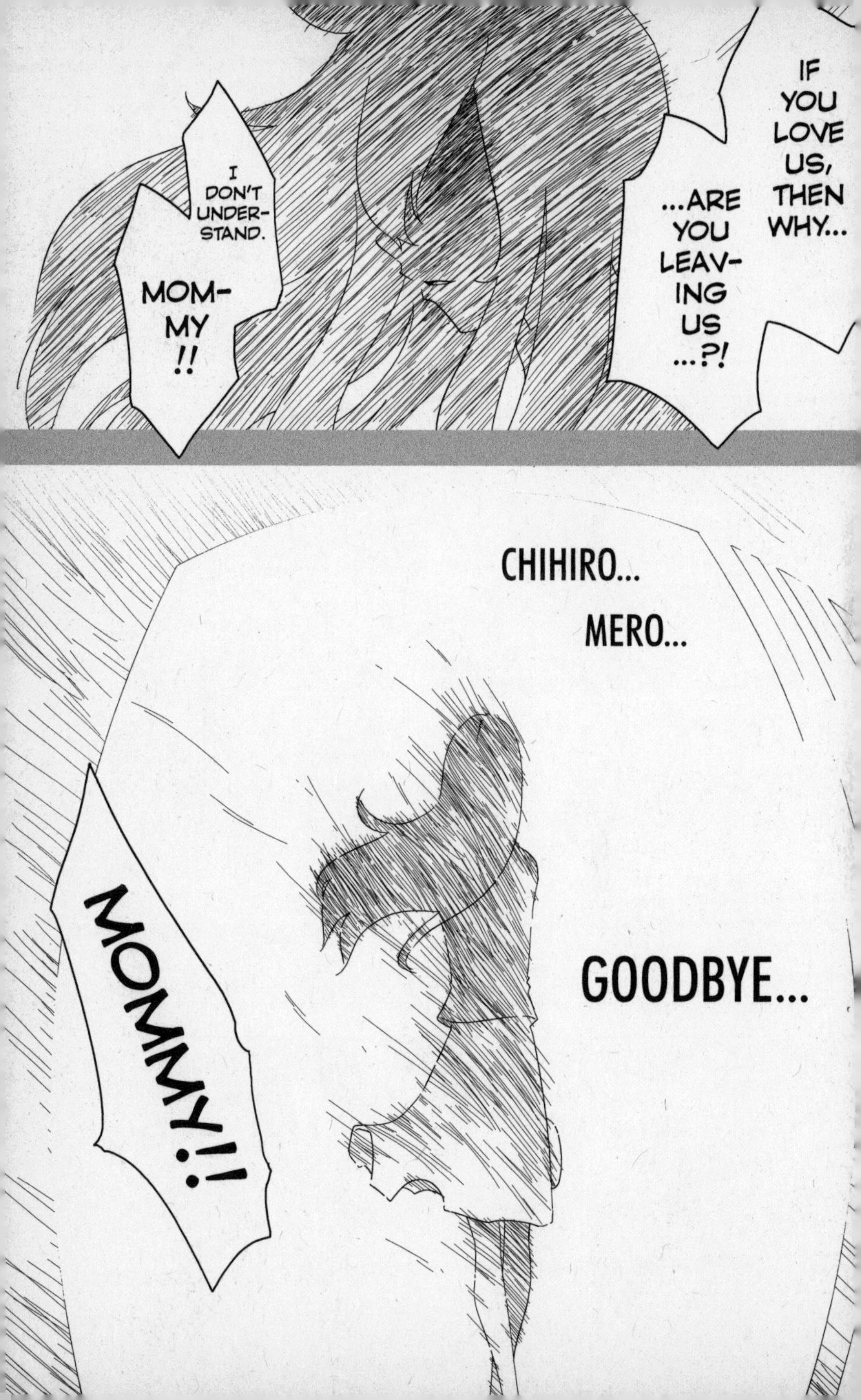
IF YOU LOVE US, THEN WHY...
...ARE YOU LEAVING US ...?!
I DON'T UNDERSTAND.
MOMMY!!
CHIHIRO...
MERO...
GOODBYE...
MOMMY!!

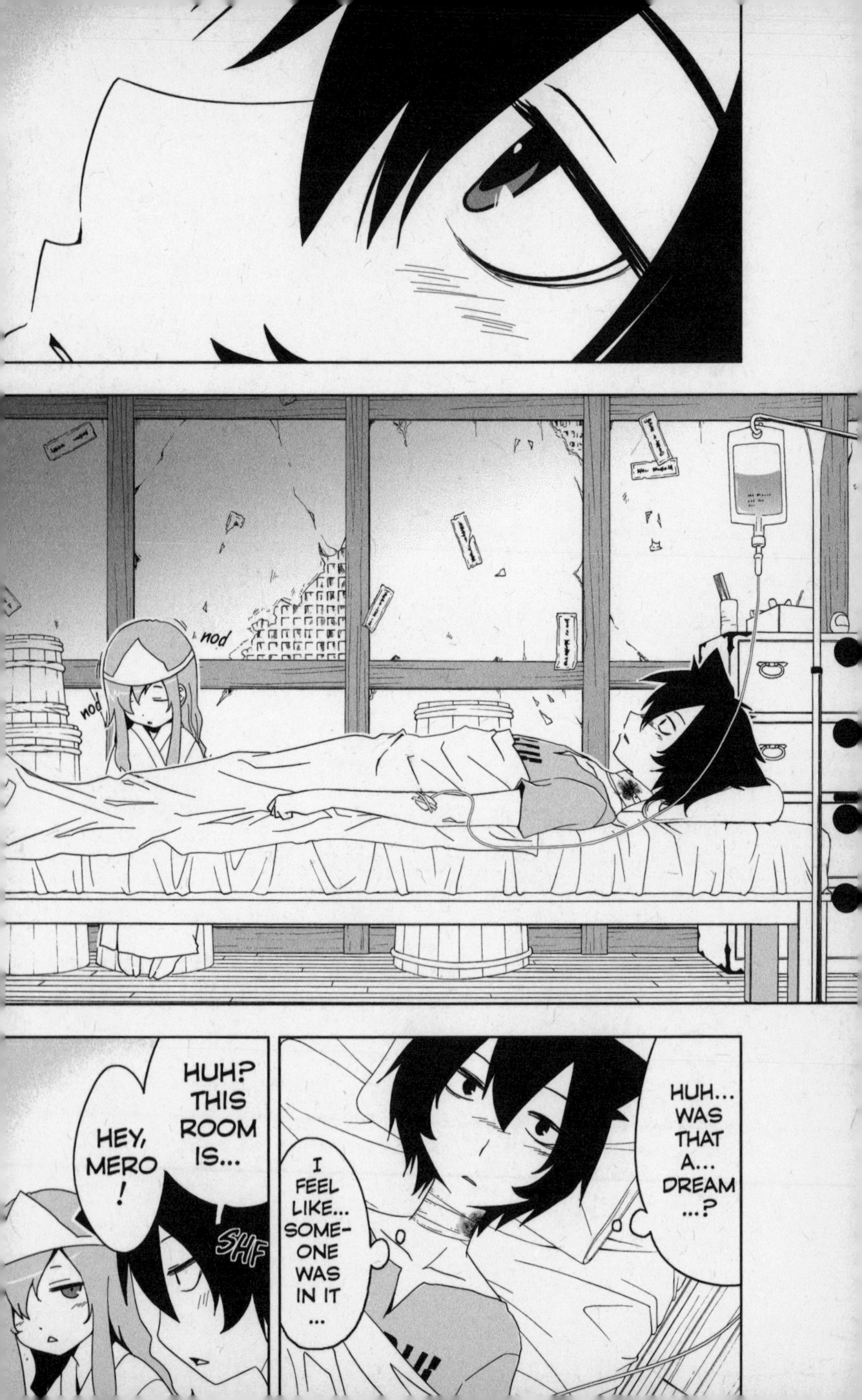
nod
nod
HUH... WAS THAT A... DREAM ...?
I FEEL LIKE... SOME-ONE WAS IN IT ...
HUH? THIS ROOM IS...
HEY, MERO!
SHF

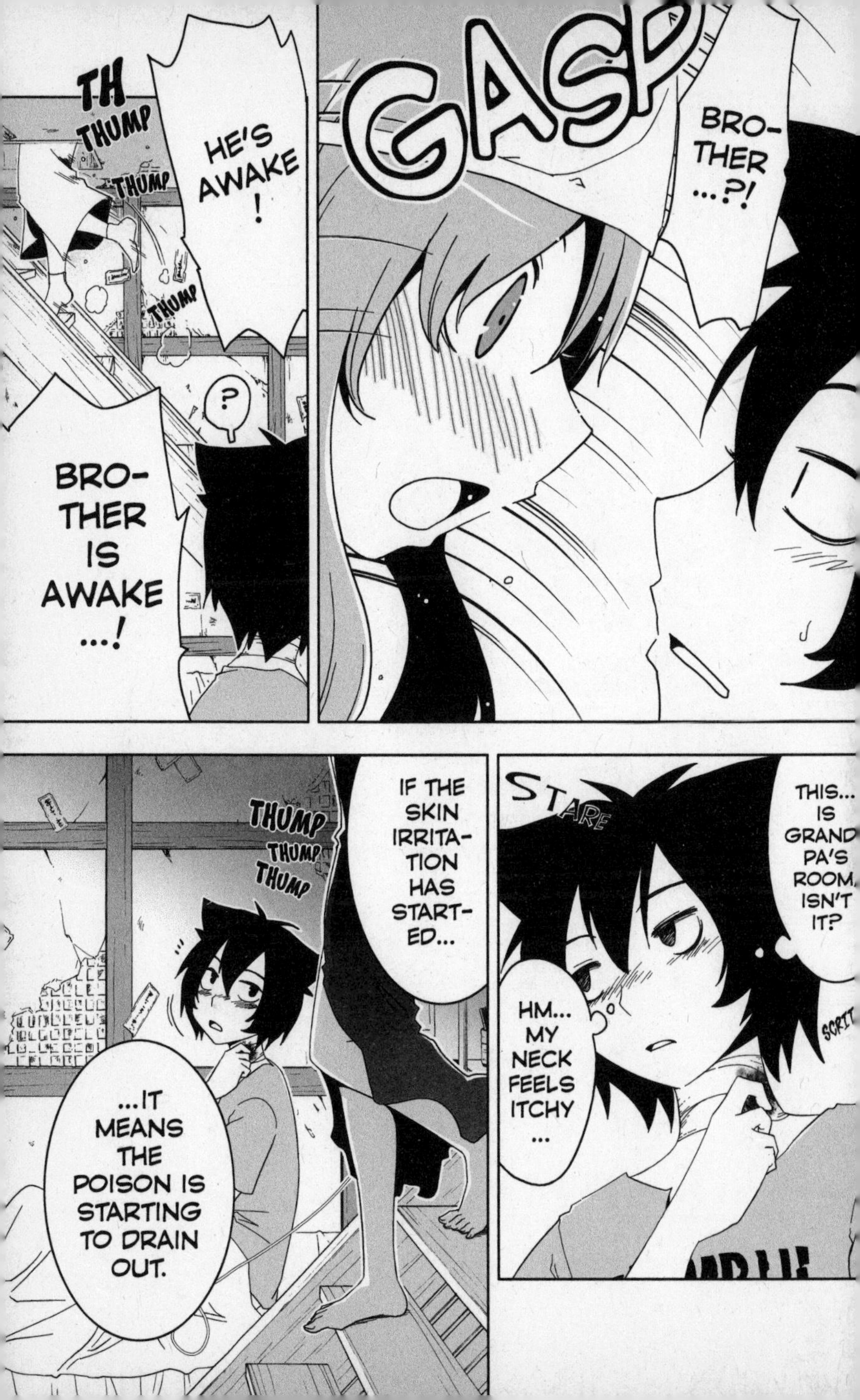
GASP
BROTHER...?!
TH THUMP
HE'S AWAKE!
THUMP
THUMP
?
BROTHER IS AWAKE...!
STARE
THIS... IS GRANDPA'S ROOM, ISN'T IT?
SCRIT
HM... MY NECK FEELS ITCHY...
IF THE SKIN IRRITATION HAS STARTED...
THUMP
THUMP
THUMP
...IT MEANS THE POISON IS STARTING TO DRAIN OUT.

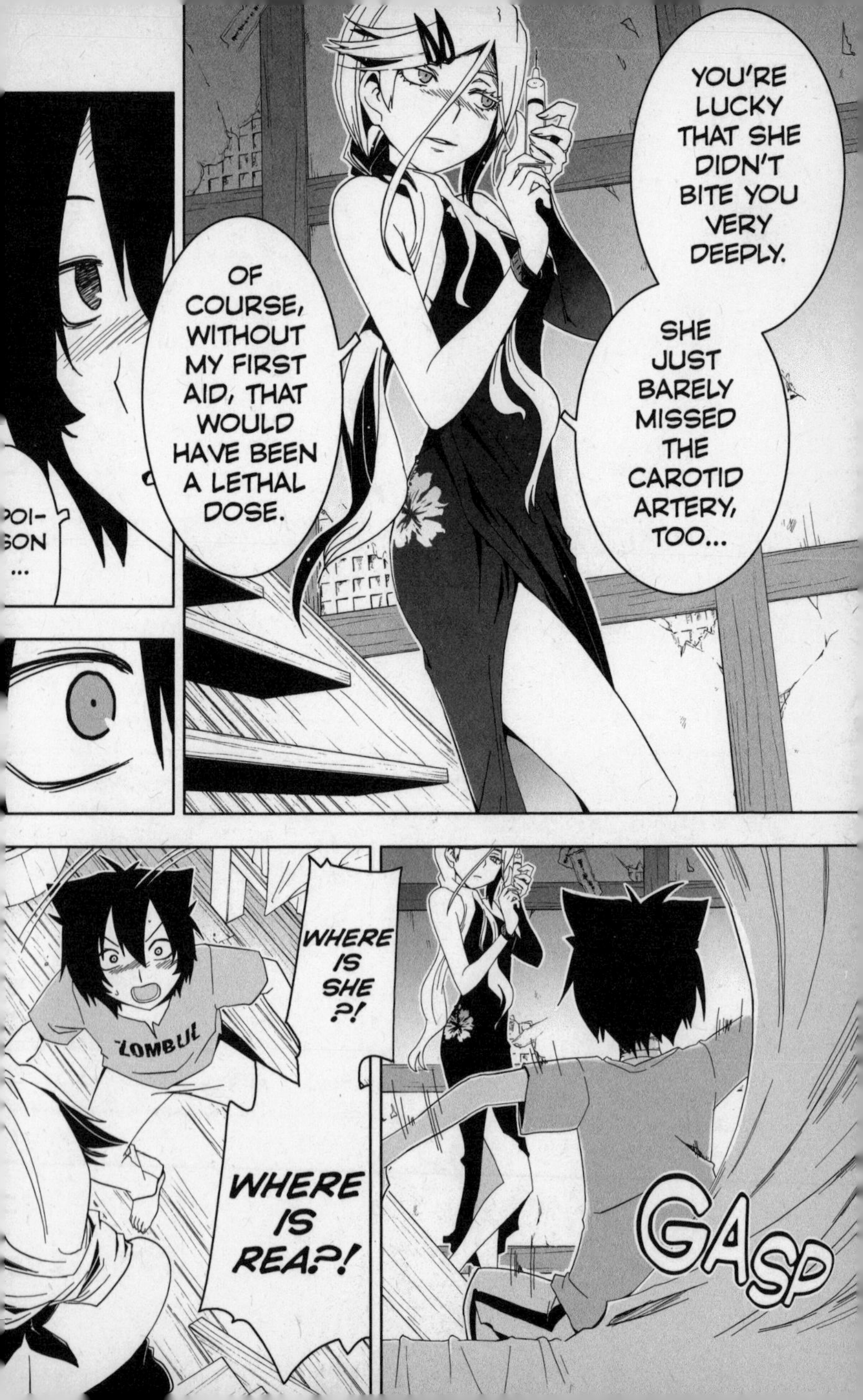
YOU'RE LUCKY THAT SHE DIDN'T BITE YOU VERY DEEPLY.
SHE JUST BARELY MISSED THE CAROTID ARTERY, TOO...
OF COURSE, WITHOUT MY FIRST AID, THAT WOULD HAVE BEEN A LETHAL DOSE.
POI-SON ...
GASP
WHERE IS SHE?!
WHERE IS REA?!

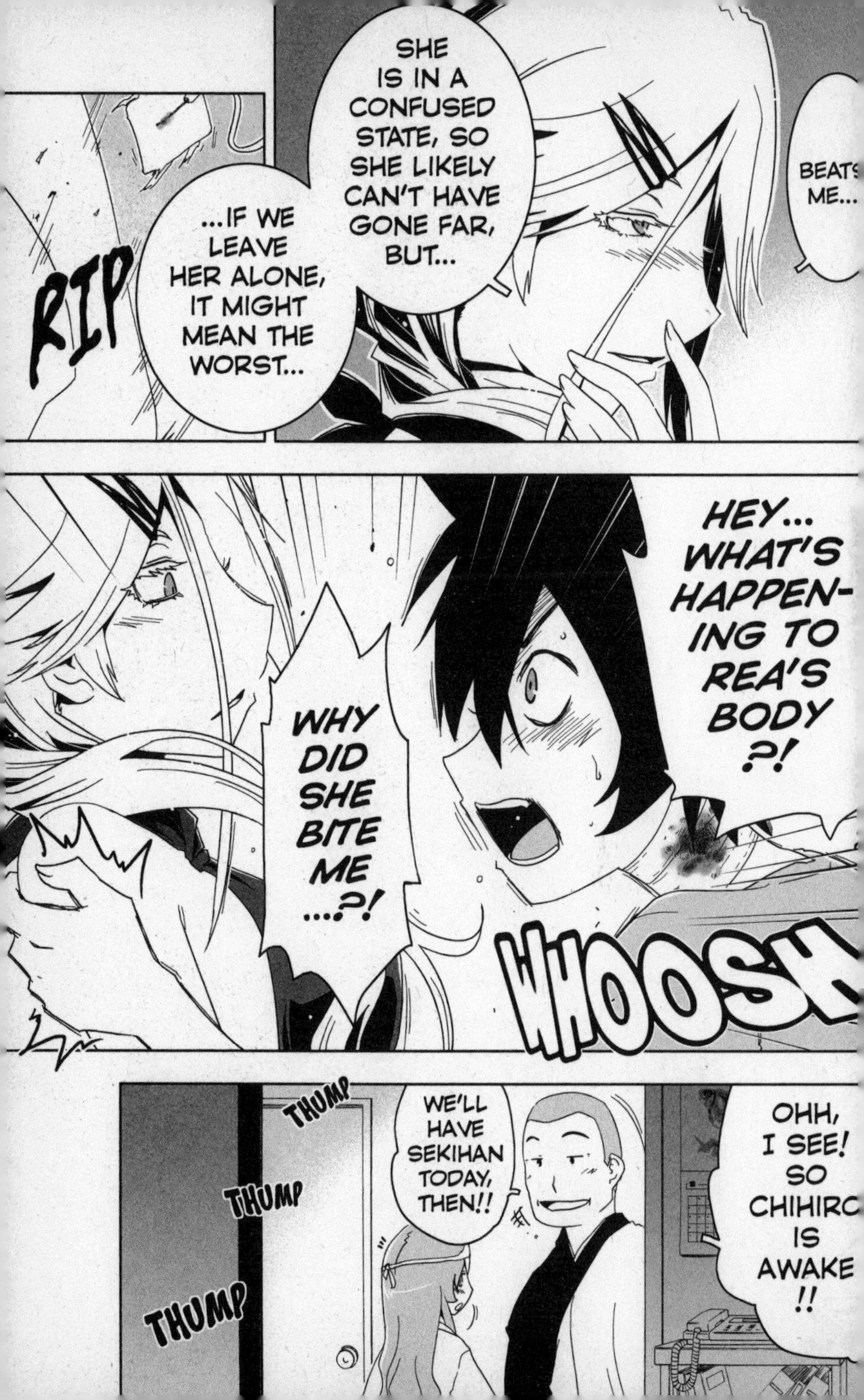
BEATS ME...
SHE IS IN A CONFUSED STATE, SO SHE LIKELY CAN'T HAVE GONE FAR, BUT...
...IF WE LEAVE HER ALONE, IT MIGHT MEAN THE WORST...
RIP
HEY... WHAT'S HAPPEN-ING TO REA'S BODY ?!
WHY DID SHE BITE ME ...?!
WHOOSH
OHH, I SEE! SO CHIHIRO IS AWAKE !!
WE'LL HAVE SEKIHAN TODAY, THEN!!
THUMP
THUMP
THUMP

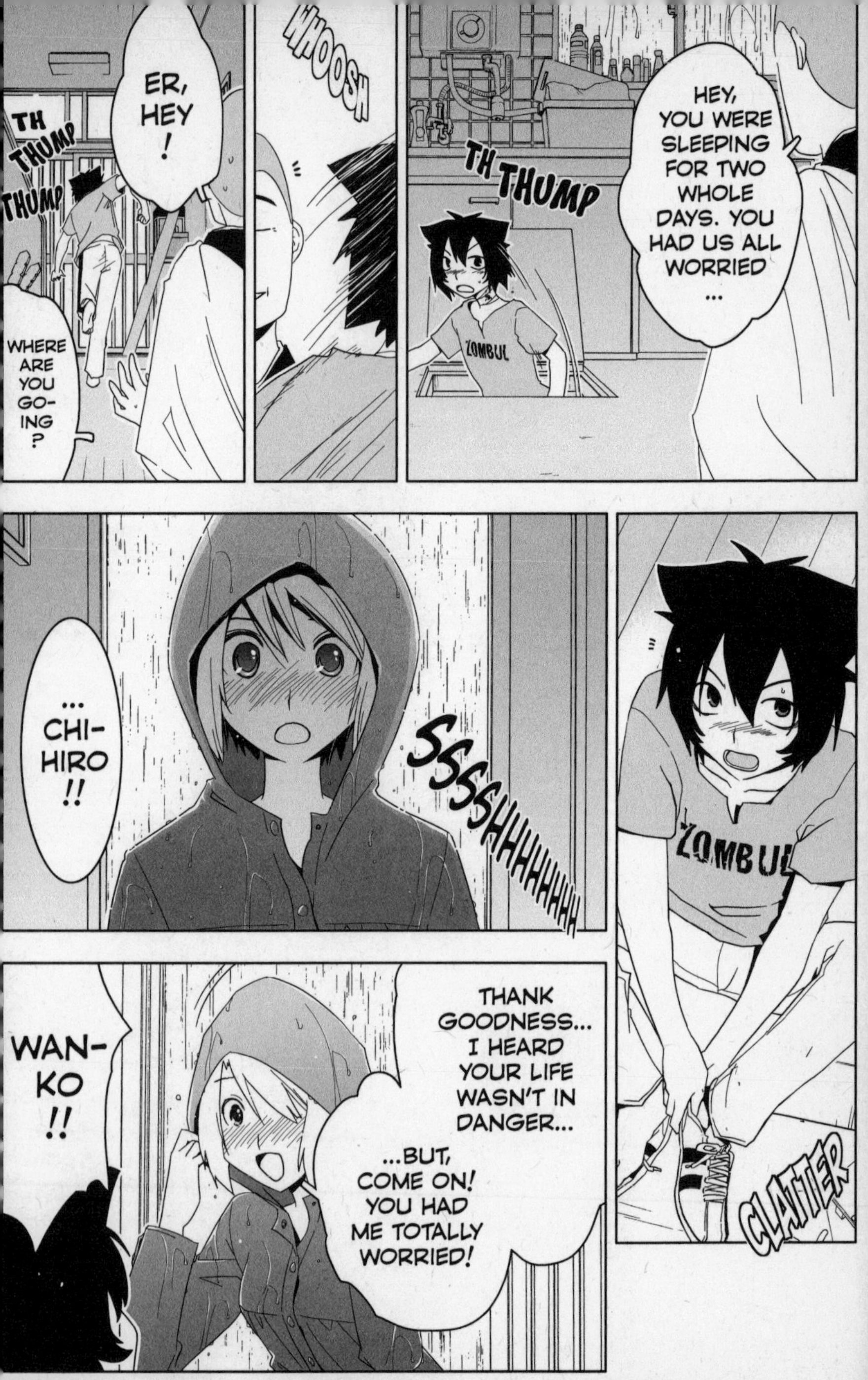
HEY, YOU WERE SLEEPING FOR TWO WHOLE DAYS. YOU HAD US ALL WORRIED ...
TH THUMP
WHOOSH
ER, HEY!
TH THUMP THUMP
WHERE ARE YOU GO-ING?
CLATTER
SSSSHHHHHHHH
... CHI-HIRO!!
THANK GOODNESS... I HEARD YOUR LIFE WASN'T IN DANGER...
...BUT, COME ON! YOU HAD ME TOTALLY WORRIED!
WAN-KO!!

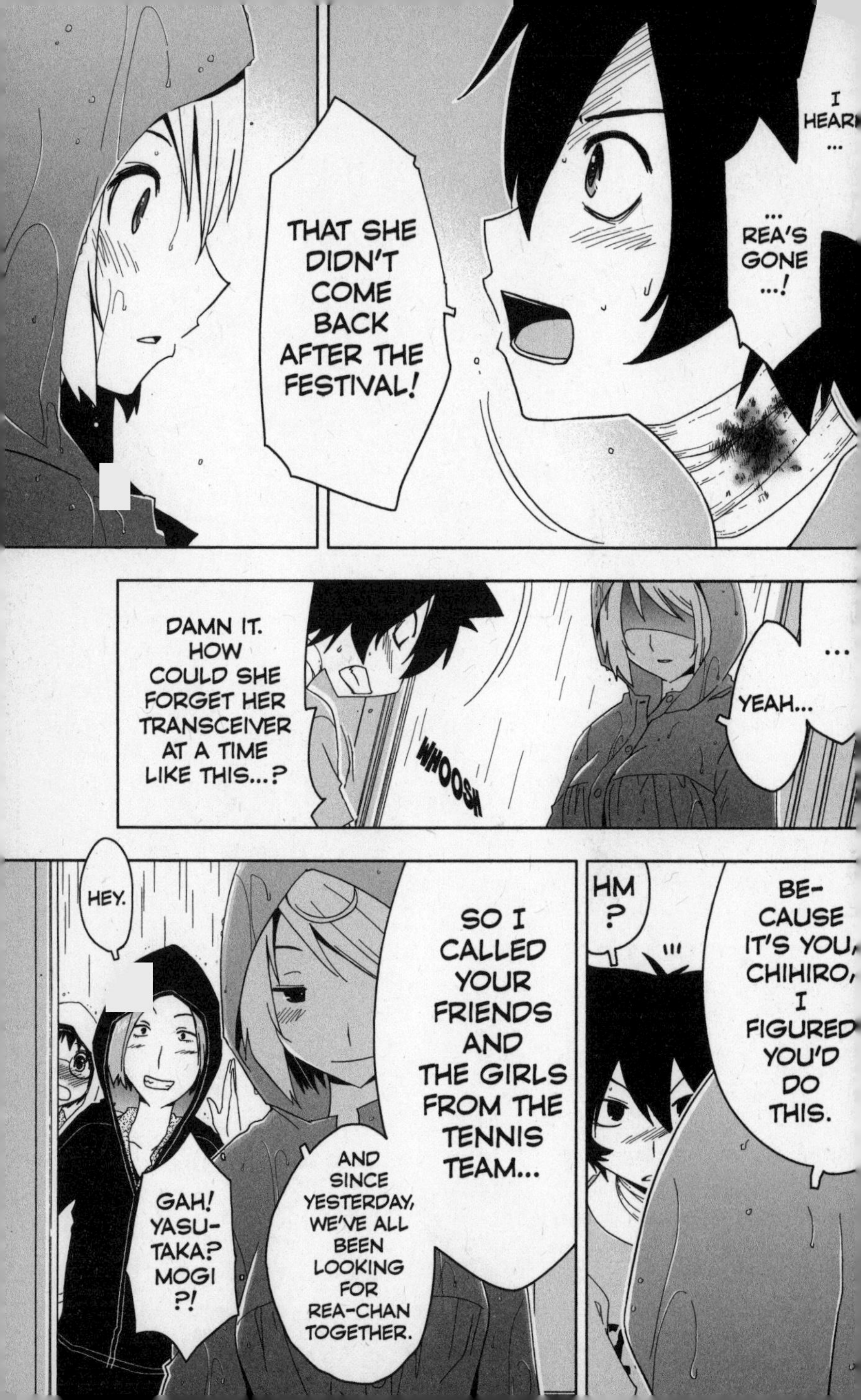
I HEAR... ...REA'S GONE...!
THAT SHE DIDN'T COME BACK AFTER THE FESTIVAL!
...
YEAH...
DAMN IT. HOW COULD SHE FORGET HER TRANSCEIVER AT A TIME LIKE THIS...?
WHOOSH
BE-CAUSE IT'S YOU, CHIHIRO, I FIGURED YOU'D DO THIS.
HM?
SO I CALLED YOUR FRIENDS AND THE GIRLS FROM THE TENNIS TEAM...
HEY.
AND SINCE YESTERDAY, WE'VE ALL BEEN LOOKING FOR REA-CHAN TOGETHER.
GAH! YASU-TAKA? MOGI?!

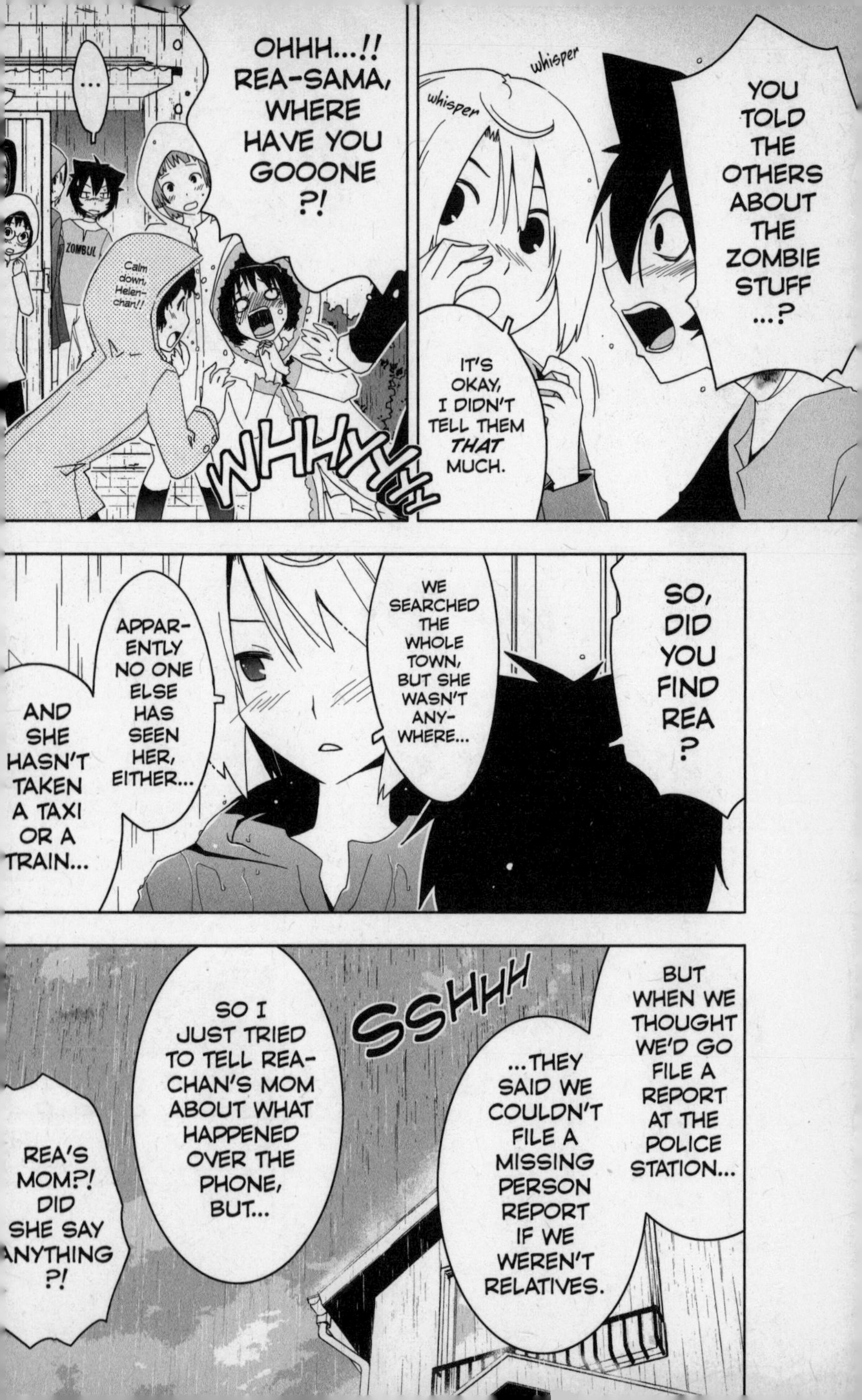
whisper
whisper
YOU TOLD THE OTHERS ABOUT THE ZOMBIE STUFF ...?
IT'S OKAY, I DIDN'T TELL THEM *THAT* MUCH.
OHHH...!! REA-SAMA, WHERE HAVE YOU GOOONE ?!
...
ZOMBUL
Calm down, Helen-chan!!
WHHYYYY
SO, DID YOU FIND REA ?
WE SEARCHED THE WHOLE TOWN, BUT SHE WASN'T ANY-WHERE...
APPAR-ENTLY NO ONE ELSE HAS SEEN HER, EITHER...
AND SHE HASN'T TAKEN A TAXI OR A TRAIN...
BUT WHEN WE THOUGHT WE'D GO FILE A REPORT AT THE POLICE STATION...
...THEY SAID WE COULDN'T FILE A MISSING PERSON REPORT IF WE WEREN'T RELATIVES.
SSHHH
SO I JUST TRIED TO TELL REA-CHAN'S MOM ABOUT WHAT HAPPENED OVER THE PHONE, BUT...
REA'S MOM?! DID SHE SAY ANYTHING ?!

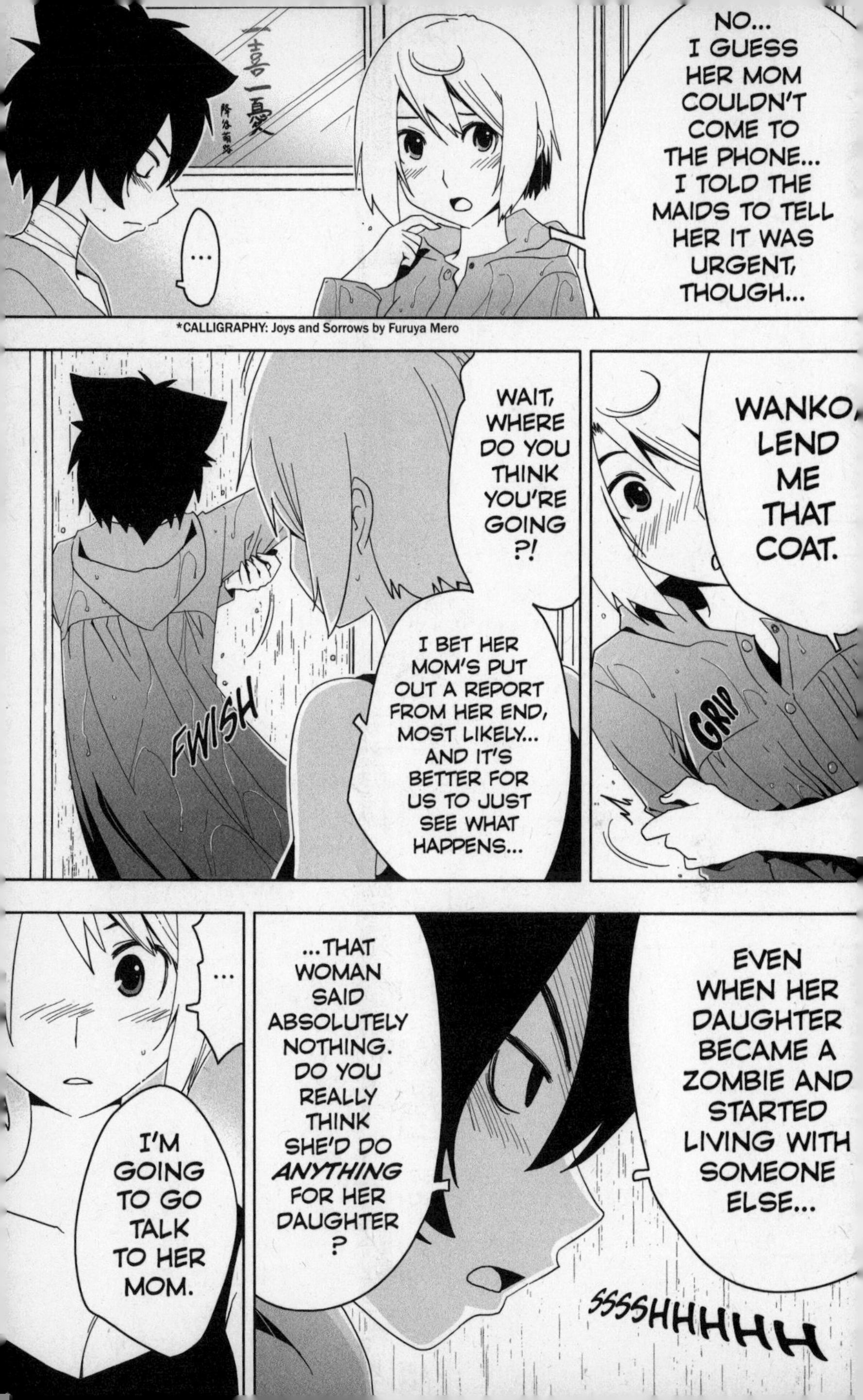

NO... I GUESS HER MOM COULDN'T COME TO THE PHONE... I TOLD THE MAIDS TO TELL HER IT WAS URGENT, THOUGH...
一喜一憂
...
*CALLIGRAPHY: Joys and Sorrows by Furuya Mero
WANKO, LEND ME THAT COAT.
GRIP
WAIT, WHERE DO YOU THINK YOU'RE GOING?!
I BET HER MOM'S PUT OUT A REPORT FROM HER END, MOST LIKELY... AND IT'S BETTER FOR US TO JUST SEE WHAT HAPPENS...
FWISH
EVEN WHEN HER DAUGHTER BECAME A ZOMBIE AND STARTED LIVING WITH SOMEONE ELSE...
...THAT WOMAN SAID ABSOLUTELY NOTHING. DO YOU REALLY THINK SHE'D DO *ANYTHING* FOR HER DAUGHTER?
SSSSHHHHHH
...
I'M GOING TO GO TALK TO HER MOM.

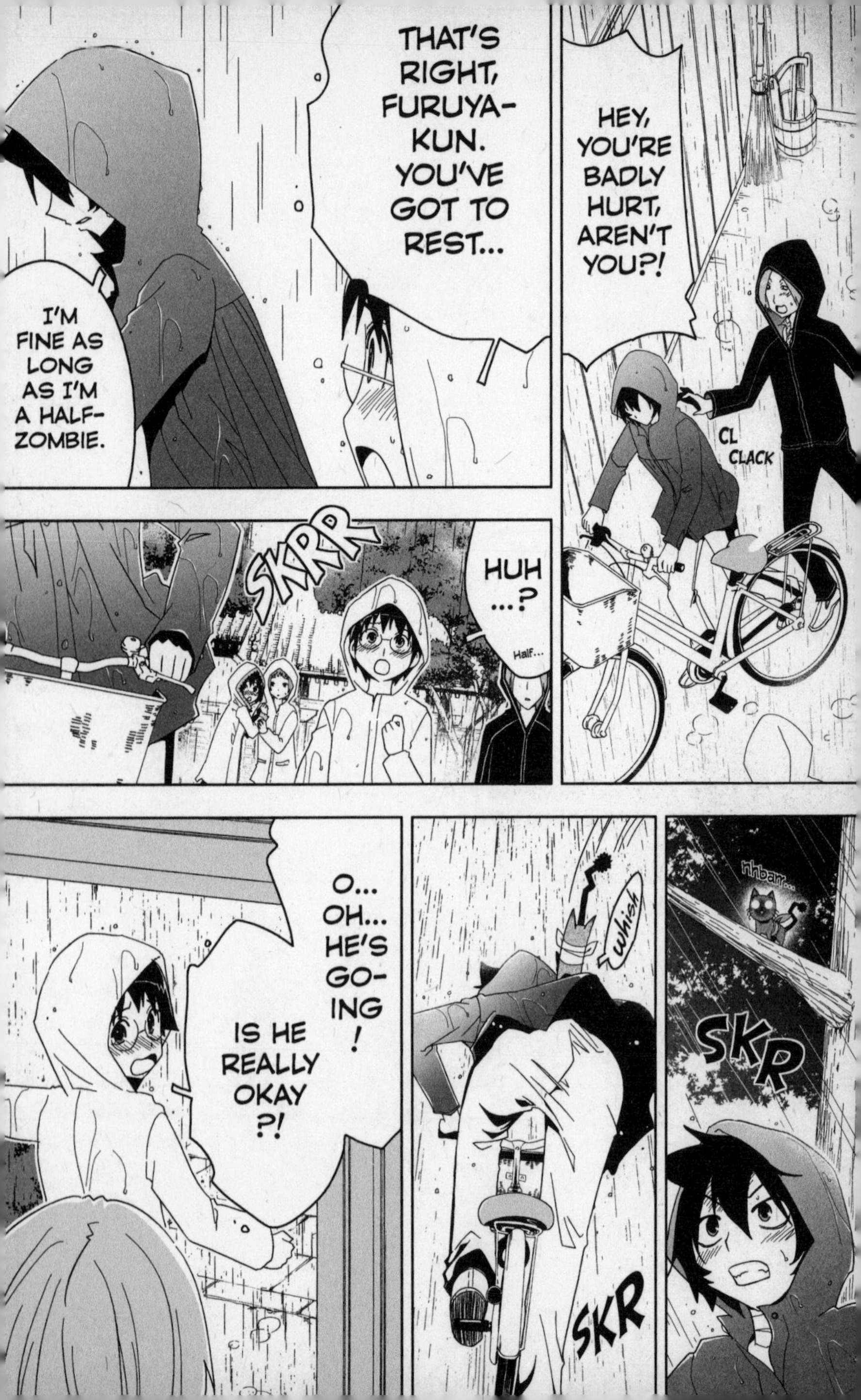
HEY, YOU'RE BADLY HURT, AREN'T YOU?!
CL CLACK
THAT'S RIGHT, FURUYA-KUN. YOU'VE GOT TO REST...
I'M FINE AS LONG AS I'M A HALF-ZOMBIE.
HUH ...?
Half...
SKRR
nhbarr...
SKR
whish
SKR
O... OH... HE'S GO-ING!
IS HE REALLY OKAY?!

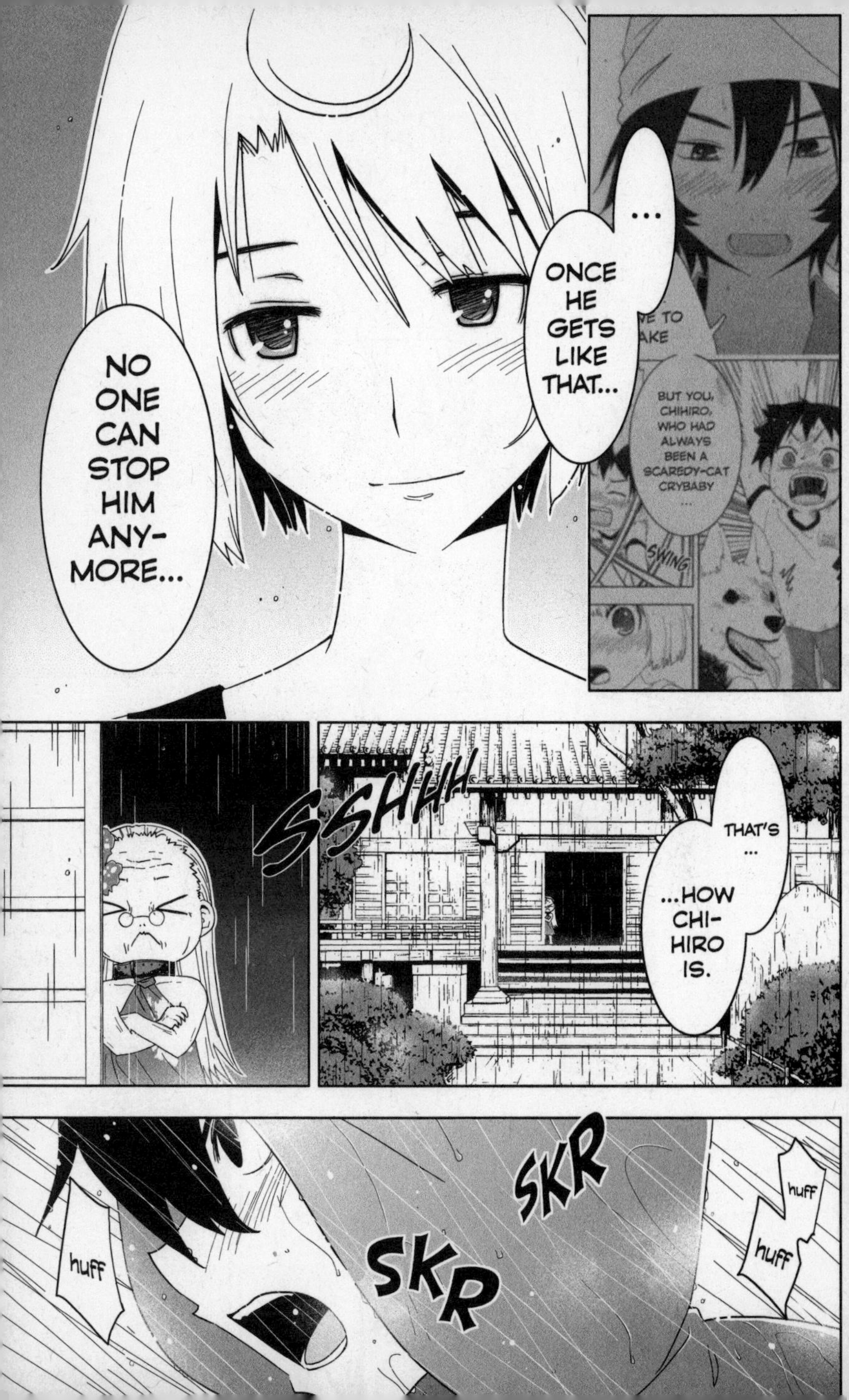
BUT YOU, CHIHIRO, WHO HAD ALWAYS BEEN A SCAREDY-CAT CRYBABY ...
SWING
...
ONCE HE GETS LIKE THAT...
NO ONE CAN STOP HIM ANY-MORE...
SSHHH
THAT'S ...
...HOW CHI-HIRO IS.
SKR
SKR
huff
huff
huff

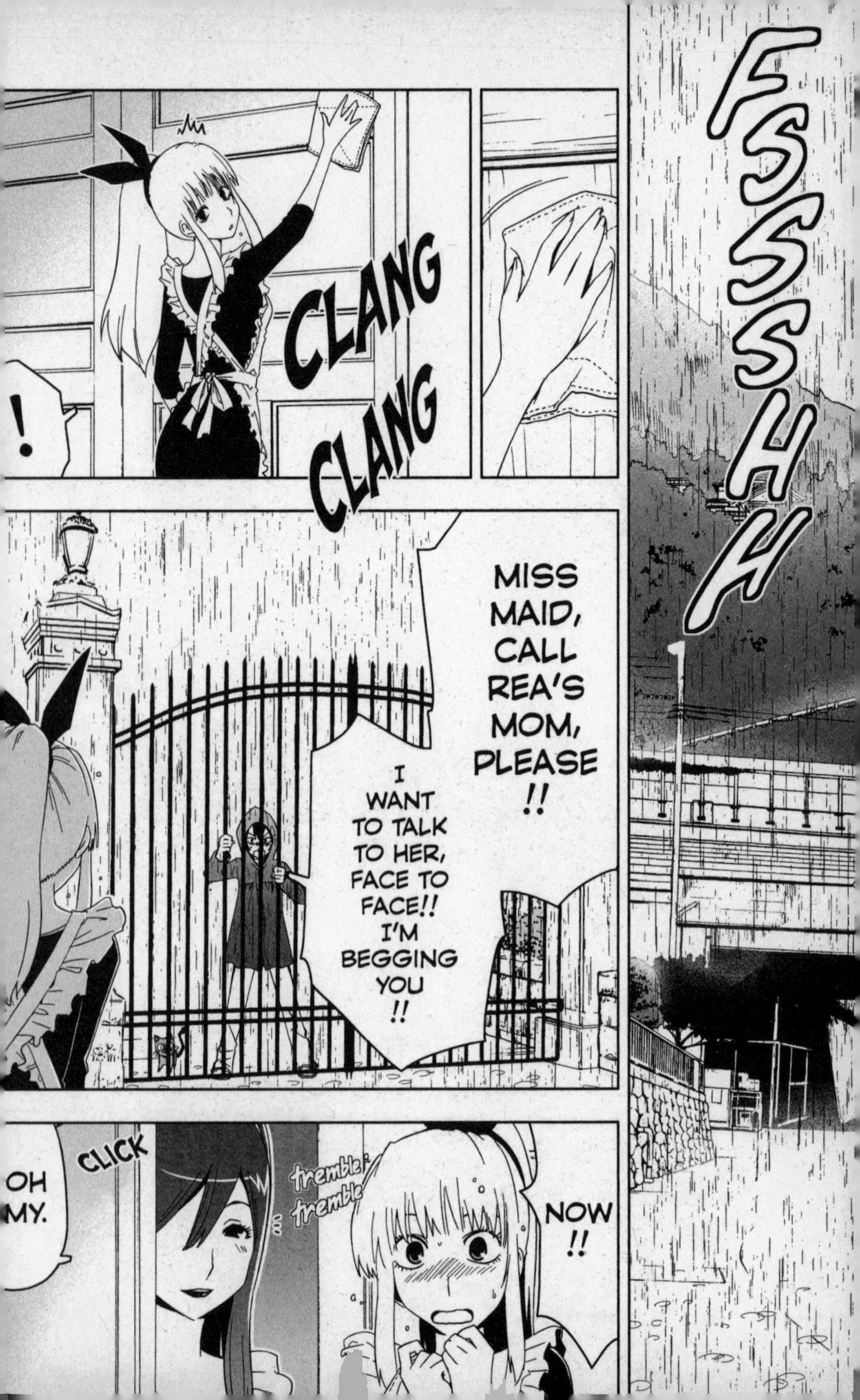
FSSSHH
CLANG CLANG
!
MISS MAID, CALL REA'S MOM, PLEASE!!
I WANT TO TALK TO HER, FACE TO FACE!! I'M BEGGING YOU!!
NOW!!
tremble tremble
CLICK
OH MY.

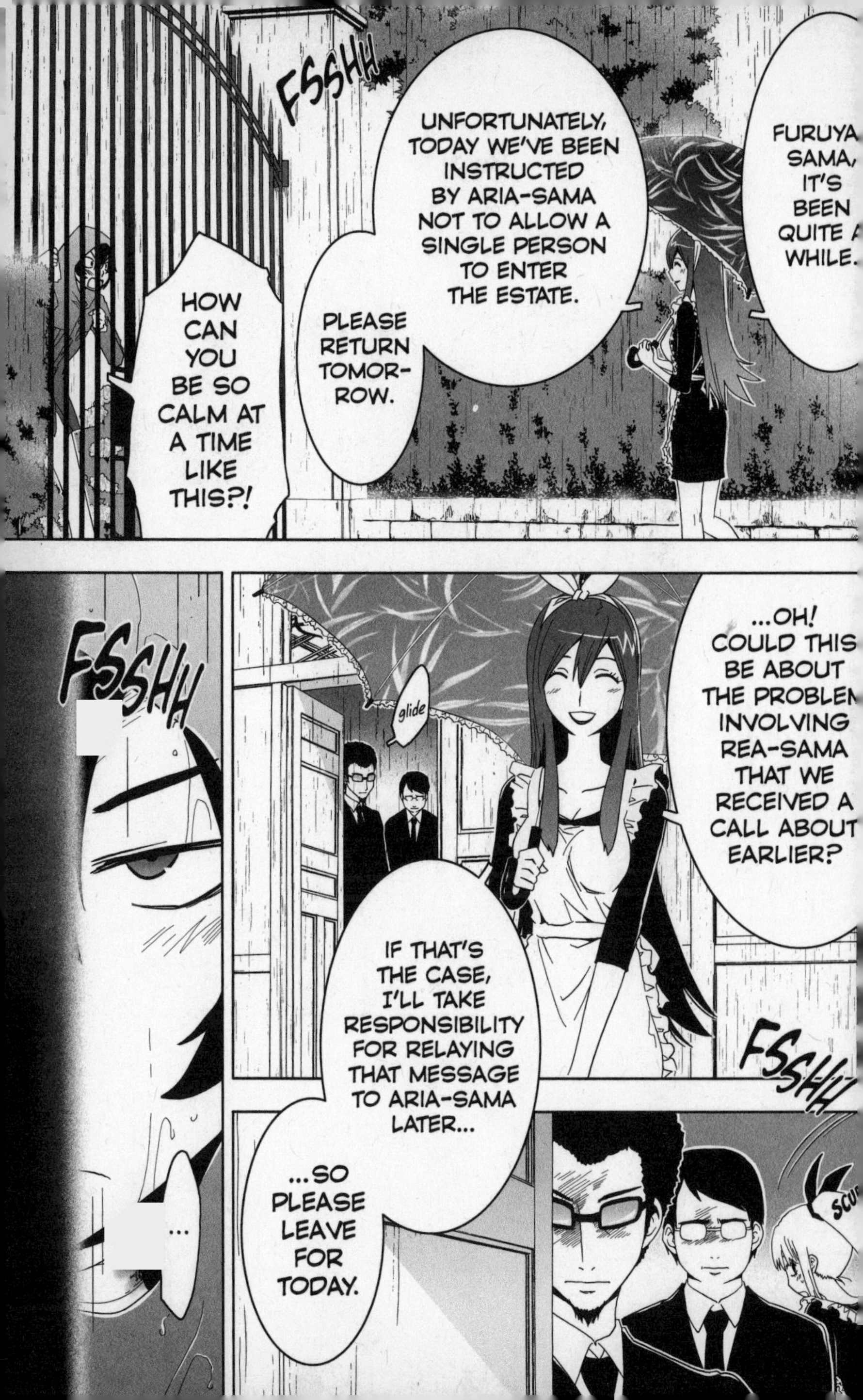
FURUYA SAMA, IT'S BEEN QUITE A WHILE.
UNFORTUNATELY, TODAY WE'VE BEEN INSTRUCTED BY ARIA-SAMA NOT TO ALLOW A SINGLE PERSON TO ENTER THE ESTATE.
PLEASE RETURN TOMORROW.
FSSHH
HOW CAN YOU BE SO CALM AT A TIME LIKE THIS?!
...OH! COULD THIS BE ABOUT THE PROBLEM INVOLVING REA-SAMA THAT WE RECEIVED A CALL ABOUT EARLIER?
glide
FSSHH
IF THAT'S THE CASE, I'LL TAKE RESPONSIBILITY FOR RELAYING THAT MESSAGE TO ARIA-SAMA LATER...
...SO PLEASE LEAVE FOR TODAY.
FSSHH
...

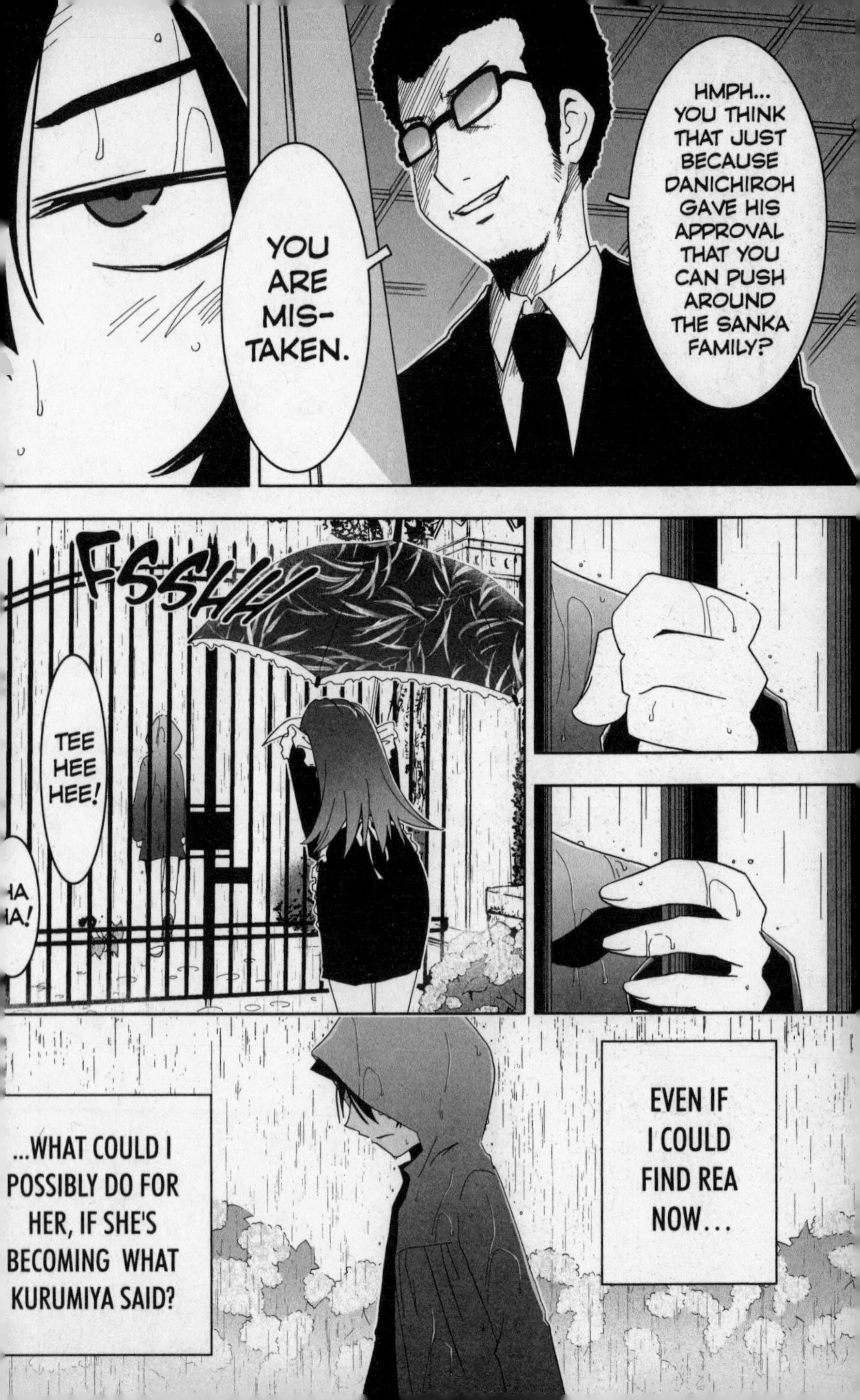

HMPH... YOU THINK THAT JUST BECAUSE DANICHIROH GAVE HIS APPROVAL THAT YOU CAN PUSH AROUND THE SANKA FAMILY?
YOU ARE MIS-TAKEN.
FSSHH
TEE HEE HEE!
HA HA!
EVEN IF I COULD FIND REA NOW...
...WHAT COULD I POSSIBLY DO FOR HER, IF SHE'S BECOMING WHAT KURUMIYA SAID?

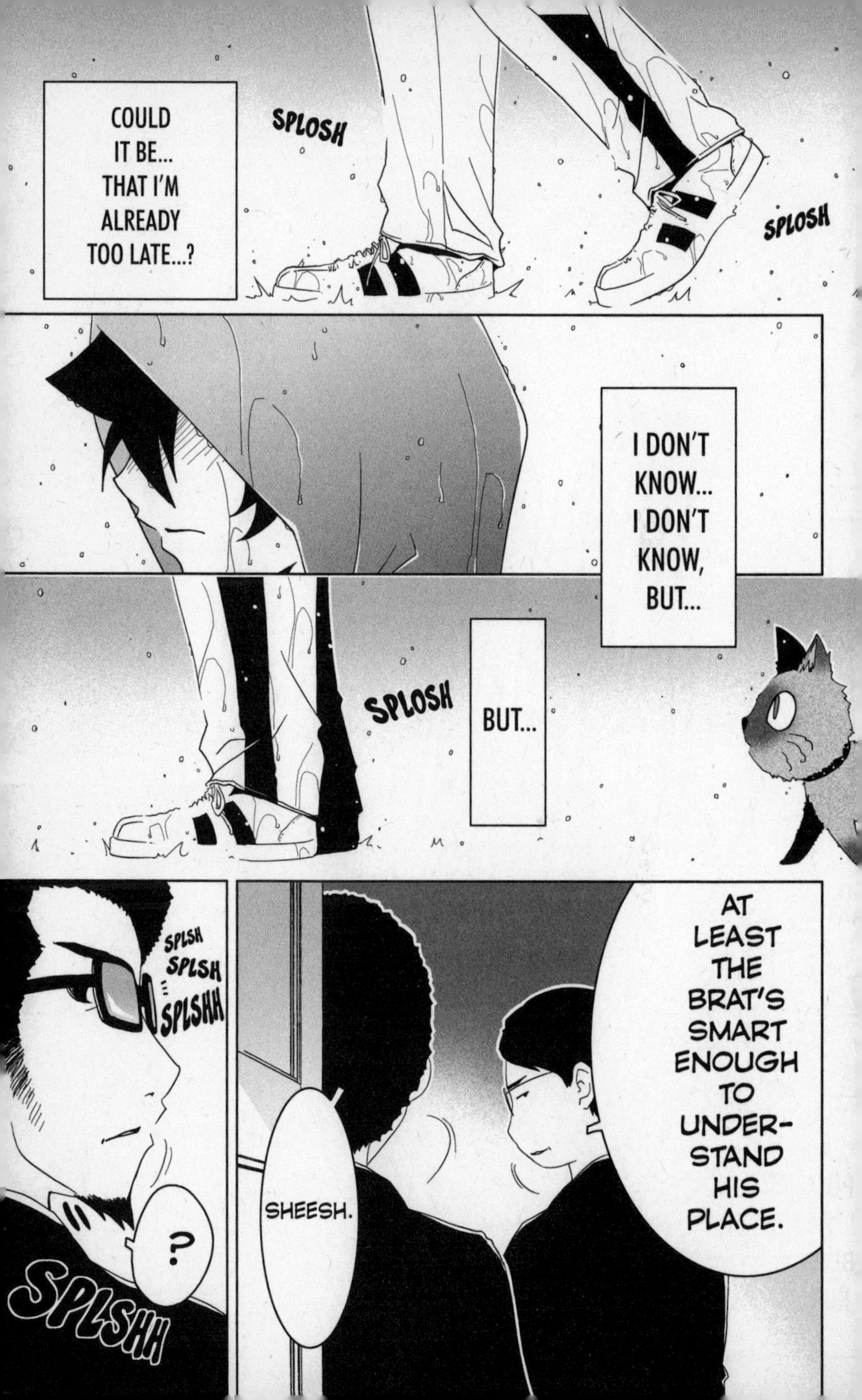
SPLOSH
SPLOSH
COULD IT BE... THAT I'M ALREADY TOO LATE...?
I DON'T KNOW... I DON'T KNOW, BUT...
BUT...
SPLOSH
AT LEAST THE BRAT'S SMART ENOUGH TO UNDER-STAND HIS PLACE.
SHEESH.
SPLSH SPLSH SPLSHH
?
SPLSHH

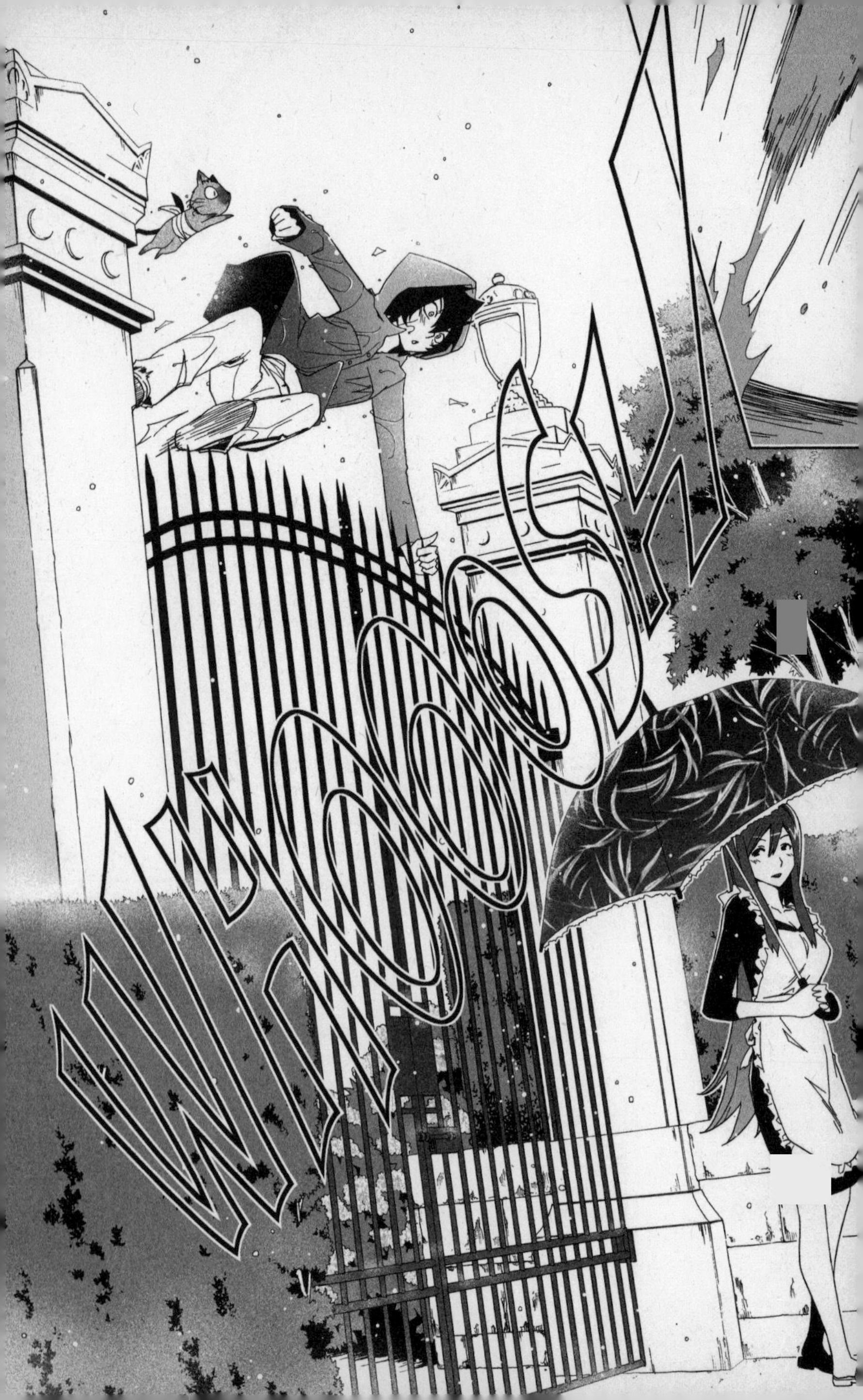
WHOOOSH

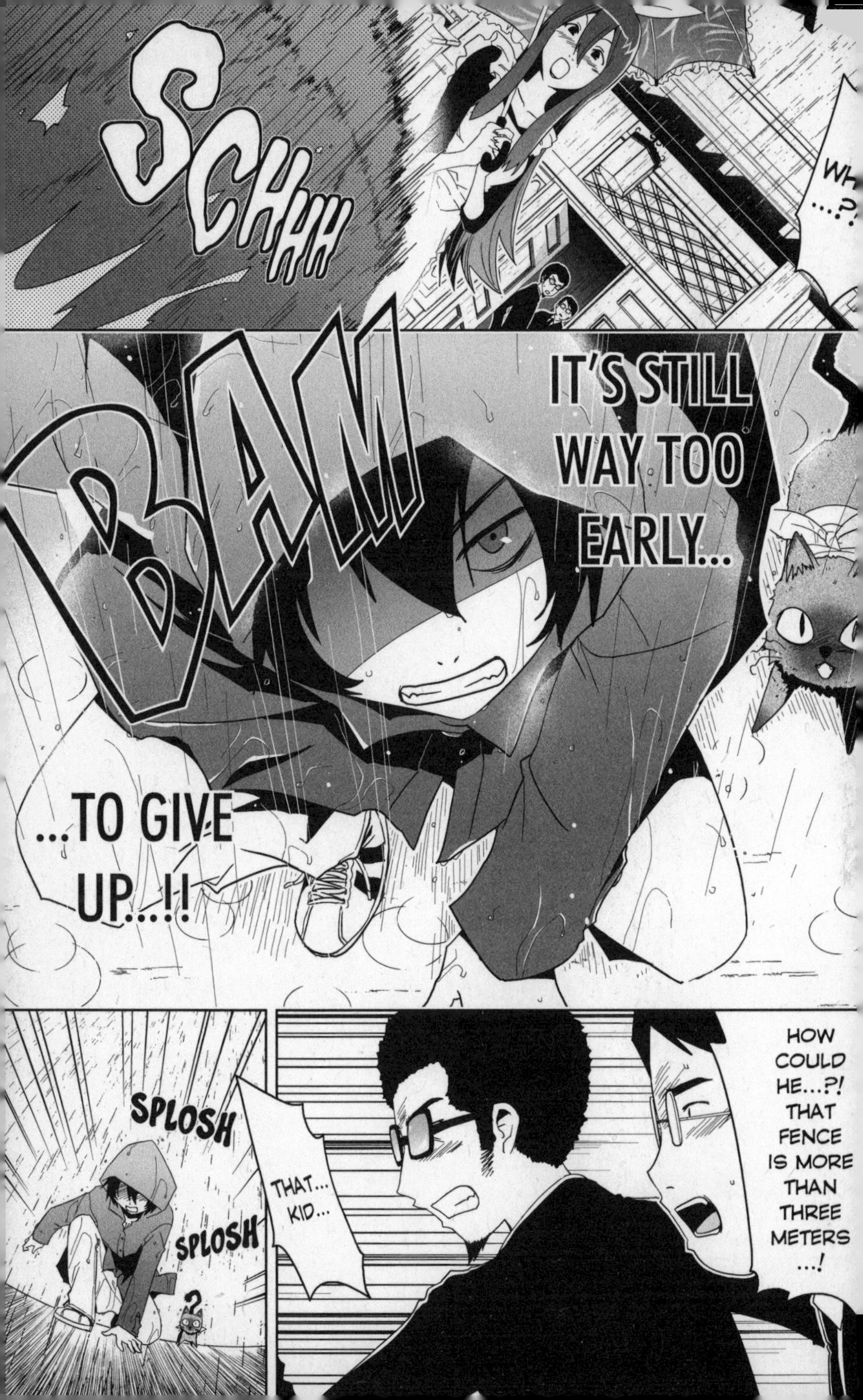
WH...?!
SCHHH
IT'S STILL WAY TOO EARLY...
BAM
...TO GIVE UP...!!
HOW COULD HE...?! THAT FENCE IS MORE THAN THREE METERS...!
THAT... KID...
SPLOSH
SPLOSH
?

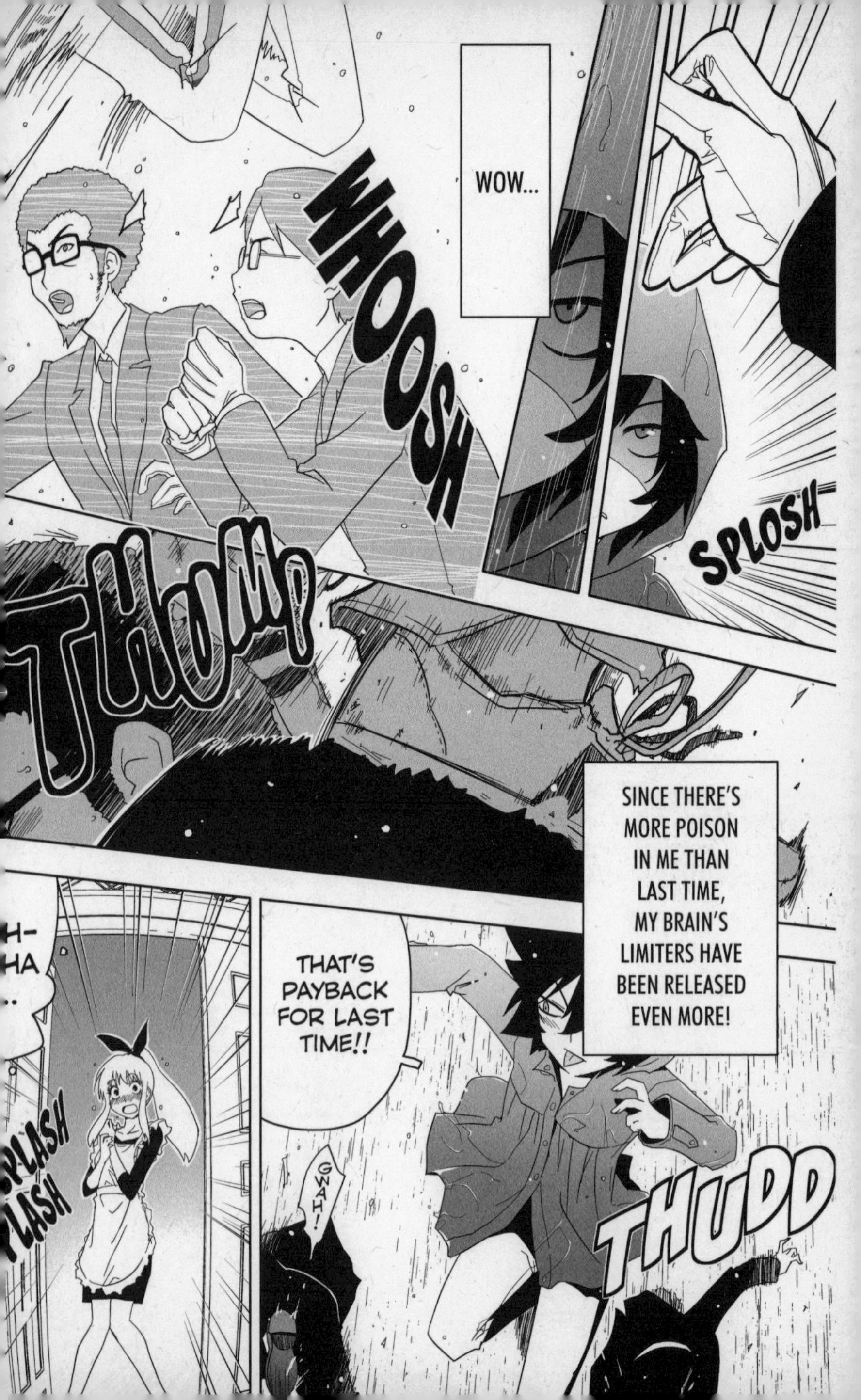
WOW...
SPLOSH
WHOOSH
THOMP
SINCE THERE'S MORE POISON IN ME THAN LAST TIME, MY BRAIN'S LIMITERS HAVE BEEN RELEASED EVEN MORE!
THAT'S PAYBACK FOR LAST TIME!!
GWAH!
THUDD

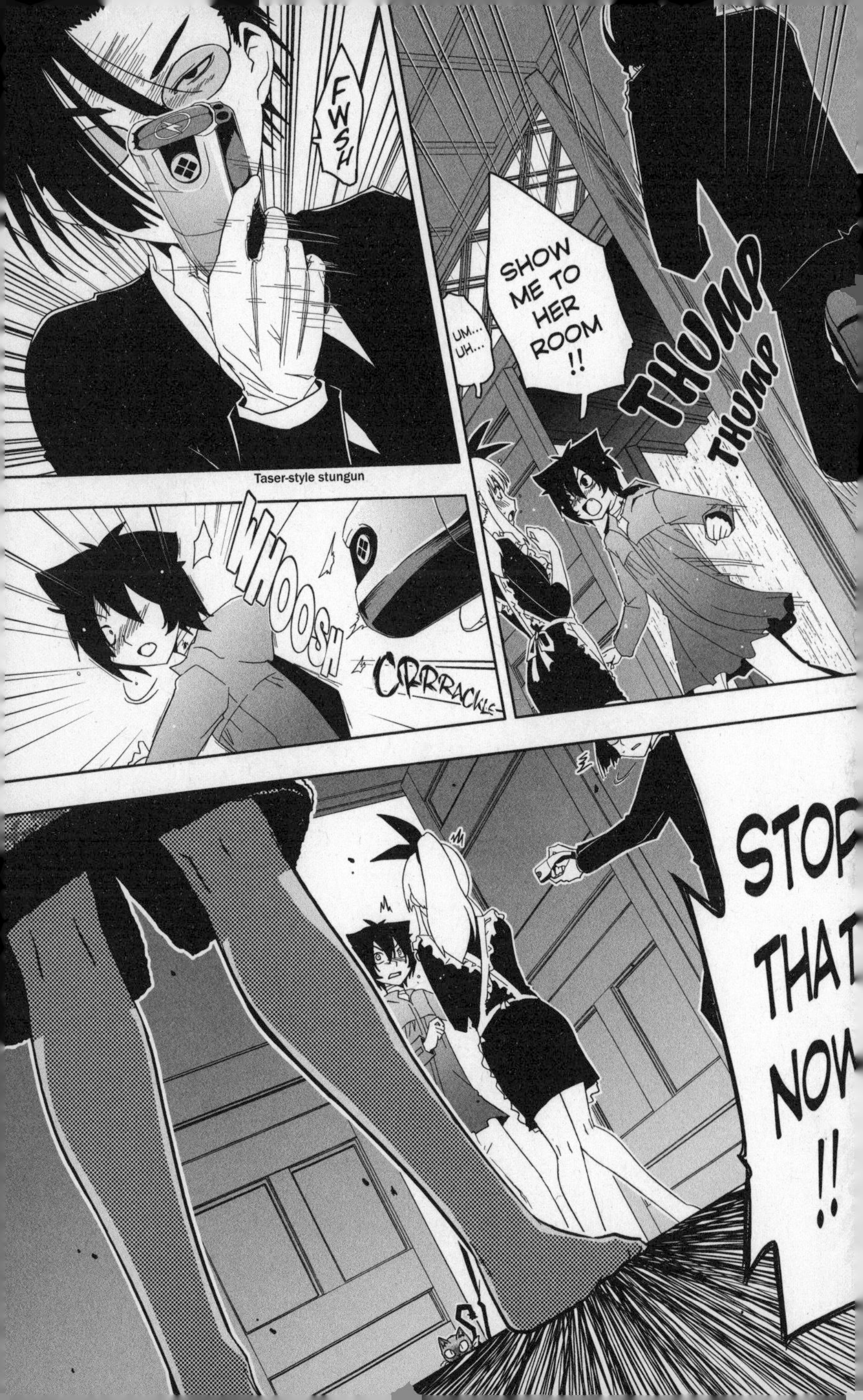
SHOW ME TO HER ROOM!!
THUMP THUMP
UM... UH...
FWSH
Taser-style stungun
WHOOSH
CRRRACKLE
STOP THAT NOW!!

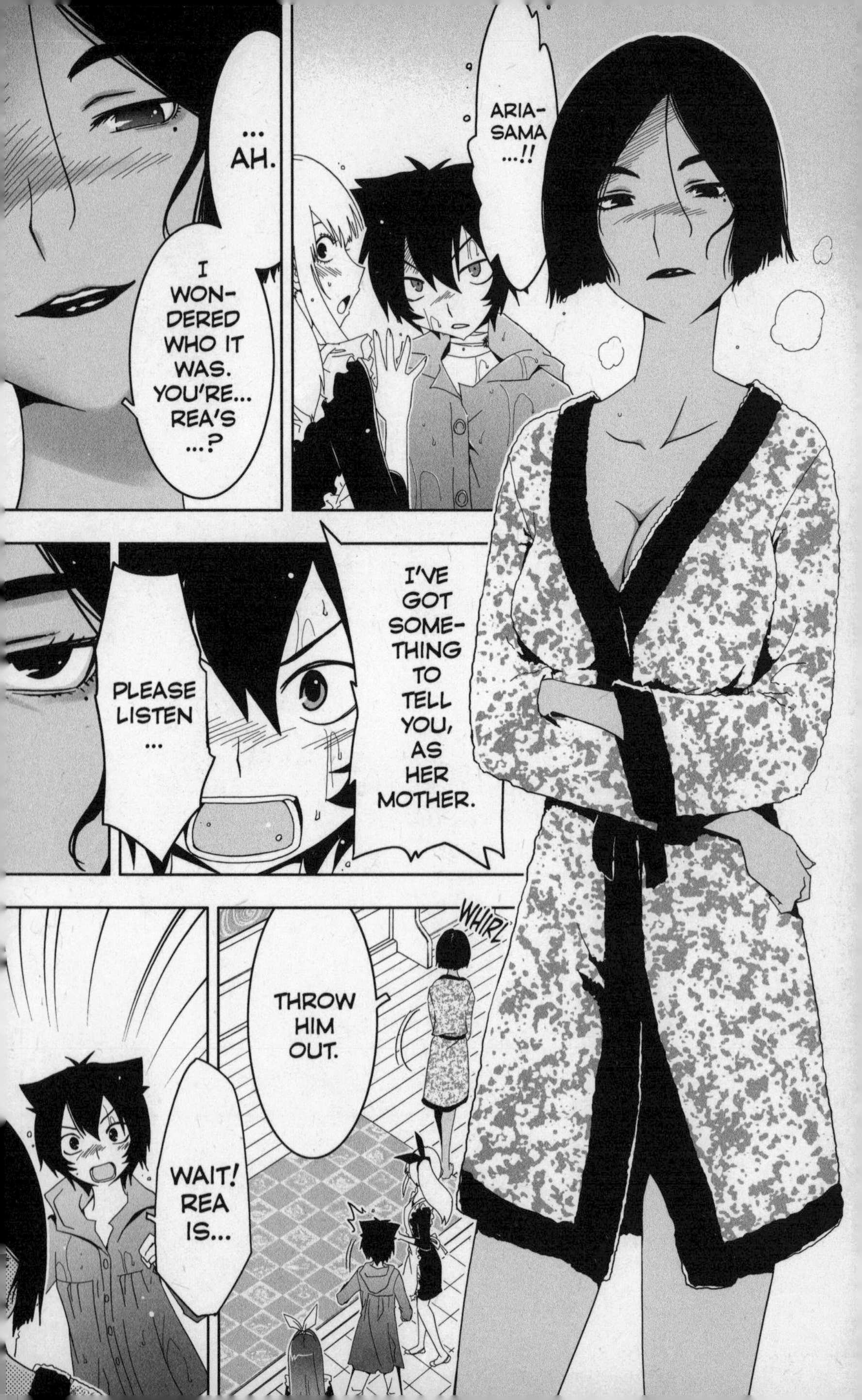

ARIA-SAMA ...!!
... AH.
I WONDERED WHO IT WAS. YOU'RE... REA'S ...?
I'VE GOT SOMETHING TO TELL YOU, AS HER MOTHER.
PLEASE LISTEN ...
WHIRL
THROW HIM OUT.
WAIT! REA IS...

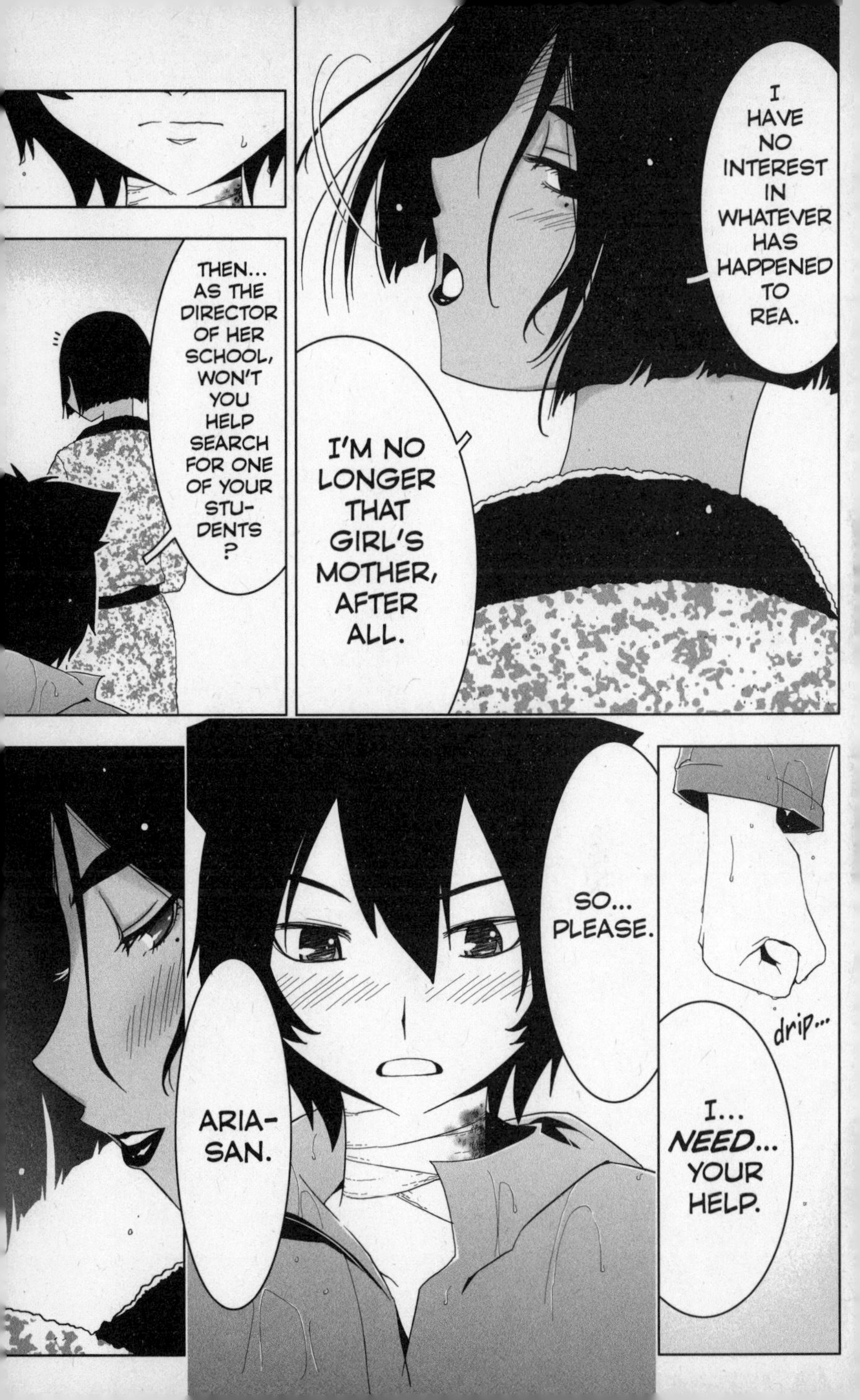
I HAVE NO INTEREST IN WHATEVER HAS HAPPENED TO REA.
I'M NO LONGER THAT GIRL'S MOTHER, AFTER ALL.
THEN... AS THE DIRECTOR OF HER SCHOOL, WON'T YOU HELP SEARCH FOR ONE OF YOUR STU-DENTS?
drip...
I... *NEED*... YOUR HELP.
SO... PLEASE.
ARIA-SAN.

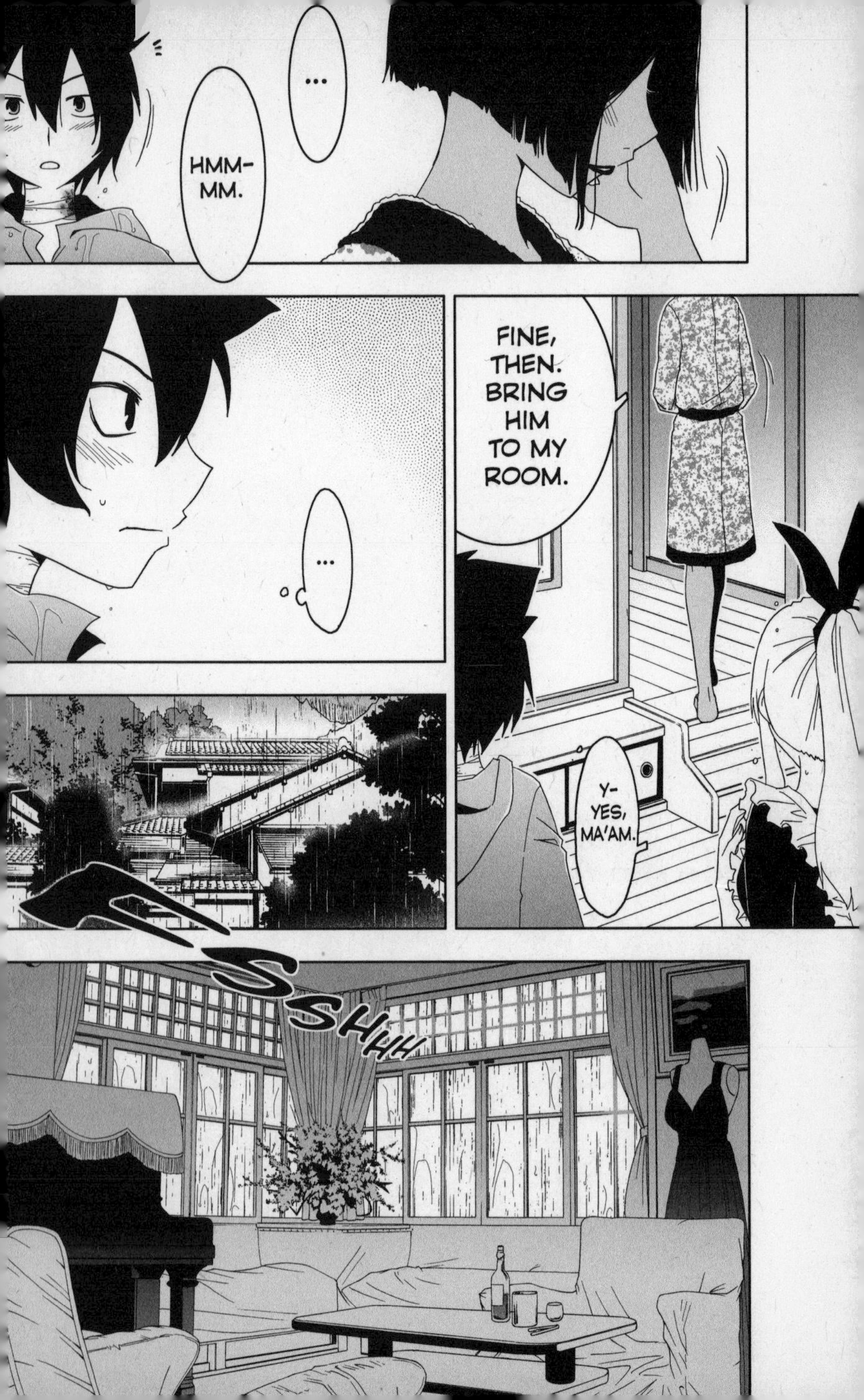
...
HMM-MM.
FINE, THEN. BRING HIM TO MY ROOM.
Y-YES, MA'AM.
...
SSHHH

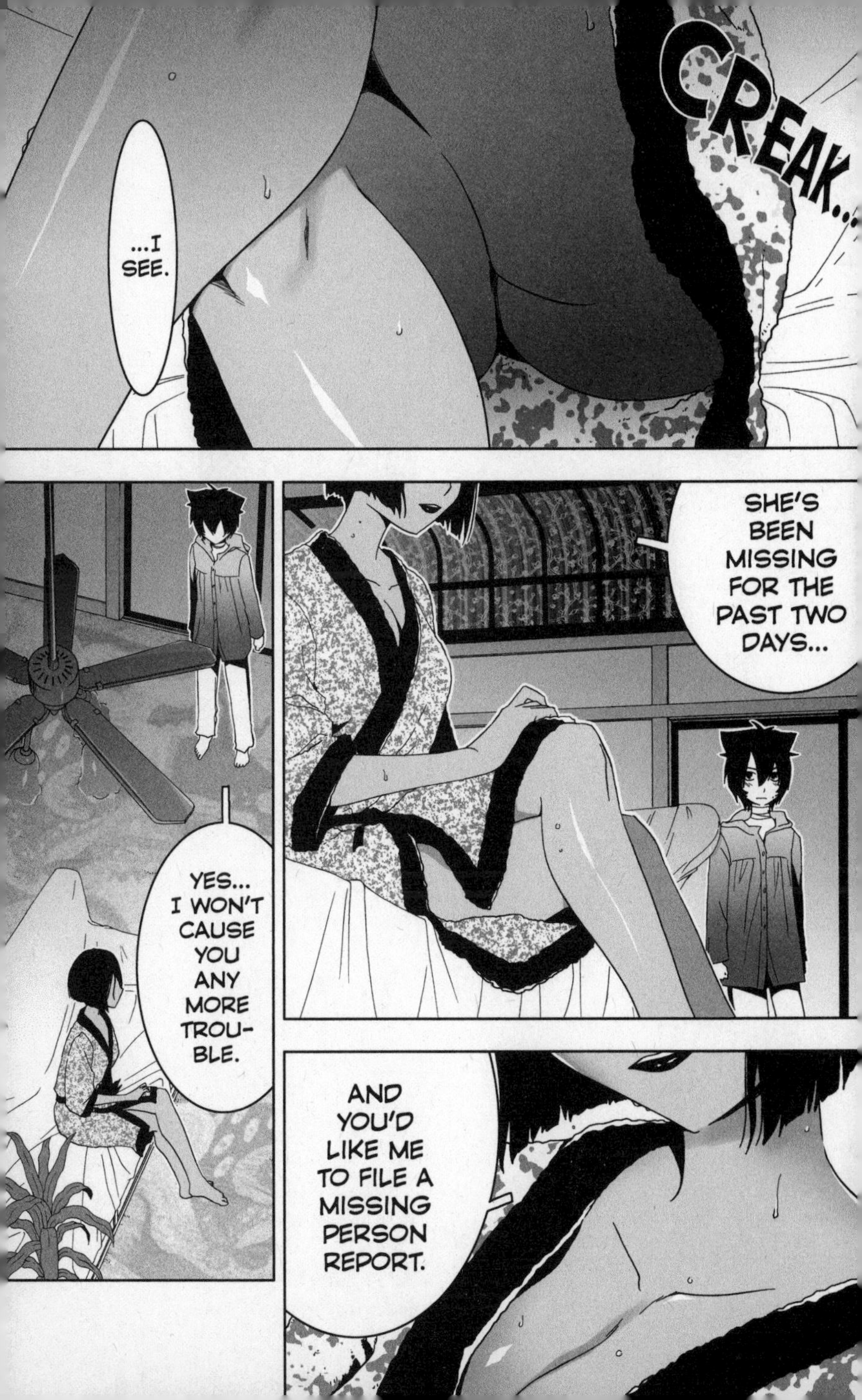
CREAK...
...I SEE.
SHE'S BEEN MISSING FOR THE PAST TWO DAYS...
AND YOU'D LIKE ME TO FILE A MISSING PERSON REPORT.
YES... I WON'T CAUSE YOU ANY MORE TROUBLE.

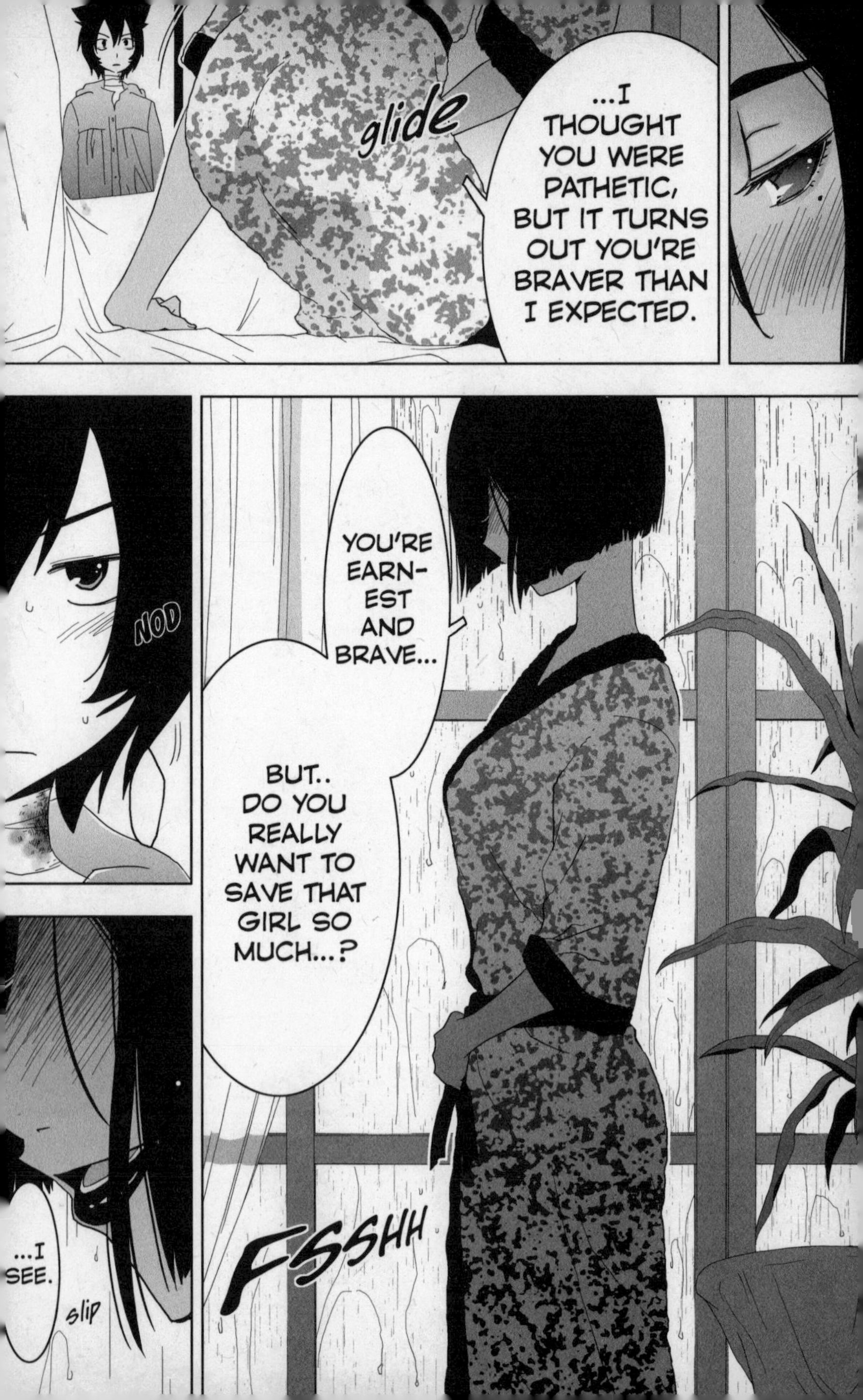
...I THOUGHT YOU WERE PATHETIC, BUT IT TURNS OUT YOU'RE BRAVER THAN I EXPECTED.
glide
YOU'RE EARNEST AND BRAVE...
BUT.. DO YOU REALLY WANT TO SAVE THAT GIRL SO MUCH...?
FSSHH
NOD
...I SEE.
slip

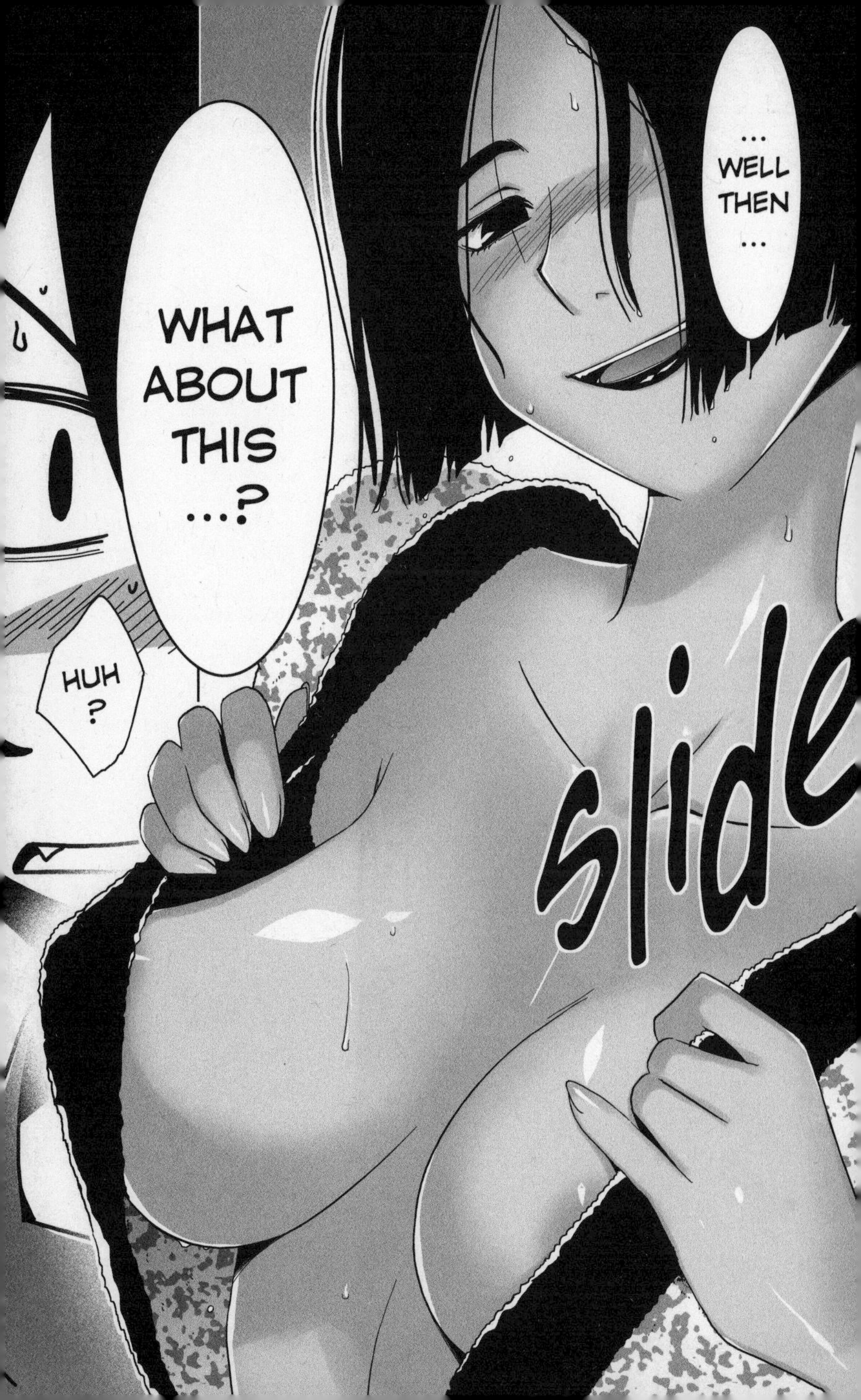
... WELL THEN ...
WHAT ABOUT THIS ...?
HUH ?
slide

SANKAREA ANECDOTES 4

About Ranko

Last time, I showed you the changes to Rea, but this time I'll go over the changes to the character design of Ranko (Wanko).

She didn't go through changes as extreme as Rea's. At first I thought I'd play with her hairstyle and accessories, but in the end, I used a rather orthodox design without going outside the lines too much.

Plan A: The atmosphere (sexiness) exuded is a bit different from the final version. This might be pretty good as it is. Even so, what a short skirt!

Plan B: This is the only version with colored hair. In plans A and B, I thought I should just put some kind of accent in the hair, but finally decided to give it up. (Rea wears a hairpin, after all).

Plan C: This is basically the final version. It's just that the sock color is different from the actual chapters? By the way, the mascot she has attached to her bag is a "zomkewpie" she got from Furuya when they were in middle school. (I just thought up the name.)

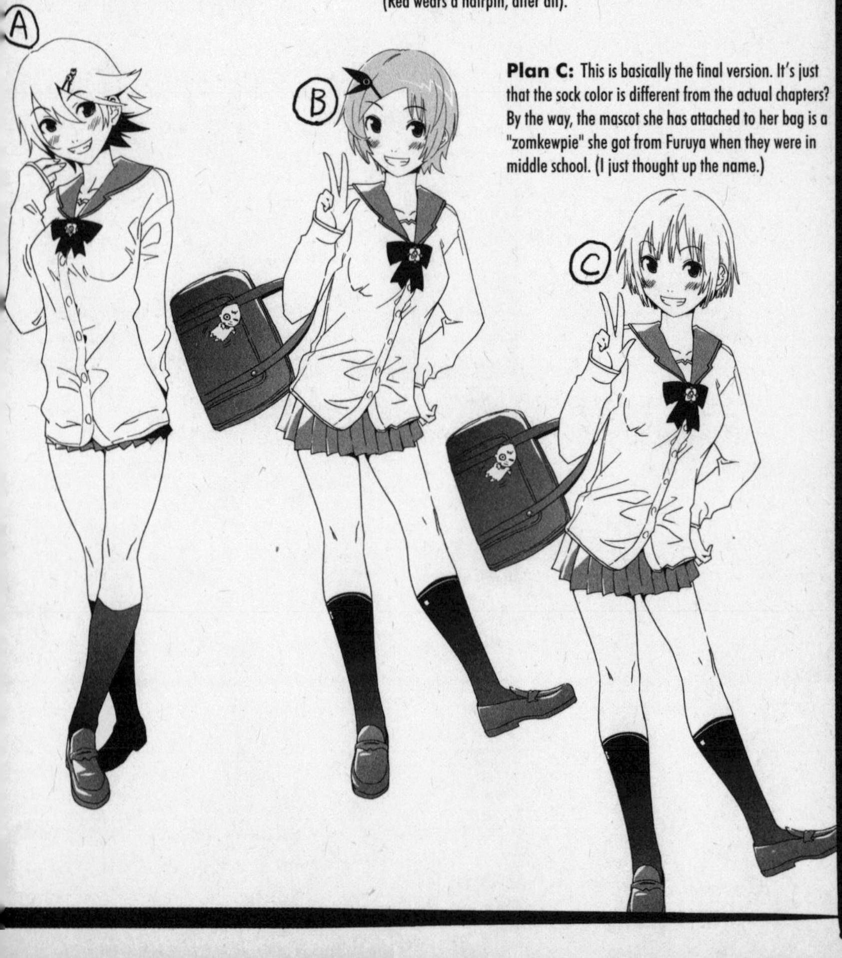
A
B
C

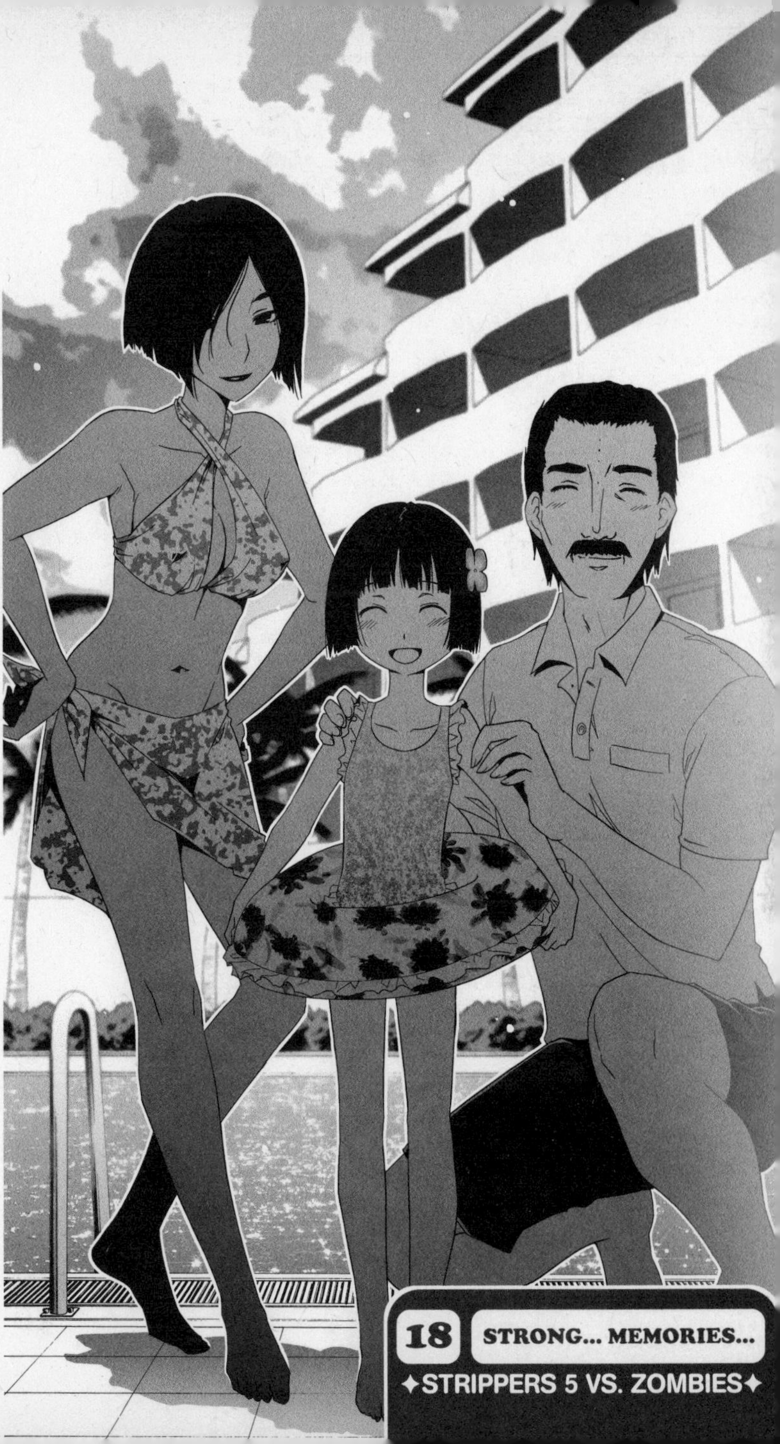
18
STRONG... MEMORIES...
✦STRIPPERS 5 VS. ZOMBIES✦

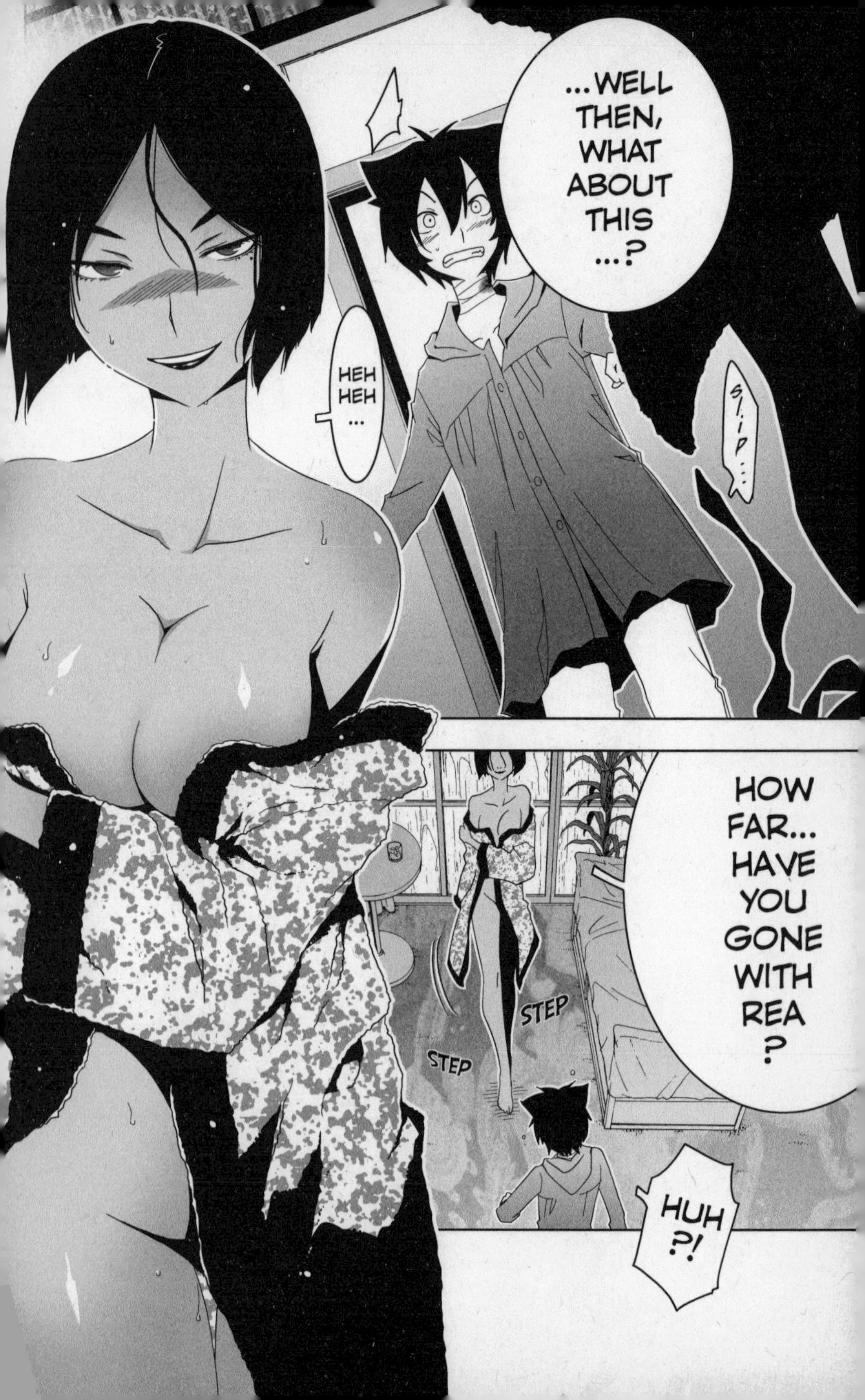
...WELL THEN, WHAT ABOUT THIS ...?
SLIP...
HEH HEH ...
HOW FAR... HAVE YOU GONE WITH REA ?
STEP
STEP
HUH ?!

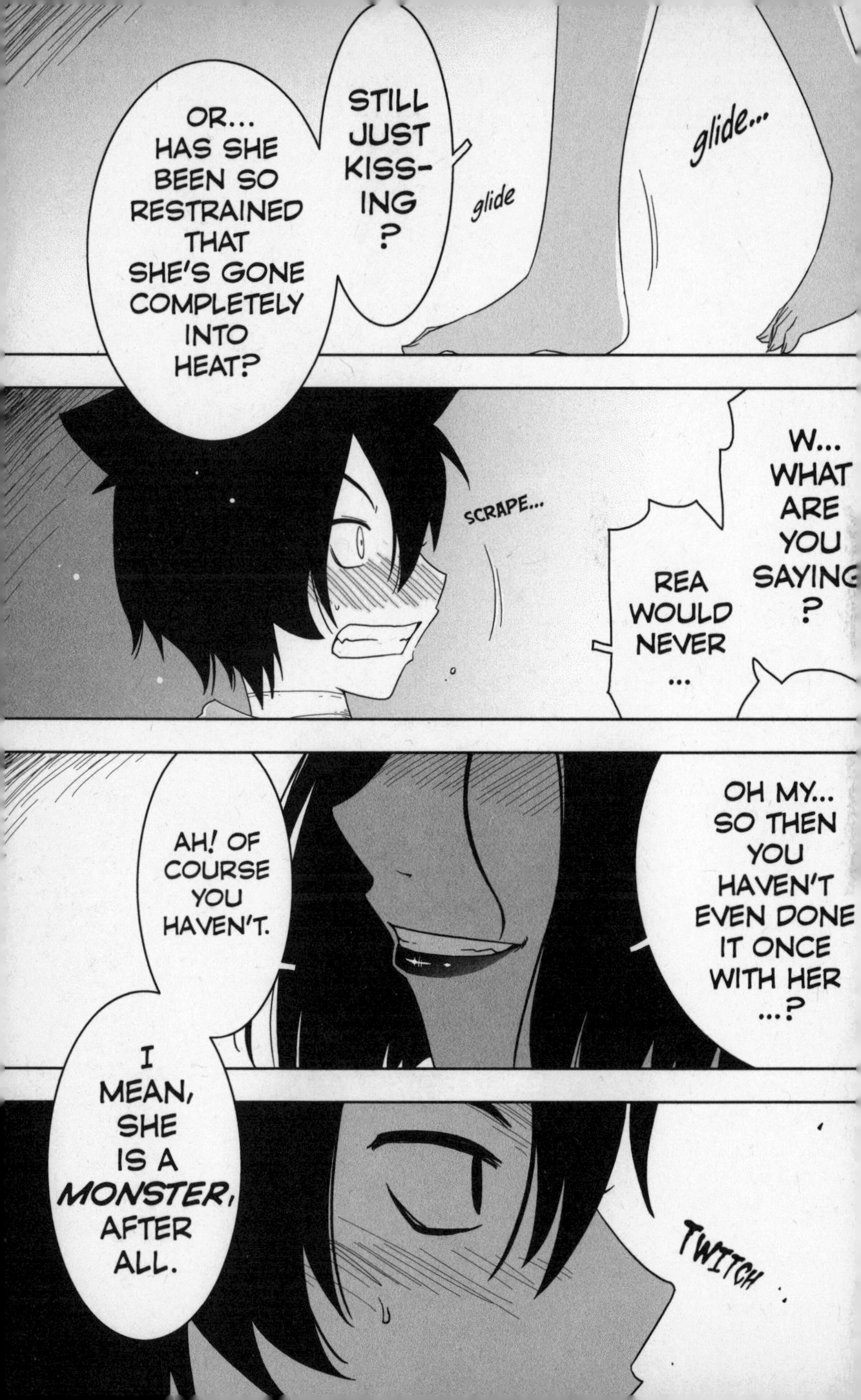
glide...
glide
STILL JUST KISSING?
OR... HAS SHE BEEN SO RESTRAINED THAT SHE'S GONE COMPLETELY INTO HEAT?
W... WHAT ARE YOU SAYING?
REA WOULD NEVER...
SCRAPE...
OH MY... SO THEN YOU HAVEN'T EVEN DONE IT ONCE WITH HER...?
AH! OF COURSE YOU HAVEN'T.
TWITCH
I MEAN, SHE IS A *MONSTER*, AFTER ALL.

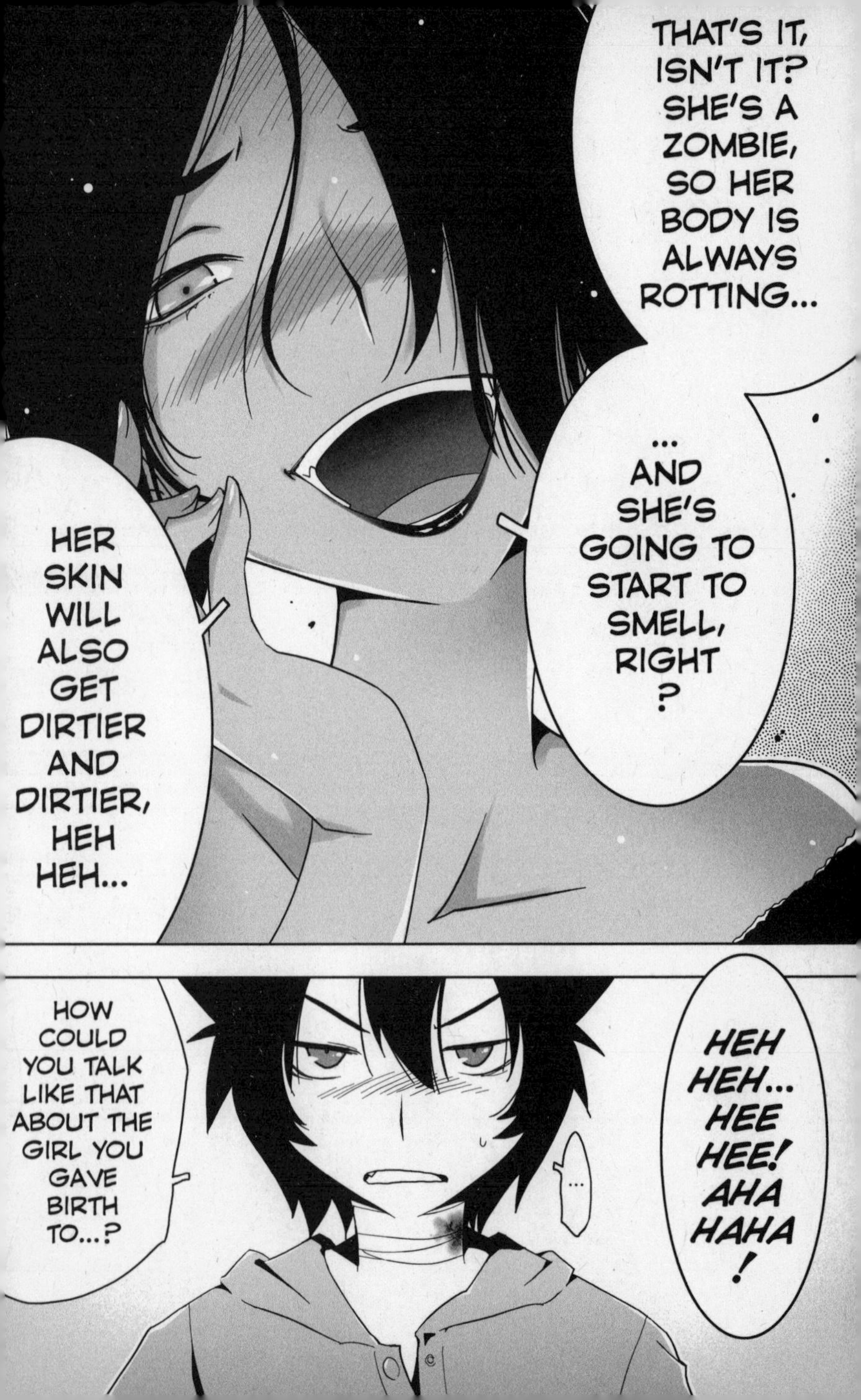
THAT'S IT, ISN'T IT? SHE'S A ZOMBIE, SO HER BODY IS ALWAYS ROTTING...
... AND SHE'S GOING TO START TO SMELL, RIGHT ?
HER SKIN WILL ALSO GET DIRTIER AND DIRTIER, HEH HEH...
HEH HEH... HEE HEE! AHA HAHA !
...
HOW COULD YOU TALK LIKE THAT ABOUT THE GIRL YOU GAVE BIRTH TO...?

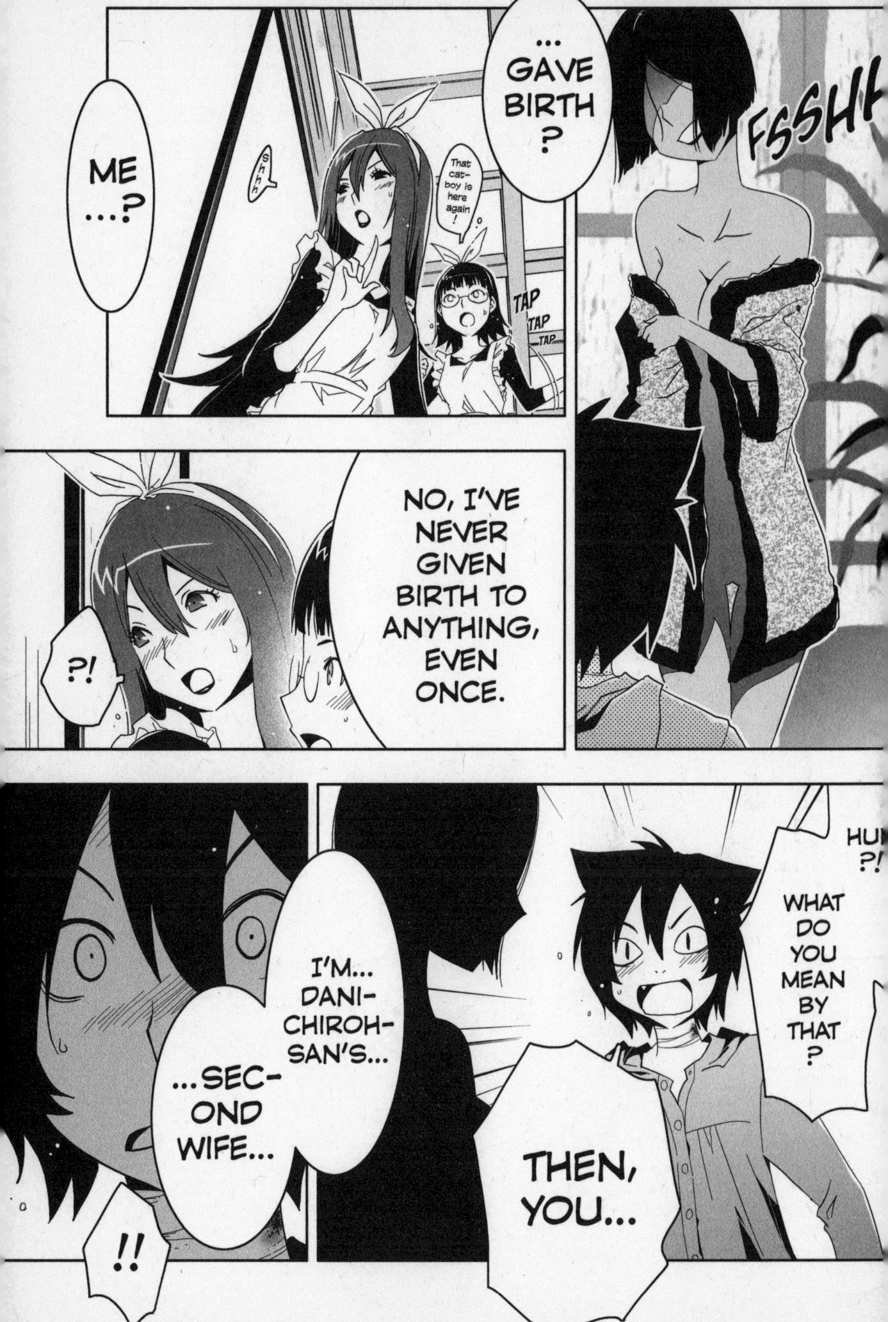
FSSHH
...GAVE BIRTH?
ME...?
shhh
That cat-boy is here again!
TAP
TAP
TAP
NO, I'VE NEVER GIVEN BIRTH TO ANYTHING, EVEN ONCE.
?!
HU ?!
WHAT DO YOU MEAN BY THAT?
THEN, YOU...
I'M... DANI-CHIROH-SAN'S...
...SEC-OND WIFE...
!!

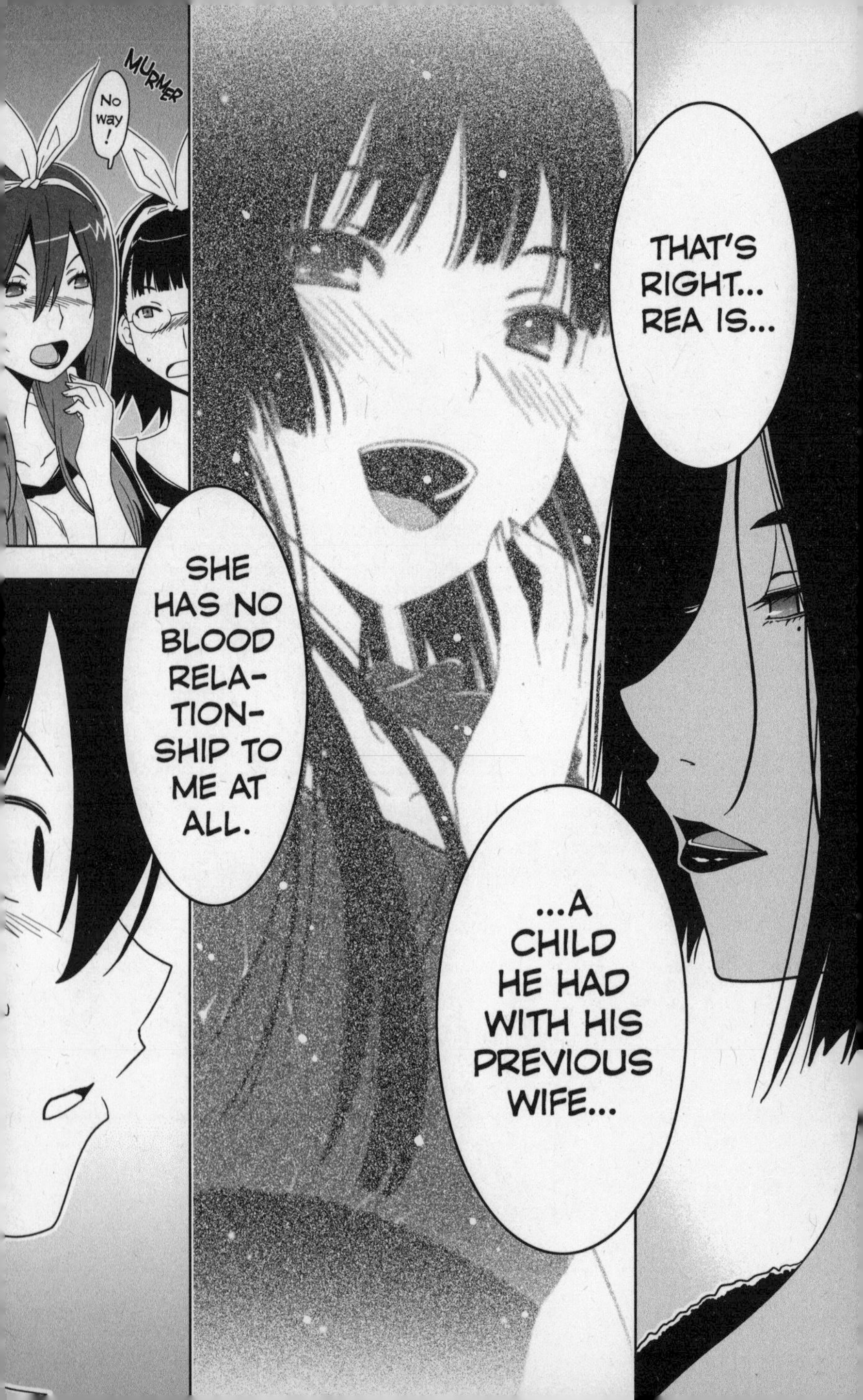
THAT'S RIGHT... REA IS...
...A CHILD HE HAD WITH HIS PREVIOUS WIFE...
SHE HAS NO BLOOD RELATIONSHIP TO ME AT ALL.
MURMER
No way!

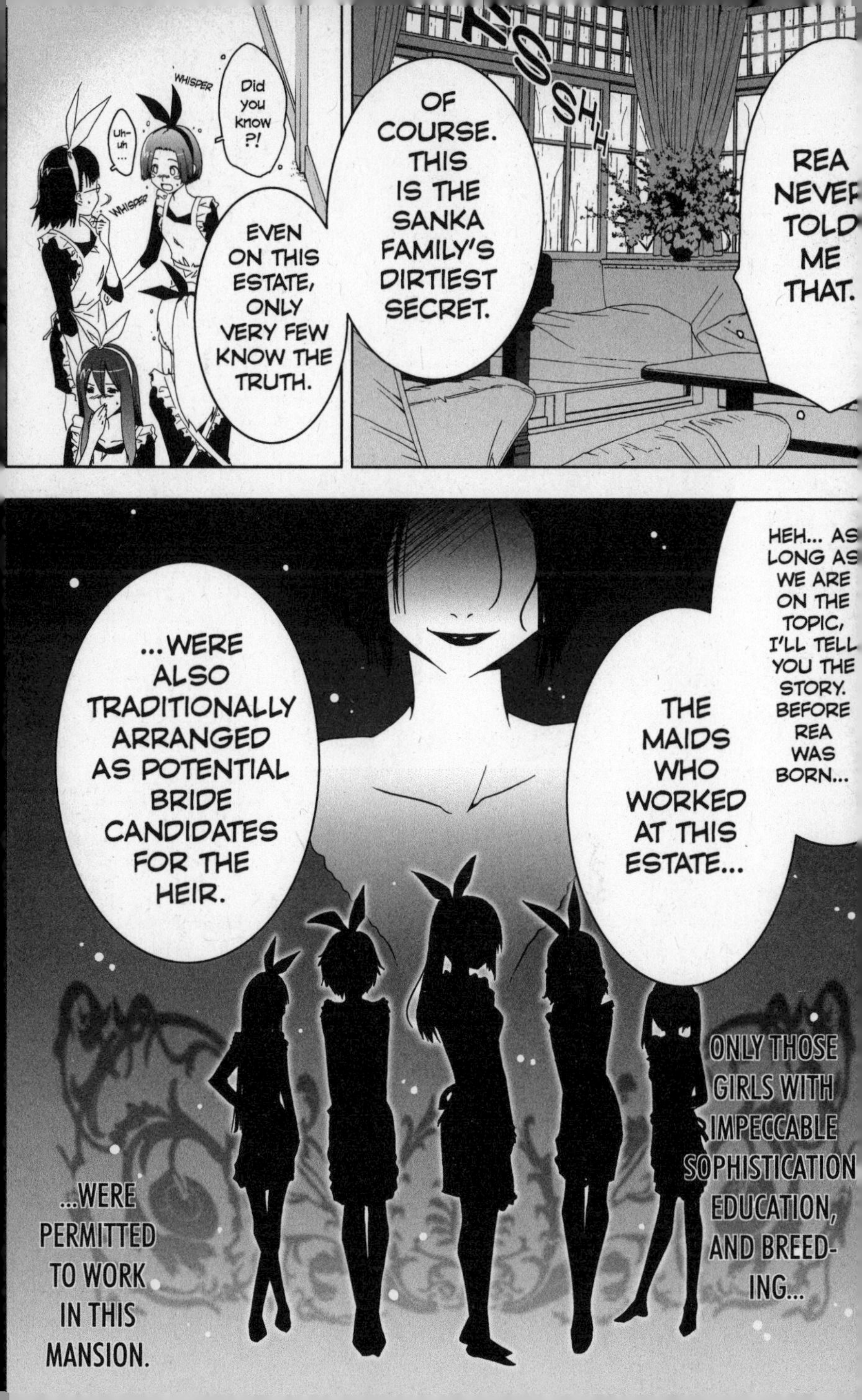SSHH
REA NEVER TOLD ME THAT.
OF COURSE. THIS IS THE SANKA FAMILY'S DIRTIEST SECRET.
EVEN ON THIS ESTATE, ONLY VERY FEW KNOW THE TRUTH.
WHISPER
Did you know ?!
Uh-uh ...
WHISPER
HEH... AS LONG AS WE ARE ON THE TOPIC, I'LL TELL YOU THE STORY. BEFORE REA WAS BORN...
THE MAIDS WHO WORKED AT THIS ESTATE...
...WERE ALSO TRADITIONALLY ARRANGED AS POTENTIAL BRIDE CANDIDATES FOR THE HEIR.
ONLY THOSE GIRLS WITH IMPECCABLE SOPHISTICATION EDUCATION, AND BREED-ING...
...WERE PERMITTED TO WORK IN THIS MANSION.

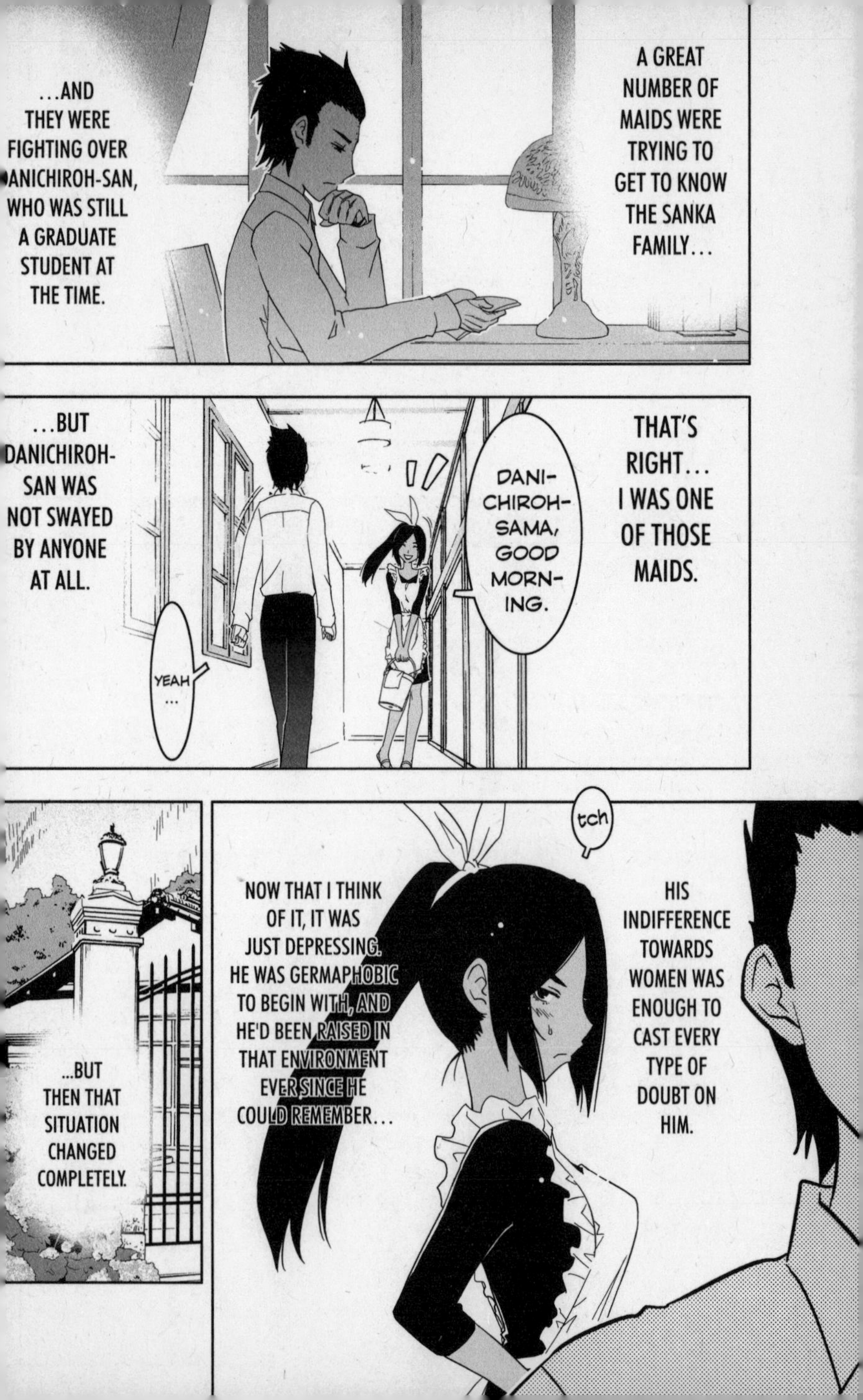
A GREAT NUMBER OF MAIDS WERE TRYING TO GET TO KNOW THE SANKA FAMILY…
…AND THEY WERE FIGHTING OVER DANICHIROH-SAN, WHO WAS STILL A GRADUATE STUDENT AT THE TIME.
THAT'S RIGHT… I WAS ONE OF THOSE MAIDS.
DANI-CHIROH-SAMA, GOOD MORN-ING.
YEAH…
…BUT DANICHIROH-SAN WAS NOT SWAYED BY ANYONE AT ALL.
tch
HIS INDIFFERENCE TOWARDS WOMEN WAS ENOUGH TO CAST EVERY TYPE OF DOUBT ON HIM.
NOW THAT I THINK OF IT, IT WAS JUST DEPRESSING. HE WAS GERMAPHOBIC TO BEGIN WITH, AND HE'D BEEN RAISED IN THAT ENVIRONMENT EVER SINCE HE COULD REMEMBER…
...BUT THEN THAT SITUATION CHANGED COMPLETELY.

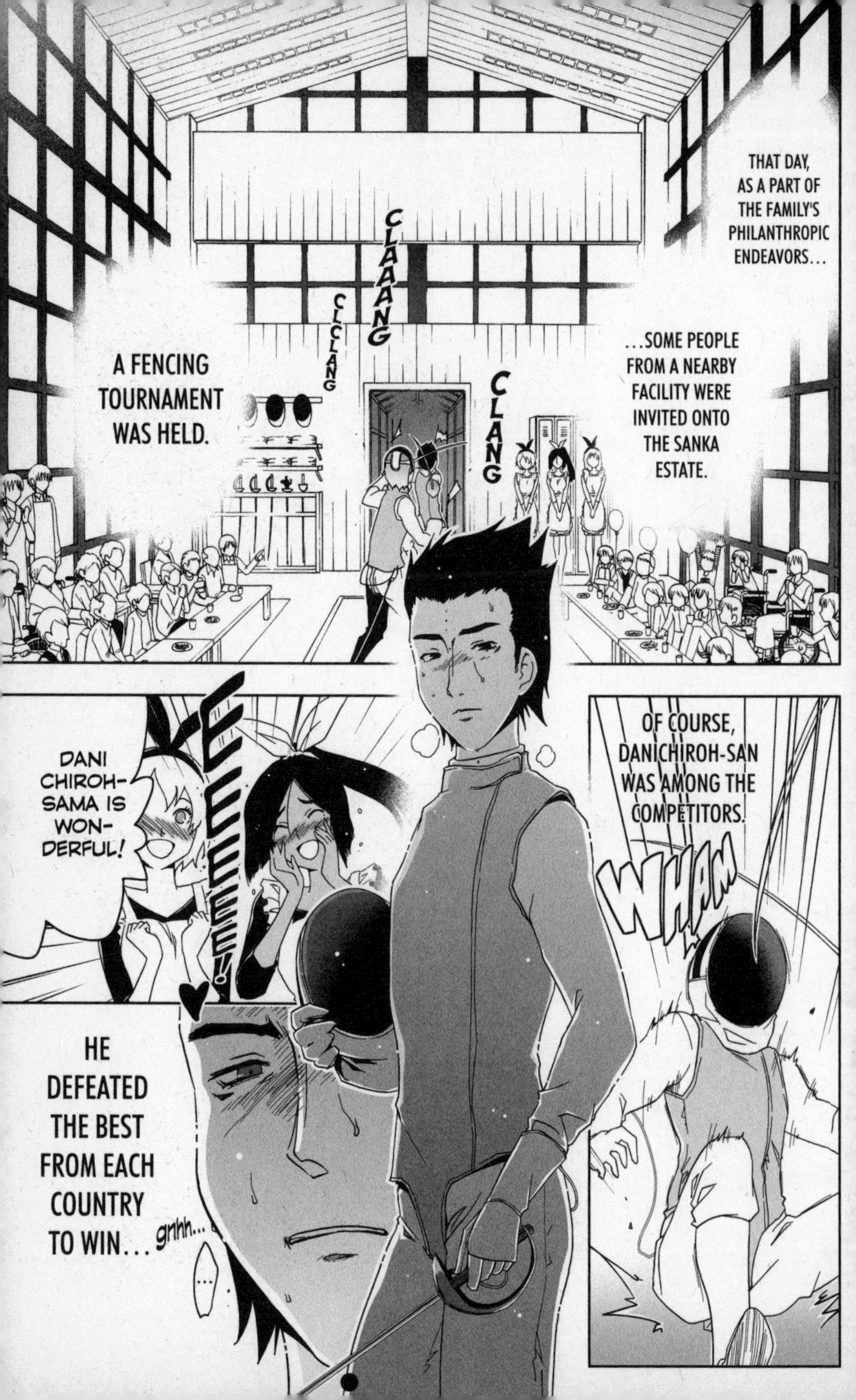
THAT DAY, AS A PART OF THE FAMILY'S PHILANTHROPIC ENDEAVORS…
…SOME PEOPLE FROM A NEARBY FACILITY WERE INVITED ONTO THE SANKA ESTATE.
CLANG
CLAAAANG
CLCLANG
A FENCING TOURNAMENT WAS HELD.
OF COURSE, DANICHIROH-SAN WAS AMONG THE COMPETITORS.
WHAM
DANI CHIROH-SAMA IS WON-DERFUL!
EEEEEEEE!!
HE DEFEATED THE BEST FROM EACH COUNTRY TO WIN…
grnh…
…

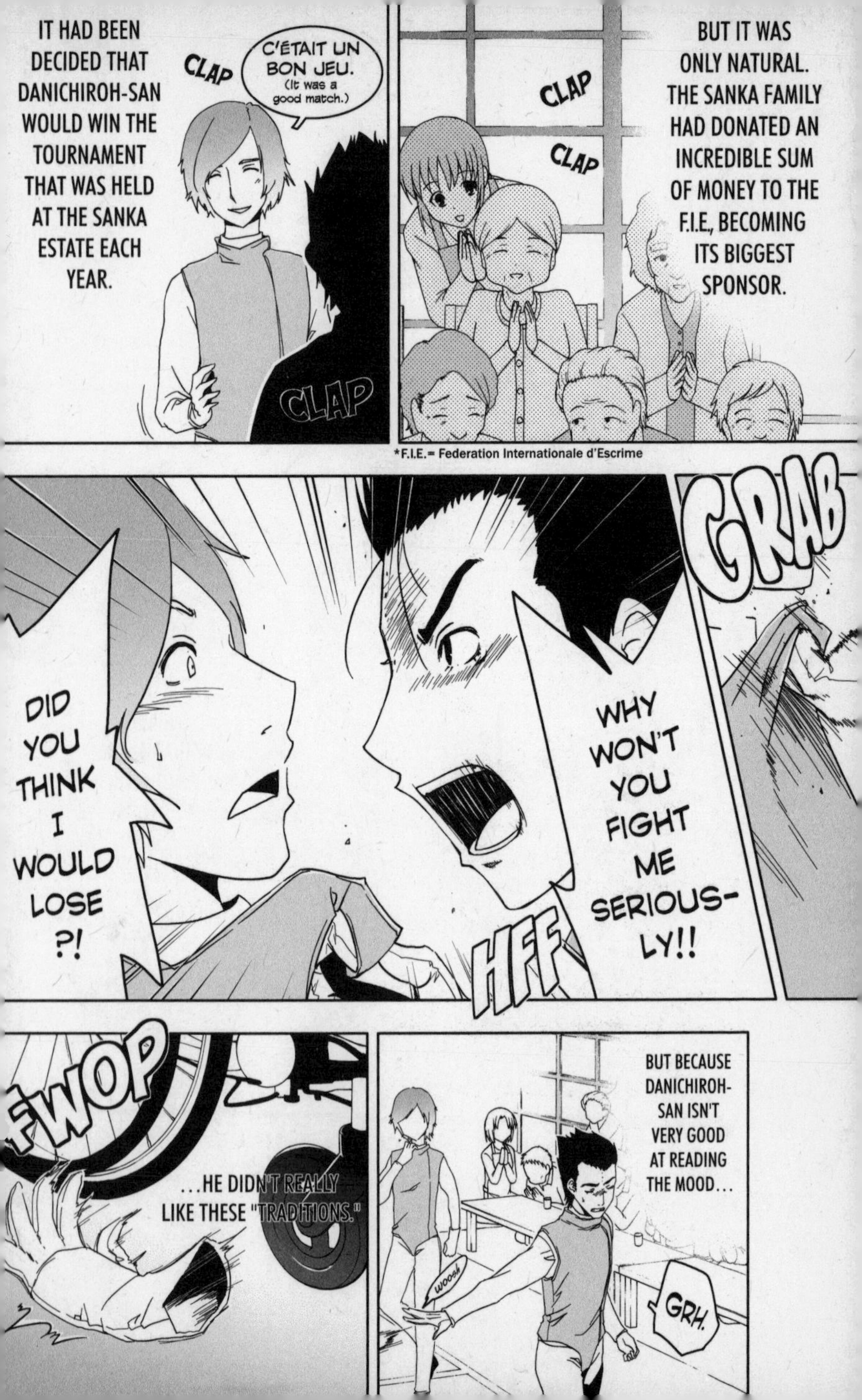
BUT IT WAS ONLY NATURAL. THE SANKA FAMILY HAD DONATED AN INCREDIBLE SUM OF MONEY TO THE F.I.E., BECOMING ITS BIGGEST SPONSOR.
CLAP
CLAP
IT HAD BEEN DECIDED THAT DANICHIROH-SAN WOULD WIN THE TOURNAMENT THAT WAS HELD AT THE SANKA ESTATE EACH YEAR.
C'ÉTAIT UN BON JEU. (It was a good match.)
CLAP
CLAP
*F.I.E.= Federation Internationale d'Escrime
GRAB
WHY WON'T YOU FIGHT ME SERIOUS-LY!!
HFF
DID YOU THINK I WOULD LOSE ?!
BUT BECAUSE DANICHIROH-SAN ISN'T VERY GOOD AT READING THE MOOD...
GRH.
WOOAH
FWOP
...HE DIDN'T REALLY LIKE THESE "TRADITIONS."

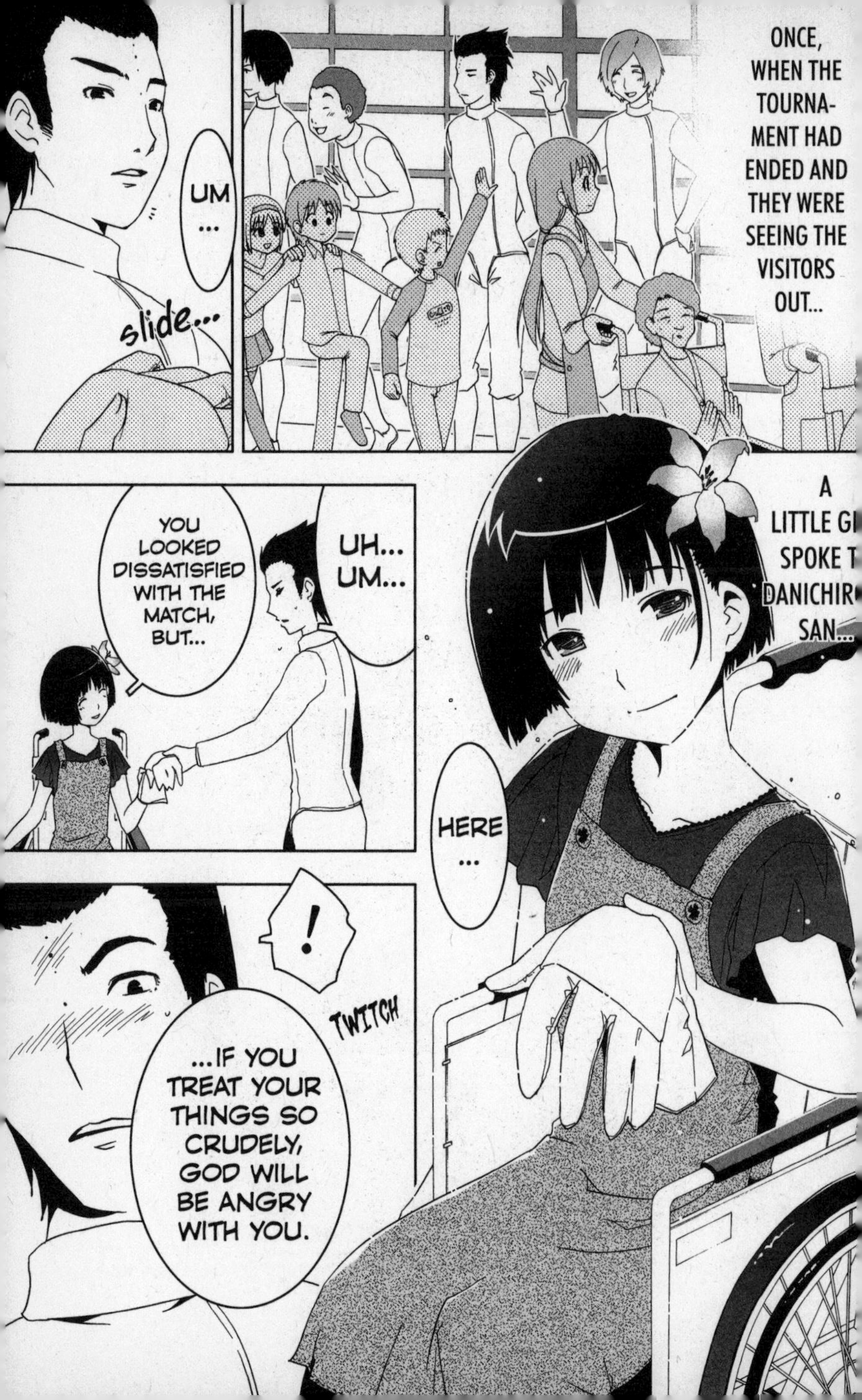
ONCE, WHEN THE TOURNA-MENT HAD ENDED AND THEY WERE SEEING THE VISITORS OUT...
UM ...
slide...
A LITTLE GI SPOKE T DANICHIR SAN...
HERE ...
UH... UM...
YOU LOOKED DISSATISFIED WITH THE MATCH, BUT...
!
TWITCH
...IF YOU TREAT YOUR THINGS SO CRUDELY, GOD WILL BE ANGRY WITH YOU.

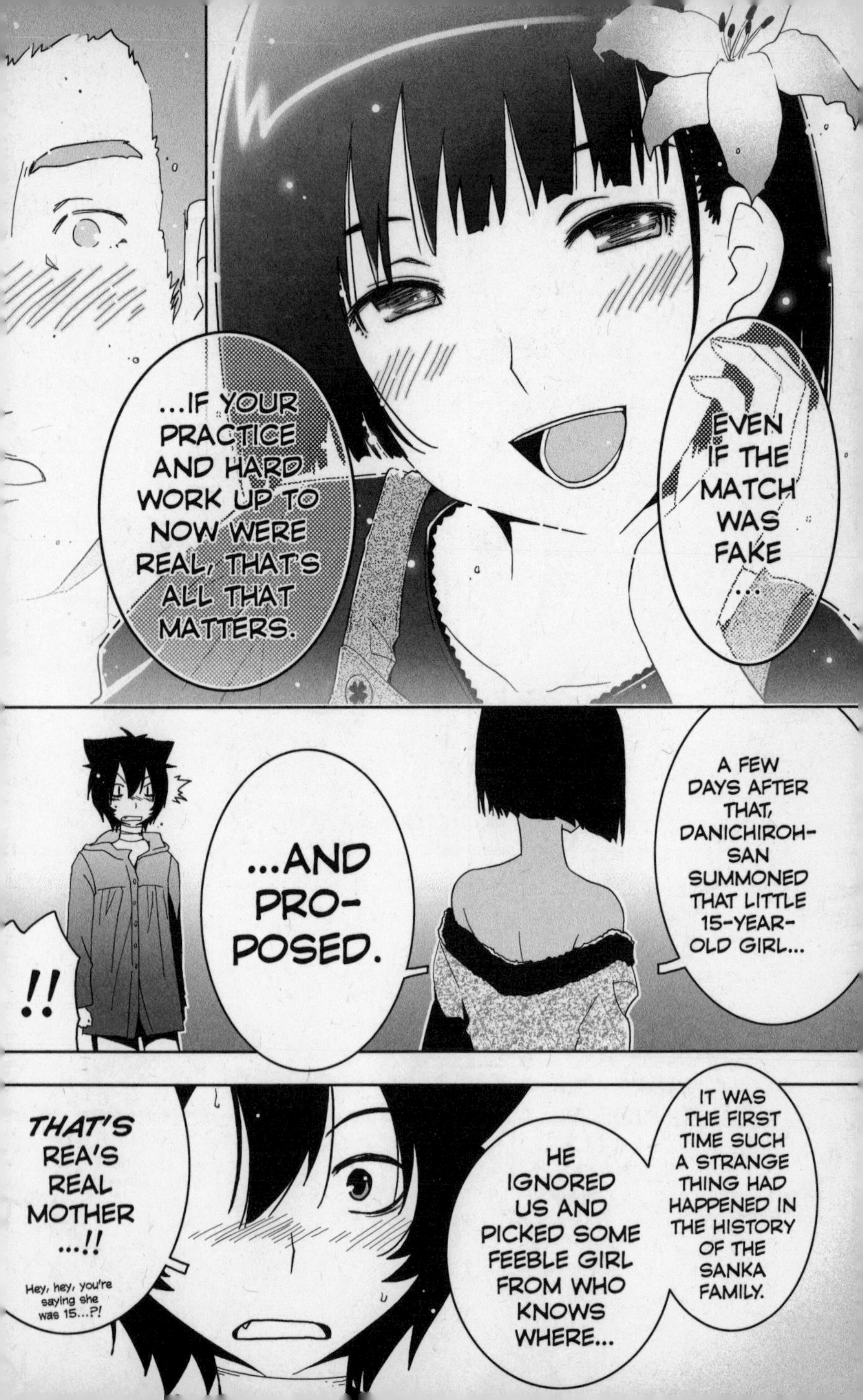
EVEN IF THE MATCH WAS FAKE
...
...IF YOUR PRACTICE AND HARD WORK UP TO NOW WERE REAL, THAT'S ALL THAT MATTERS.
A FEW DAYS AFTER THAT, DANICHIROH-SAN SUMMONED THAT LITTLE 15-YEAR-OLD GIRL...
...AND PRO-POSED.
!!
IT WAS THE FIRST TIME SUCH A STRANGE THING HAD HAPPENED IN THE HISTORY OF THE SANKA FAMILY.
HE IGNORED US AND PICKED SOME FEEBLE GIRL FROM WHO KNOWS WHERE...
THAT'S REA'S REAL MOTHER ...!!
Hey, hey, you're saying she was 15...?!

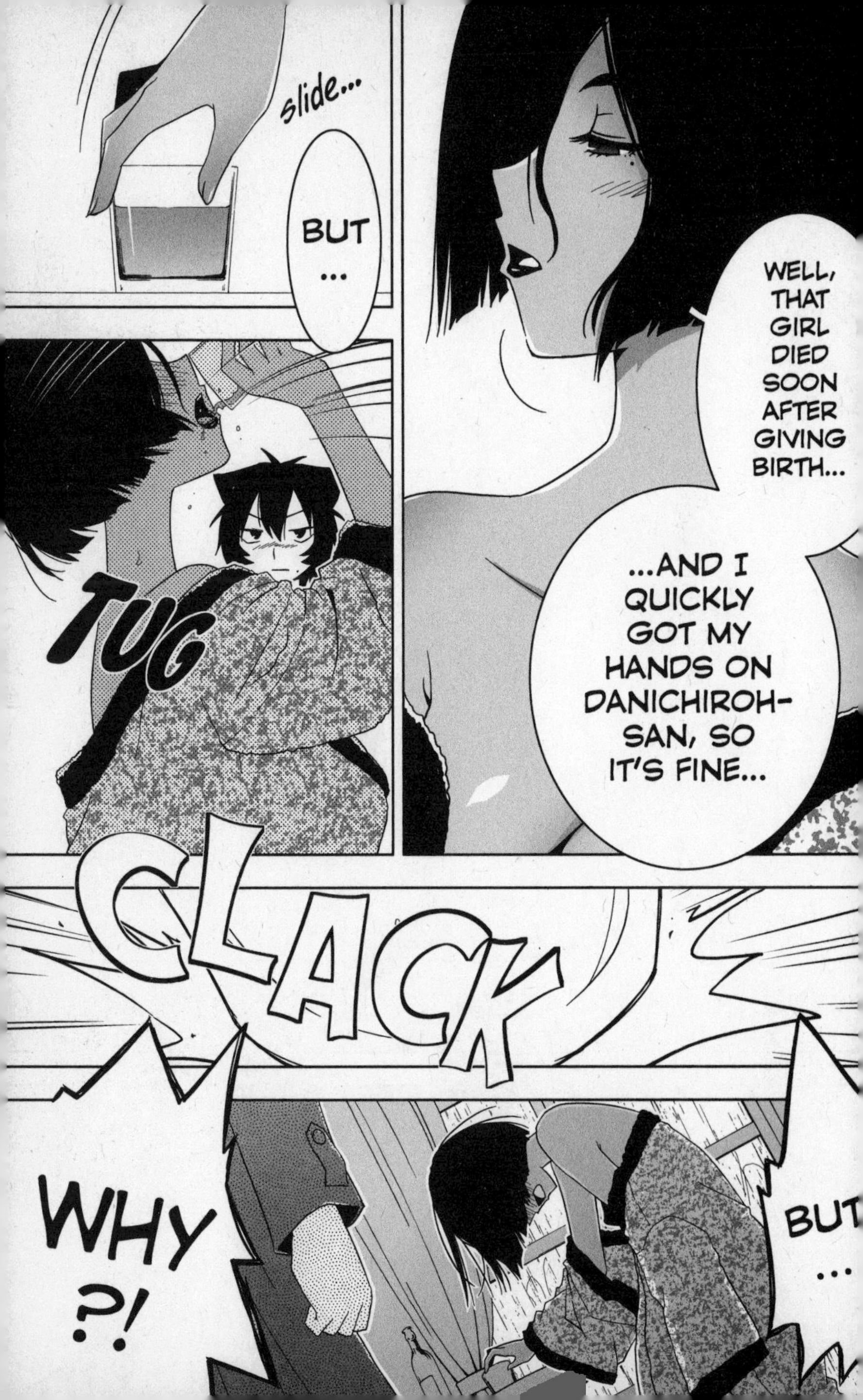
WELL, THAT GIRL DIED SOON AFTER GIVING BIRTH...
...AND I QUICKLY GOT MY HANDS ON DANICHIROH-SAN, SO IT'S FINE...
slide...
BUT ...
TUG
CLACK
BUT ...
WHY ?!

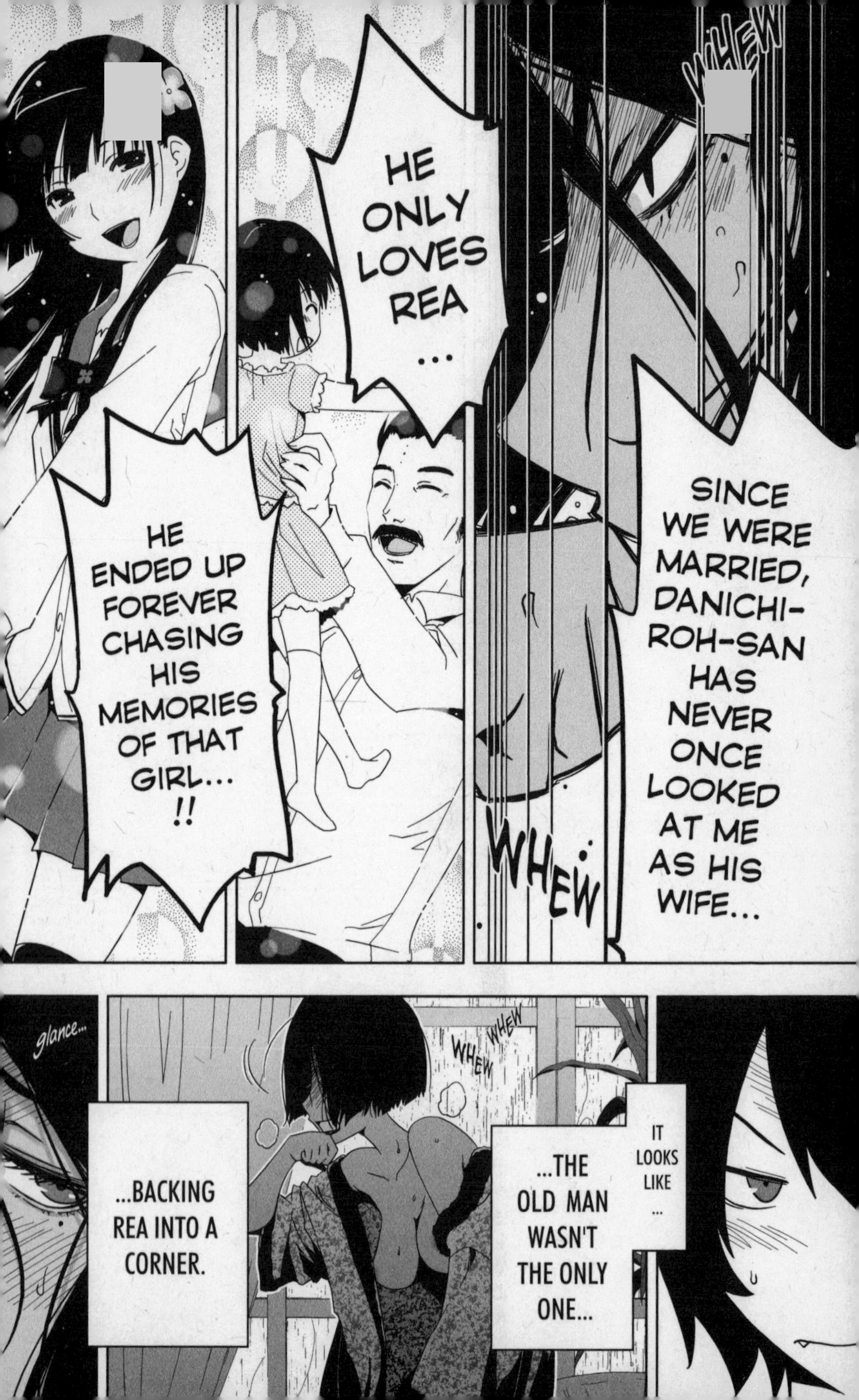
WHEW
SINCE WE WERE MARRIED, DANICHI-ROH-SAN HAS NEVER ONCE LOOKED AT ME AS HIS WIFE...
WHEW
HE ONLY LOVES REA ...
HE ENDED UP FOREVER CHASING HIS MEMORIES OF THAT GIRL... !!
IT LOOKS LIKE ...
...THE OLD MAN WASN'T THE ONLY ONE...
WHEW
WHEW
...BACKING REA INTO A CORNER.
glance...

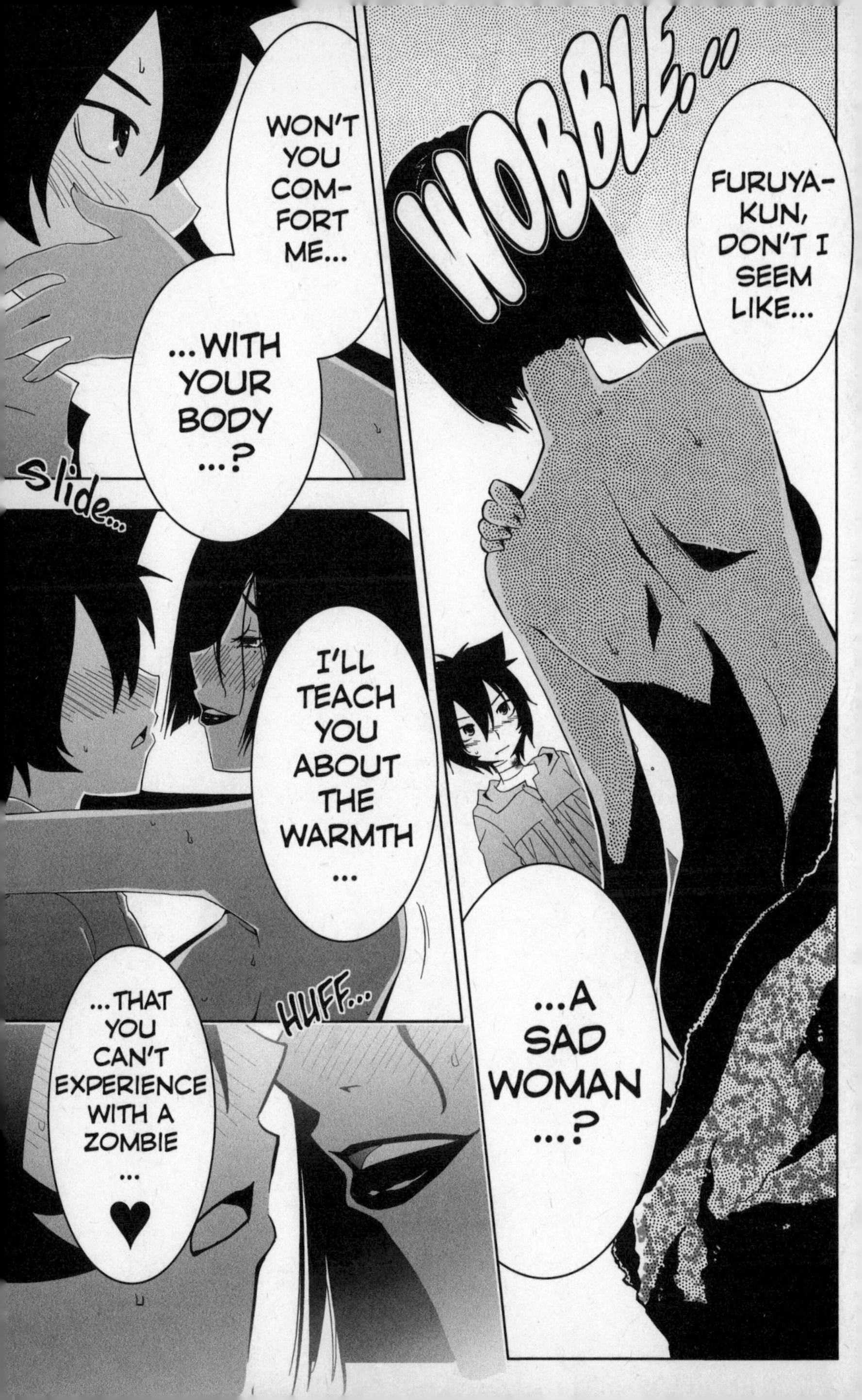
WOBBLE...
FURUYA-KUN, DON'T I SEEM LIKE...
...A SAD WOMAN ...?
WON'T YOU COM-FORT ME...
...WITH YOUR BODY ...?
slide...
I'LL TEACH YOU ABOUT THE WARMTH ...
HUFF...
...THAT YOU CAN'T EXPERIENCE WITH A ZOMBIE ... ♥

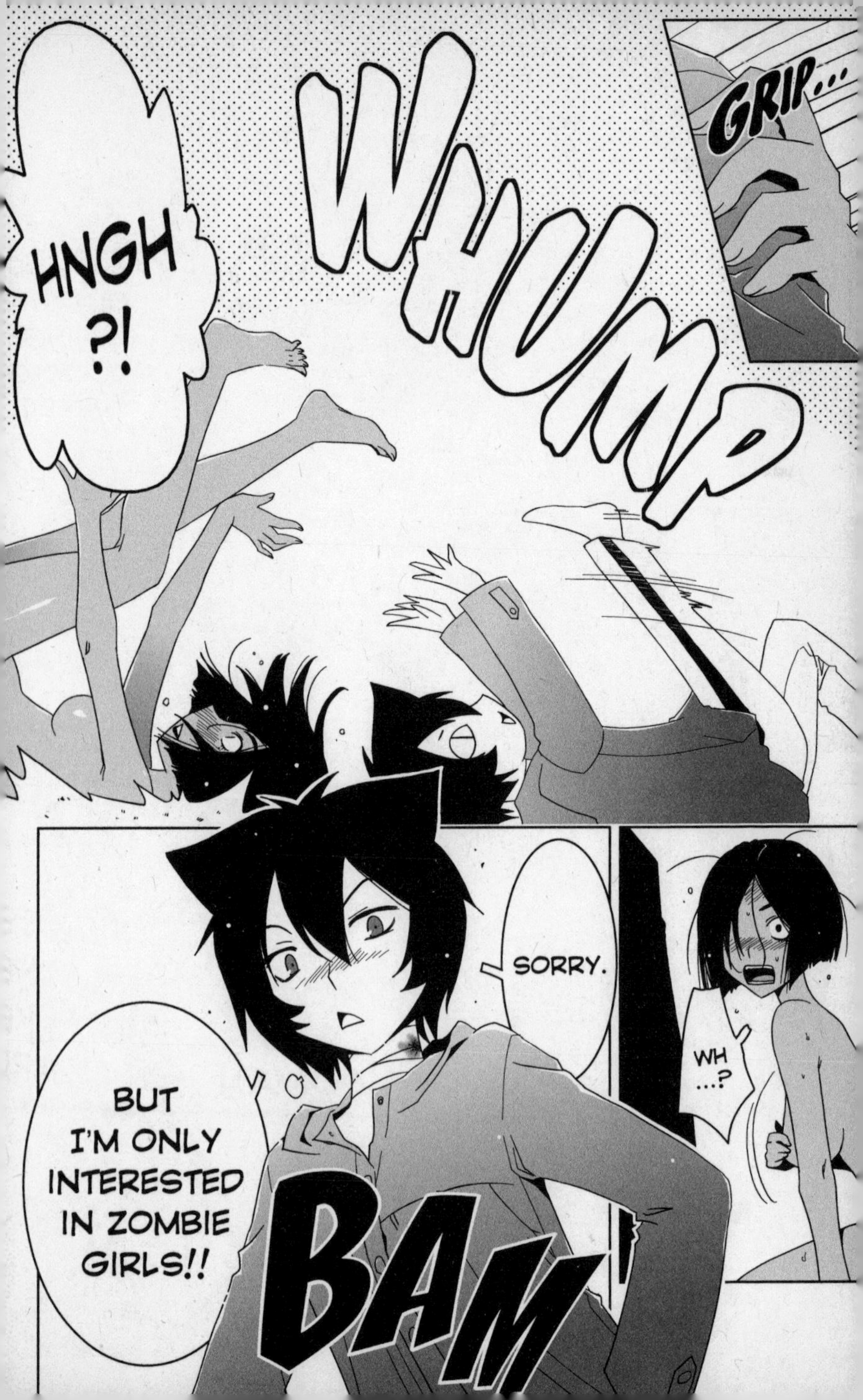
GRIP...
WHUMP
HNGH ?!
WH ...?
SORRY.
BUT I'M ONLY INTERESTED IN ZOMBIE GIRLS!!
BAM

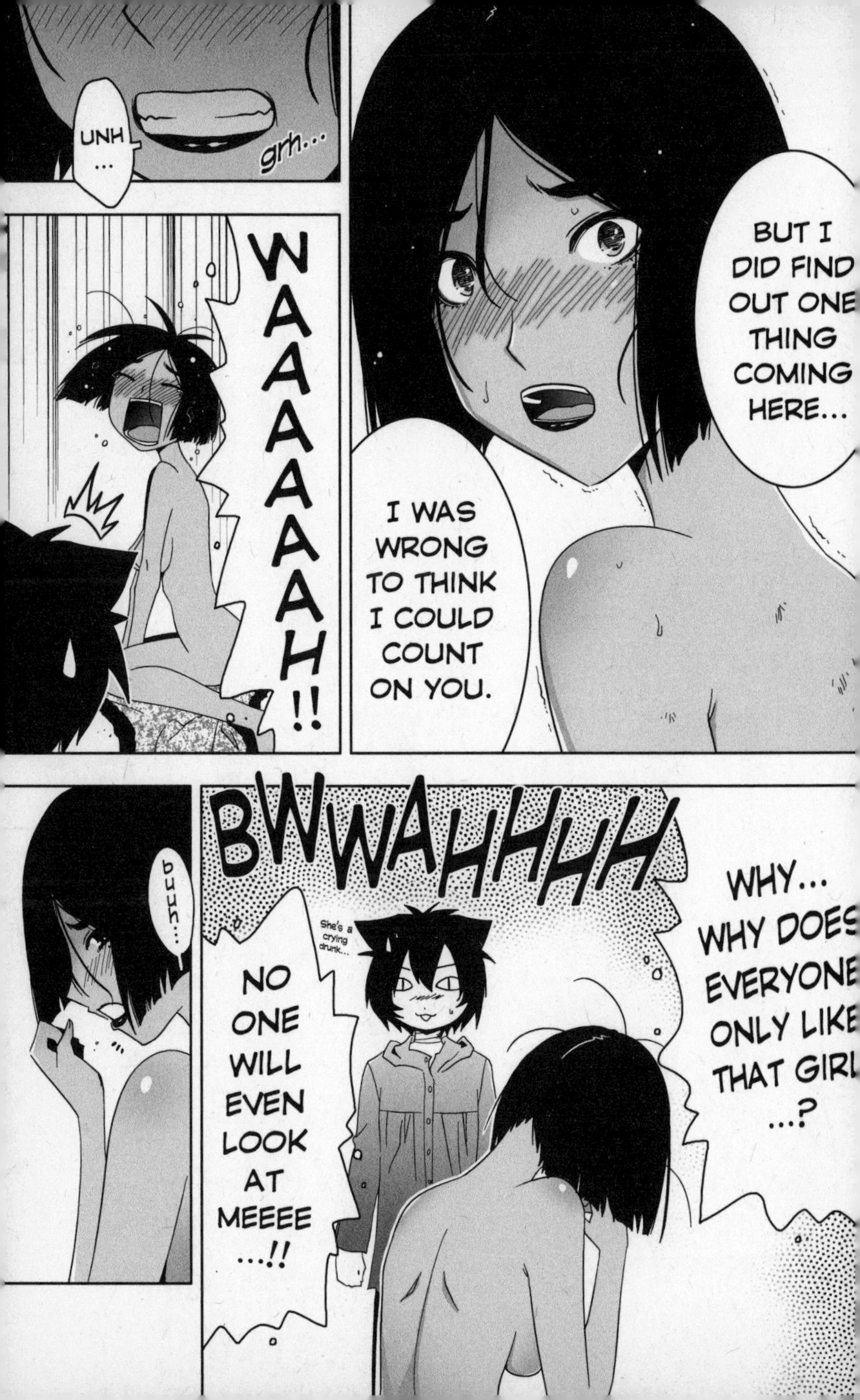
BUT I DID FIND OUT ONE THING COMING HERE...
I WAS WRONG TO THINK I COULD COUNT ON YOU.
UNH ...
grh...
WAAAAAAAH!!
BWAHHHHH
WHY... WHY DOES EVERYONE ONLY LIKE THAT GIRL ...?
She's a crying drunk...
NO ONE WILL EVEN LOOK AT MEEEE ...!!
buuh...

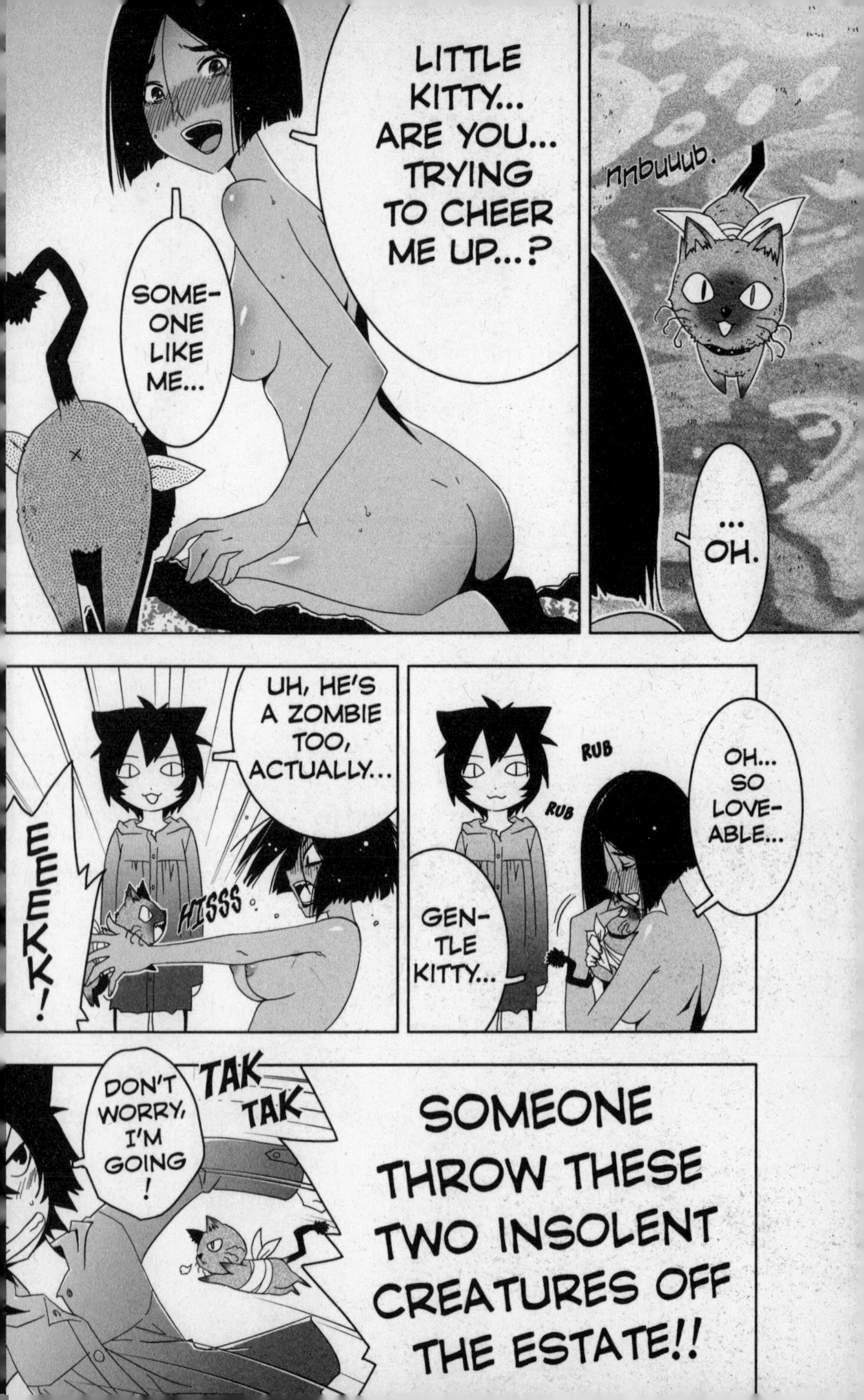
nnbuuub.
...OH.
LITTLE KITTY... ARE YOU... TRYING TO CHEER ME UP...?
SOME-ONE LIKE ME...
RUB
RUB
OH... SO LOVE-ABLE...
GEN-TLE KITTY...
UH, HE'S A ZOMBIE TOO, ACTUALLY...
HISSS
EEEEKK!
SOMEONE THROW THESE TWO INSOLENT CREATURES OFF THE ESTATE!!
DON'T WORRY, I'M GOING!
TAK
TAK

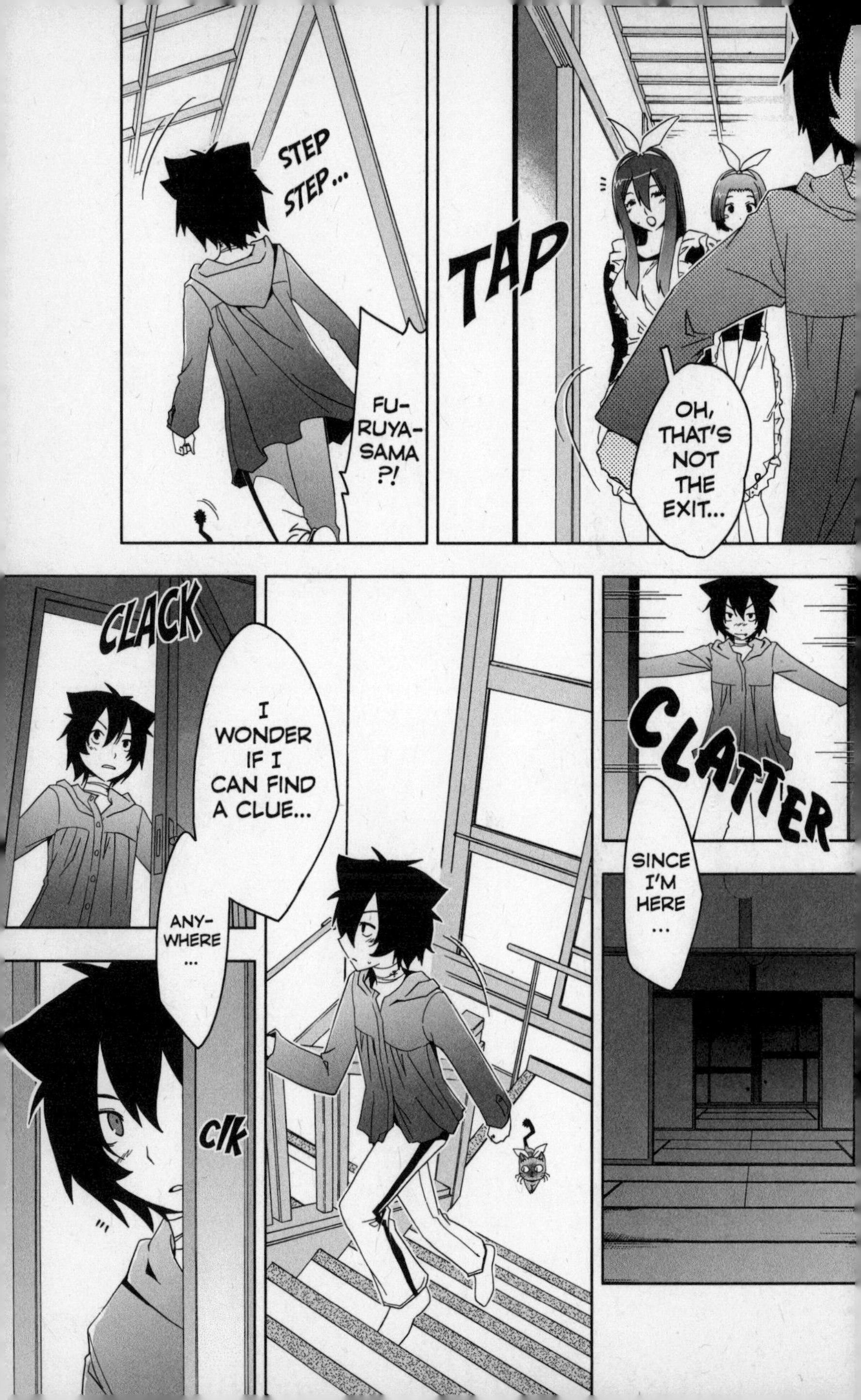

TAP
OH, THAT'S NOT THE EXIT...
STEP STEP...
FU-RUYA-SAMA?!
CLATTER
SINCE I'M HERE...
I WONDER IF I CAN FIND A CLUE...
ANY-WHERE...
CLACK
CIK

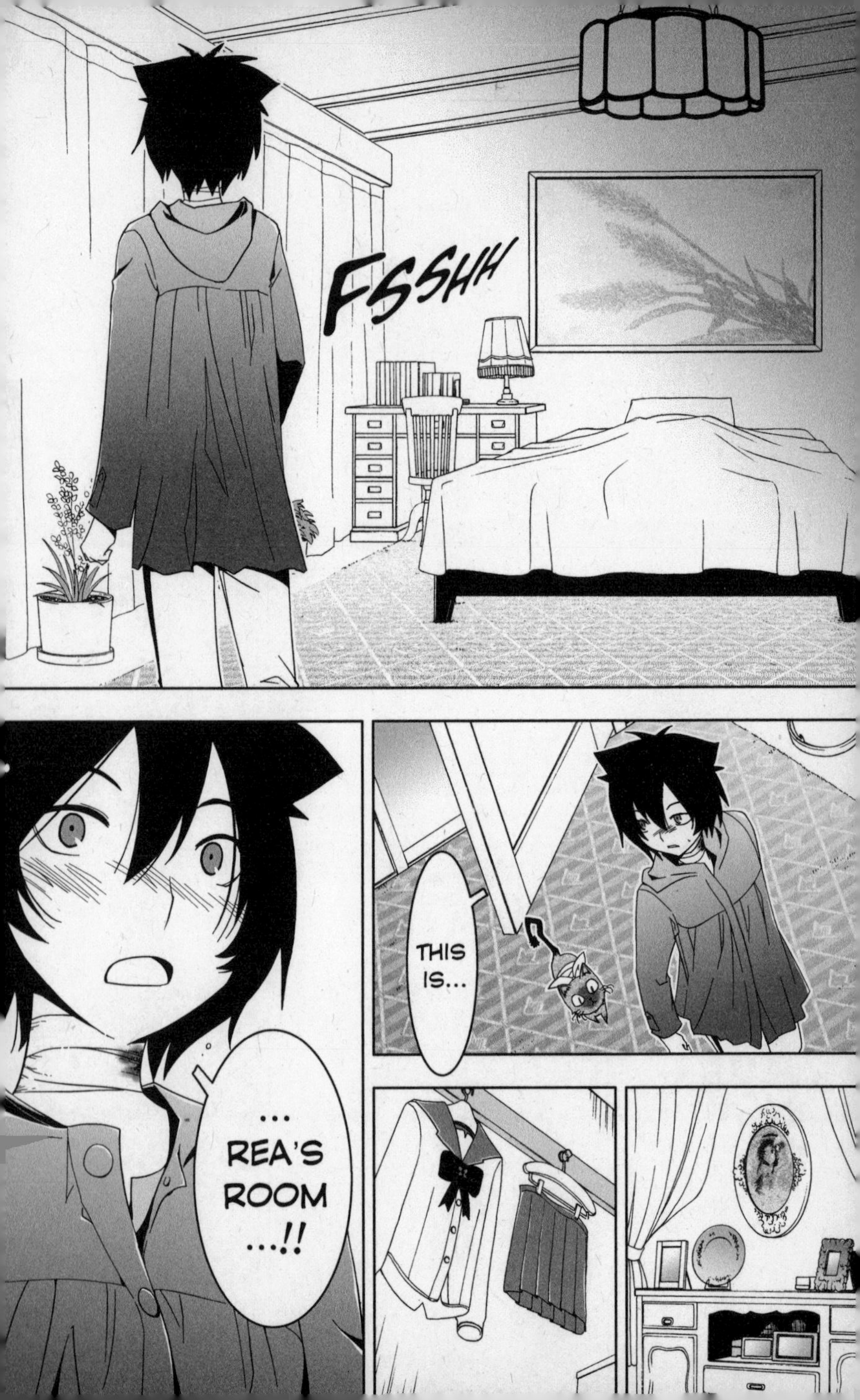
FSSHH
THIS IS...
... REA'S ROOM ...!!

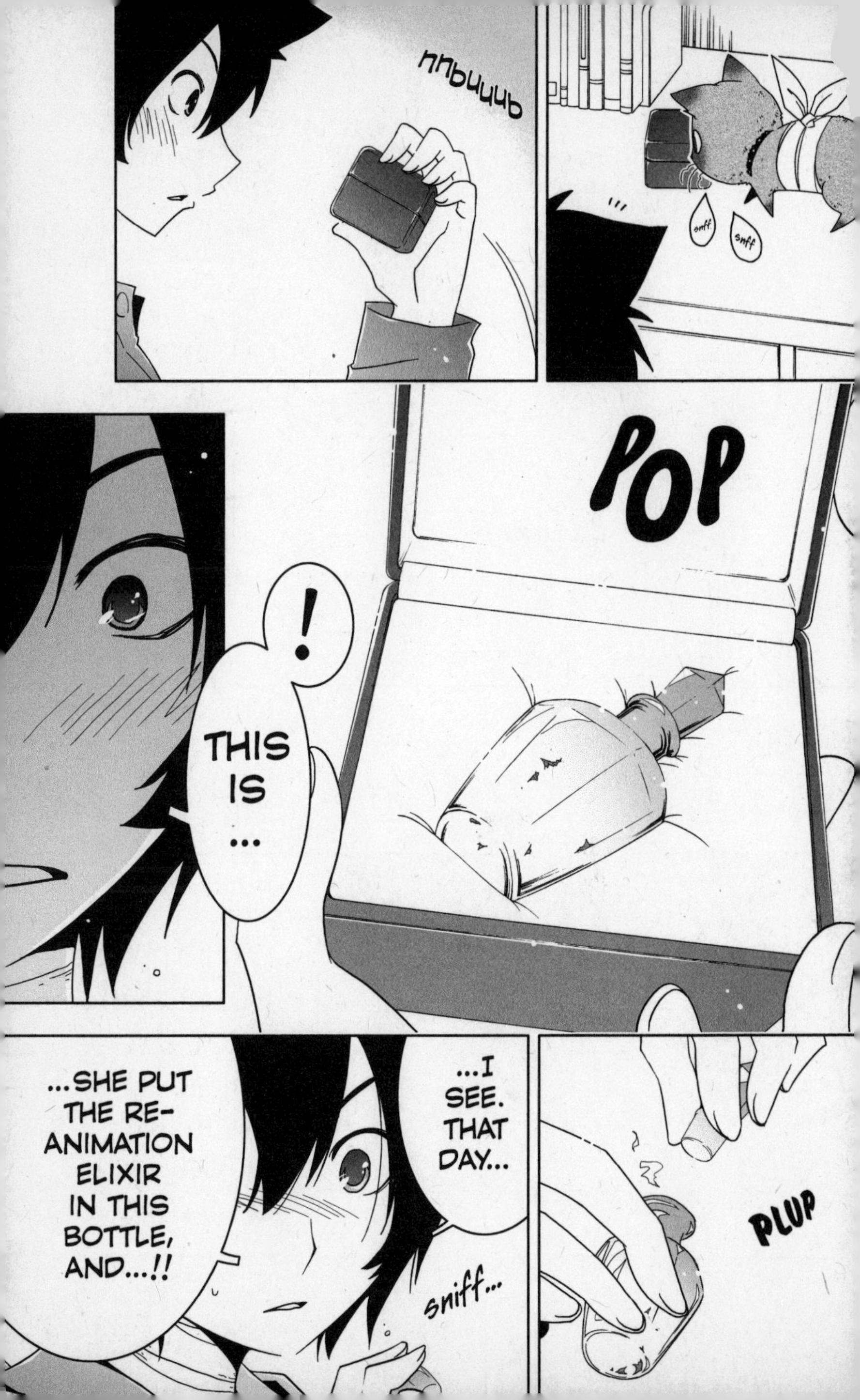
sniff
sniff
nnguuuh
POP
!
THIS IS ...
PLUP
...I SEE. THAT DAY...
sniff...
...SHE PUT THE RE-ANIMATION ELIXIR IN THIS BOTTLE, AND...!!

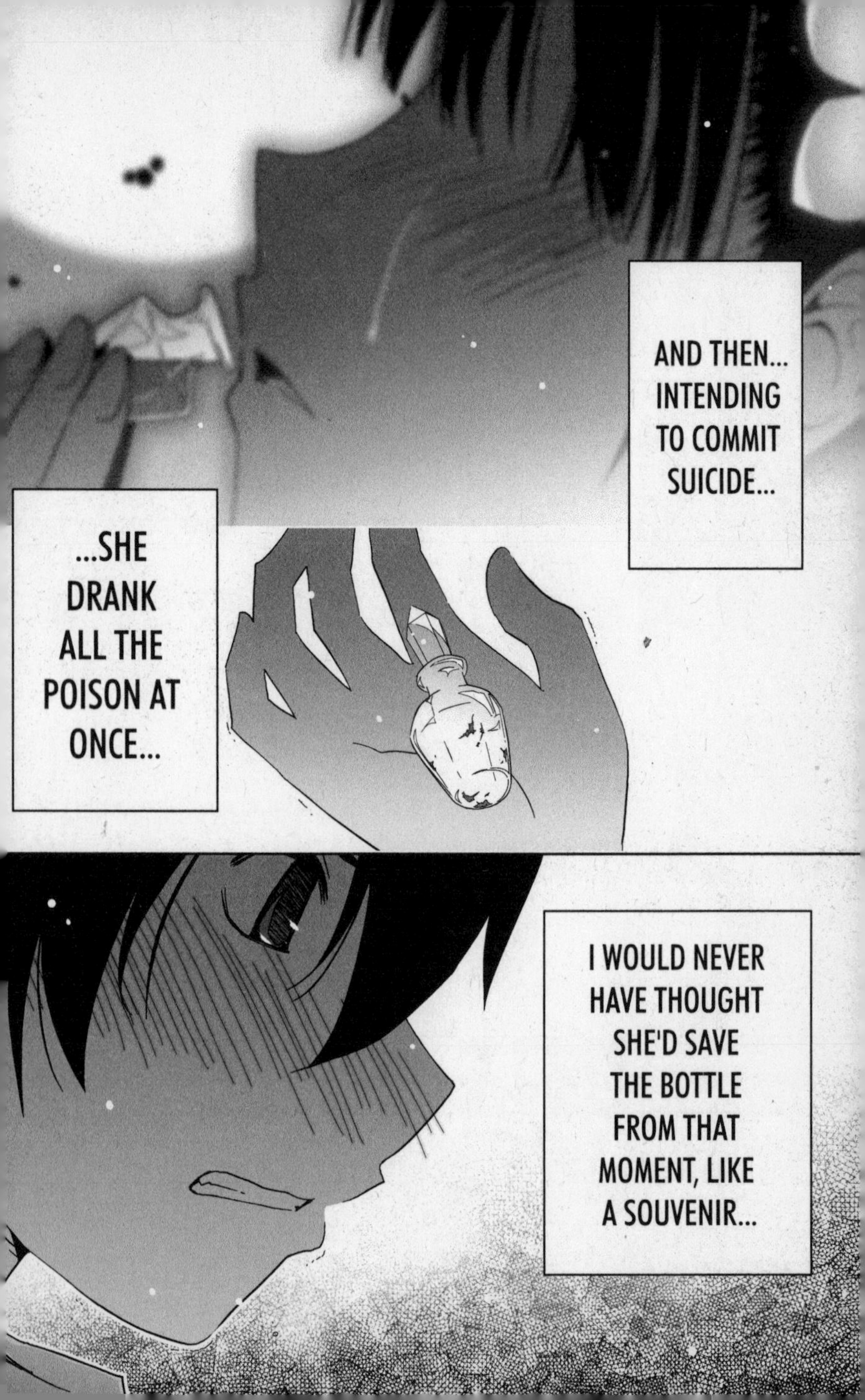
AND THEN... INTENDING TO COMMIT SUICIDE...
...SHE DRANK ALL THE POISON AT ONCE...
I WOULD NEVER HAVE THOUGHT SHE'D SAVE THE BOTTLE FROM THAT MOMENT, LIKE A SOUVENIR...

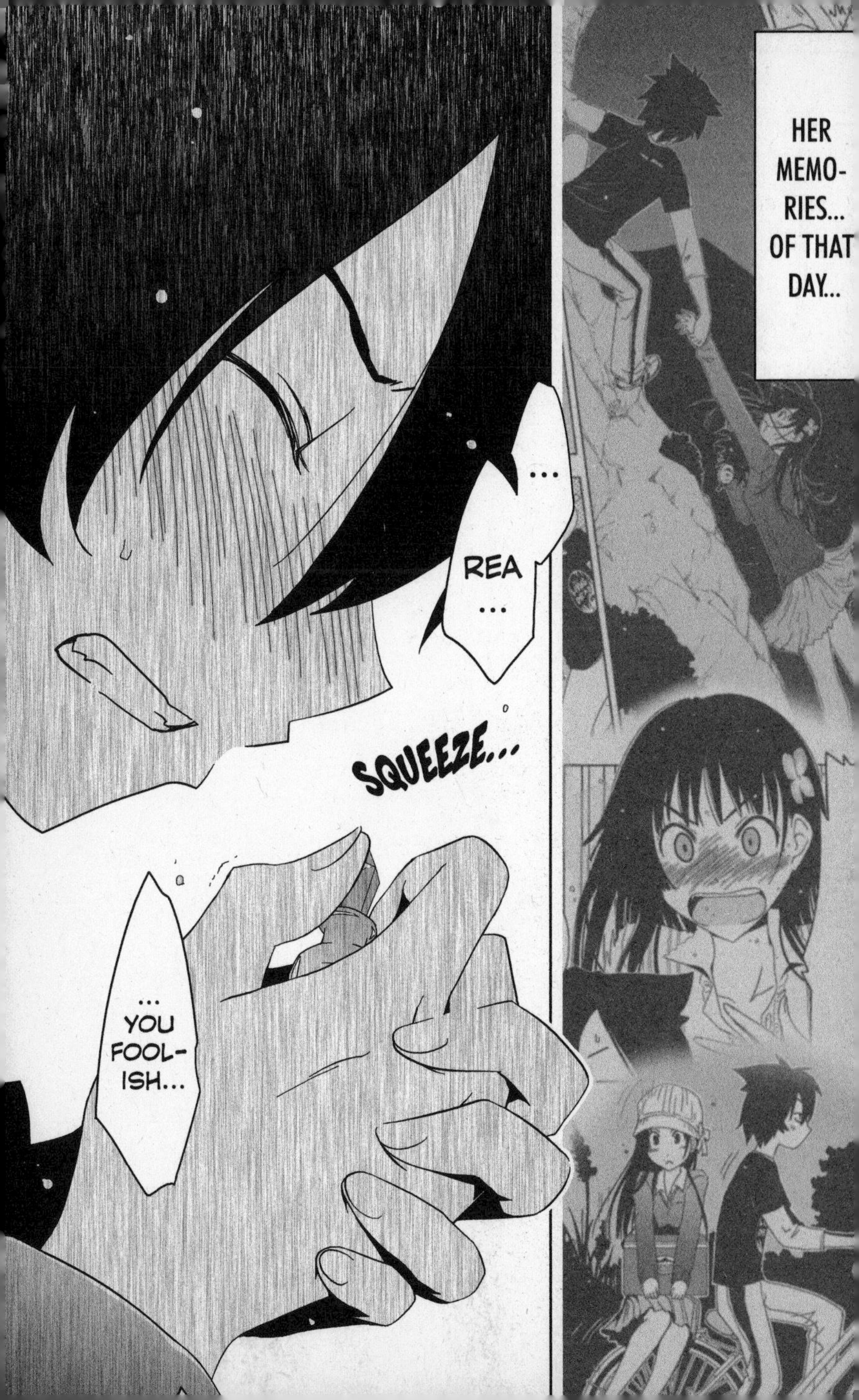
HER MEMO-RIES... OF THAT DAY...
... REA ...
SQUEEZE...
... YOU FOOL-ISH...

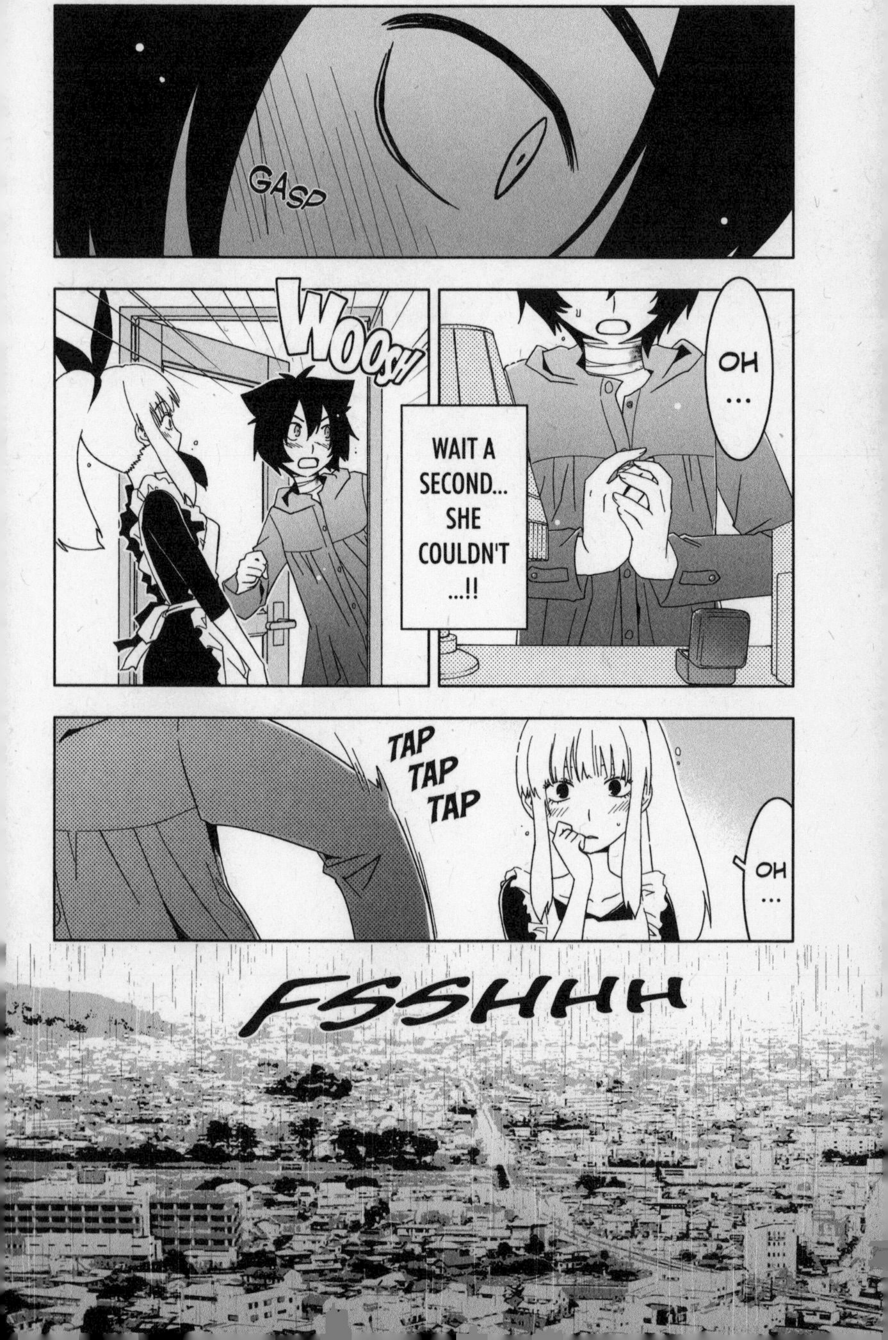
GASP
OH ...
WAIT A SECOND... SHE COULDN'T ...!!
WOOSH
OH ...
TAP TAP TAP
FSSHHH

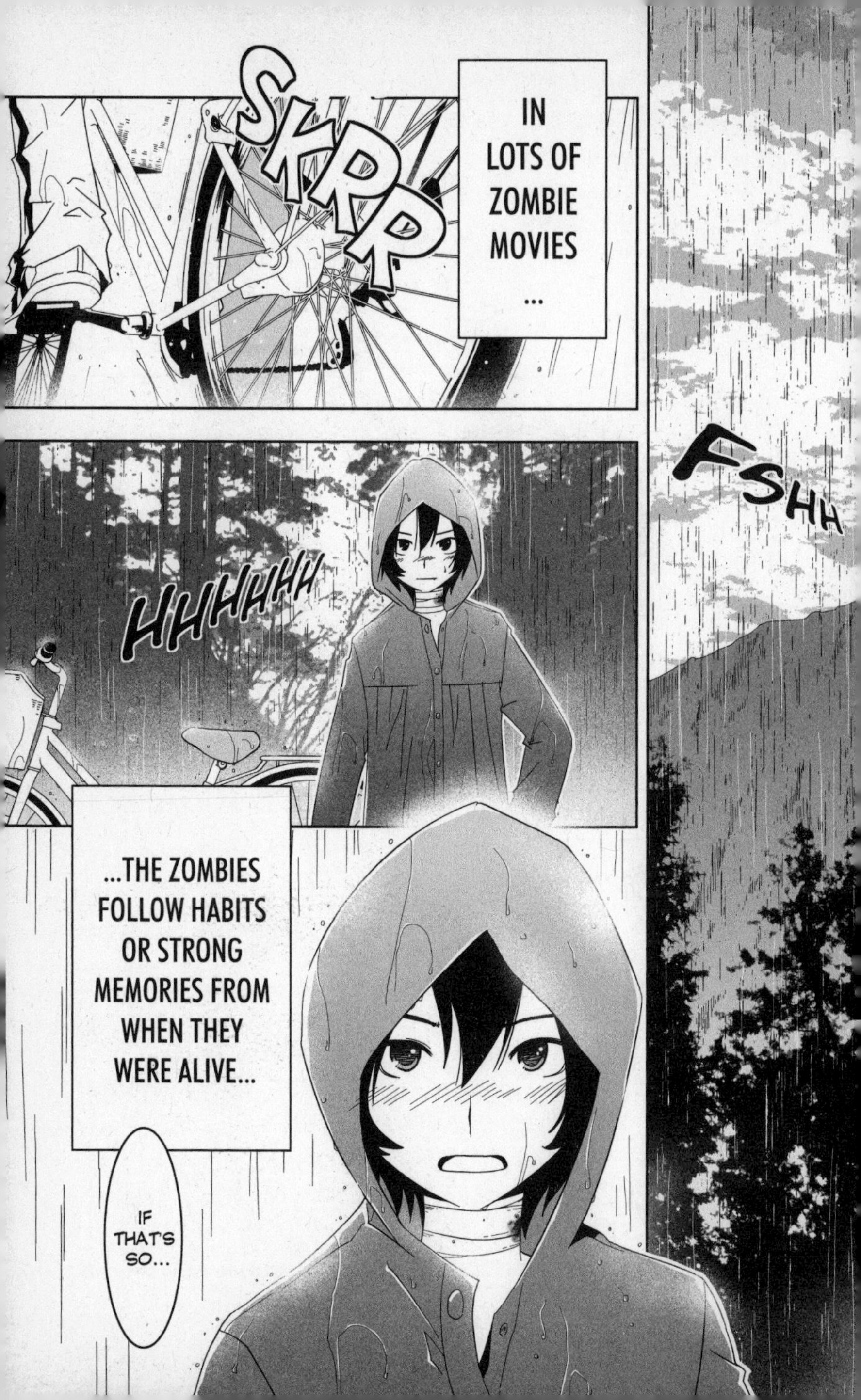
FSHH
IN LOTS OF ZOMBIE MOVIES ...
SKRP
HHHHHH
...THE ZOMBIES FOLLOW HABITS OR STRONG MEMORIES FROM WHEN THEY WERE ALIVE...
IF THAT'S SO...

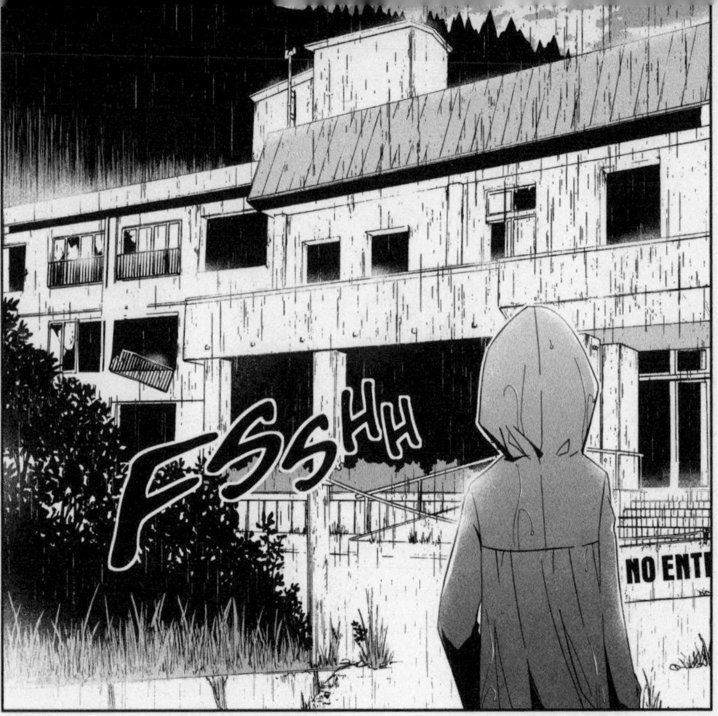
NO ENT
FSSHH
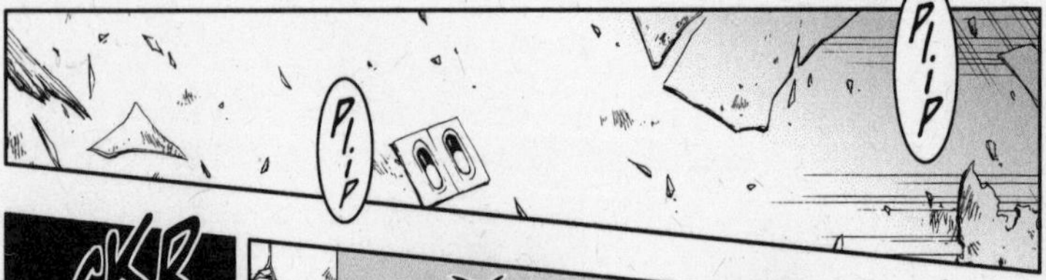
PLIP
PLIP
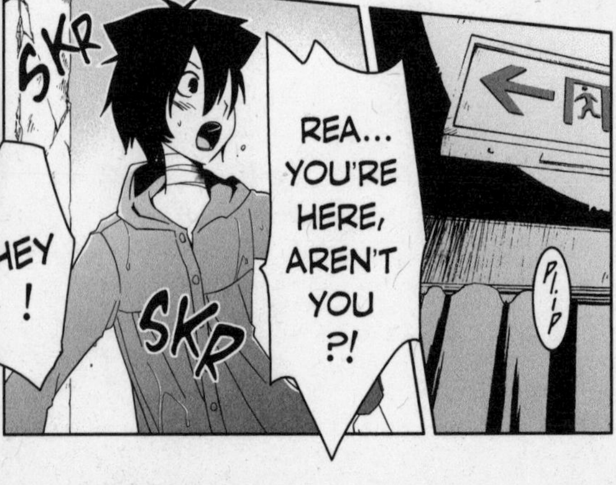
PLIP
REA... YOU'RE HERE, AREN'T YOU ?!
HEY !
SKR
SKR
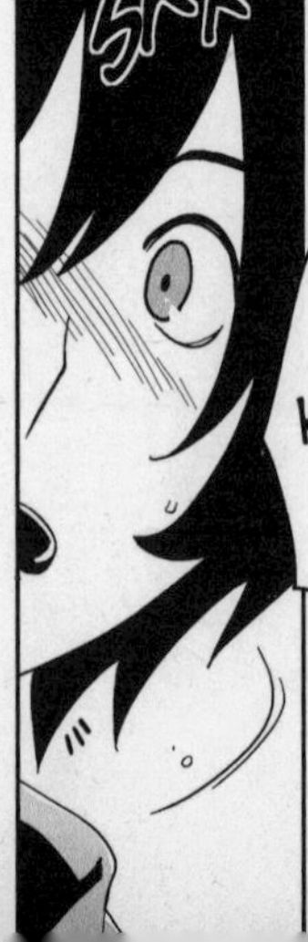
SKR

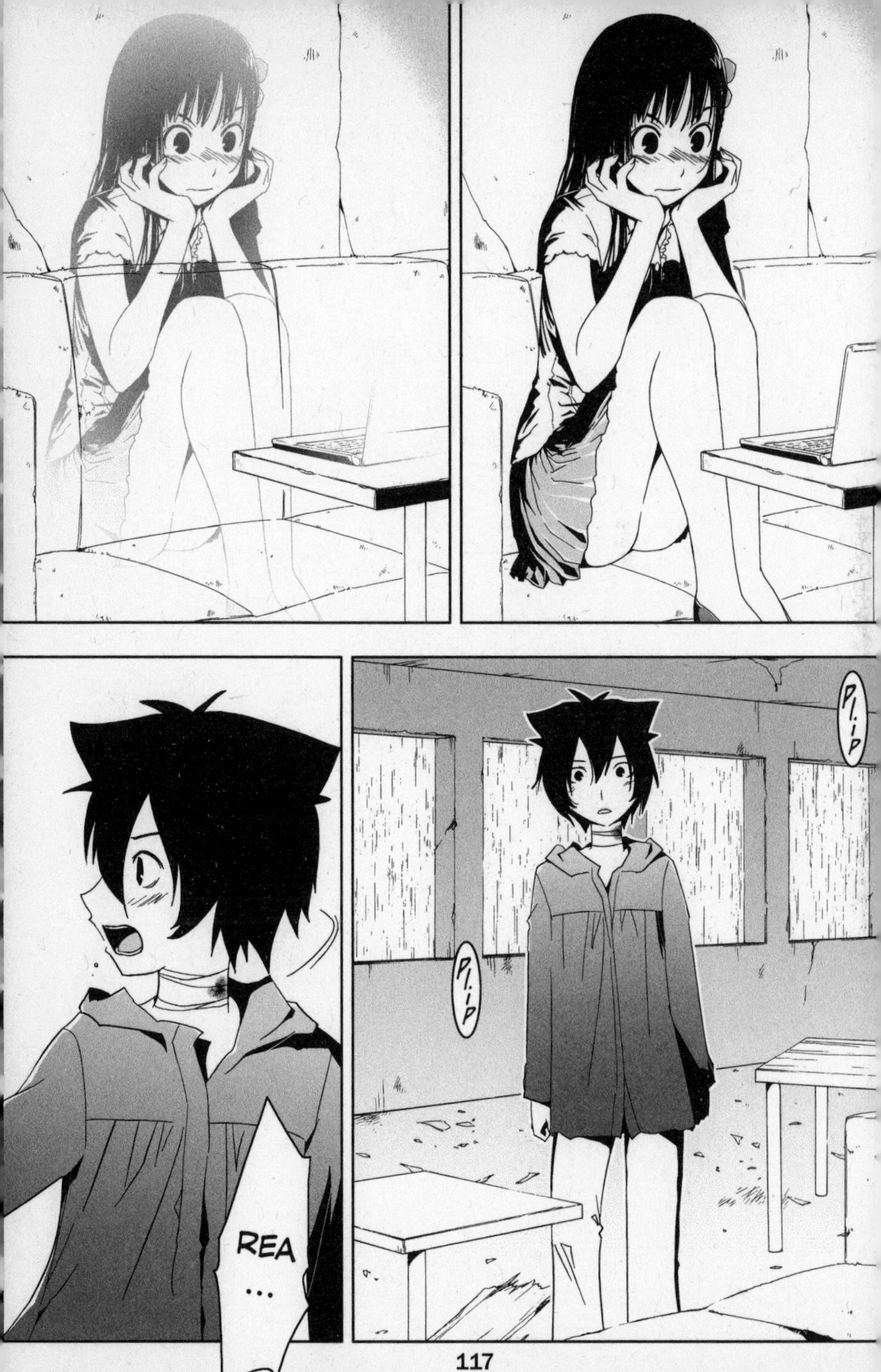
PI.IP
PI.IP
REA ...

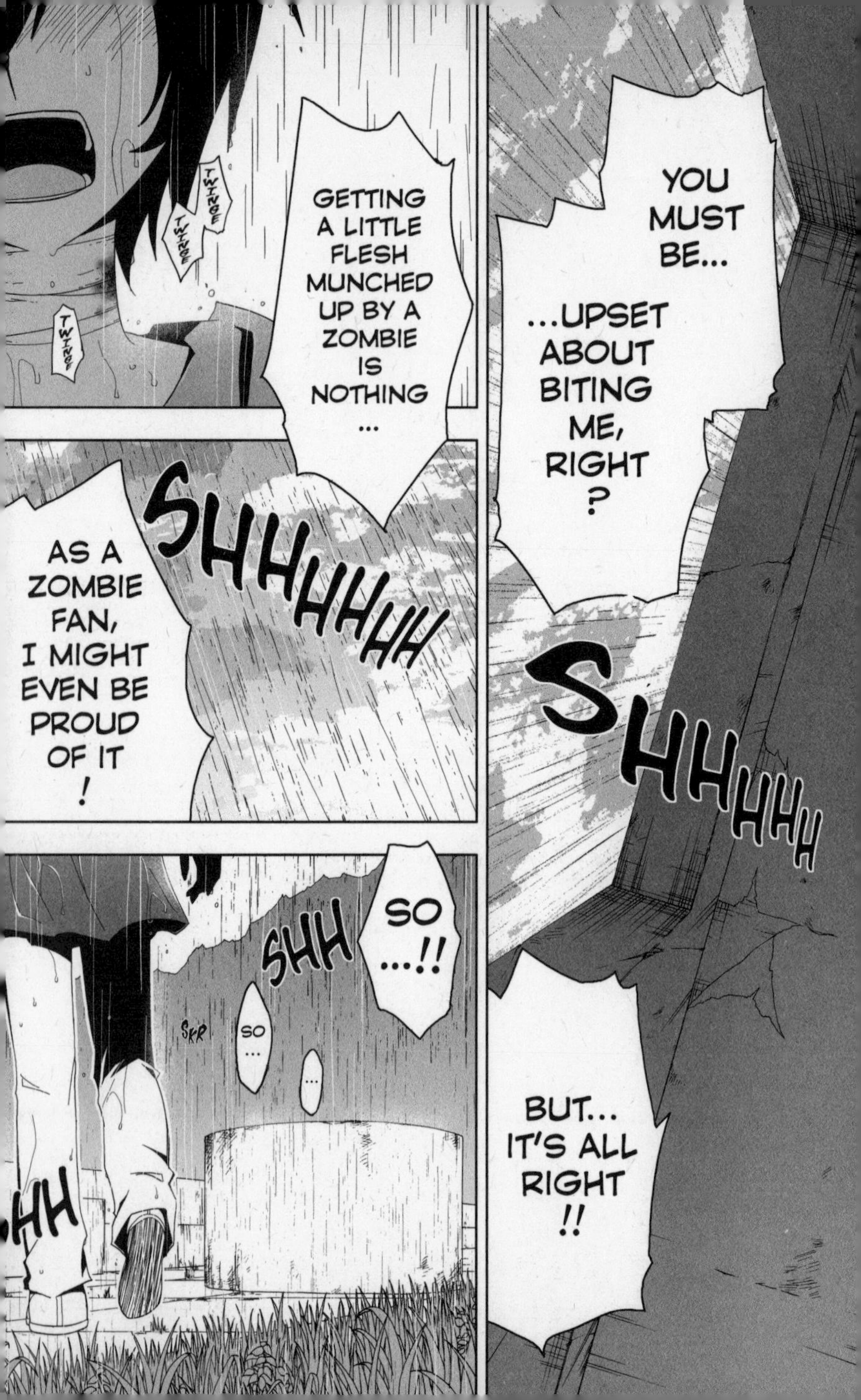

YOU MUST BE...
...UPSET ABOUT BITING ME, RIGHT?
SHHHHHH
BUT... IT'S ALL RIGHT!!
TWINGE
TWINGE
TWINGE
GETTING A LITTLE FLESH MUNCHED UP BY A ZOMBIE IS NOTHING...
SHHHHHHH
AS A ZOMBIE FAN, I MIGHT EVEN BE PROUD OF IT!
SO...!!
SHH
SO...
...
SKR
HH

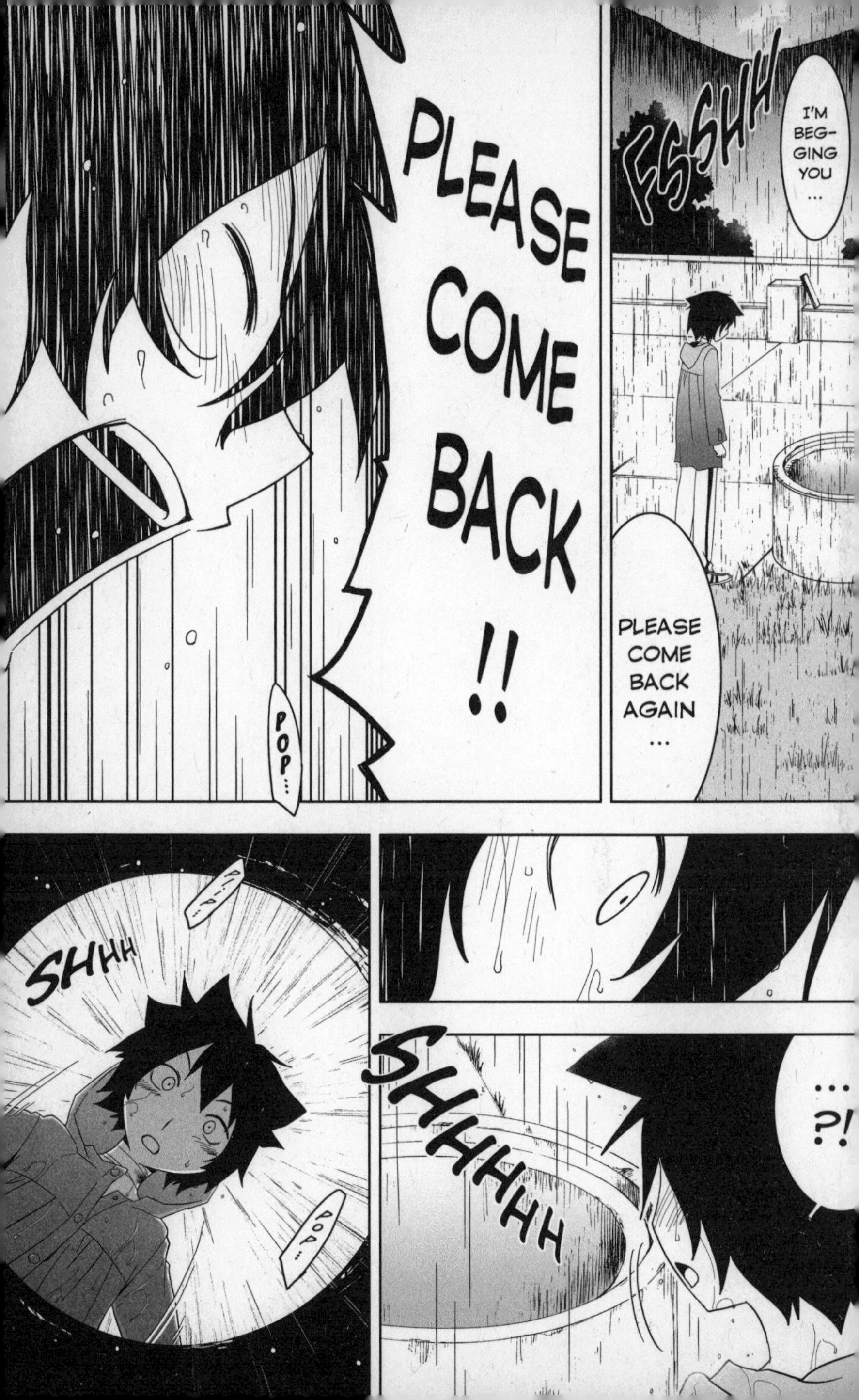
FSSHH
I'M BEG-GING YOU ...
PLEASE COME BACK AGAIN ...
PLEASE COME BACK!!
POP...
SHHHHH
...?!
SHHH
POP...

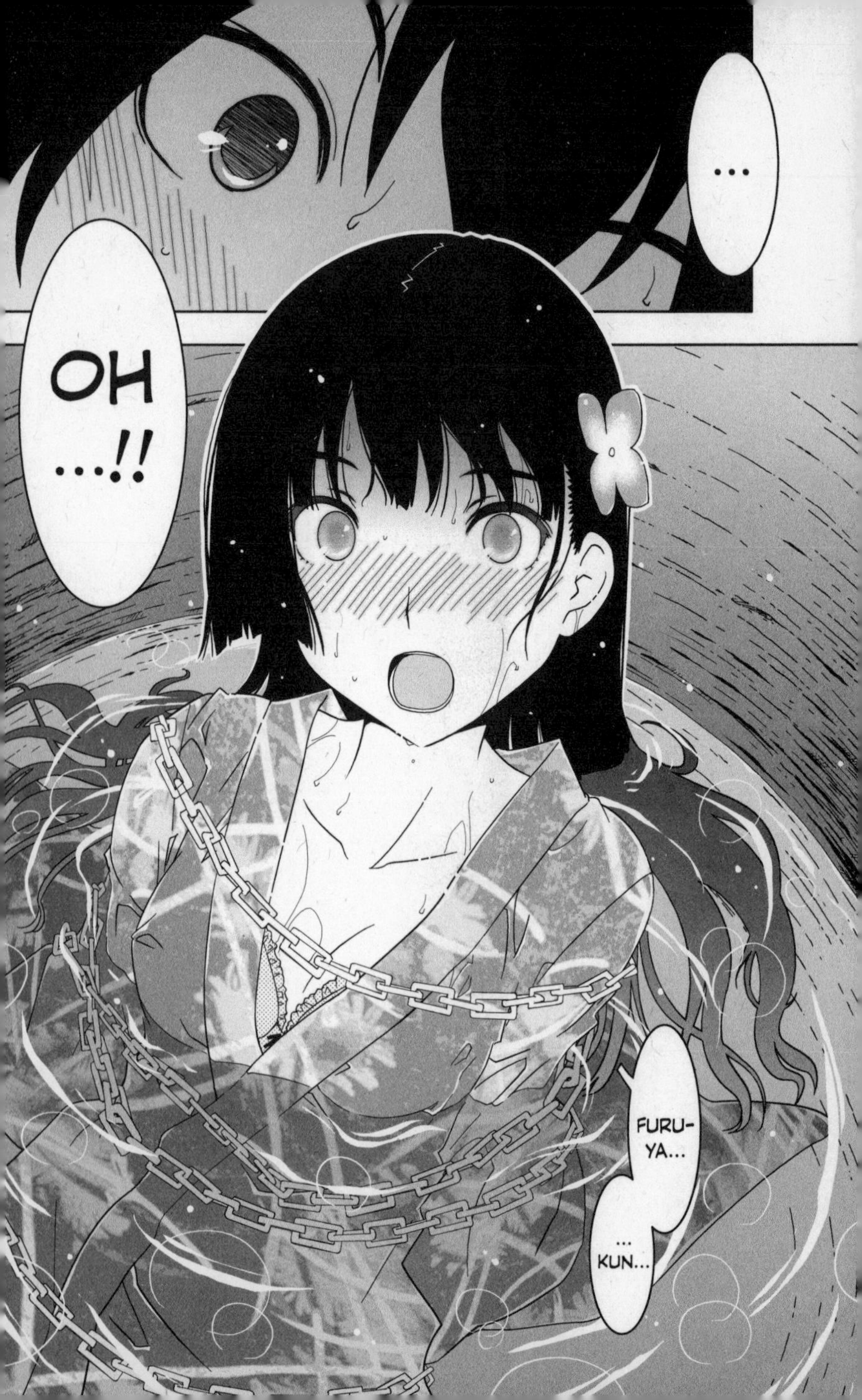
...
OH ...!!
FURU-YA...
...KUN...

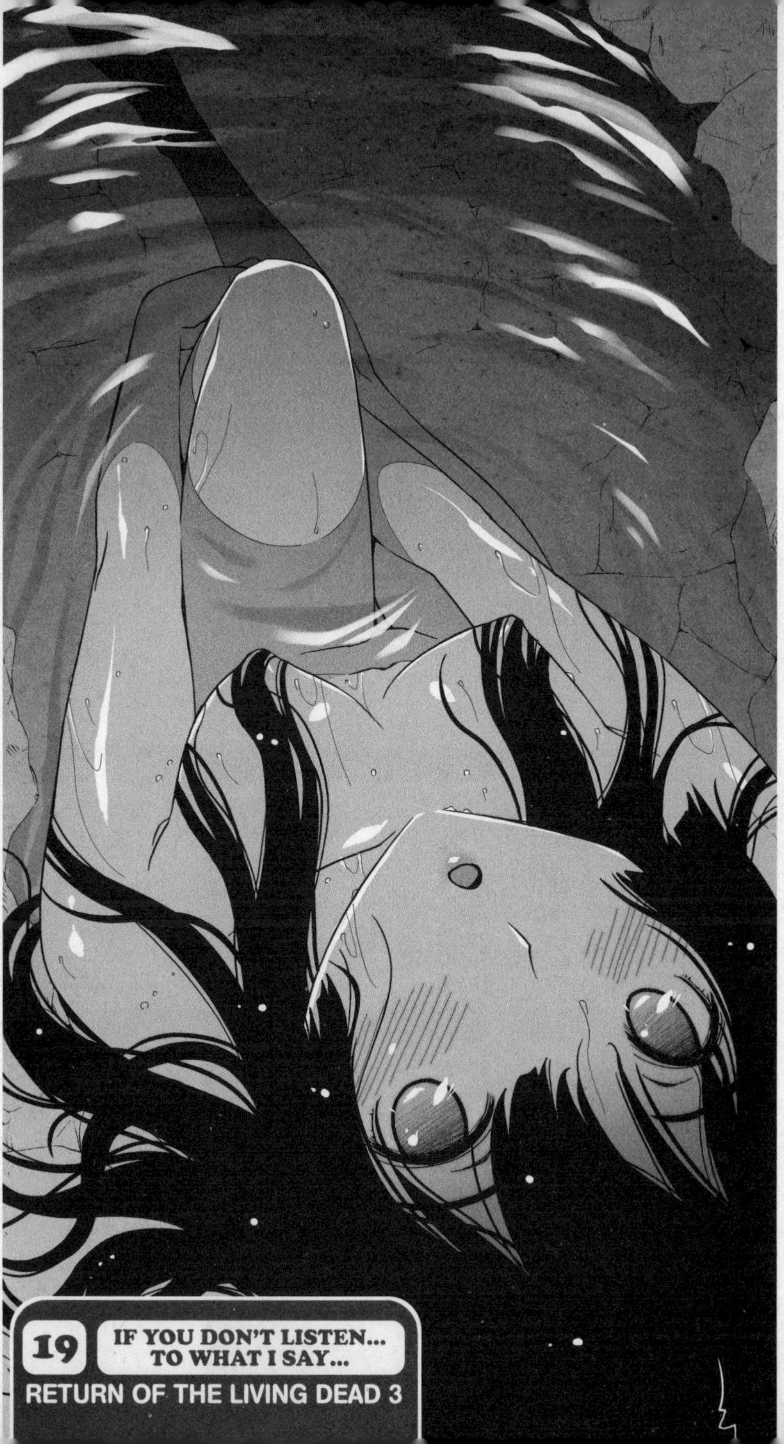
19
IF YOU DON'T LISTEN... TO WHAT I SAY...
RETURN OF THE LIVING DEAD 3

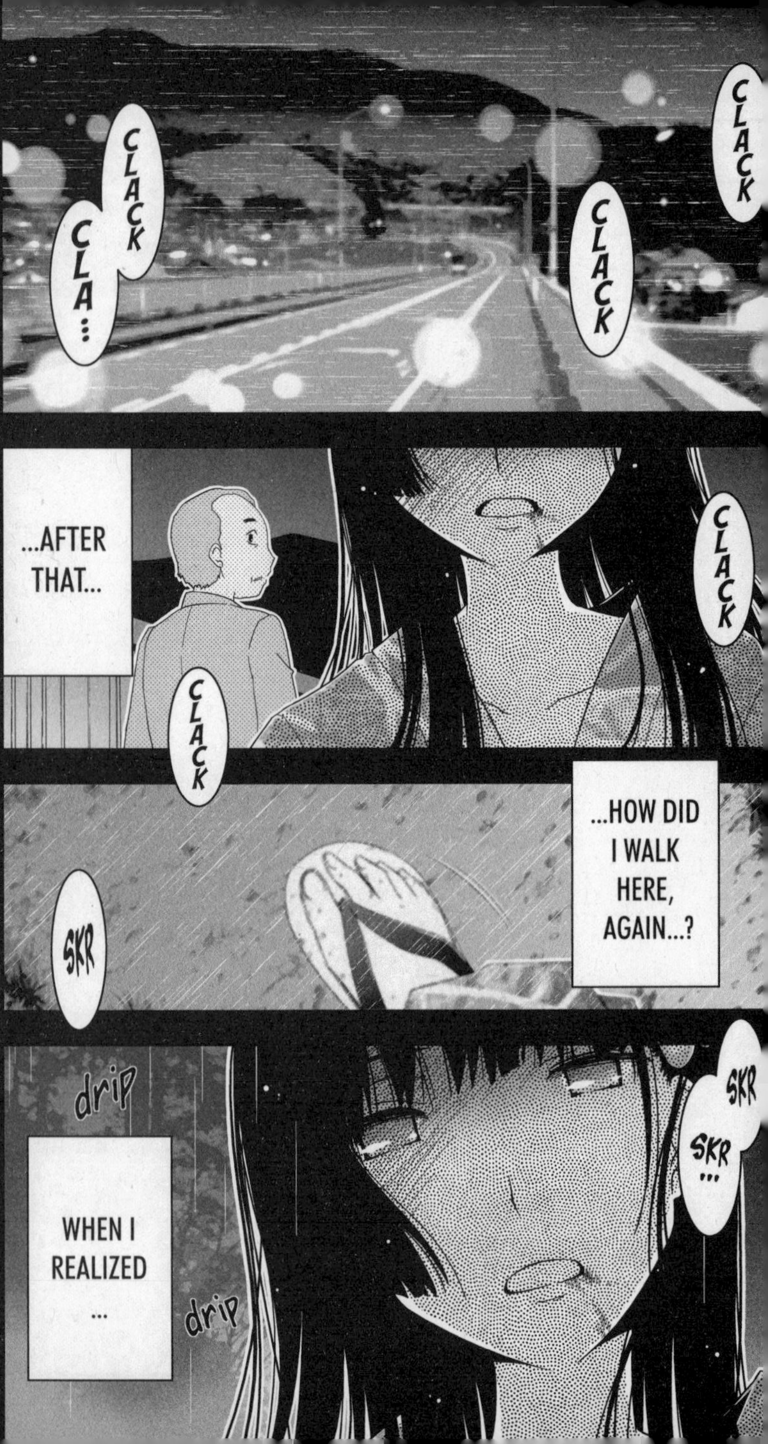
CLACK
CLACK
CLACK
CLA...
CLACK
...AFTER THAT...
CLACK
...HOW DID I WALK HERE, AGAIN...?
SKR
SKR
SKR...
drip
WHEN I REALIZED ...
drip

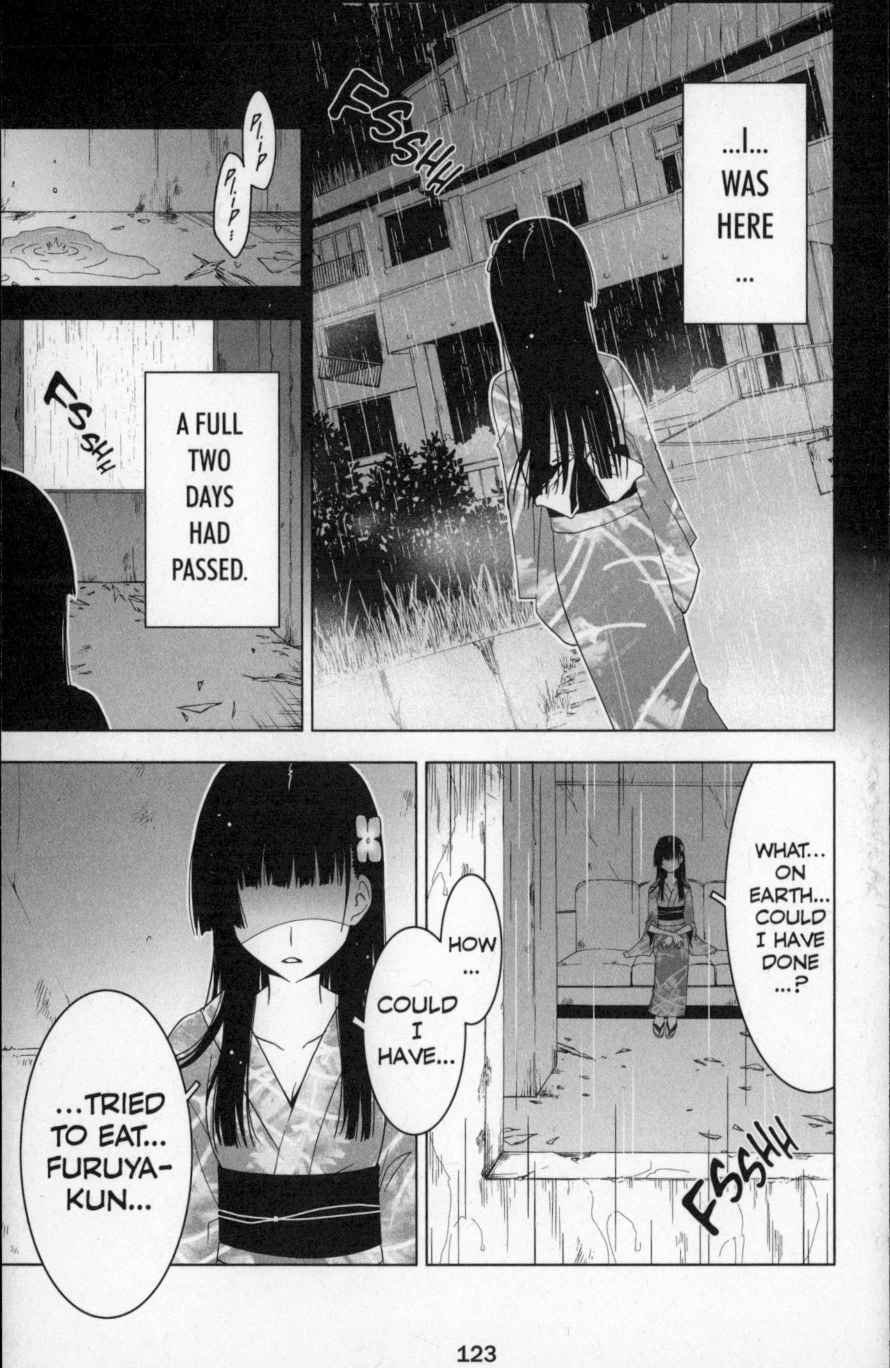
FSSHH
...I... WAS HERE ...
PI.IP
PI.IP...
FSSHH
A FULL TWO DAYS HAD PASSED.
WHAT... ON EARTH... COULD I HAVE DONE ...?
FSSHH
HOW ... COULD I HAVE...
...TRIED TO EAT... FURUYA-KUN...

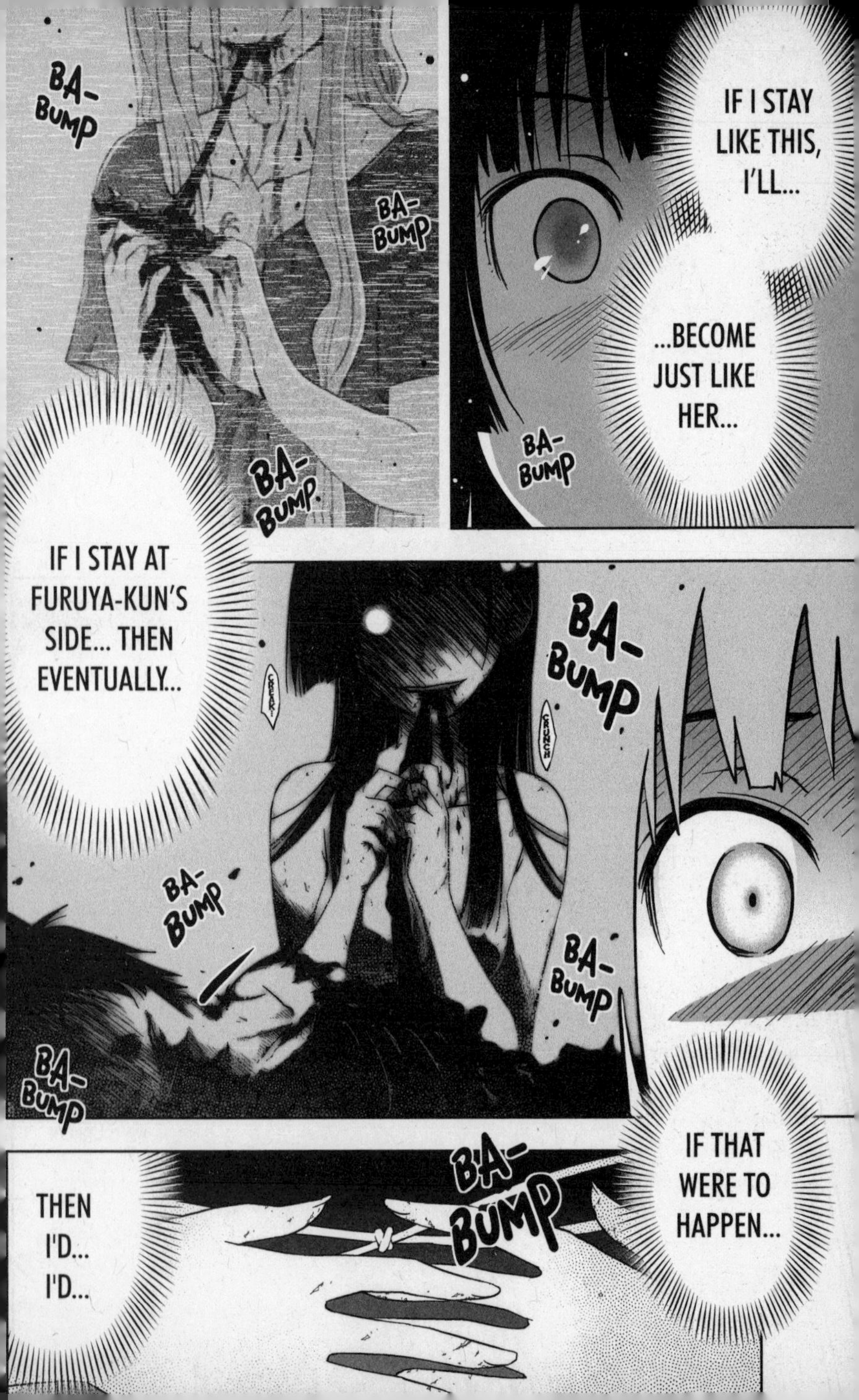
IF I STAY LIKE THIS, I'LL...
...BECOME JUST LIKE HER...
BA-BUMP
BA-BUMP
BA-BUMP
BA-BUMP
BA-BUMP
BA-BUMP
BA-BUMP
CRUNCH
CREAK...
BA-BUMP
IF I STAY AT FURUYA-KUN'S SIDE... THEN EVENTUALLY...
BA-BUMP
IF THAT WERE TO HAPPEN...
BA-BUMP
THEN I'D... I'D... I'D...

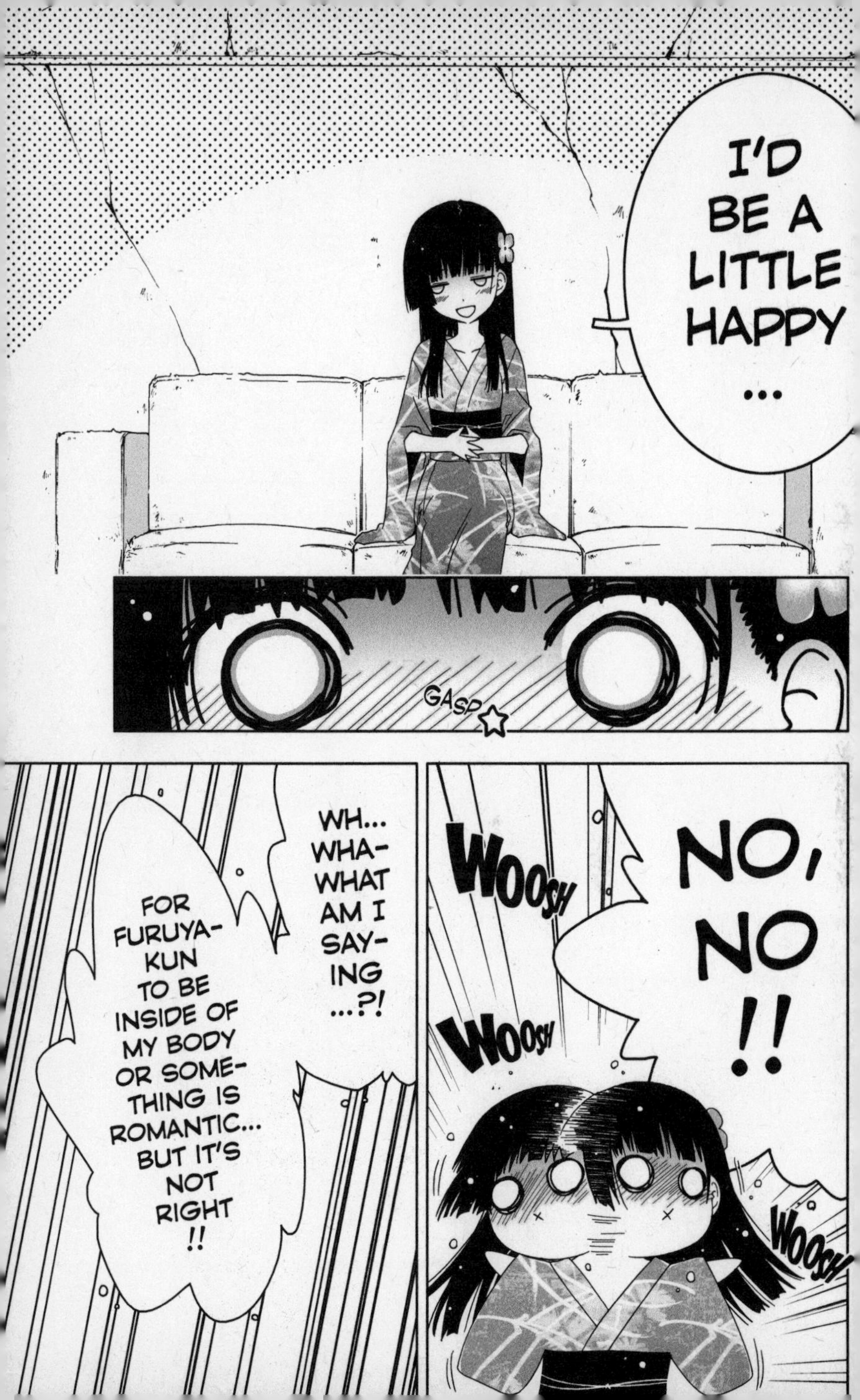
I'D BE A LITTLE HAPPY ...
GASP
WH... WHA-WHAT AM I SAY-ING ...?!
FOR FURUYA-KUN TO BE INSIDE OF MY BODY OR SOME-THING IS ROMANTIC... BUT IT'S NOT RIGHT !!
NO, NO !!
WOOSH
WOOSH
WOOSH

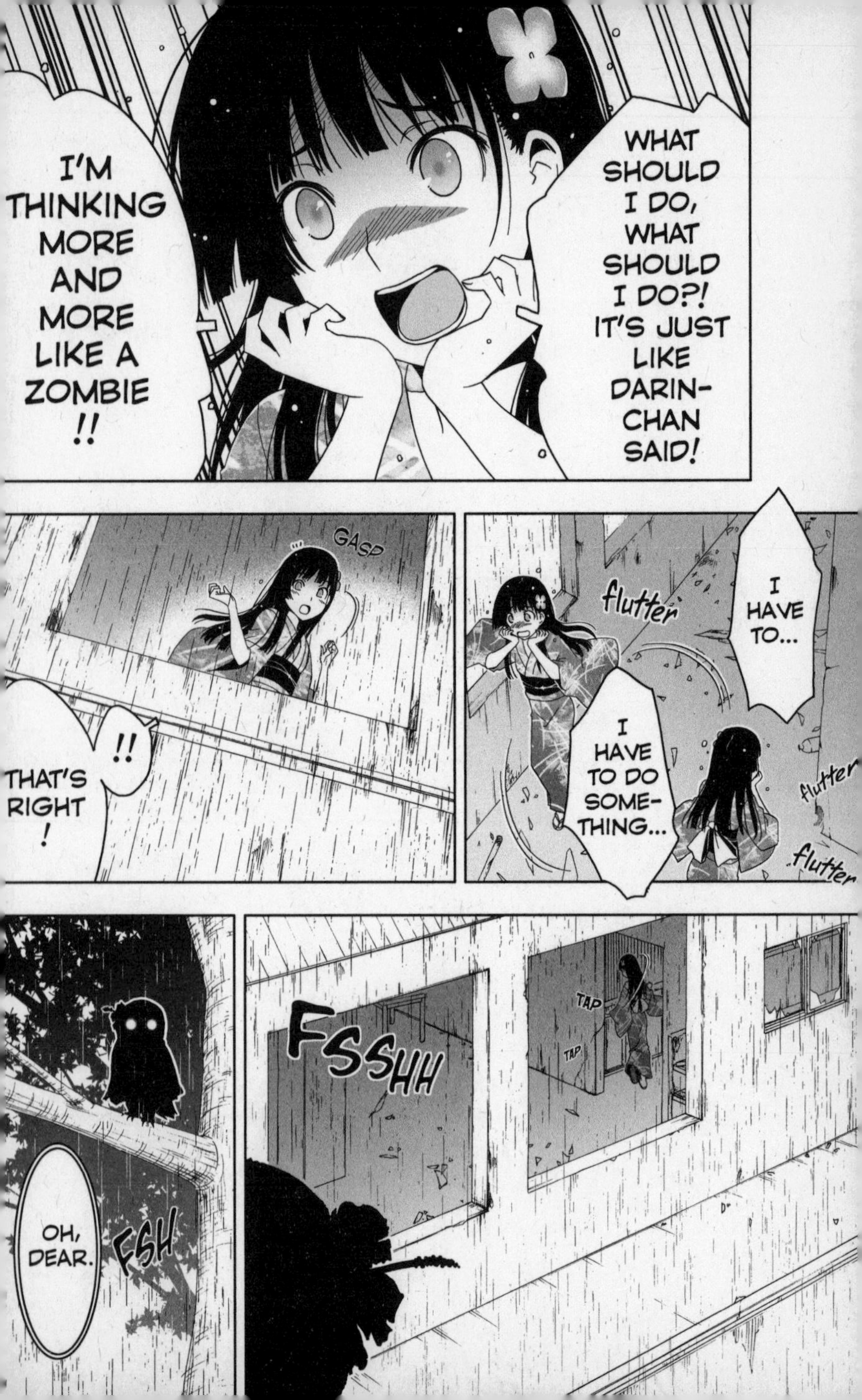
WHAT SHOULD I DO, WHAT SHOULD I DO?! IT'S JUST LIKE DARIN-CHAN SAID!
I'M THINKING MORE AND MORE LIKE A ZOMBIE !!
I HAVE TO...
flutter
I HAVE TO DO SOME-THING...
flutter
flutter
GASP
!!
THAT'S RIGHT!
TAP
TAP
FSSHH
FSH
OH, DEAR.

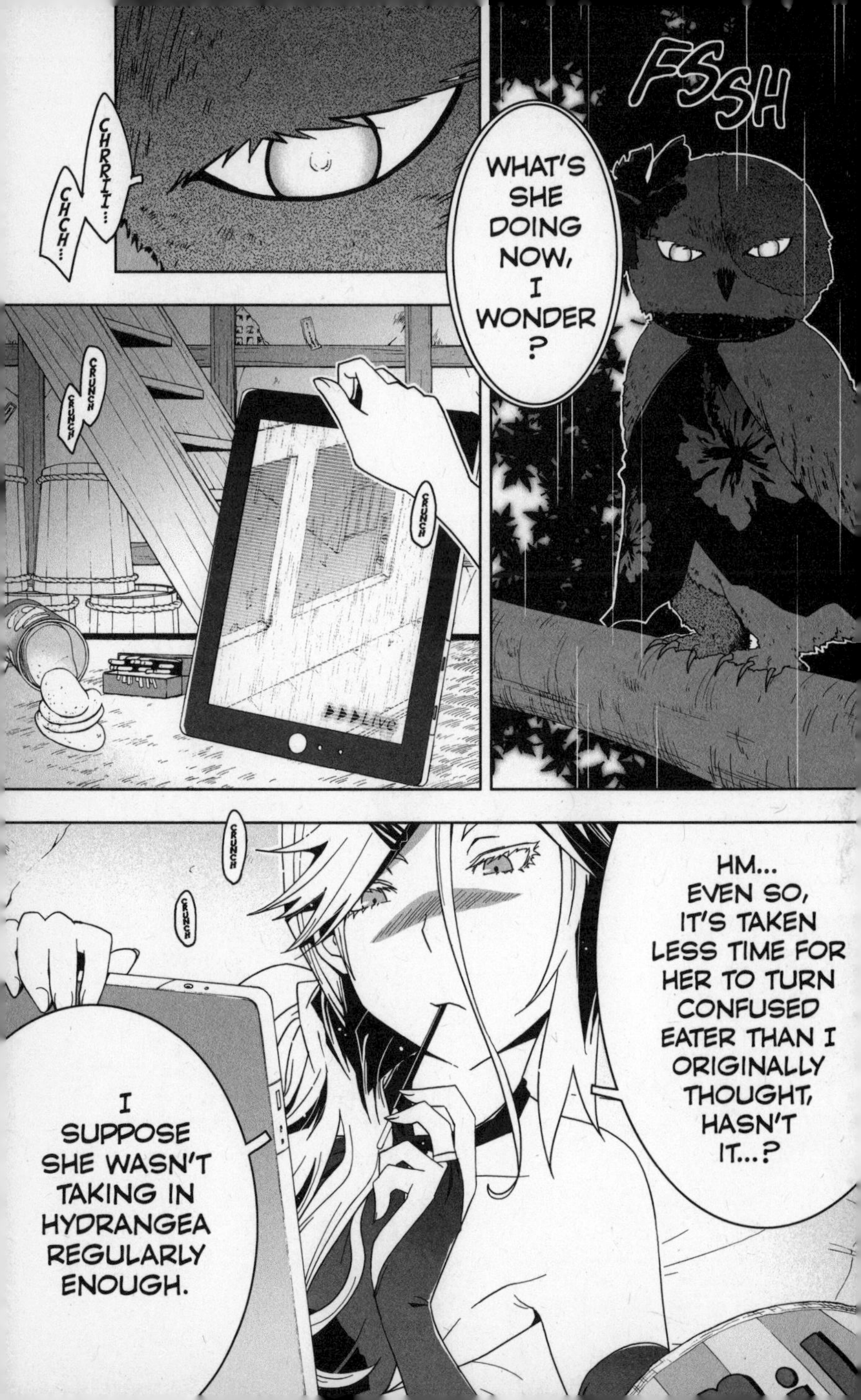
FSSH
WHAT'S SHE DOING NOW, I WONDER?
CHRRII...
CHCH...
CRUNCH
CRUNCH
CRUNCH
CRUNCH
CRUNCH
HM... EVEN SO, IT'S TAKEN LESS TIME FOR HER TO TURN CONFUSED EATER THAN I ORIGINALLY THOUGHT, HASN'T IT...?
I SUPPOSE SHE WASN'T TAKING IN HYDRANGEA REGULARLY ENOUGH.

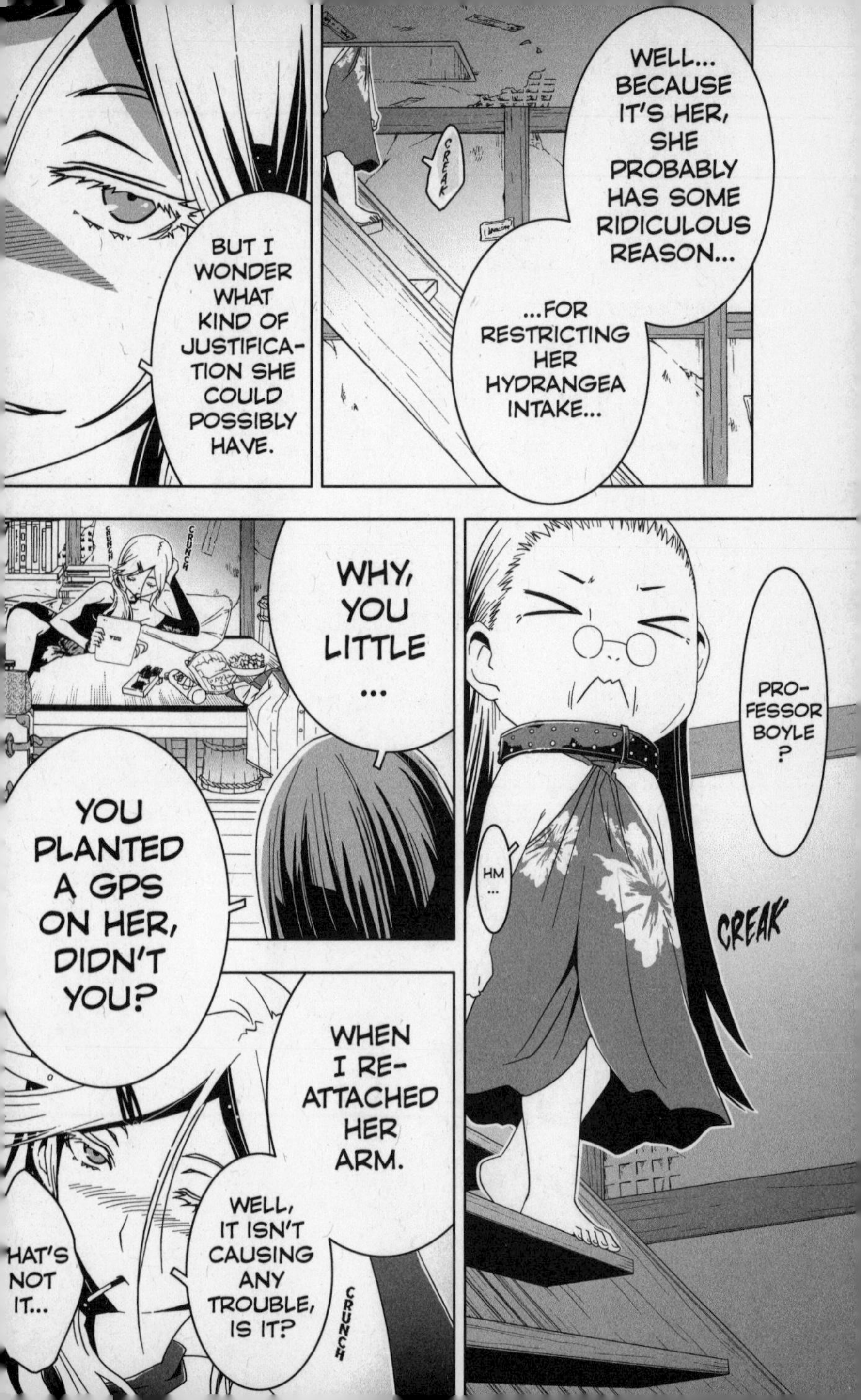
CREAK
WELL... BECAUSE IT'S HER, SHE PROBABLY HAS SOME RIDICULOUS REASON...
...FOR RESTRICTING HER HYDRANGEA INTAKE...
BUT I WONDER WHAT KIND OF JUSTIFICATION SHE COULD POSSIBLY HAVE.
PRO-FESSOR BOYLE ?
HM ...
CREAK
WHY, YOU LITTLE ...
CRUNCH
CRUNCH
YOU PLANTED A GPS ON HER, DIDN'T YOU?
WHEN I RE-ATTACHED HER ARM.
WELL, IT ISN'T CAUSING ANY TROUBLE, IS IT?
HAT'S NOT IT...
CRUNCH

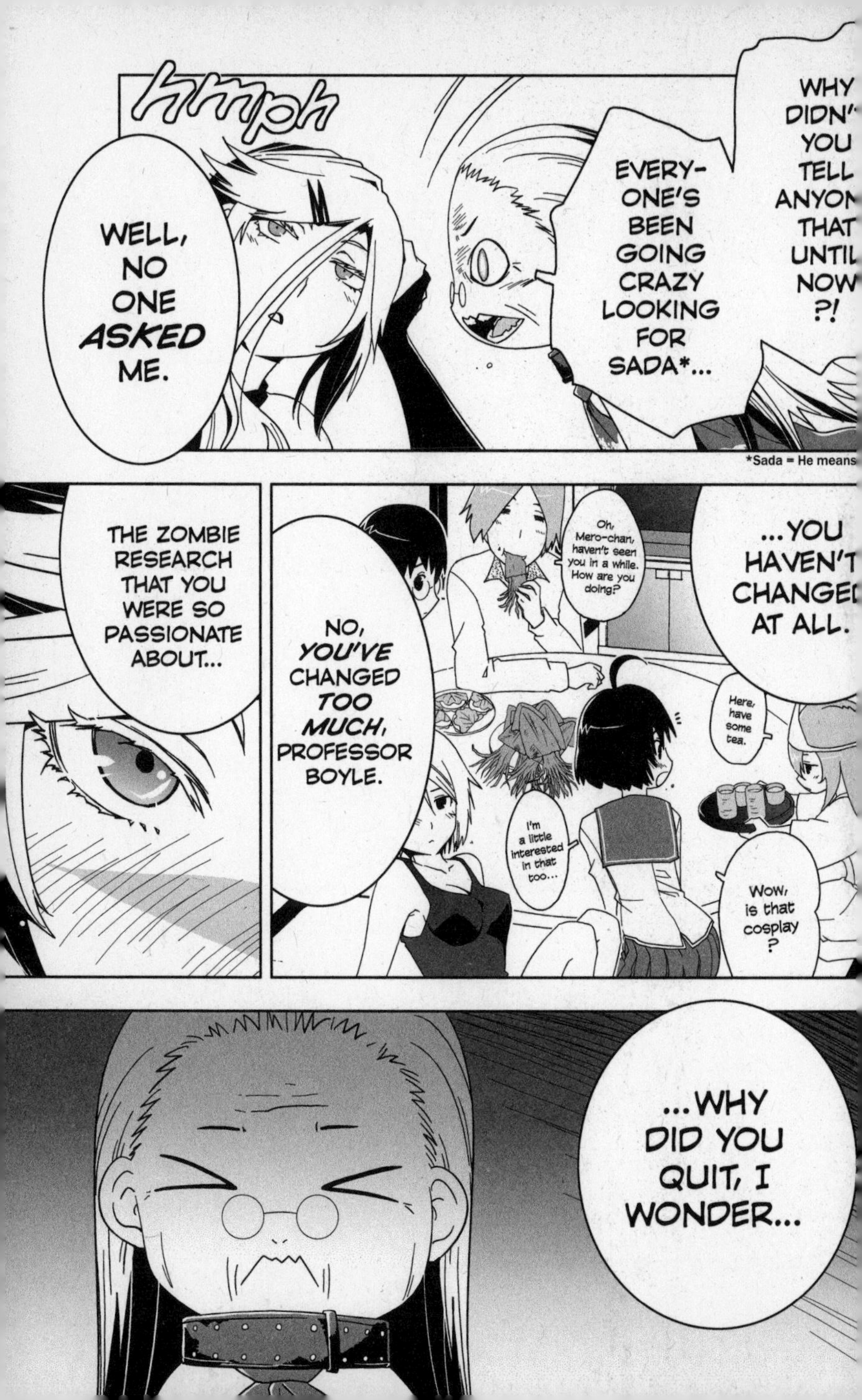
WHY DIDN' YOU TELL ANYON THAT UNTIL NOW ?!
EVERY-ONE'S BEEN GOING CRAZY LOOKING FOR SADA*...
hmph
WELL, NO ONE *ASKED* ME.
...YOU HAVEN'T CHANGE AT ALL.
Oh, Mero-chan, haven't seen you in a while. How are you doing?
Here, have some tea.
NO, *YOU'VE* CHANGED *TOO MUCH*, PROFESSOR BOYLE.
Wow, is that cosplay?
I'm a little interested in that too...
THE ZOMBIE RESEARCH THAT YOU WERE SO PASSIONATE ABOUT...
...WHY DID YOU QUIT, I WONDER...

*Sada = He means

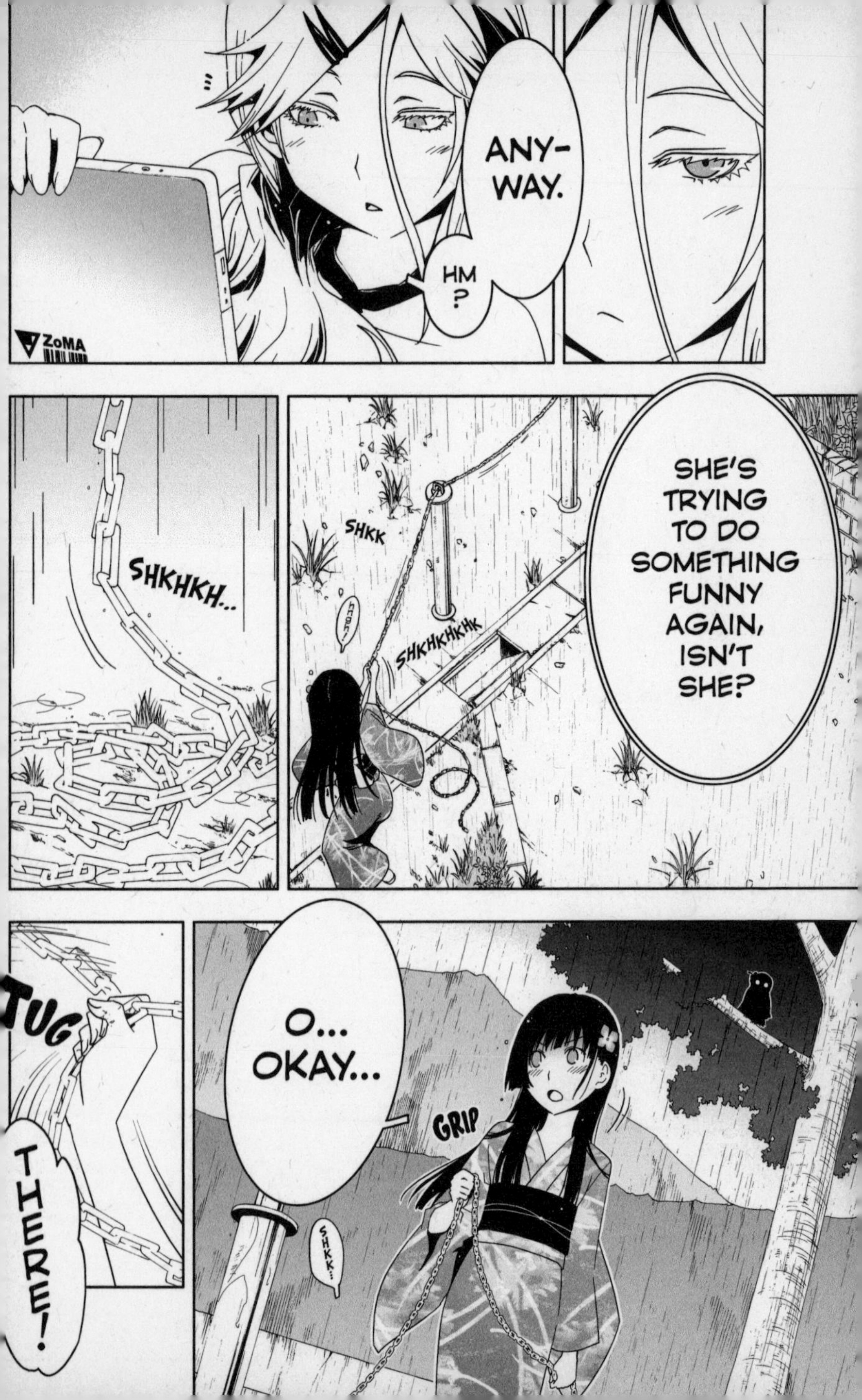
ANY-WAY.
HM?
SHE'S TRYING TO DO SOMETHING FUNNY AGAIN, ISN'T SHE?
SHKK
hngh!
SHKHKHKHK
SHKHKH...
O... OKAY...
GRIP
SHKK...
TUG
THERE!

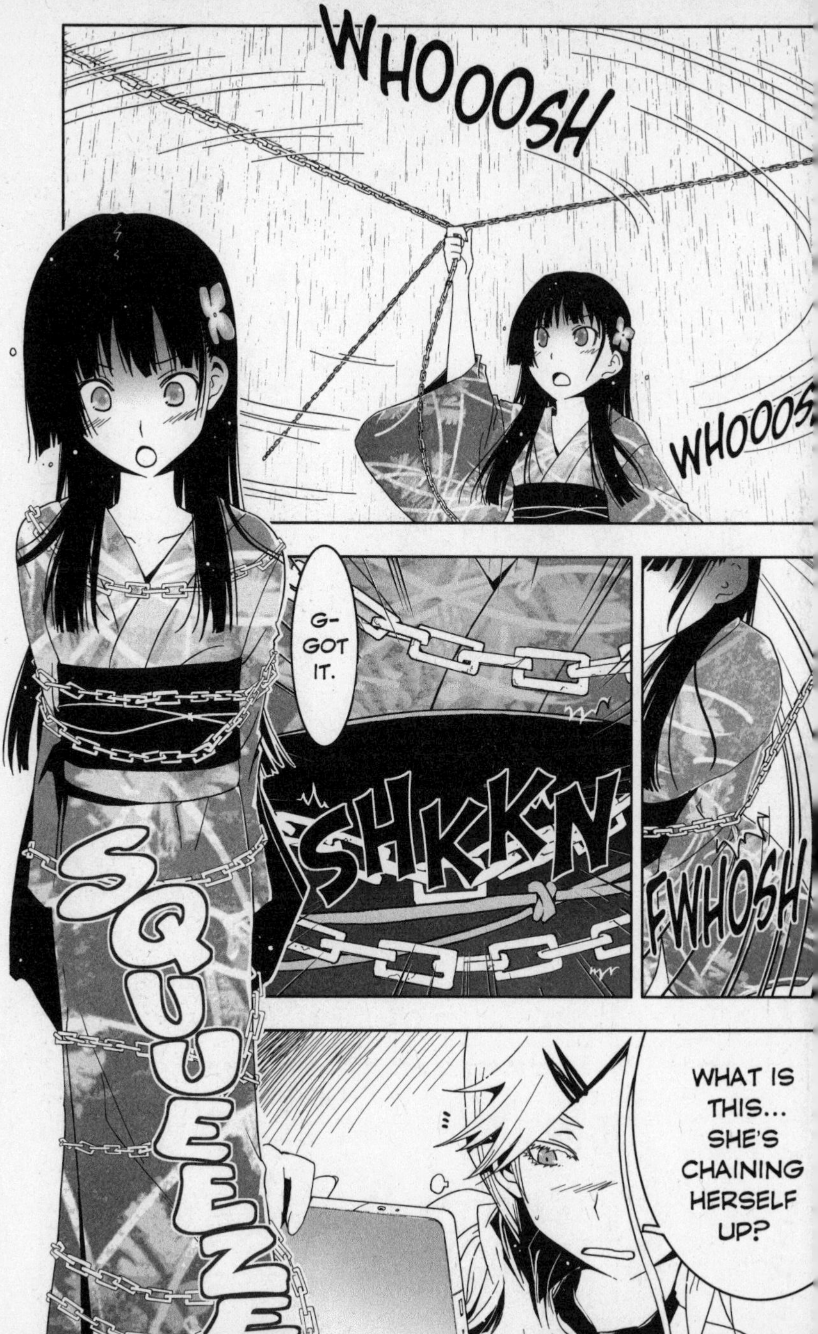
WHOOOSH
WHOOOS
FWHOSH
G-GOT IT.
SHKKN
WHAT IS THIS... SHE'S CHAINING HERSELF UP?
SQUEEZE

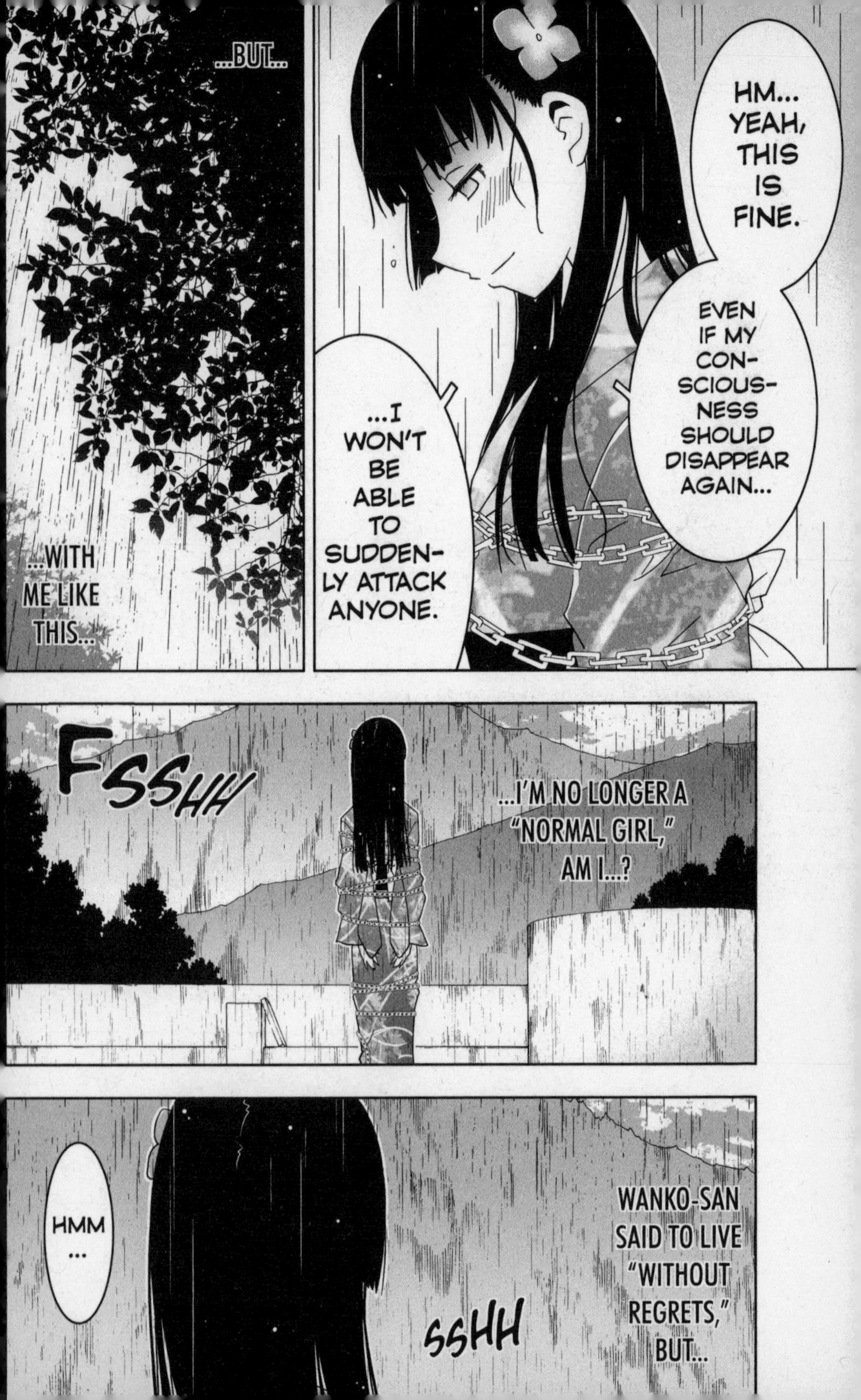
HM... YEAH, THIS IS FINE.
EVEN IF MY CON-SCIOUS-NESS SHOULD DISAPPEAR AGAIN...
...I WON'T BE ABLE TO SUDDEN-LY ATTACK ANYONE.
...BUT...
...WITH ME LIKE THIS...
FSSHH
...I'M NO LONGER A "NORMAL GIRL," AM I...?
WANKO-SAN SAID TO LIVE "WITHOUT REGRETS," BUT...
HMM...
SSHH

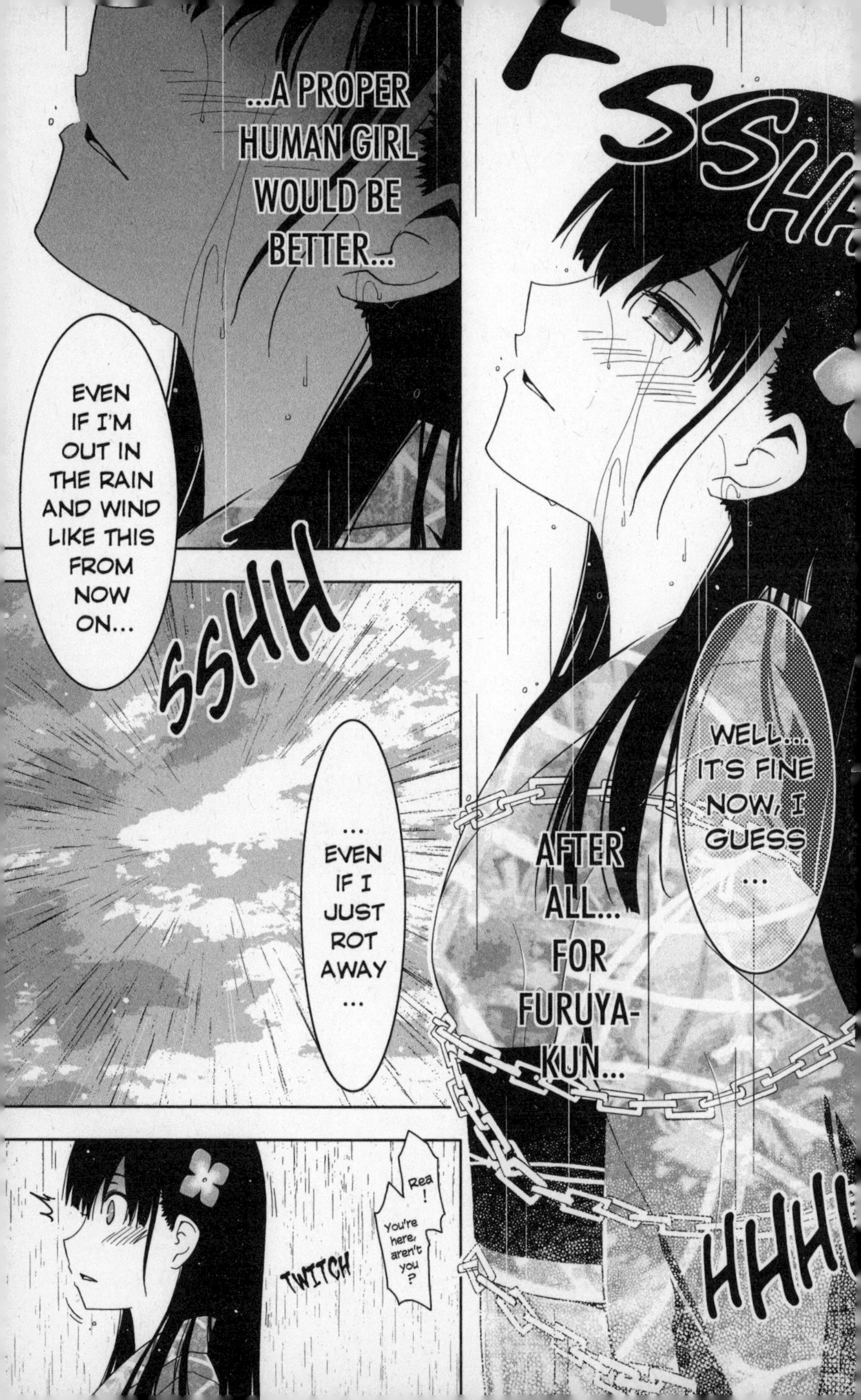
SSH
WELL... IT'S FINE NOW, I GUESS...
AFTER ALL... FOR FURUYA-KUN...
HHH
...A PROPER HUMAN GIRL WOULD BE BETTER...
EVEN IF I'M OUT IN THE RAIN AND WIND LIKE THIS FROM NOW ON...
SSHH
...EVEN IF I JUST ROT AWAY...
Rea! You're here, aren't you?
TWITCH

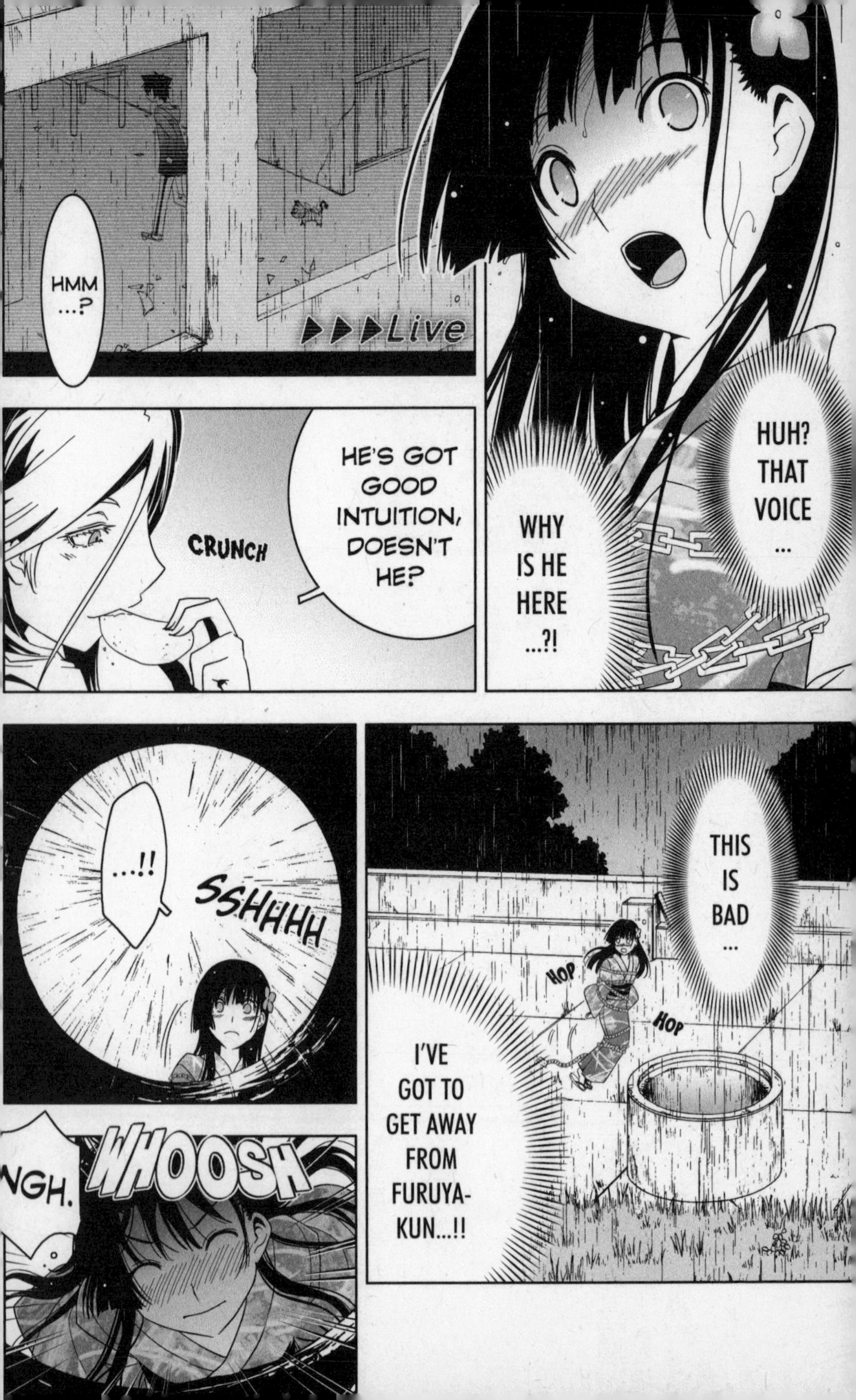
HUH? THAT VOICE ...
WHY IS HE HERE ...?!
HMM ...?
▶▶▶Live
HE'S GOT GOOD INTUITION, DOESN'T HE?
CRUNCH
THIS IS BAD ...
I'VE GOT TO GET AWAY FROM FURUYA-KUN...!!
HOP
HOP
...!!
SSHHHH
NGH.
WHOOSH

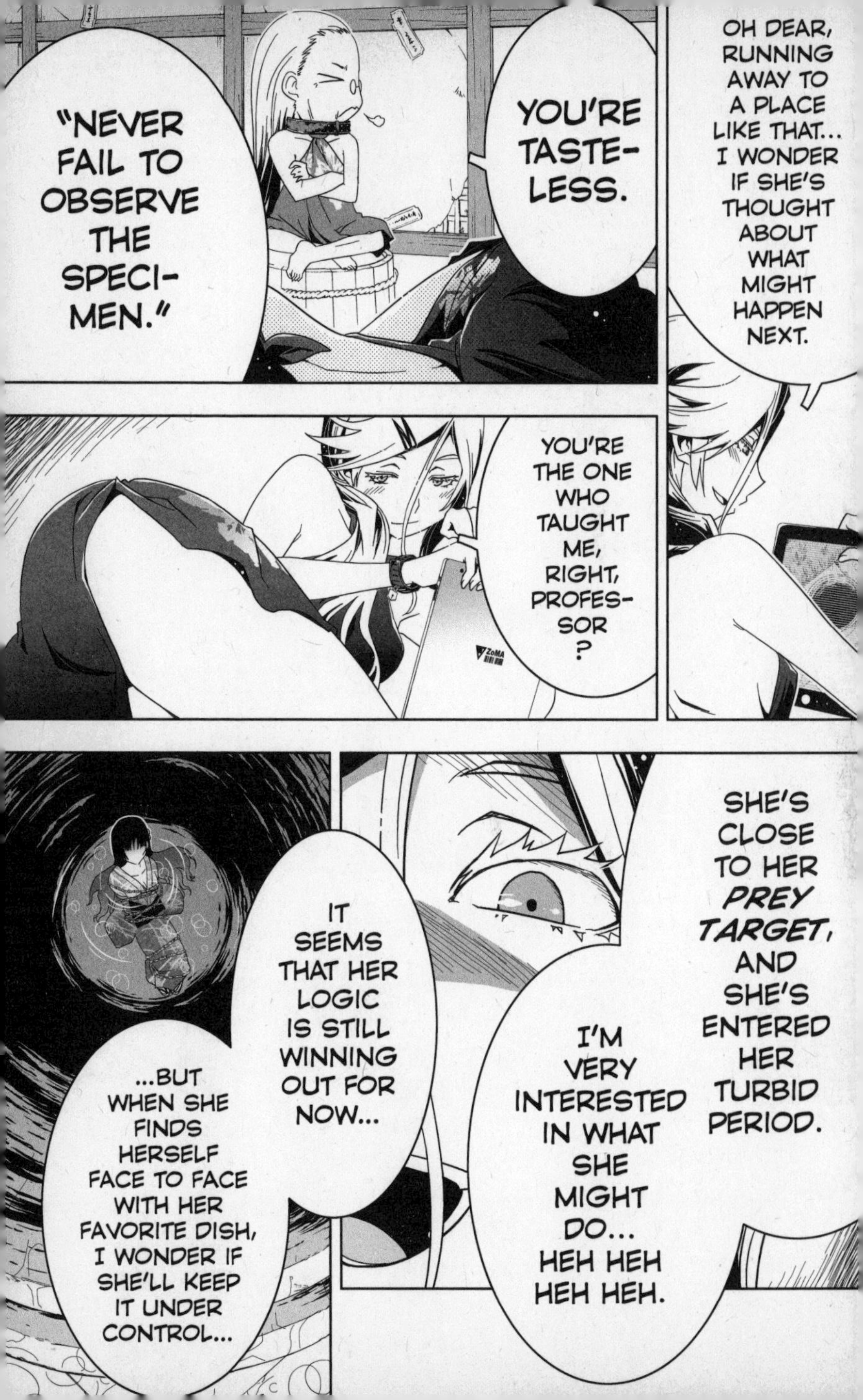
OH DEAR, RUNNING AWAY TO A PLACE LIKE THAT... I WONDER IF SHE'S THOUGHT ABOUT WHAT MIGHT HAPPEN NEXT.
YOU'RE TASTE-LESS.
"NEVER FAIL TO OBSERVE THE SPECI-MEN."
YOU'RE THE ONE WHO TAUGHT ME, RIGHT, PROFES-SOR?
SHE'S CLOSE TO HER *PREY TARGET*, AND SHE'S ENTERED HER TURBID PERIOD.
I'M VERY INTERESTED IN WHAT SHE MIGHT DO... HEH HEH HEH HEH.
IT SEEMS THAT HER LOGIC IS STILL WINNING OUT FOR NOW...
...BUT WHEN SHE FINDS HERSELF FACE TO FACE WITH HER FAVORITE DISH, I WONDER IF SHE'LL KEEP IT UNDER CONTROL...

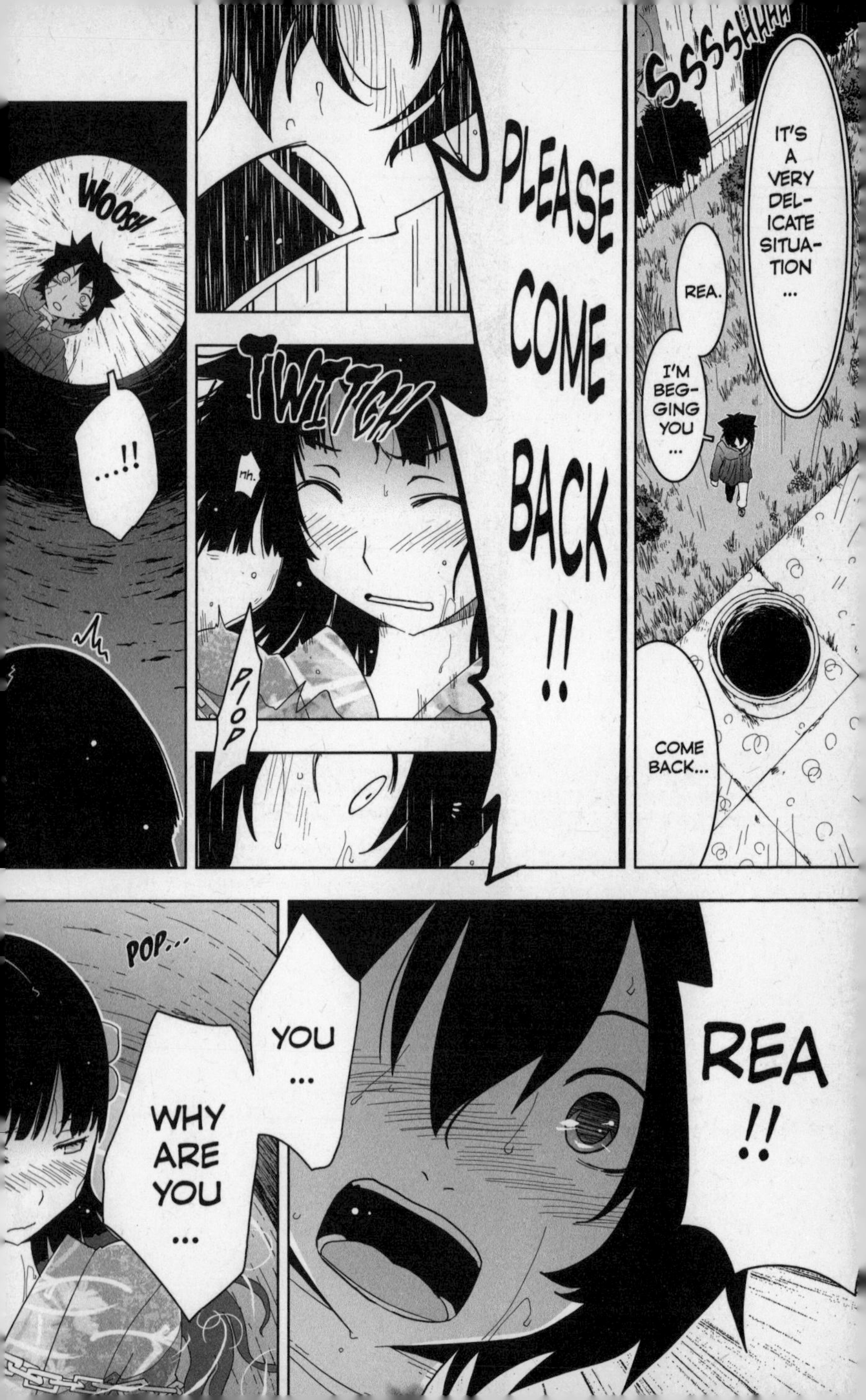
SSSSHHHH
IT'S A VERY DELICATE SITUATION...
REA.
I'M BEGGING YOU...
COME BACK...
TWITCH
nh.
PLEASE COME BACK!!
PLOP
WOOSH
...!!
REA!!
POP...
YOU...
WHY ARE YOU...

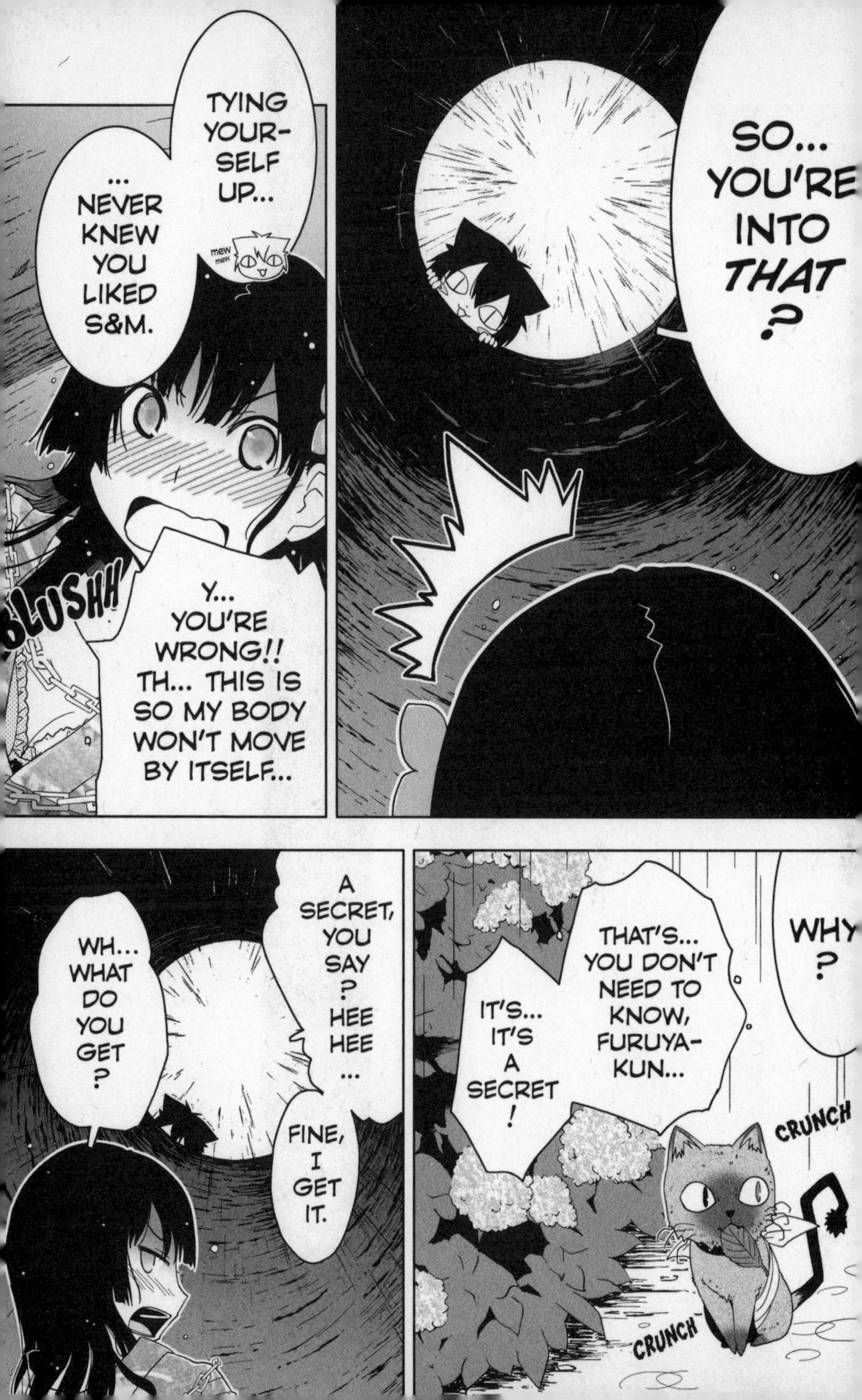
SO... YOU'RE INTO THAT?
TYING YOUR-SELF UP...
...NEVER KNEW YOU LIKED S&M.
mew mew
BLUSHH
Y... YOU'RE WRONG!! TH... THIS IS SO MY BODY WON'T MOVE BY ITSELF...
WHY?
THAT'S... YOU DON'T NEED TO KNOW, FURUYA-KUN...
IT'S... IT'S A SECRET!
CRUNCH
CRUNCH
A SECRET, YOU SAY? HEE HEE...
WH... WHAT DO YOU GET?
FINE, I GET IT.

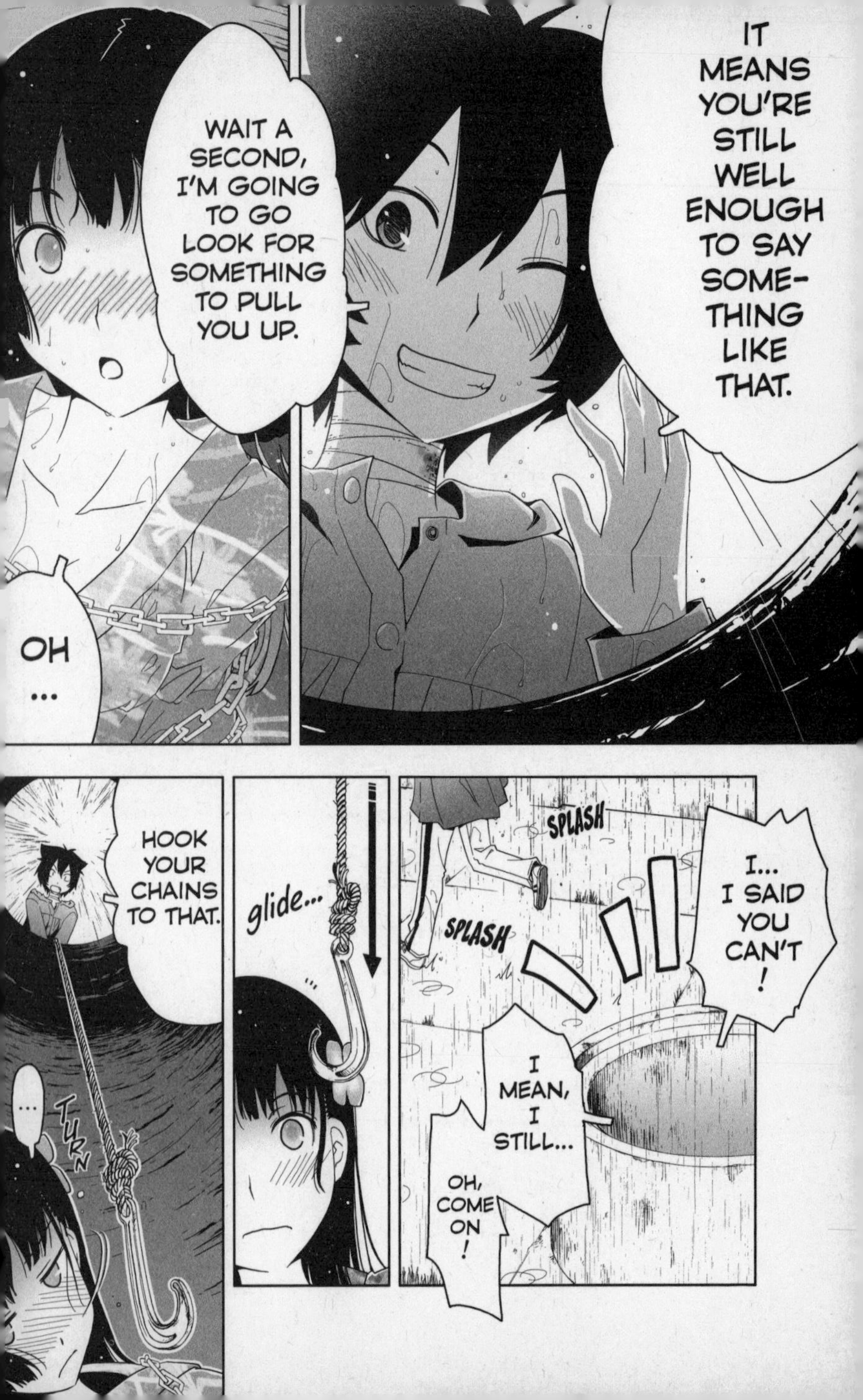
IT MEANS YOU'RE STILL WELL ENOUGH TO SAY SOME-THING LIKE THAT.
WAIT A SECOND, I'M GOING TO GO LOOK FOR SOMETHING TO PULL YOU UP.
OH ...
I... I SAID YOU CAN'T!
SPLASH
SPLASH
I MEAN, I STILL...
OH, COME ON!
glide...
...
HOOK YOUR CHAINS TO THAT.
...
TURN

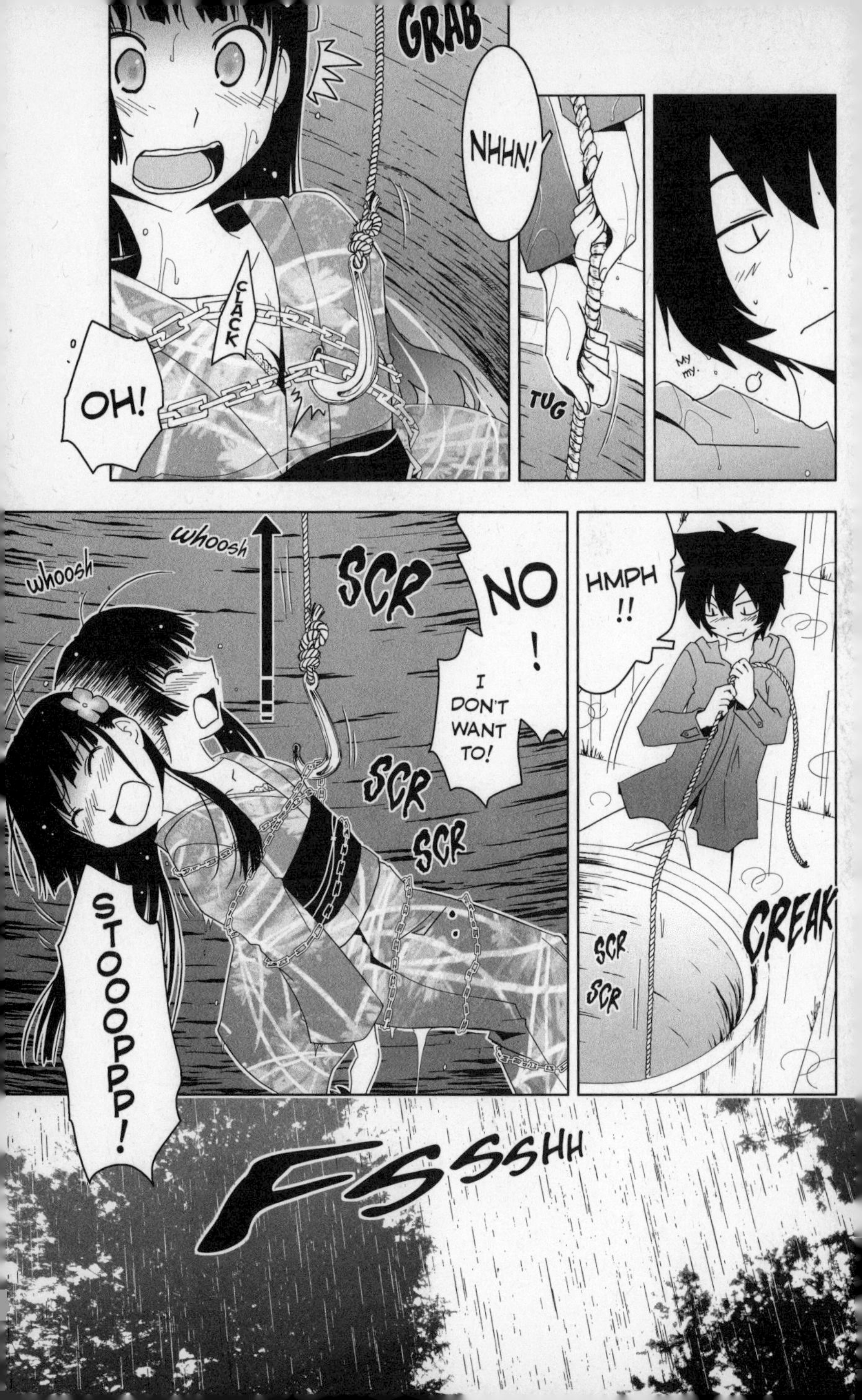
My my.
NHHN!
TUG
GRAB
CLACK
OH!
HMPH !!
CREAK
SCR
SCR
NO!
I DON'T WANT TO!
SCR
SCR
SCR
whoosh
whoosh
STOOOPPP!
FSSSHH

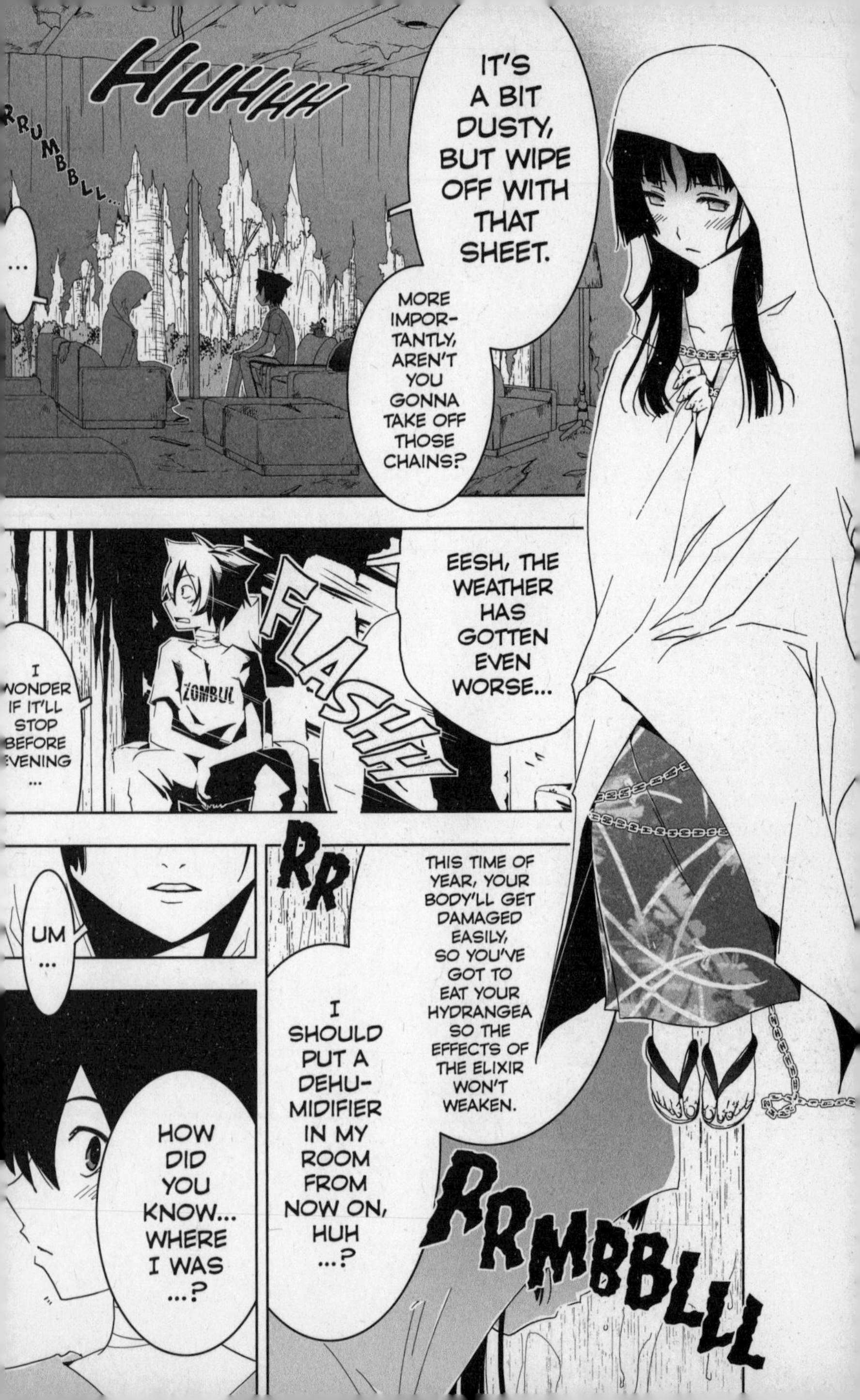

IT'S A BIT DUSTY, BUT WIPE OFF WITH THAT SHEET.
MORE IMPORTANTLY, AREN'T YOU GONNA TAKE OFF THOSE CHAINS?
HHHHHH
RRUMBBLLL...
...
EESH, THE WEATHER HAS GOTTEN EVEN WORSE...
FLASHH
I WONDER IF IT'LL STOP BEFORE EVENING...
ZOMBUL
THIS TIME OF YEAR, YOUR BODY'LL GET DAMAGED EASILY, SO YOU'VE GOT TO EAT YOUR HYDRANGEA SO THE EFFECTS OF THE ELIXIR WON'T WEAKEN.
RR
UM...
I SHOULD PUT A DEHU-MIDIFIER IN MY ROOM FROM NOW ON, HUH...?
HOW DID YOU KNOW... WHERE I WAS...?
RRMBBLLL

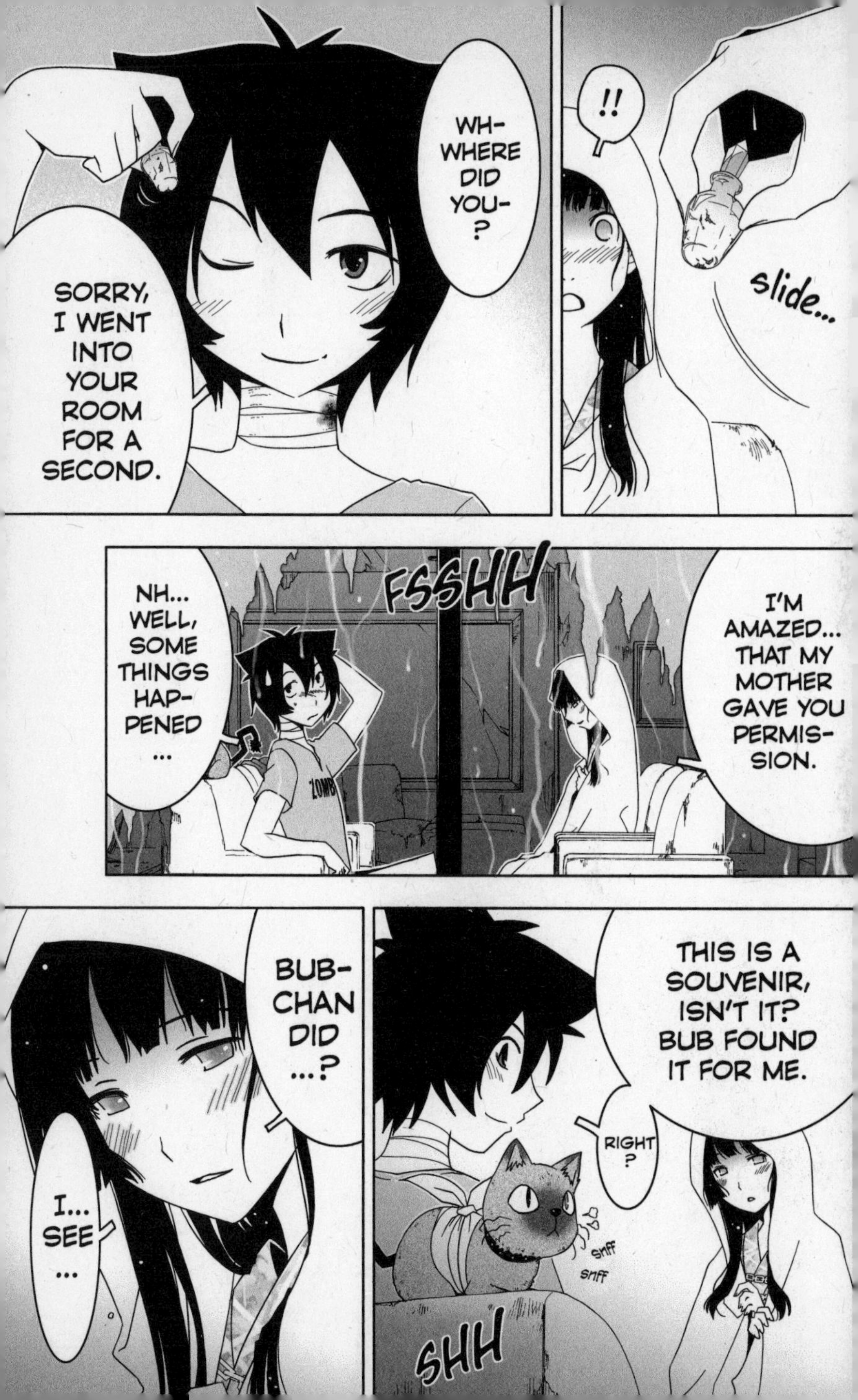
!!
slide...
WH- WHERE DID YOU- ?
SORRY, I WENT INTO YOUR ROOM FOR A SECOND.
I'M AMAZED... THAT MY MOTHER GAVE YOU PERMISSION.
FSSHH
NH... WELL, SOME THINGS HAPPENED ...
ZOMB
THIS IS A SOUVENIR, ISN'T IT? BUB FOUND IT FOR ME.
RIGHT ?
SNFF
SNFF
SHH
BUB-CHAN DID ...?
I... SEE ...

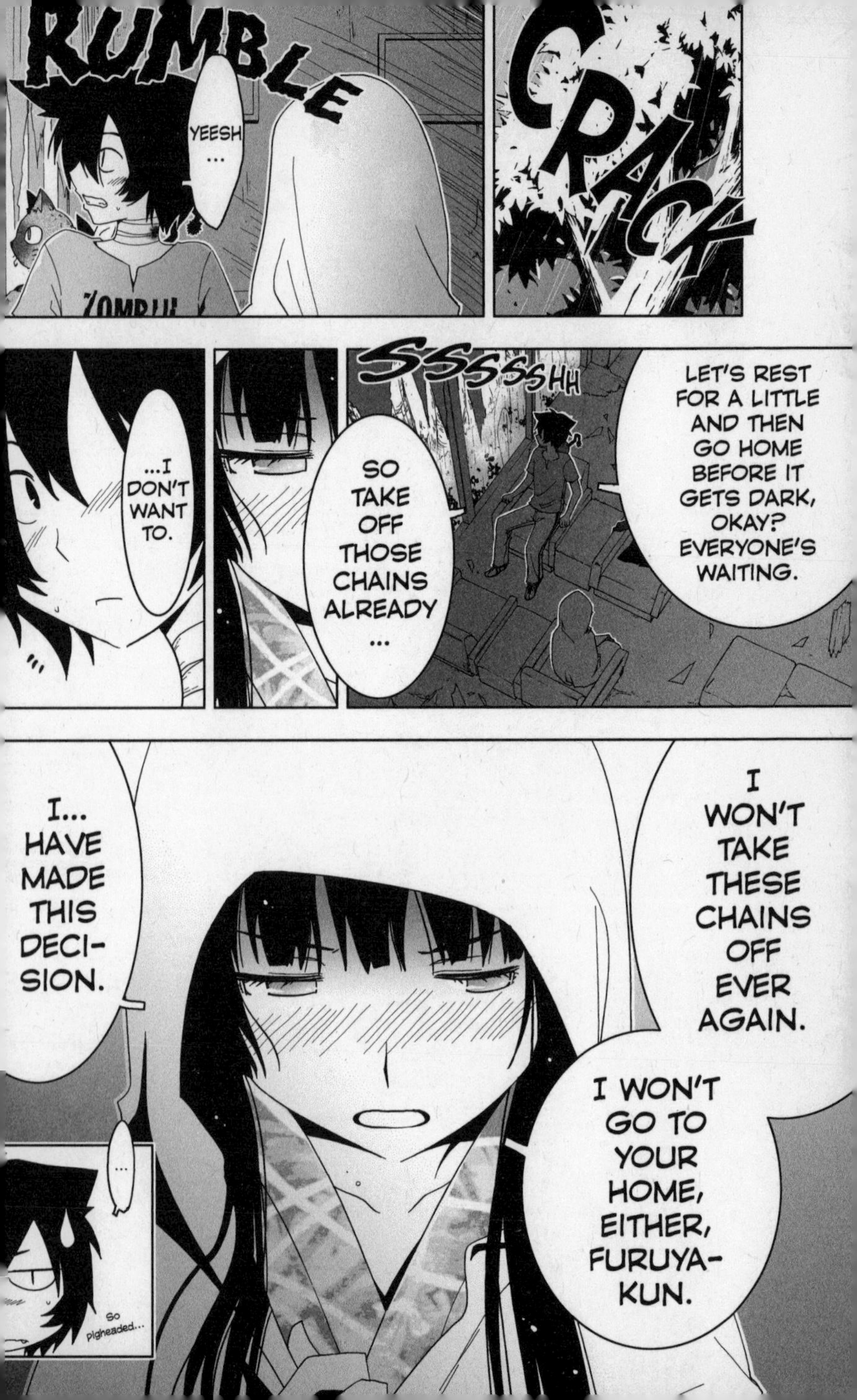
CRACK
RUMBLE
YEESH ...
SSSSSHH
LET'S REST FOR A LITTLE AND THEN GO HOME BEFORE IT GETS DARK, OKAY? EVERYONE'S WAITING.
SO TAKE OFF THOSE CHAINS ALREADY ...
...I DON'T WANT TO.
I WON'T TAKE THESE CHAINS OFF EVER AGAIN.
I WON'T GO TO YOUR HOME, EITHER, FURUYA-KUN.
I... HAVE MADE THIS DECI-SION.
...
So pigheaded...

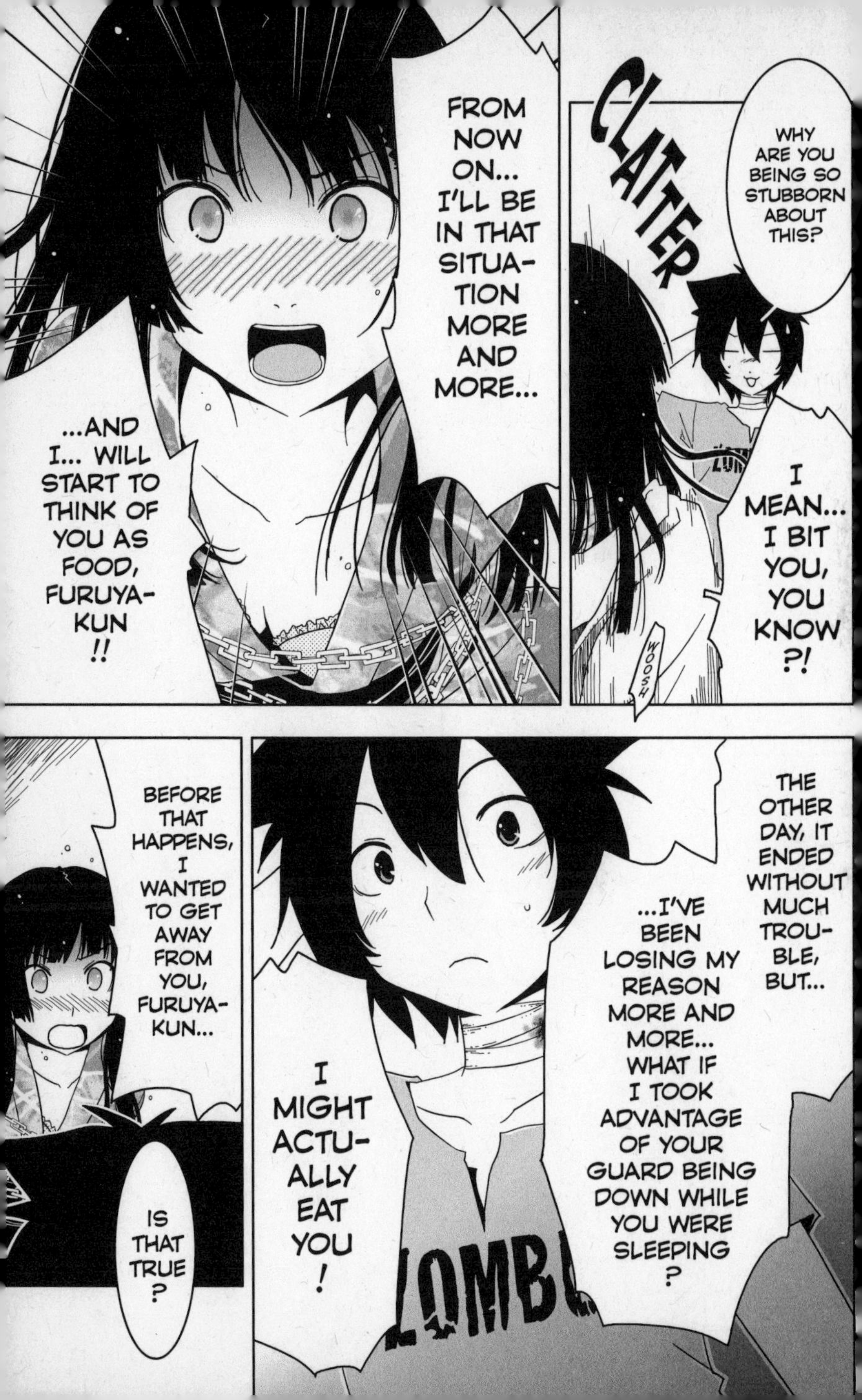
WHY ARE YOU BEING SO STUBBORN ABOUT THIS?
CLATER
I MEAN... I BIT YOU, YOU KNOW?!
WOOSH
FROM NOW ON... I'LL BE IN THAT SITUATION MORE AND MORE...
...AND I... WILL START TO THINK OF YOU AS FOOD, FURUYA-KUN!!
THE OTHER DAY, IT ENDED WITHOUT MUCH TROUBLE, BUT...
...I'VE BEEN LOSING MY REASON MORE AND MORE... WHAT IF I TOOK ADVANTAGE OF YOUR GUARD BEING DOWN WHILE YOU WERE SLEEPING?
I MIGHT ACTUALLY EAT YOU!
BEFORE THAT HAPPENS, I WANTED TO GET AWAY FROM YOU, FURUYA-KUN...
IS THAT TRUE?

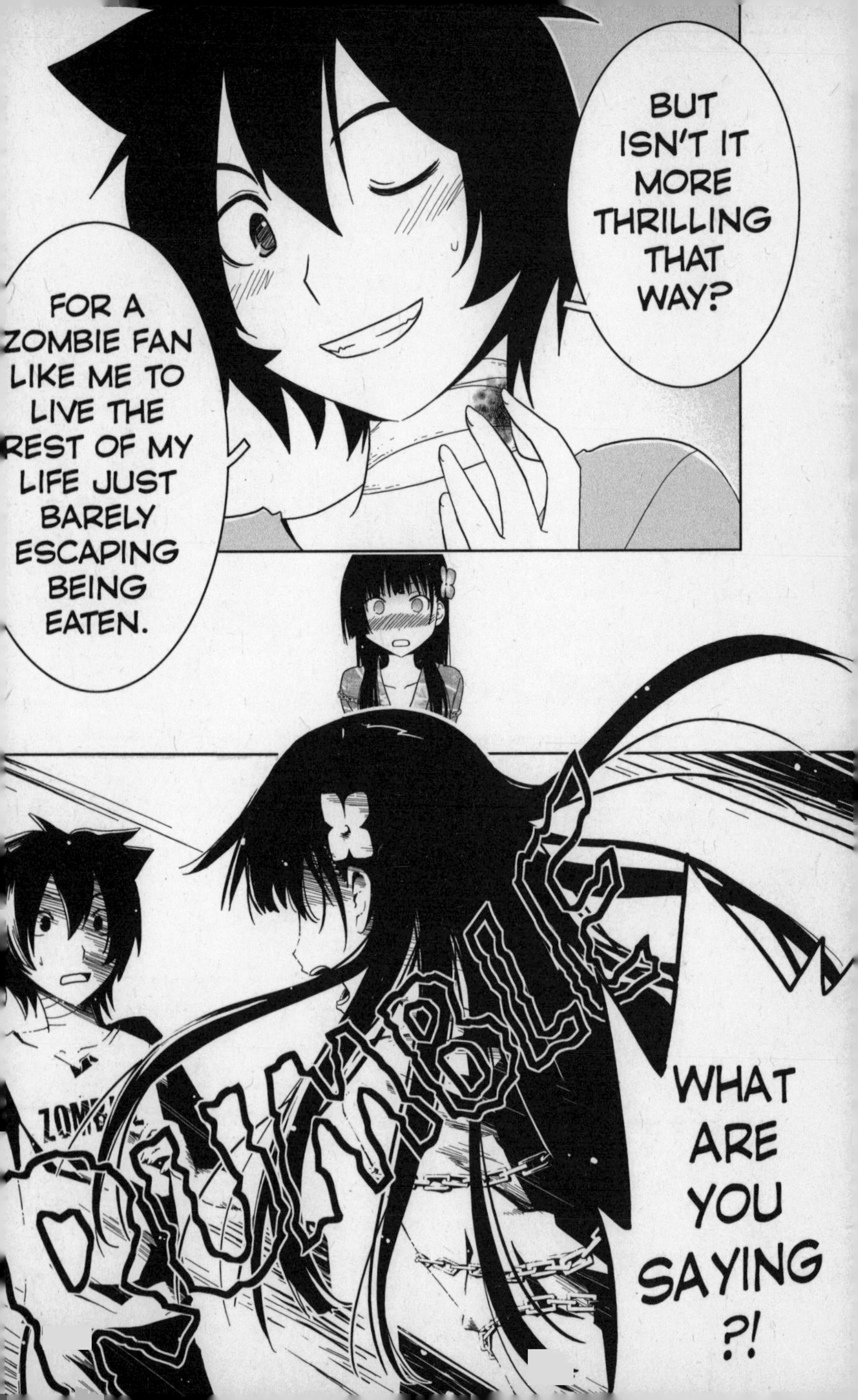
BUT ISN'T IT MORE THRILLING THAT WAY?
FOR A ZOMBIE FAN LIKE ME TO LIVE THE REST OF MY LIFE JUST BARELY ESCAPING BEING EATEN.
WHAT ARE YOU SAYING?!

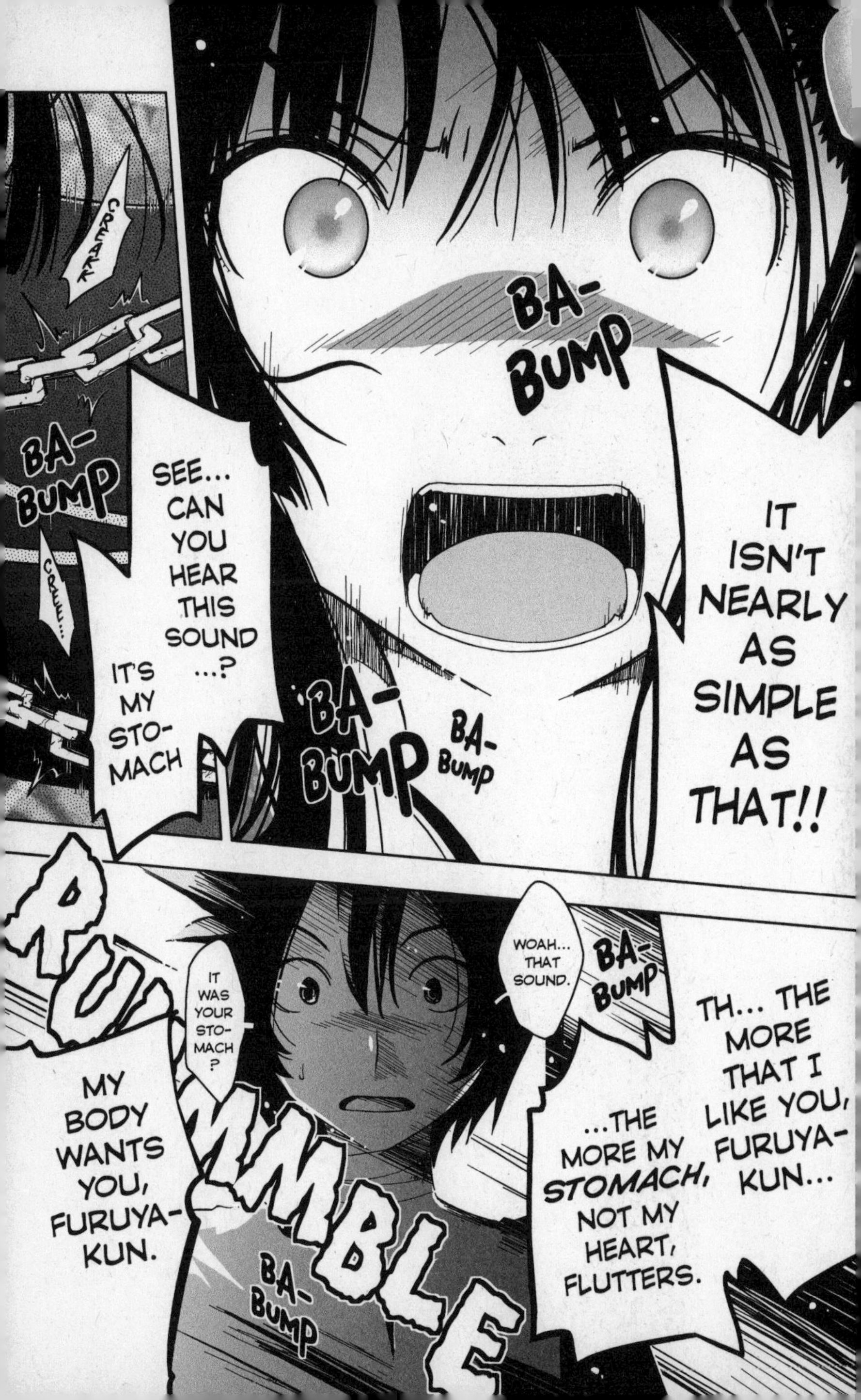
IT ISN'T NEARLY AS SIMPLE AS THAT!!
BA-BUMP
SEE... CAN YOU HEAR THIS SOUND ...?
IT'S MY STO-MACH
BA-BUMP
BA-BUMP
CREAKK
BA-BUMP
CREE...
TH... THE MORE THAT I LIKE YOU, FURUYA-KUN...
...THE MORE MY STOMACH, NOT MY HEART, FLUTTERS.
BA-BUMP
WOAH... THAT SOUND.
IT WAS YOUR STO-MACH ?
RUMMBLE
MY BODY WANTS YOU, FURUYA-KUN.
BA-BUMP

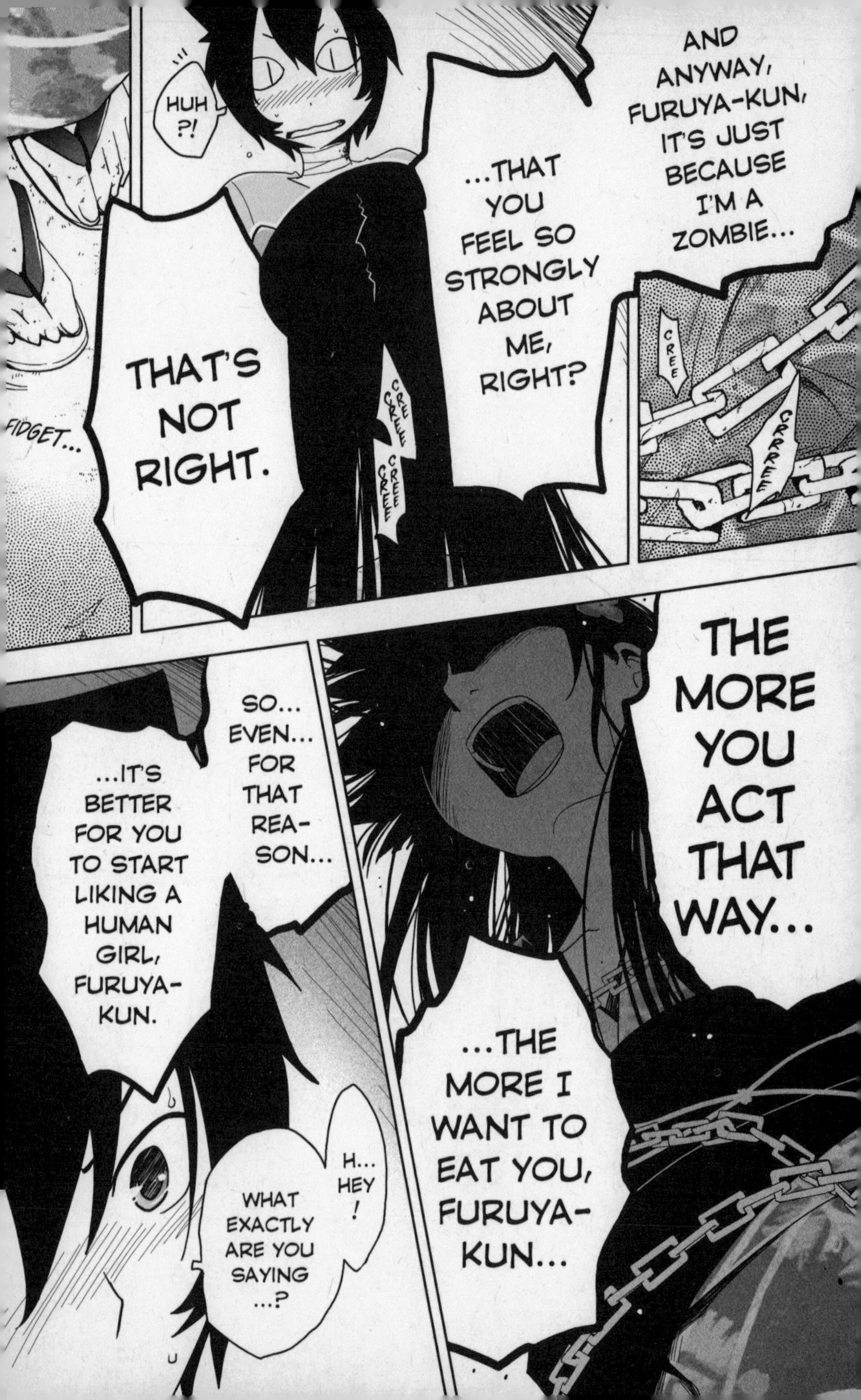
AND ANYWAY, FURUYA-KUN, IT'S JUST BECAUSE I'M A ZOMBIE...
CREE
CRRREE
...THAT YOU FEEL SO STRONGLY ABOUT ME, RIGHT?
HUH ?!
THAT'S NOT RIGHT.
CREE CREE
CREE CREE
FIDGET...
THE MORE YOU ACT THAT WAY...
...THE MORE I WANT TO EAT YOU, FURUYA-KUN...
SO... EVEN... FOR THAT REA-SON...
...IT'S BETTER FOR YOU TO START LIKING A HUMAN GIRL, FURUYA-KUN.
H... HEY!
WHAT EXACTLY ARE YOU SAYING ...?

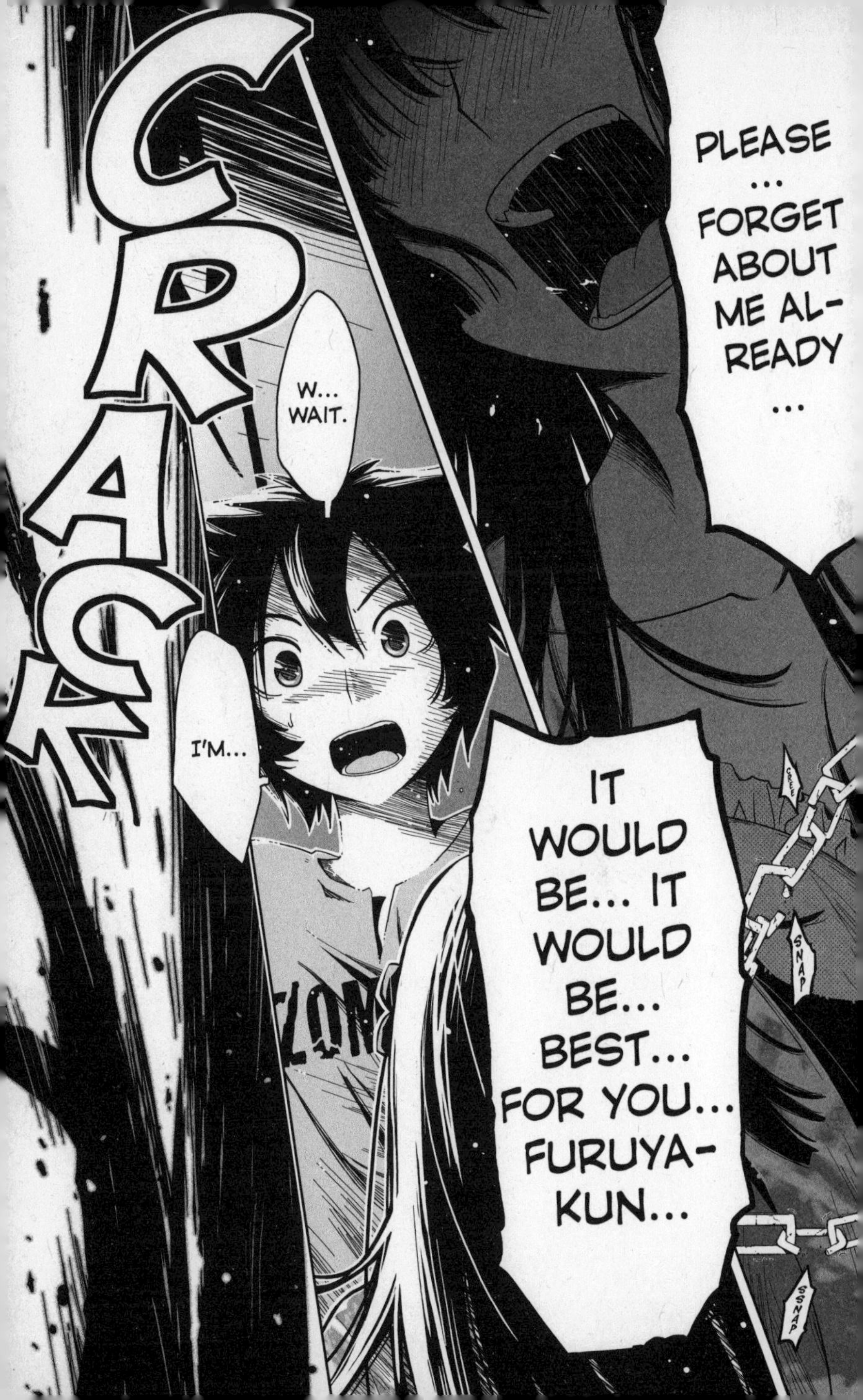
PLEASE ... FORGET ABOUT ME AL-READY ...
CREE
IT WOULD BE... IT WOULD BE... BEST... FOR YOU... FURUYA-KUN...
SNAP
SSNAP
W... WAIT.
I'M...
CRACK

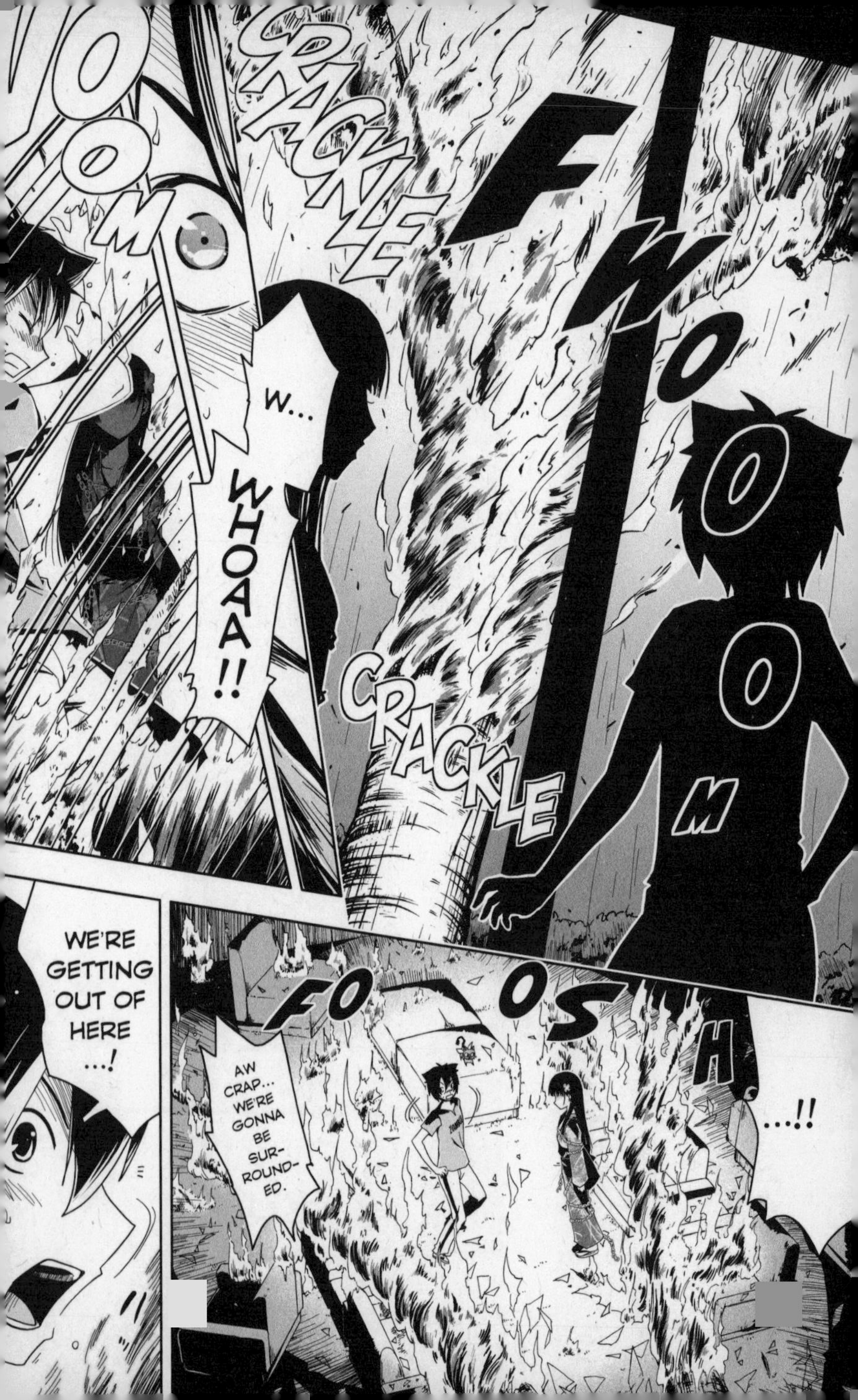
FWOOOOM
CRACKLE
W...
WHOAA!!
CRACKLE
OOM
FOOSH
AW CRAP... WE'RE GONNA BE SUR-ROUND-ED.
...!!
WE'RE GETTING OUT OF HERE ...!

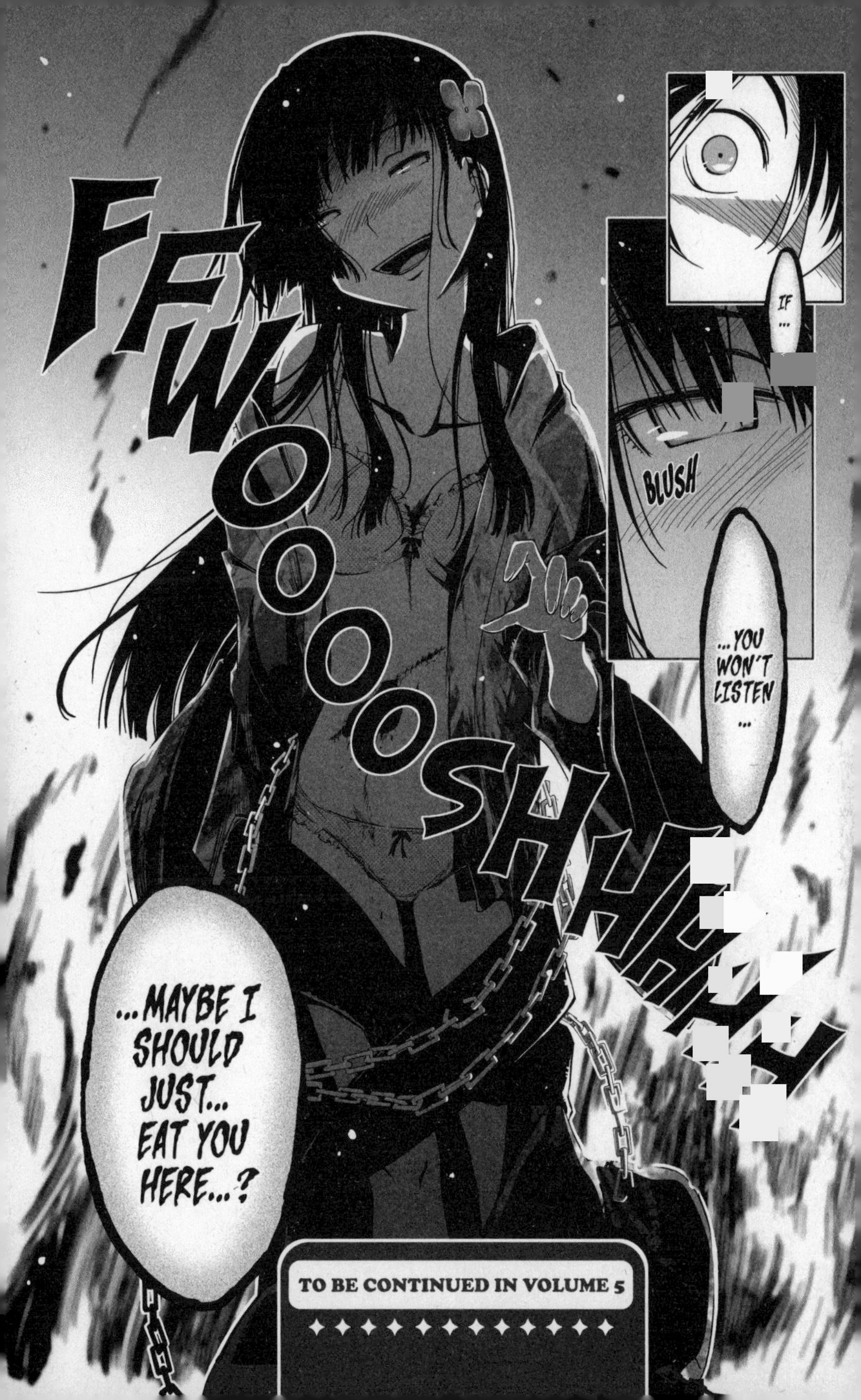
IF...
BLUSH
...YOU WON'T LISTEN...
FFWOOOOOSHH
...MAYBE I SHOULD JUST... EAT YOU HERE...?
TO BE CONTINUED IN VOLUME 5

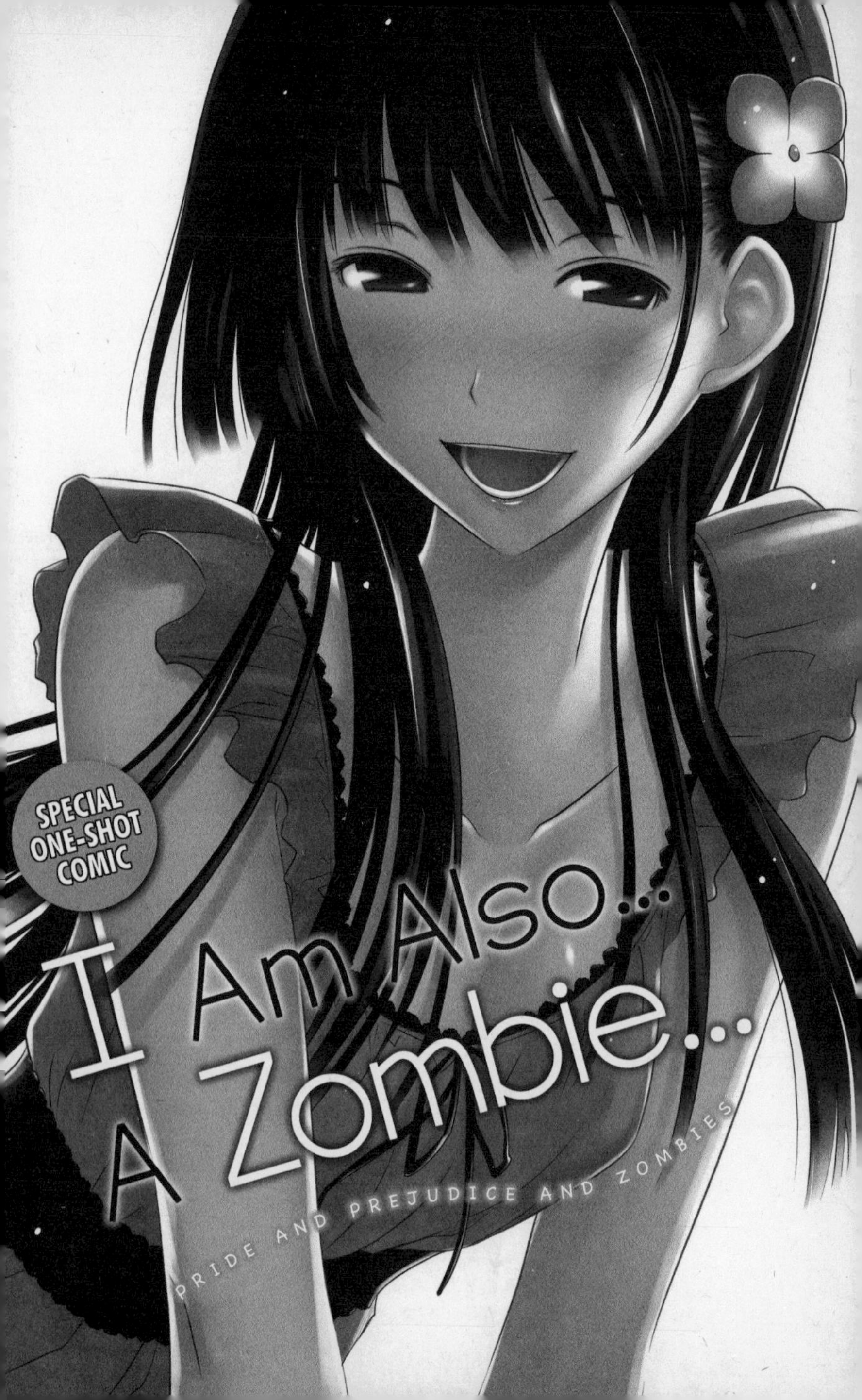
SPECIAL
ONE-SHOT
COMIC
I Am Also...
A Zombie...
PRIDE AND PREJUDICE AND ZOMBIES

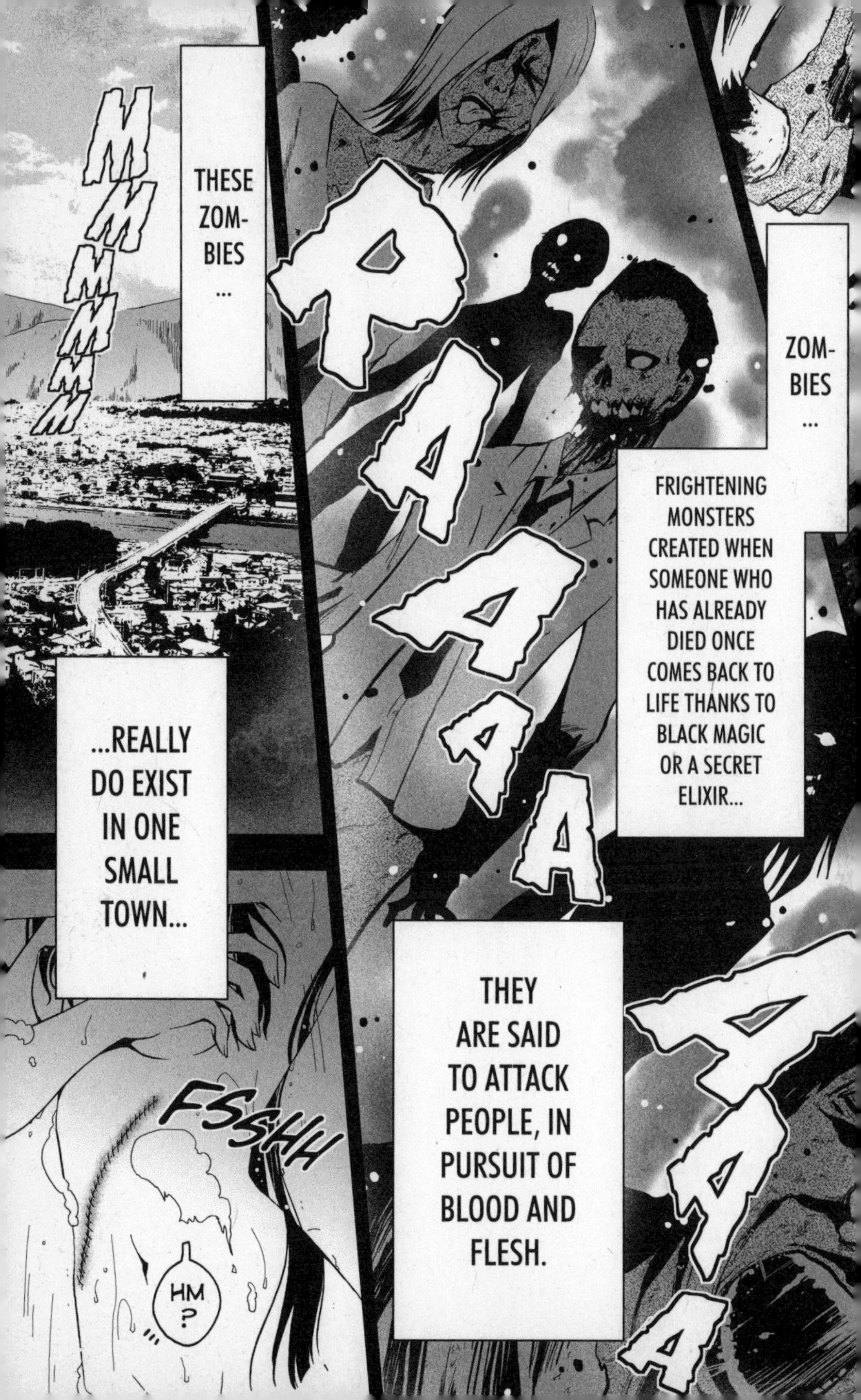
ZOMBIES...
FRIGHTENING MONSTERS CREATED WHEN SOMEONE WHO HAS ALREADY DIED ONCE COMES BACK TO LIFE THANKS TO BLACK MAGIC OR A SECRET ELIXIR...
THEY ARE SAID TO ATTACK PEOPLE, IN PURSUIT OF BLOOD AND FLESH.
AAA
RAAAAA
THESE ZOMBIES...
MMMMMMM
...REALLY DO EXIST IN ONE SMALL TOWN...
FSSHH
HM?

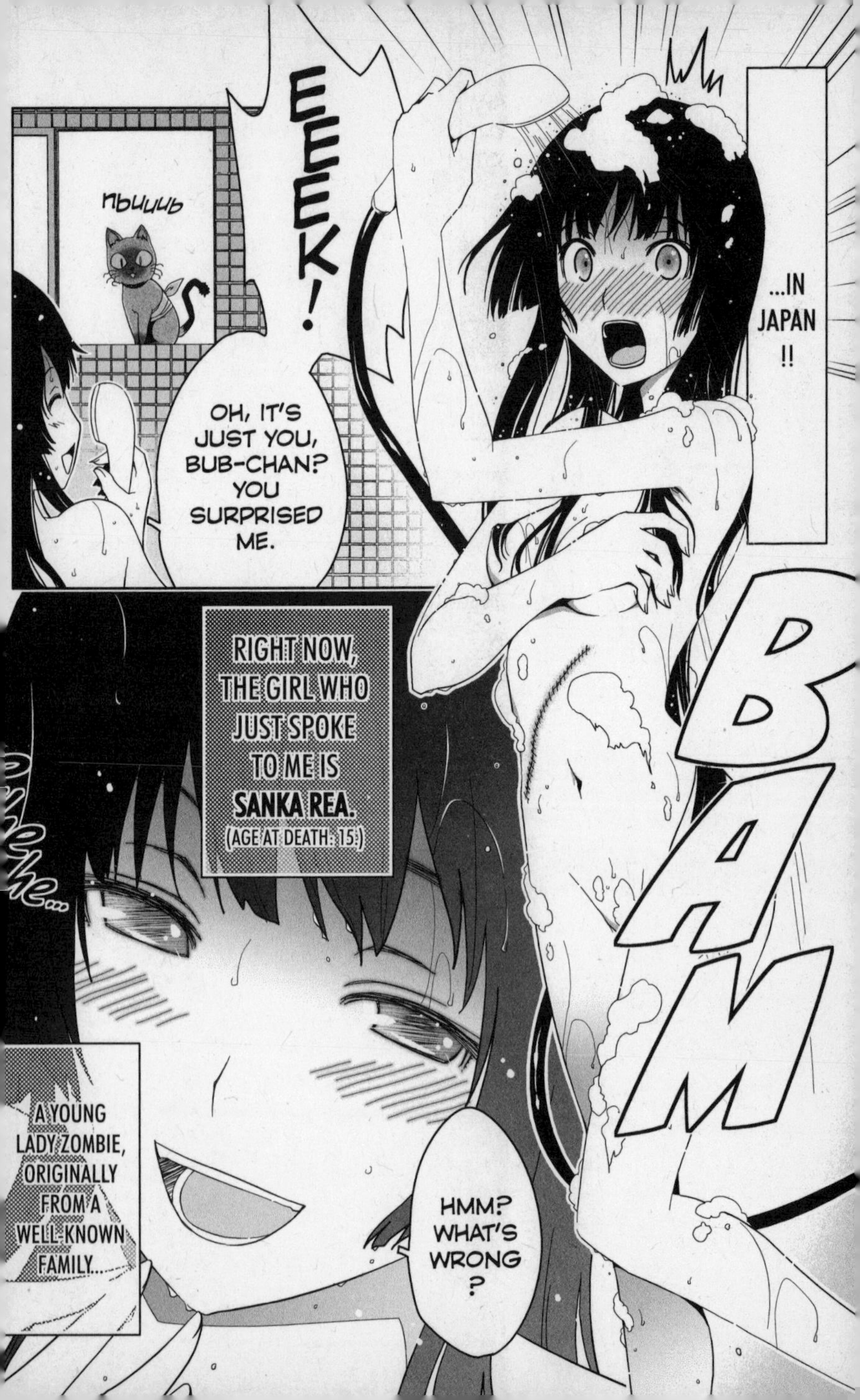

...IN JAPAN !!
EEEK!
BAM
OH, IT'S JUST YOU, BUB-CHAN? YOU SURPRISED ME.
RIGHT NOW, THE GIRL WHO JUST SPOKE TO ME IS **SANKA REA.** (AGE AT DEATH: 15.)
HMM? WHAT'S WRONG?
A YOUNG LADY ZOMBIE, ORIGINALLY FROM A WELL-KNOWN FAMILY...

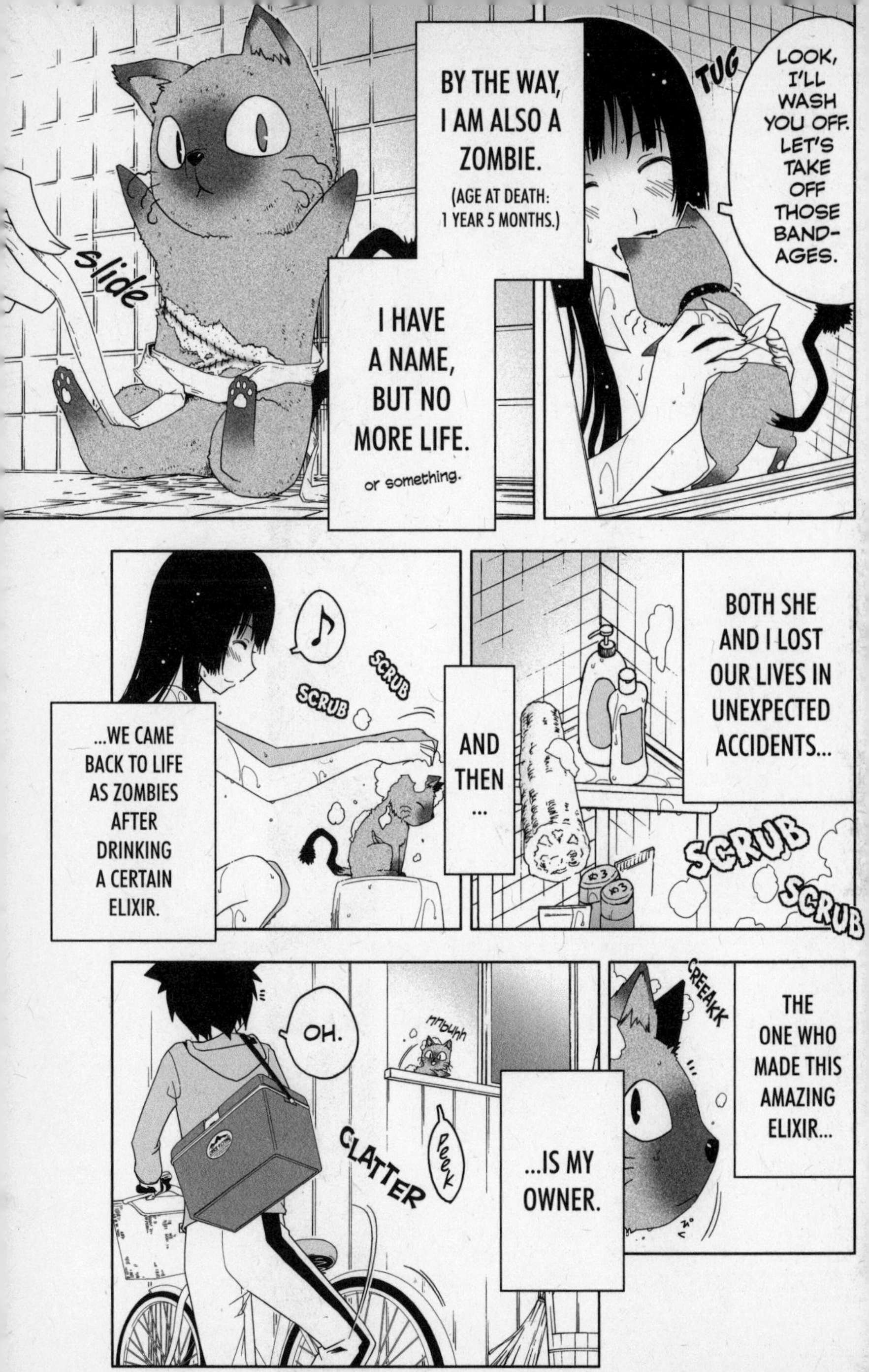
TUG
LOOK, I'LL WASH YOU OFF. LET'S TAKE OFF THOSE BAND-AGES.
BY THE WAY, I AM ALSO A ZOMBIE.
(AGE AT DEATH: 1 YEAR 5 MONTHS.)
slide
I HAVE A NAME, BUT NO MORE LIFE.
or something.
BOTH SHE AND I LOST OUR LIVES IN UNEXPECTED ACCIDENTS...
SCRUB
SCRUB
AND THEN ...
♪
SCRUB
SCRUB
...WE CAME BACK TO LIFE AS ZOMBIES AFTER DRINKING A CERTAIN ELIXIR.
CREEAKK
THE ONE WHO MADE THIS AMAZING ELIXIR...
...IS MY OWNER.
OH.
peek
CLATTER

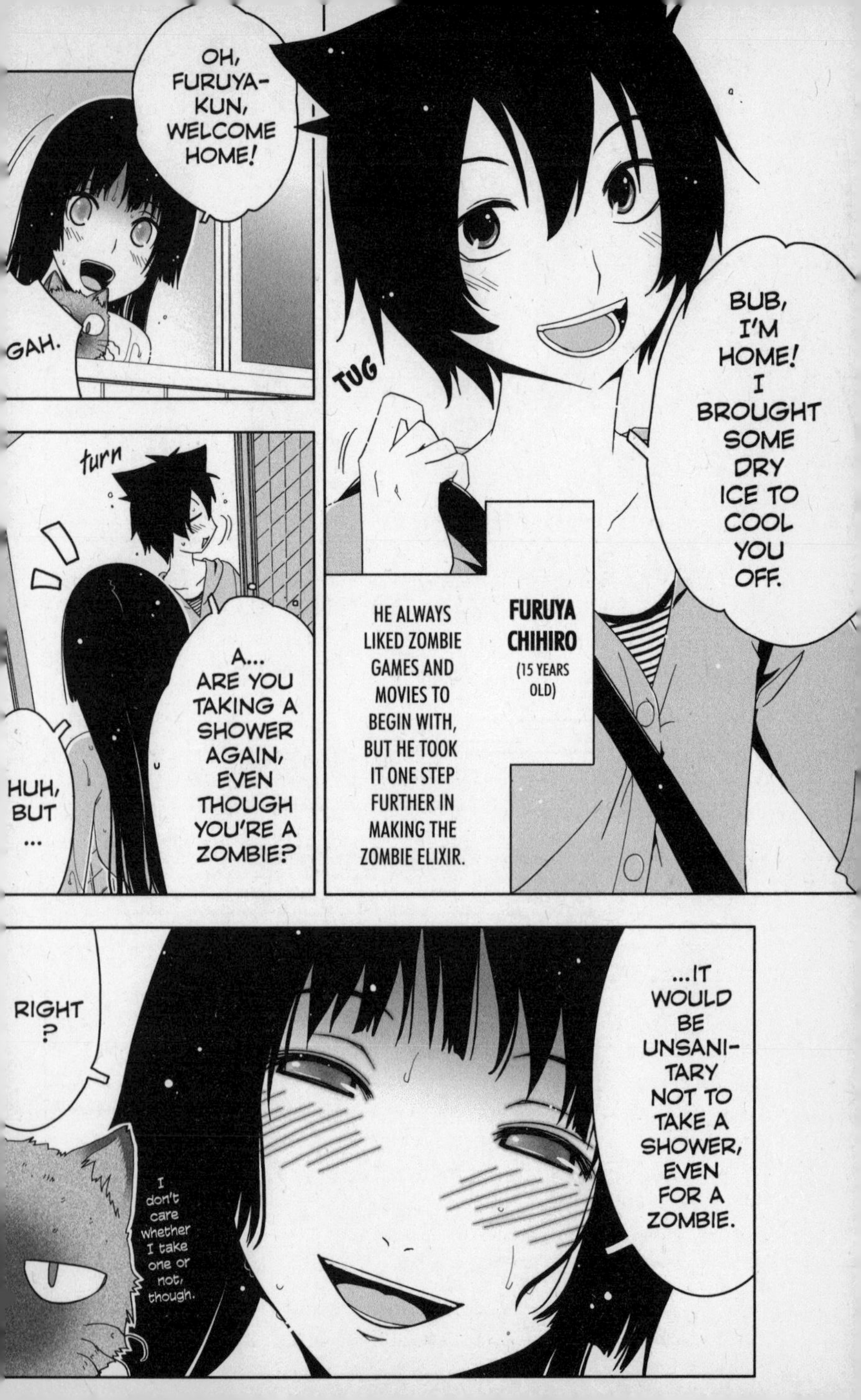
BUB, I'M HOME! I BROUGHT SOME DRY ICE TO COOL YOU OFF.
TUG
FURUYA CHIHIRO (15 YEARS OLD)
HE ALWAYS LIKED ZOMBIE GAMES AND MOVIES TO BEGIN WITH, BUT HE TOOK IT ONE STEP FURTHER IN MAKING THE ZOMBIE ELIXIR.
OH, FURUYA-KUN, WELCOME HOME!
GAH.
turn
A... ARE YOU TAKING A SHOWER AGAIN, EVEN THOUGH YOU'RE A ZOMBIE?
HUH, BUT ...
...IT WOULD BE UNSANITARY NOT TO TAKE A SHOWER, EVEN FOR A ZOMBIE.
RIGHT?
I don't care whether I take one or not, though.

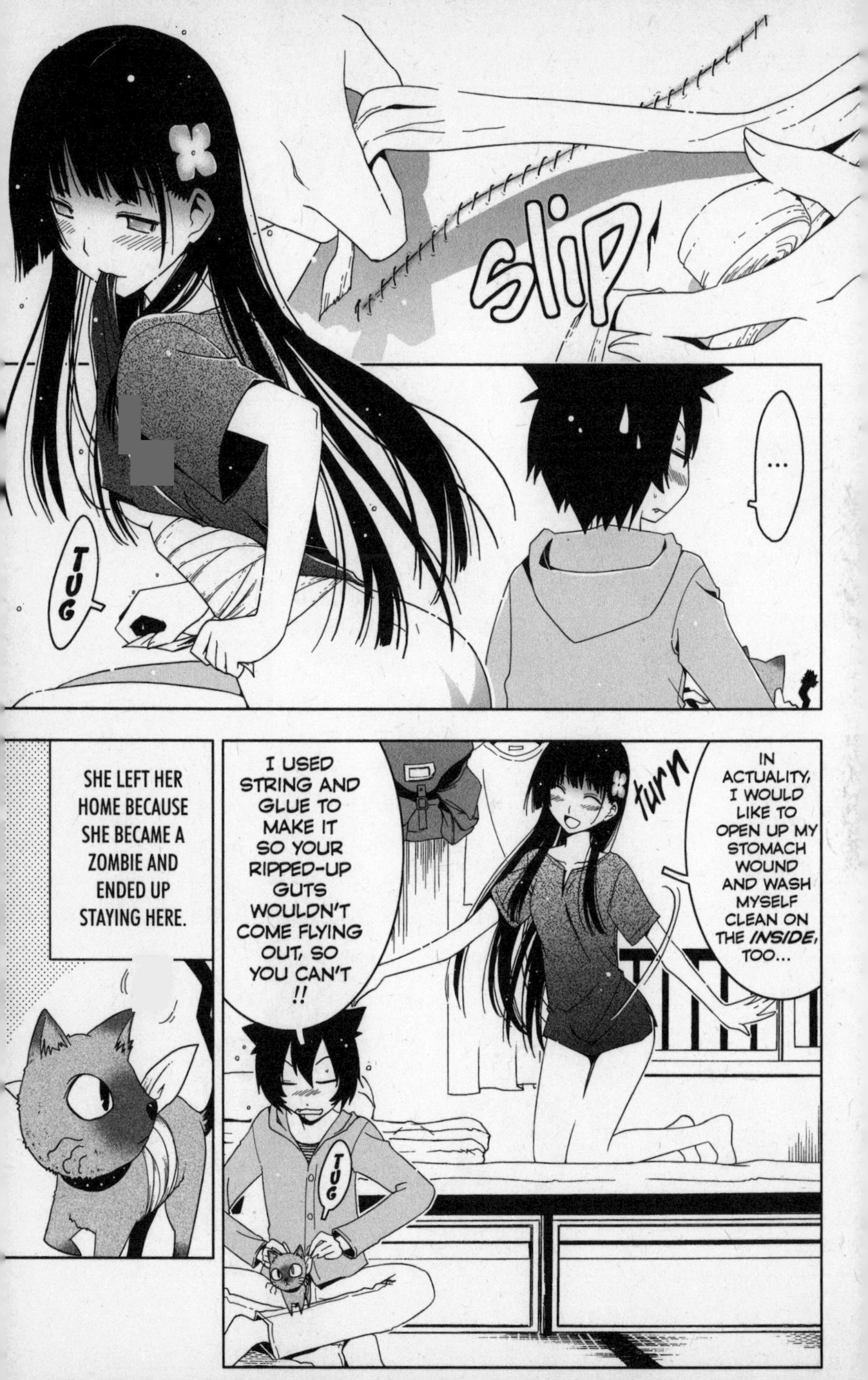
slip
…
TUG
IN ACTUALITY, I WOULD LIKE TO OPEN UP MY STOMACH WOUND AND WASH MYSELF CLEAN ON THE *INSIDE*, TOO…
turn
I USED STRING AND GLUE TO MAKE IT SO YOUR RIPPED-UP GUTS WOULDN'T COME FLYING OUT, SO YOU CAN'T!!
TUG
SHE LEFT HER HOME BECAUSE SHE BECAME A ZOMBIE AND ENDED UP STAYING HERE.

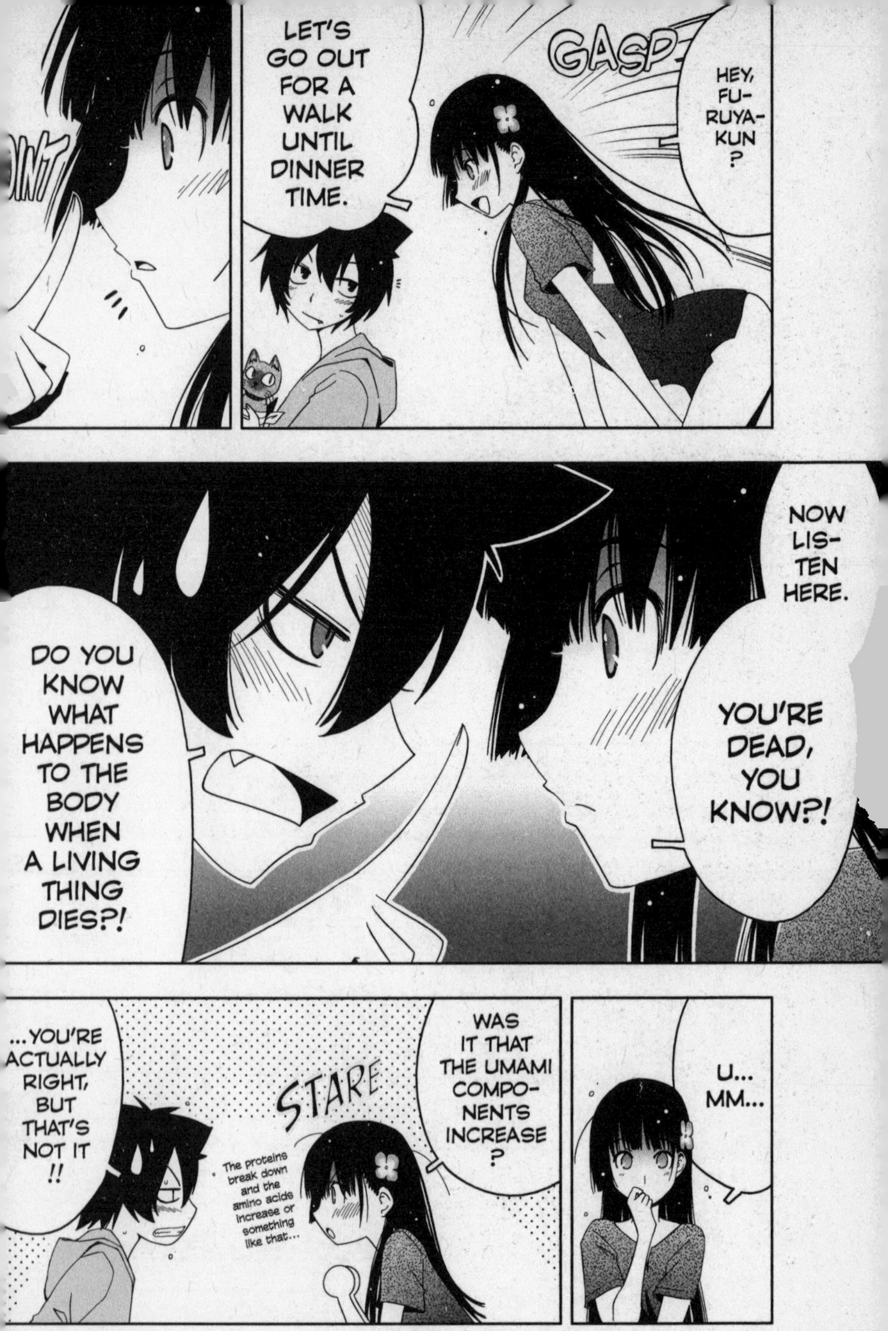
GASP
HEY, FU-RUYA-KUN?
LET'S GO OUT FOR A WALK UNTIL DINNER TIME.
NOW LIS-TEN HERE.
YOU'RE DEAD, YOU KNOW?!
DO YOU KNOW WHAT HAPPENS TO THE BODY WHEN A LIVING THING DIES?!
U... MM...
WAS IT THAT THE UMAMI COMPO-NENTS INCREASE?
STARE
The proteins break down and the amino acids increase or something like that...
...YOU'RE ACTUALLY RIGHT, BUT THAT'S NOT IT!!

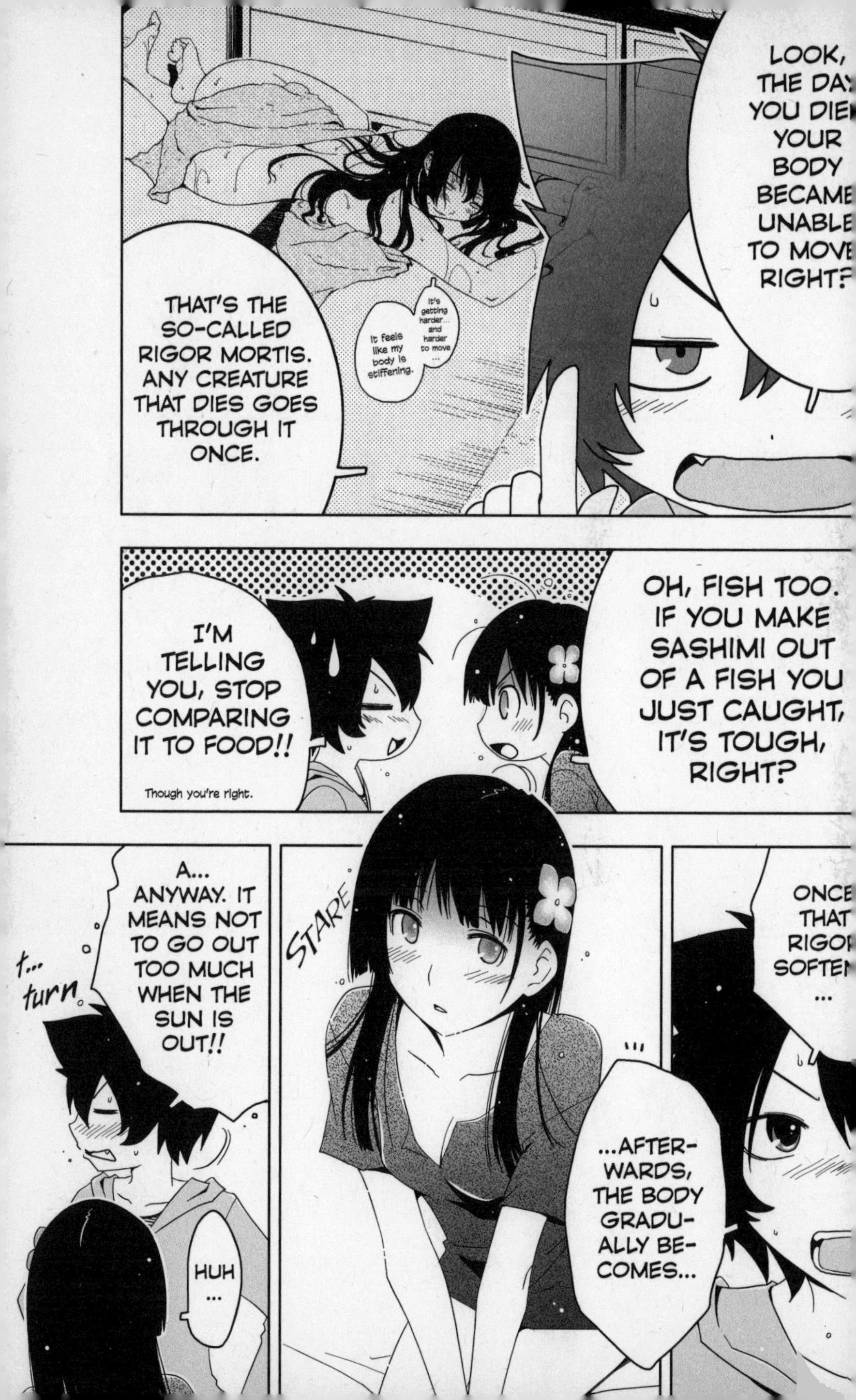
LOOK, THE DAY YOU DIE YOUR BODY BECAME UNABLE TO MOVE RIGHT?
It's getting harder... and harder to move...
It feels like my body is stiffening.
THAT'S THE SO-CALLED RIGOR MORTIS. ANY CREATURE THAT DIES GOES THROUGH IT ONCE.
OH, FISH TOO. IF YOU MAKE SASHIMI OUT OF A FISH YOU JUST CAUGHT, IT'S TOUGH, RIGHT?
I'M TELLING YOU, STOP COMPARING IT TO FOOD!!
Though you're right.
ONCE THAT RIGOR SOFTEN...
...AFTER-WARDS, THE BODY GRADU-ALLY BE-COMES...
STARE
A... ANYWAY. IT MEANS NOT TO GO OUT TOO MUCH WHEN THE SUN IS OUT!!
t... turn
HUH...

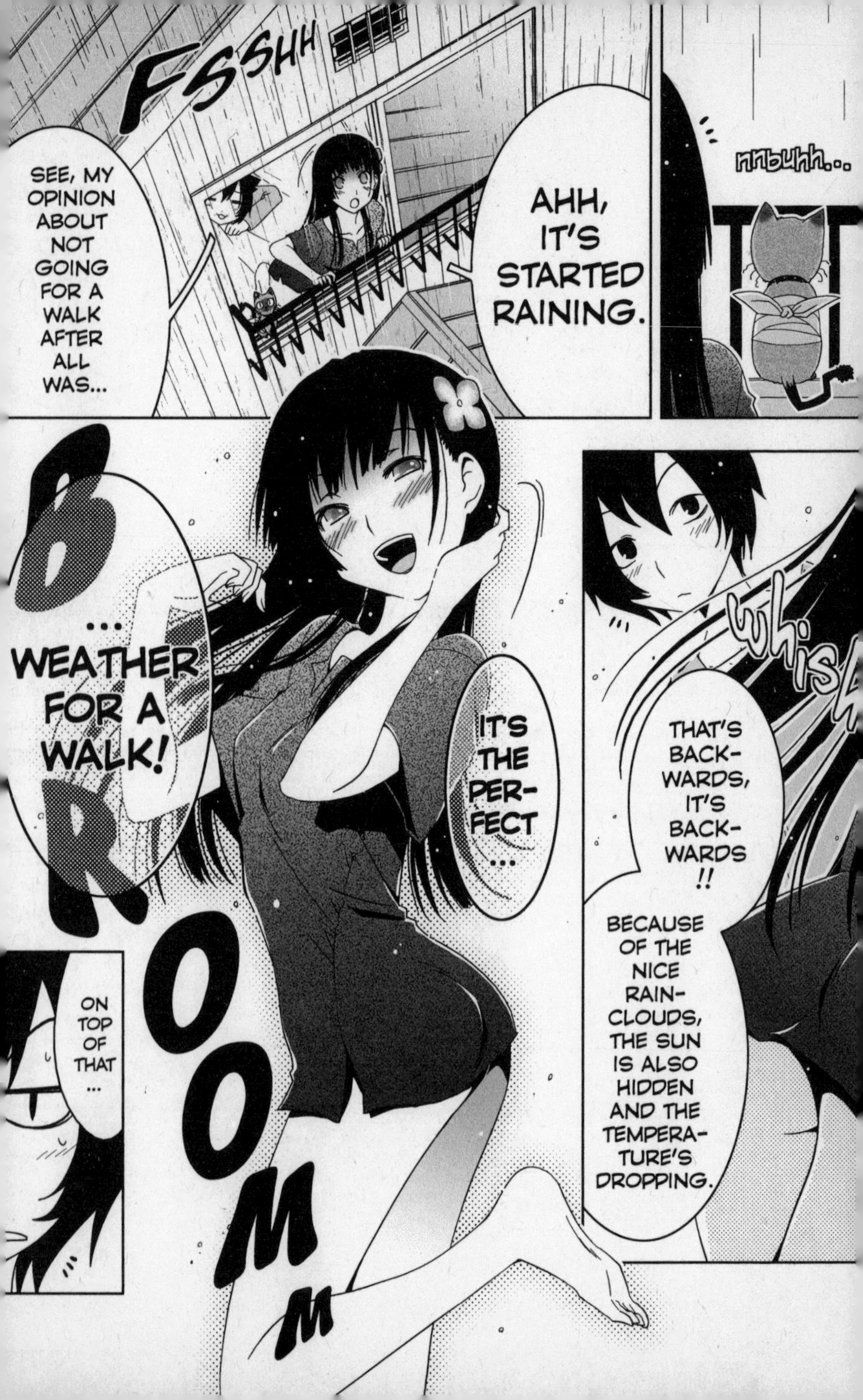
nnbuhh...
FSSHH
AHH, IT'S STARTED RAINING.
SEE, MY OPINION ABOUT NOT GOING FOR A WALK AFTER ALL WAS...
whisk
THAT'S BACKWARDS, IT'S BACKWARDS!!
BECAUSE OF THE NICE RAINCLOUDS, THE SUN IS ALSO HIDDEN AND THE TEMPERATURE'S DROPPING.
BROOMM
IT'S THE PERFECT...
...WEATHER FOR A WALK!
ON TOP OF THAT...

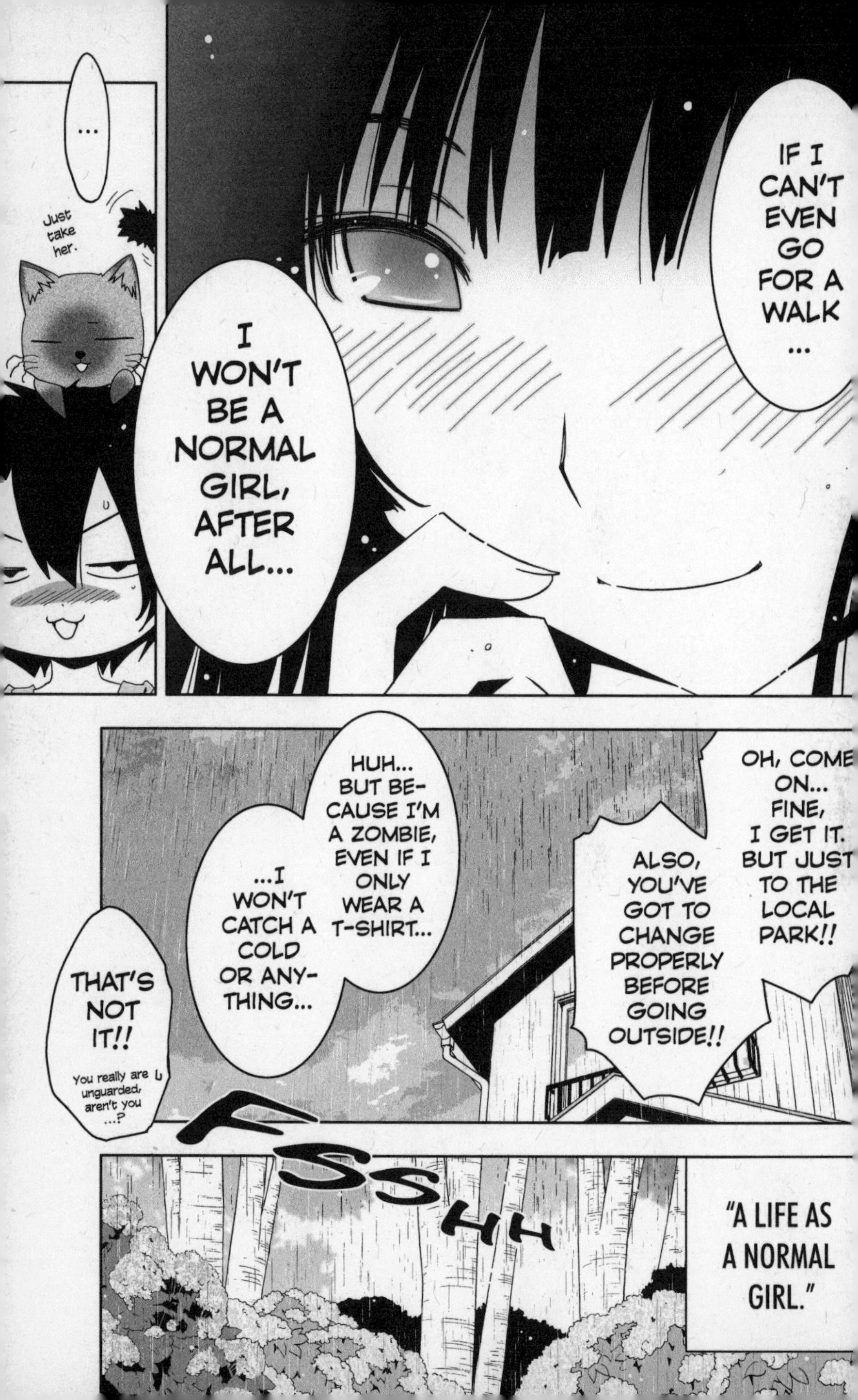
IF I CAN'T EVEN GO FOR A WALK ...
I WON'T BE A NORMAL GIRL, AFTER ALL...
...
Just take her.
OH, COME ON... FINE, I GET IT. BUT JUST TO THE LOCAL PARK!!
ALSO, YOU'VE GOT TO CHANGE PROPERLY BEFORE GOING OUTSIDE!!
HUH... BUT BE-CAUSE I'M A ZOMBIE, EVEN IF I ONLY WEAR A T-SHIRT...
...I WON'T CATCH A COLD OR ANY-THING...
THAT'S NOT IT!!
You really are unguarded, aren't you ...?
FSSHH
"A LIFE AS A NORMAL GIRL."

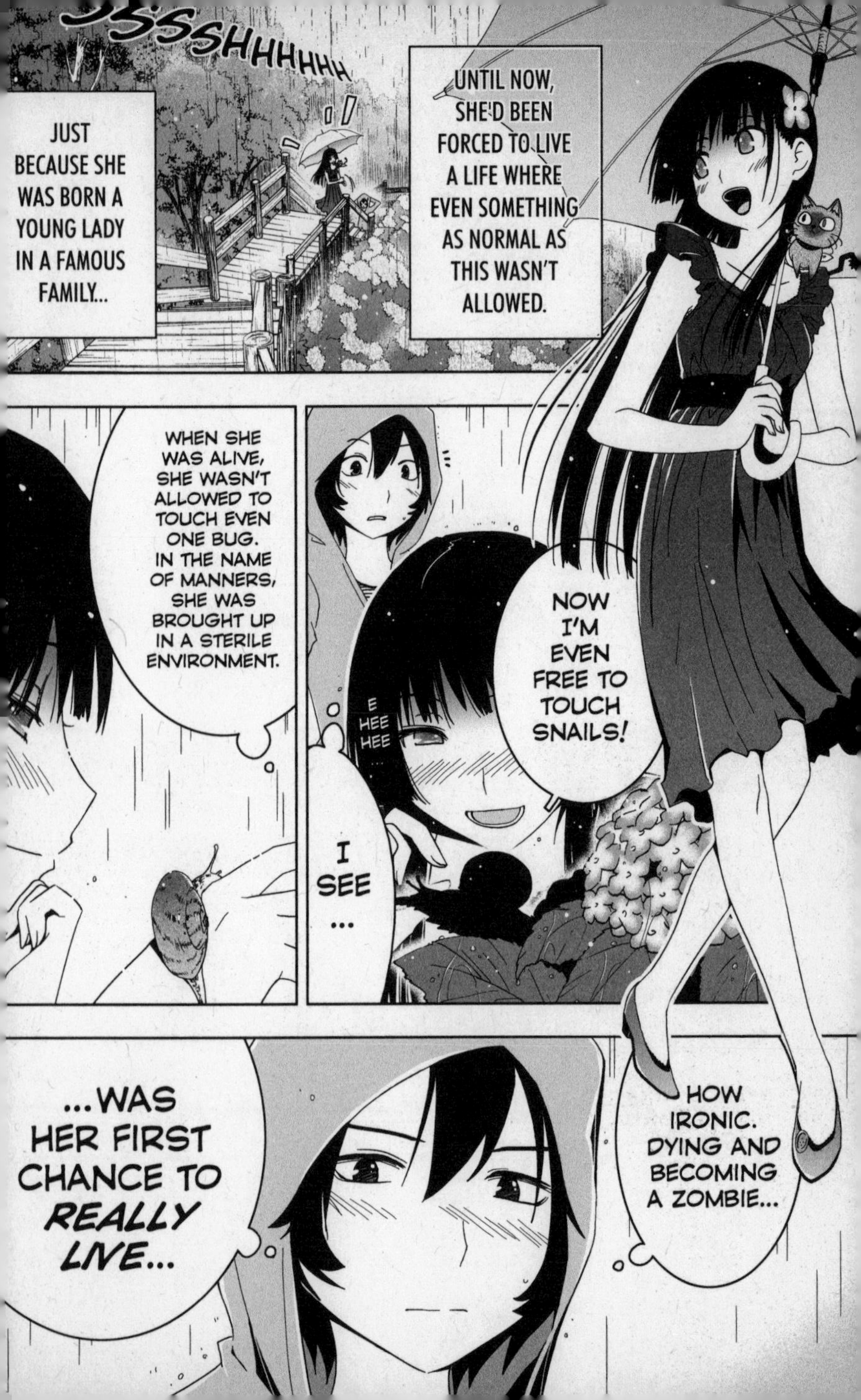
UNTIL NOW, SHE'D BEEN FORCED TO LIVE A LIFE WHERE EVEN SOMETHING AS NORMAL AS THIS WASN'T ALLOWED.
SSSHHHHHH
JUST BECAUSE SHE WAS BORN A YOUNG LADY IN A FAMOUS FAMILY...
NOW I'M EVEN FREE TO TOUCH SNAILS!
E HEE HEE
I SEE ...
WHEN SHE WAS ALIVE, SHE WASN'T ALLOWED TO TOUCH EVEN ONE BUG. IN THE NAME OF MANNERS, SHE WAS BROUGHT UP IN A STERILE ENVIRONMENT.
HOW IRONIC. DYING AND BECOMING A ZOMBIE...
...WAS HER FIRST CHANCE TO *REALLY LIVE*...

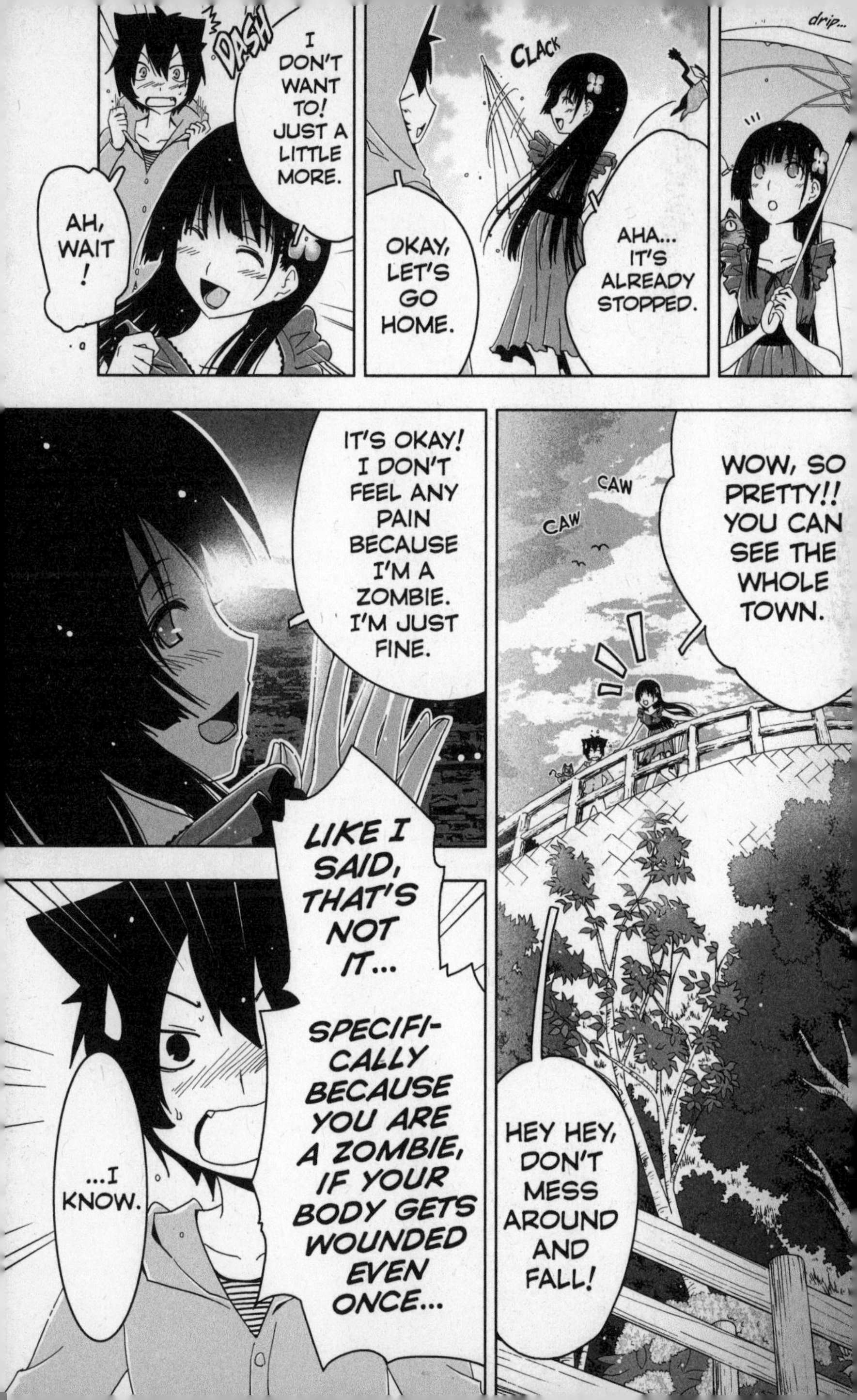
drip...
CLACK
AHA... IT'S ALREADY STOPPED.
OKAY, LET'S GO HOME.
I DON'T WANT TO! JUST A LITTLE MORE.
DASH
AH, WAIT!
WOW, SO PRETTY!! YOU CAN SEE THE WHOLE TOWN.
CAW
CAW
HEY HEY, DON'T MESS AROUND AND FALL!
IT'S OKAY! I DON'T FEEL ANY PAIN BECAUSE I'M A ZOMBIE. I'M JUST FINE.
LIKE I SAID, THAT'S NOT IT...
SPECIFI-CALLY BECAUSE YOU ARE A ZOMBIE, IF YOUR BODY GETS WOUNDED EVEN ONCE...
...I KNOW.

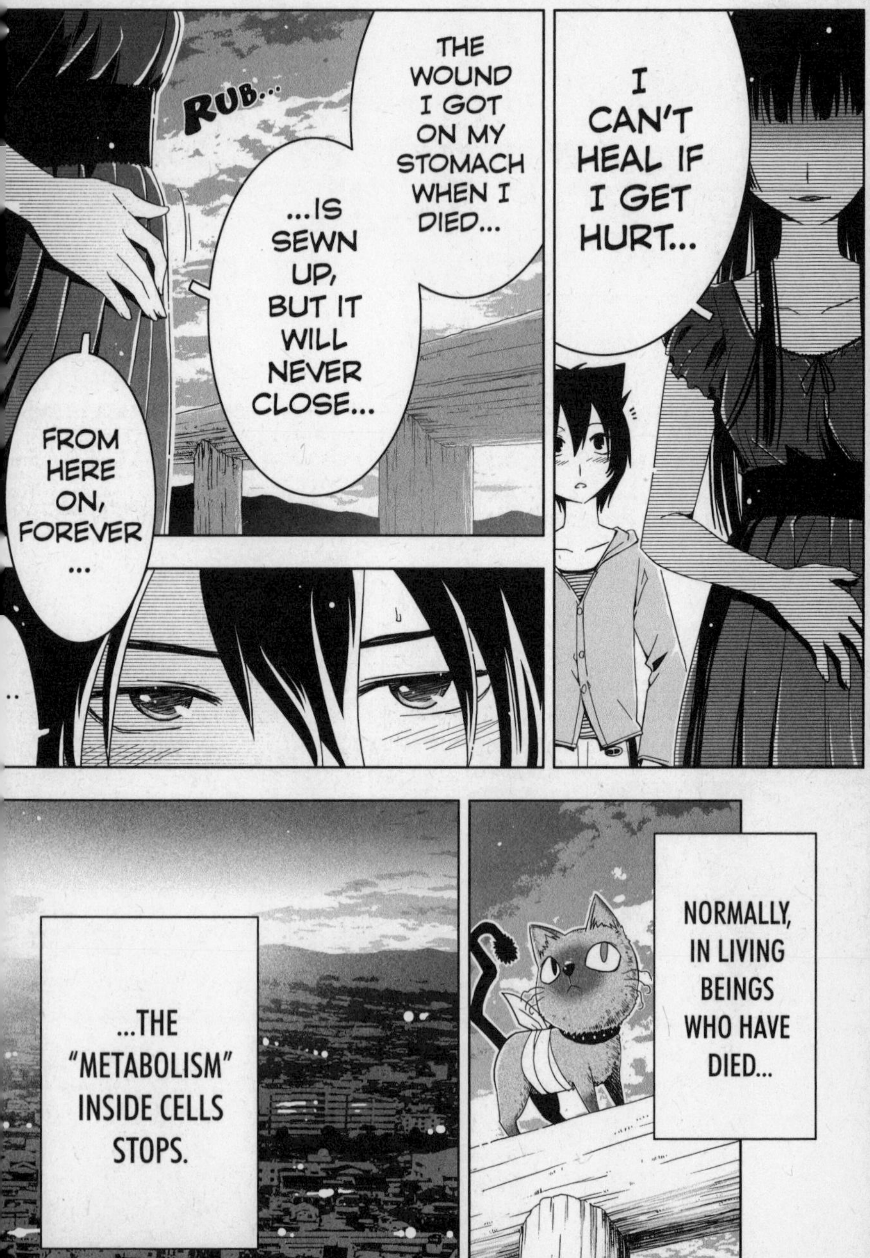
I CAN'T HEAL IF I GET HURT...
THE WOUND I GOT ON MY STOMACH WHEN I DIED...
...IS SEWN UP, BUT IT WILL NEVER CLOSE...
RUB...
FROM HERE ON, FOREVER...
NORMALLY, IN LIVING BEINGS WHO HAVE DIED...
...THE "METABOLISM" INSIDE CELLS STOPS.

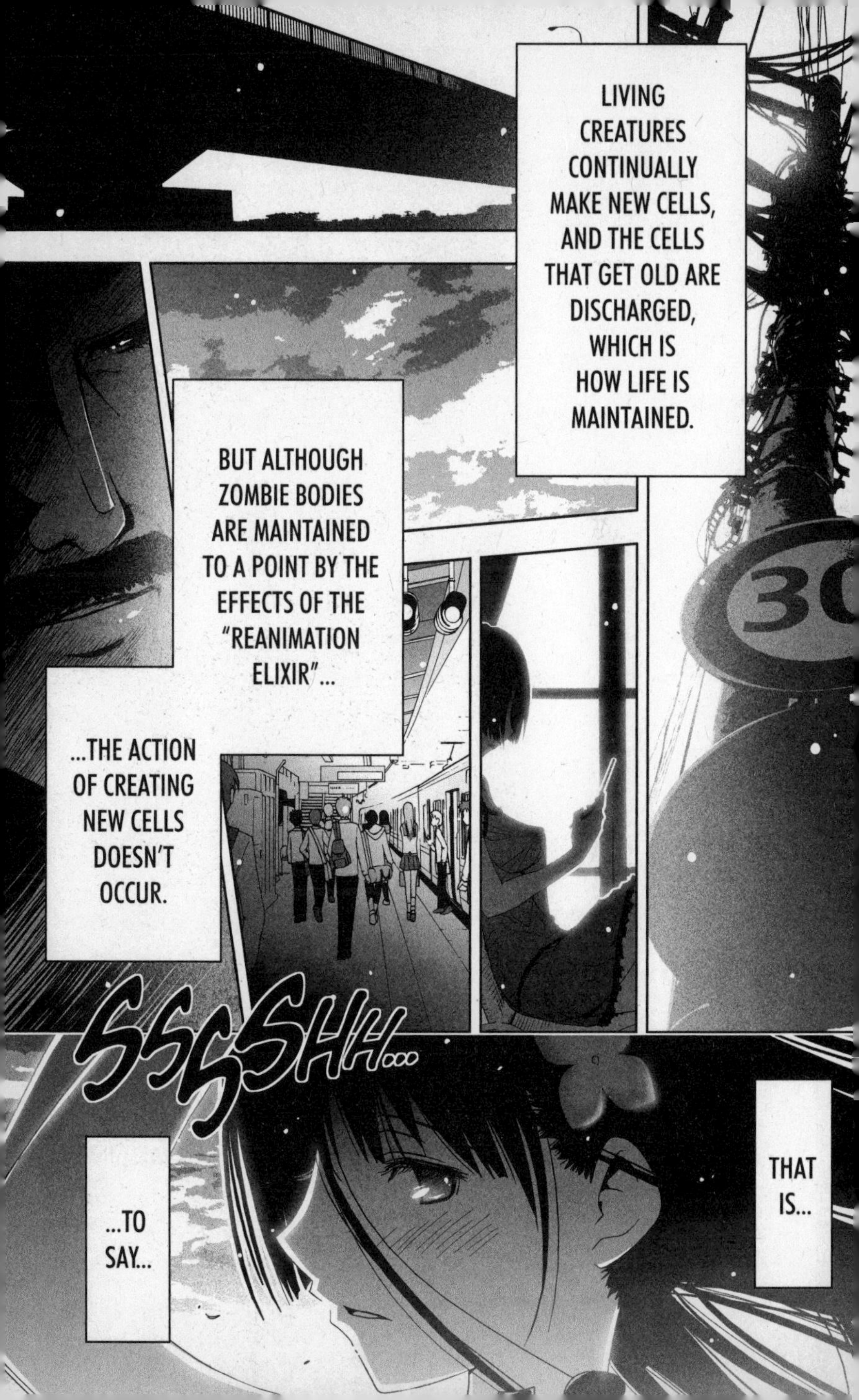
LIVING CREATURES CONTINUALLY MAKE NEW CELLS, AND THE CELLS THAT GET OLD ARE DISCHARGED, WHICH IS HOW LIFE IS MAINTAINED.
BUT ALTHOUGH ZOMBIE BODIES ARE MAINTAINED TO A POINT BY THE EFFECTS OF THE "REANIMATION ELIXIR"...
...THE ACTION OF CREATING NEW CELLS DOESN'T OCCUR.
SSSSHH...
THAT IS...
...TO SAY...

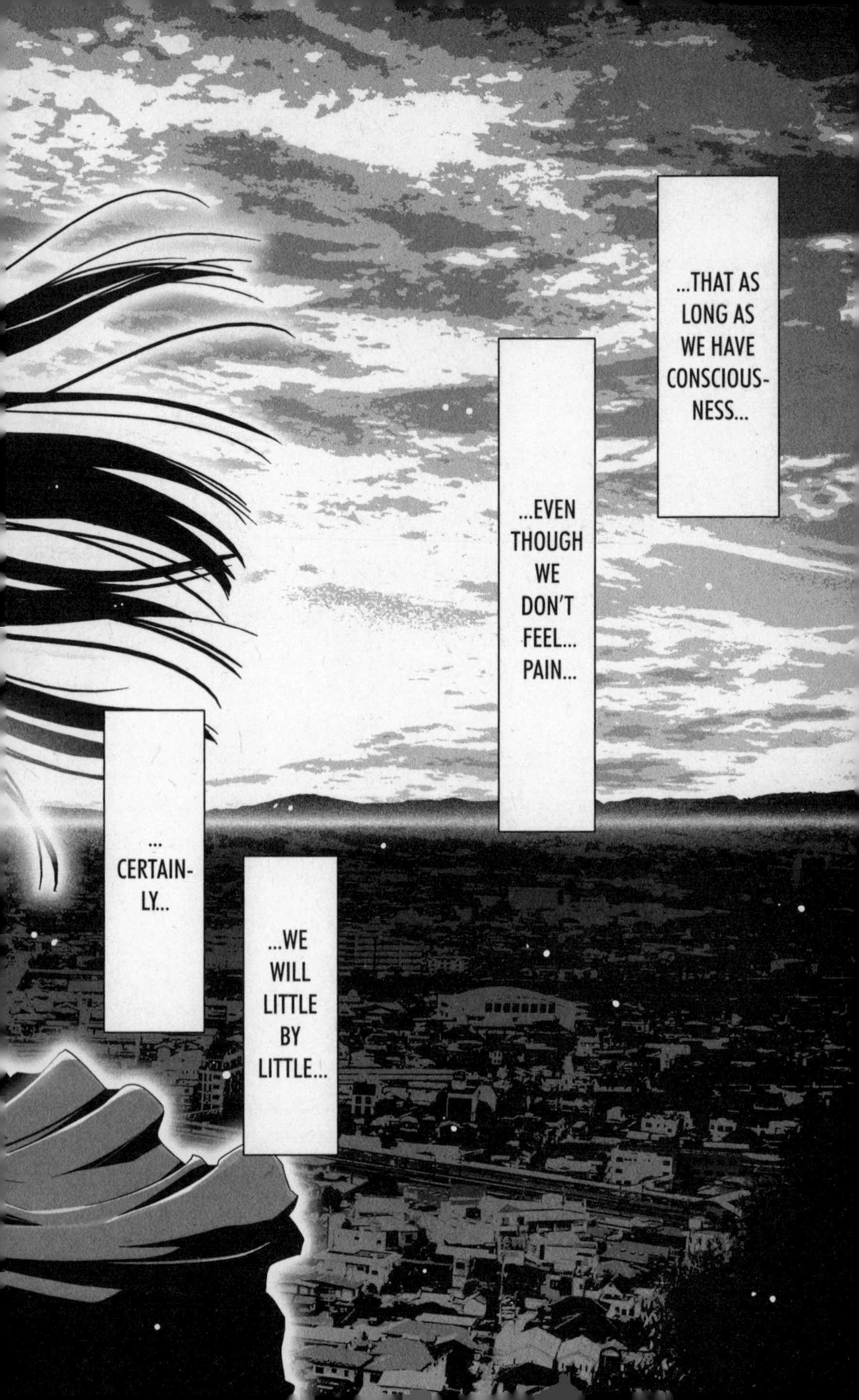
...THAT AS LONG AS WE HAVE CONSCIOUS-NESS...
...EVEN THOUGH WE DON'T FEEL... PAIN...
... CERTAIN-LY...
...WE WILL LITTLE BY LITTLE...

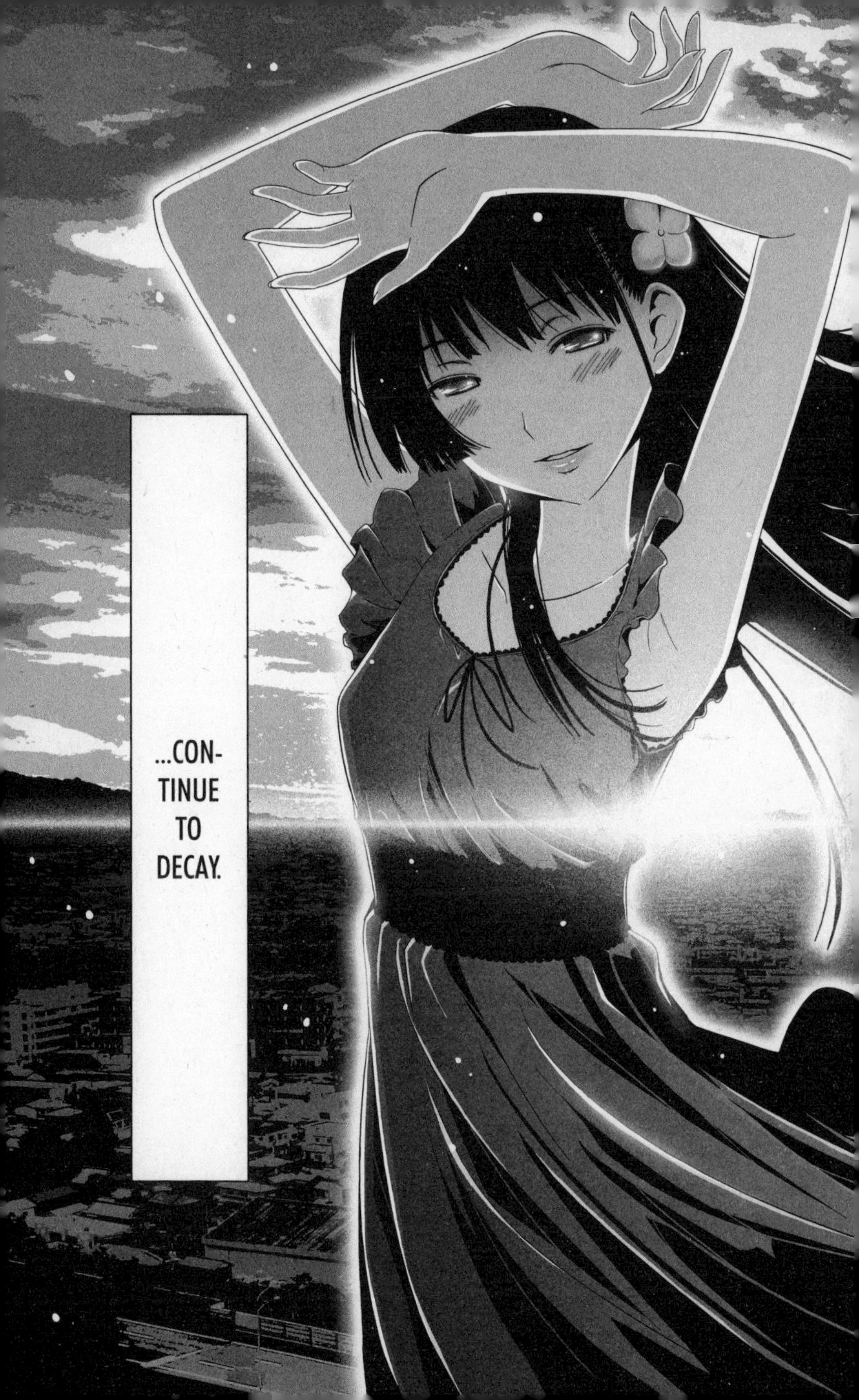
...CON-TINUE TO DECAY.

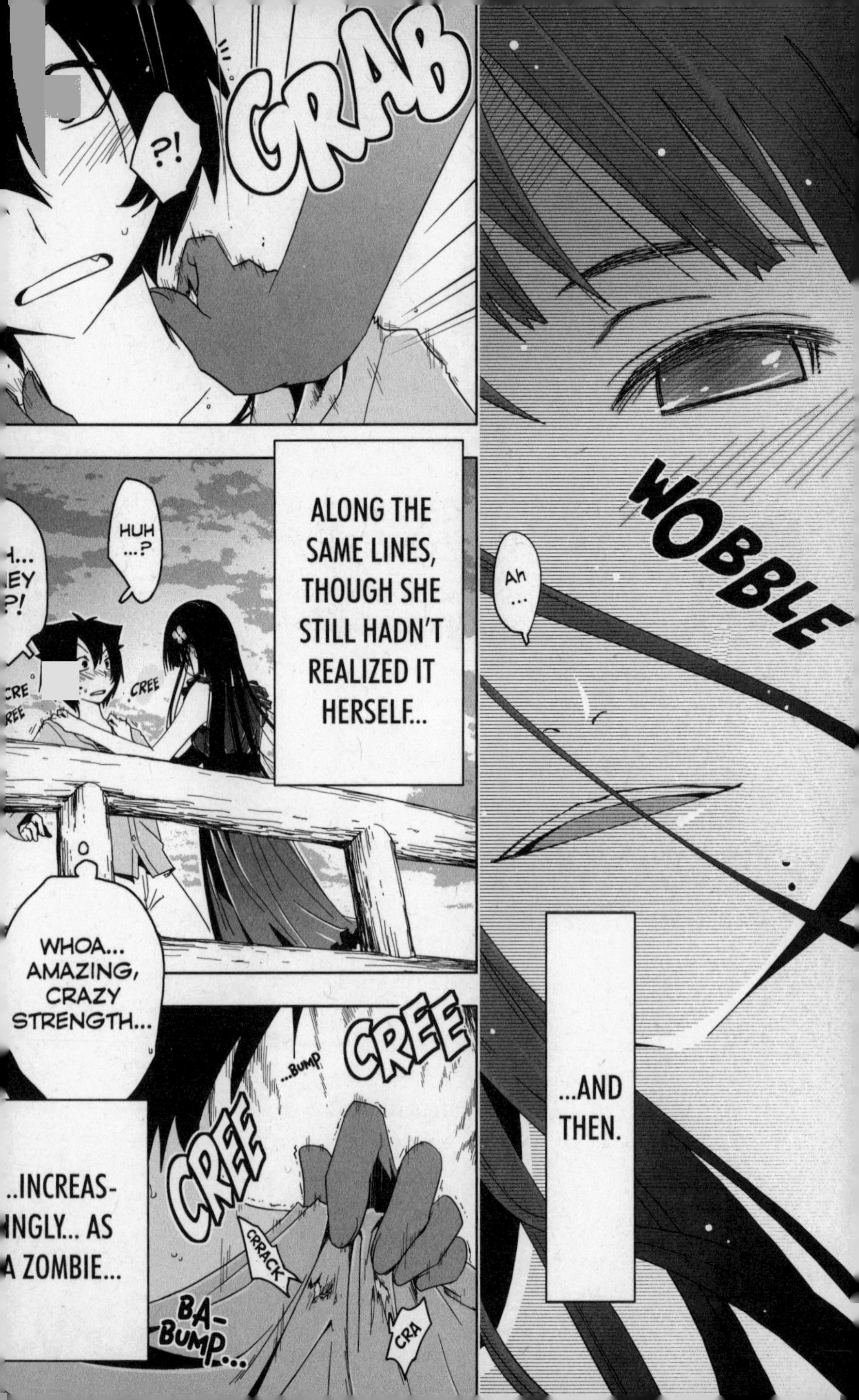
WOBBLE
Ah ...
...AND THEN.
?!
GRAB
ALONG THE SAME LINES, THOUGH SHE STILL HADN'T REALIZED IT HERSELF...
HUH ...?
CREE
WHOA... AMAZING, CRAZY STRENGTH...
CREE
...BUMP
CREE
..INCREAS-INGLY... AS A ZOMBIE...
CRRACK
BA-BUMP...
CRA

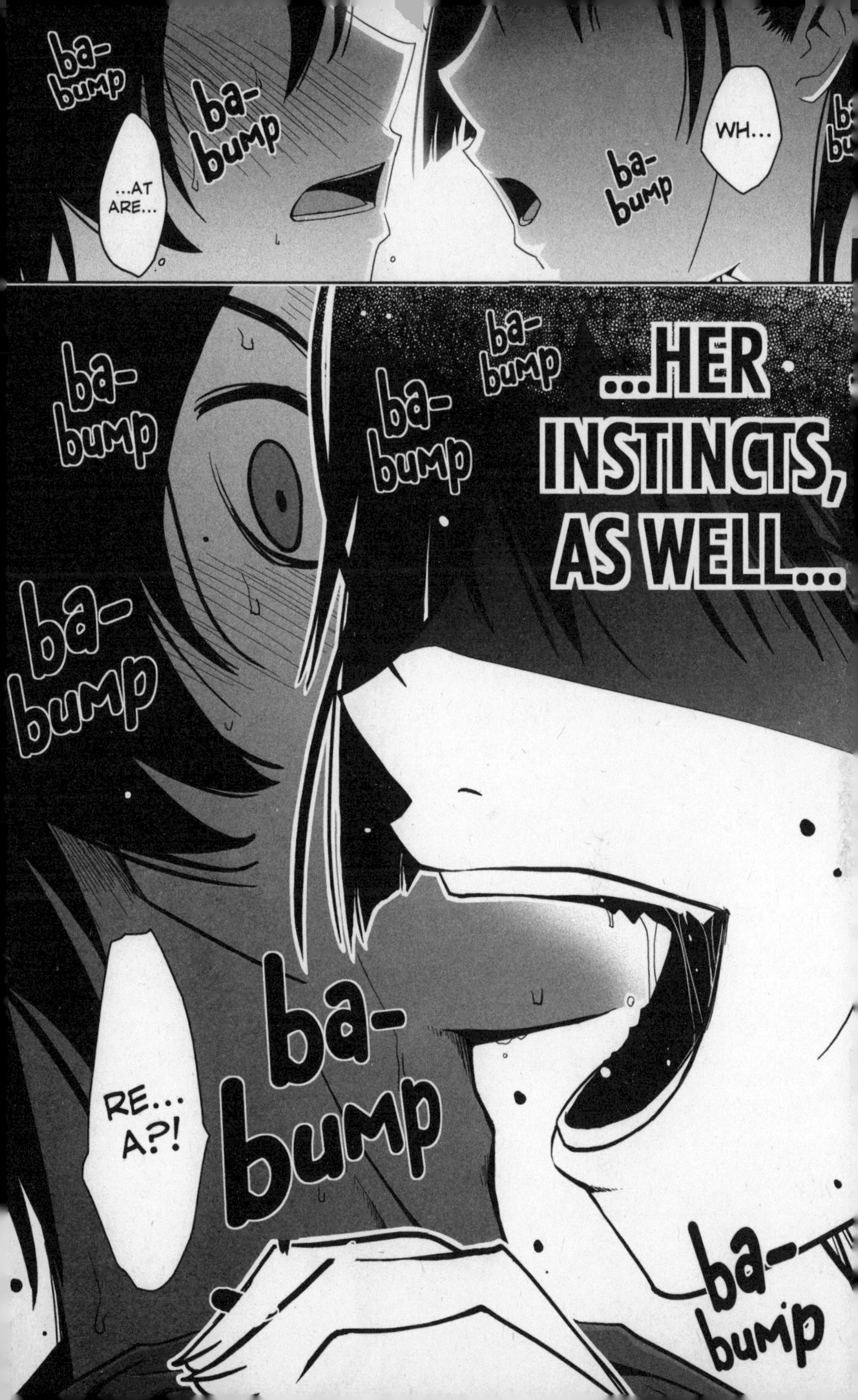
WH...
ba-bump
ba-bump
ba-bump
...AT ARE...
...HER INSTINCTS, AS WELL...
ba-bump
ba-bump
ba-bump
ba-bump
ba-bump
ba-bump
RE... A?!

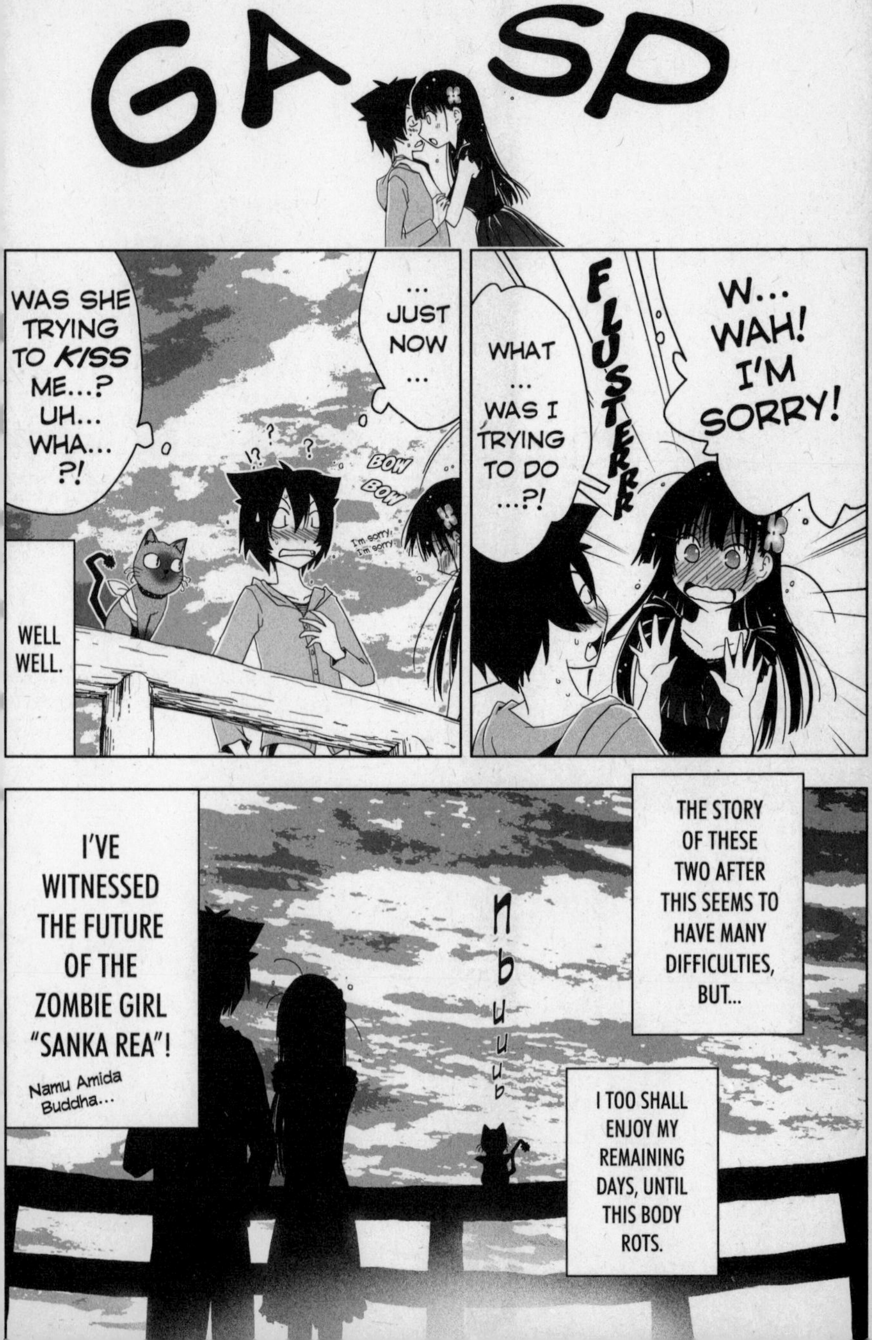
GASP
W... WAH! I'M SORRY!
FLUSTERRR
WHAT ... WAS I TRYING TO DO ...?!
... JUST NOW ...
WAS SHE TRYING TO KISS ME...? UH... WHA...?!
!? ? ?
BOW BOW
I'm sorry, I'm sorry
WELL WELL.
THE STORY OF THESE TWO AFTER THIS SEEMS TO HAVE MANY DIFFICULTIES, BUT...
I TOO SHALL ENJOY MY REMAINING DAYS, UNTIL THIS BODY ROTS.
I'VE WITNESSED THE FUTURE OF THE ZOMBIE GIRL "SANKA REA"!
Namu Amida Buddha...

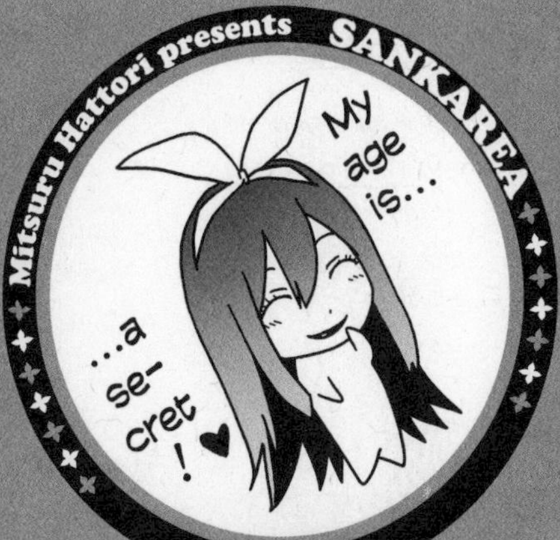
Mitsuru Hattori presents SANKAREA
My age is...
...a se-cret! ♥

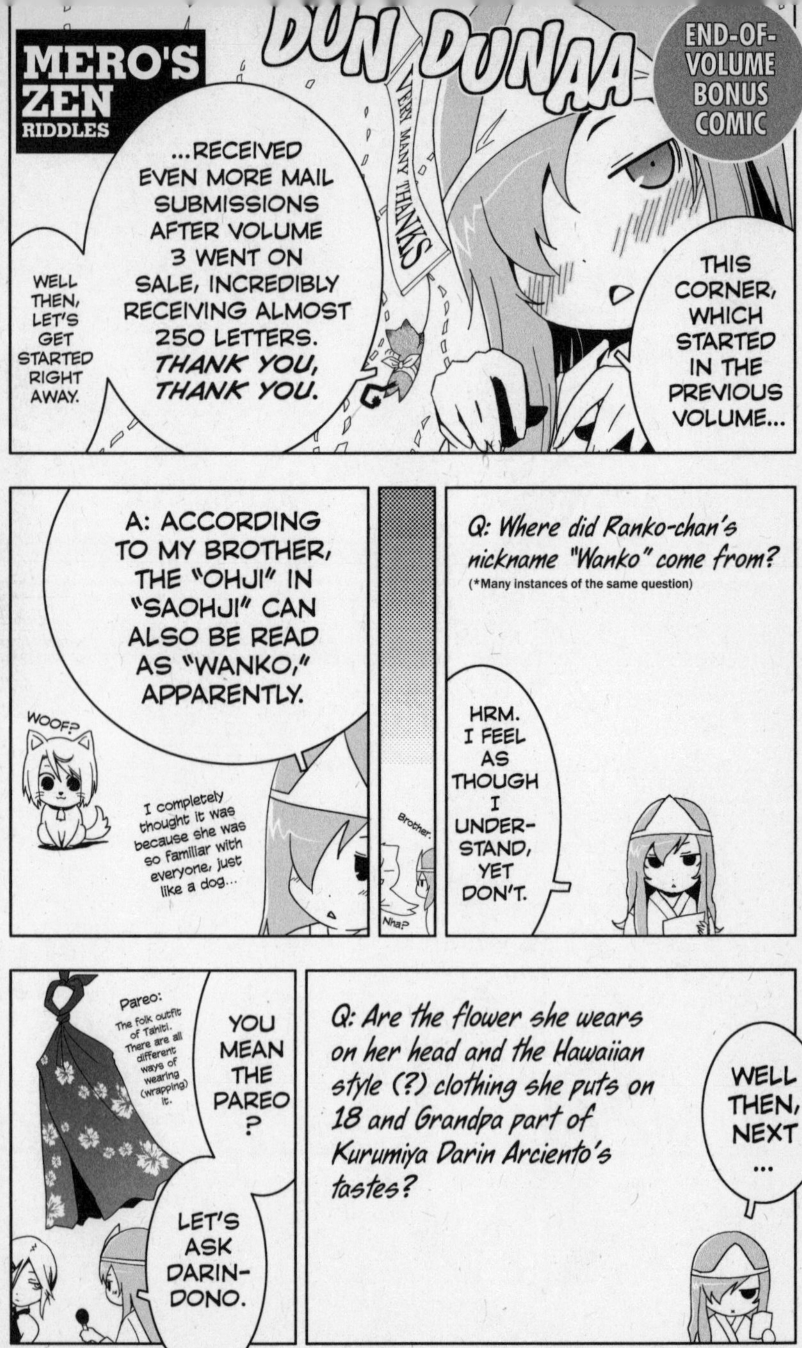
END-OF-VOLUME BONUS COMIC
DUN DUNAA
MERO'S ZEN RIDDLES
VERY MANY THANKS
THIS CORNER, WHICH STARTED IN THE PREVIOUS VOLUME...
...RECEIVED EVEN MORE MAIL SUBMISSIONS AFTER VOLUME 3 WENT ON SALE, INCREDIBLY RECEIVING ALMOST 250 LETTERS. THANK YOU, THANK YOU.
WELL THEN, LET'S GET STARTED RIGHT AWAY.
Q: Where did Ranko-chan's nickname "Wanko" come from?
(*Many instances of the same question)
HRM. I FEEL AS THOUGH I UNDERSTAND, YET DON'T.
Brother.
Nha?
A: ACCORDING TO MY BROTHER, THE "OHJI" IN "SAOHJI" CAN ALSO BE READ AS "WANKO," APPARENTLY.
WOOF?
I completely thought it was because she was so familiar with everyone, just like a dog...
WELL THEN, NEXT...
Q: Are the flower she wears on her head and the Hawaiian style (?) clothing she puts on 18 and Grandpa part of Kurumiya Darin Arciento's tastes?
YOU MEAN THE PAREO?
Pareo: The folk outfit of Tahiti. There are all different ways of wearing (wrapping) it.
LET'S ASK DARIN-DONO.

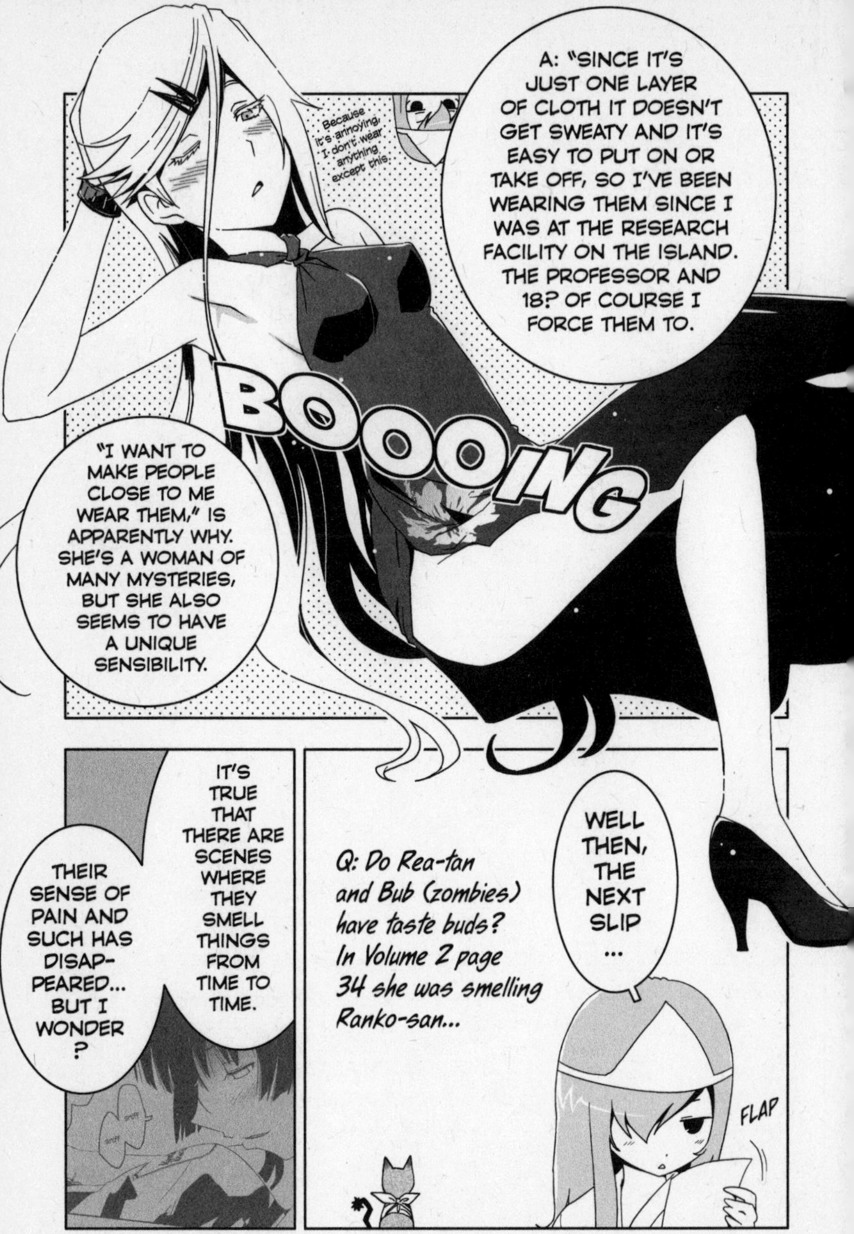
A: "SINCE IT'S JUST ONE LAYER OF CLOTH IT DOESN'T GET SWEATY AND IT'S EASY TO PUT ON OR TAKE OFF, SO I'VE BEEN WEARING THEM SINCE I WAS AT THE RESEARCH FACILITY ON THE ISLAND. THE PROFESSOR AND 18? OF COURSE I FORCE THEM TO.
Because it's annoying, I don't wear anything except this.
BOOOING
"I WANT TO MAKE PEOPLE CLOSE TO ME WEAR THEM," IS APPARENTLY WHY. SHE'S A WOMAN OF MANY MYSTERIES, BUT SHE ALSO SEEMS TO HAVE A UNIQUE SENSIBILITY.
WELL THEN, THE NEXT SLIP ...
Q: Do Rea-tan and Bub (zombies) have taste buds? In Volume 2 page 34 she was smelling Ranko-san...
FLAP
IT'S TRUE THAT THERE ARE SCENES WHERE THEY SMELL THINGS FROM TIME TO TIME.
THEIR SENSE OF PAIN AND SUCH HAS DISAPPEARED... BUT I WONDER ?
sniff
sniff

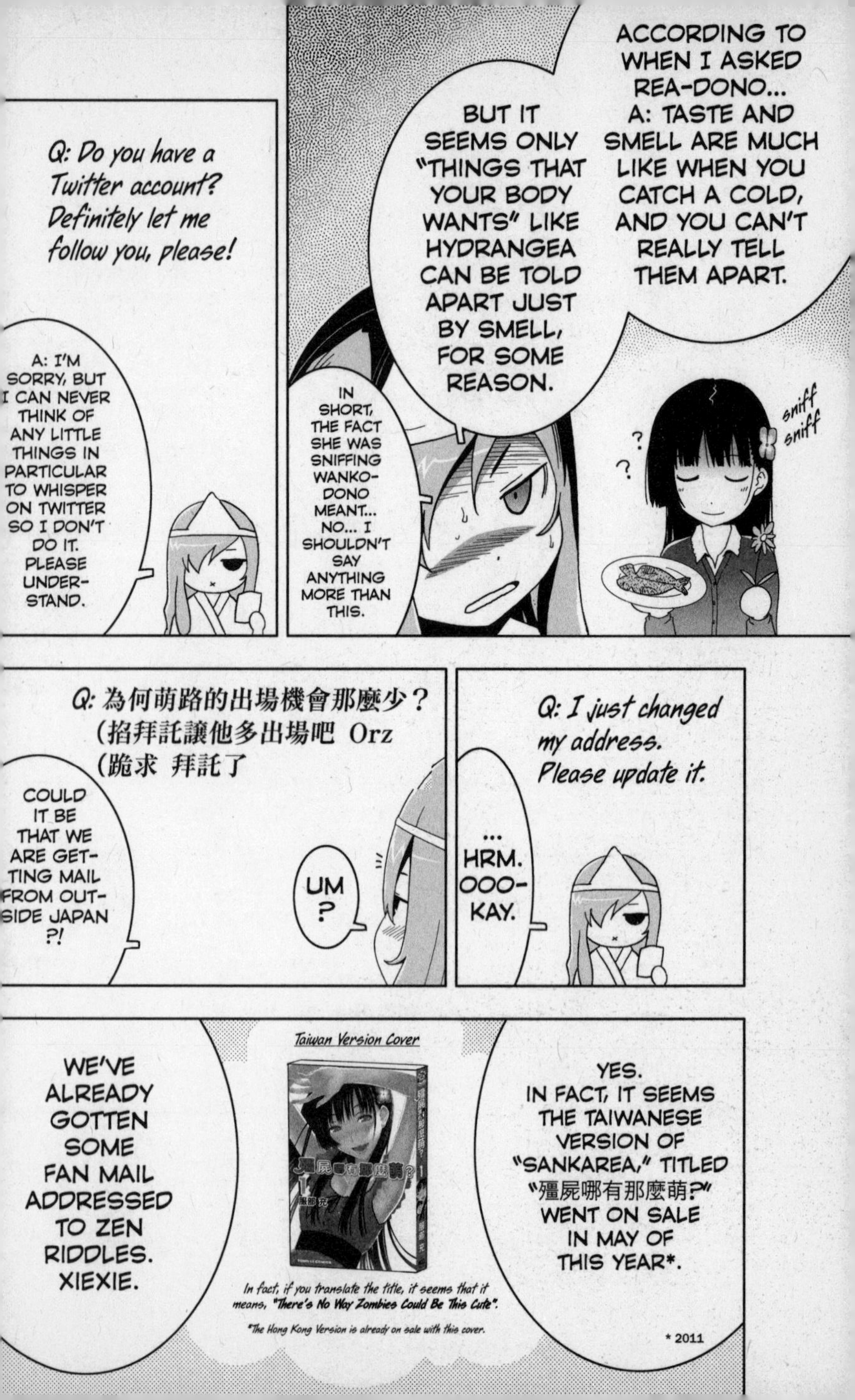
ACCORDING TO WHEN I ASKED REA-DONO... A: TASTE AND SMELL ARE MUCH LIKE WHEN YOU CATCH A COLD, AND YOU CAN'T REALLY TELL THEM APART.
BUT IT SEEMS ONLY "THINGS THAT YOUR BODY WANTS" LIKE HYDRANGEA CAN BE TOLD APART JUST BY SMELL, FOR SOME REASON.
sniff sniff
??
IN SHORT, THE FACT SHE WAS SNIFFING WANKO-DONO MEANT... NO... I SHOULDN'T SAY ANYTHING MORE THAN THIS.
Q: Do you have a Twitter account? Definitely let me follow you, please!
A: I'M SORRY, BUT I CAN NEVER THINK OF ANY LITTLE THINGS IN PARTICULAR TO WHISPER ON TWITTER SO I DON'T DO IT. PLEASE UNDER-STAND.
Q: I just changed my address. Please update it.
... HRM. OOO-KAY.
Q: 為何萌路的出場機會那麼少？
(掐拜託讓他多出場吧 Orz
(跪求 拜託了
UM ?
COULD IT BE THAT WE ARE GET-TING MAIL FROM OUT-SIDE JAPAN ?!
YES. IN FACT, IT SEEMS THE TAIWANESE VERSION OF "SANKAREA," TITLED "殭屍哪有那麼萌?" WENT ON SALE IN MAY OF THIS YEAR*.
Taiwan Version Cover
殭屍哪有那麼萌?
1
服部充
In fact, if you translate the title, it seems that it means, "There's No Way Zombies Could Be This Cute".
*The Hong Kong Version is already on sale with this cover.
* 2011
WE'VE ALREADY GOTTEN SOME FAN MAIL ADDRESSED TO ZEN RIDDLES. XIEXIE.

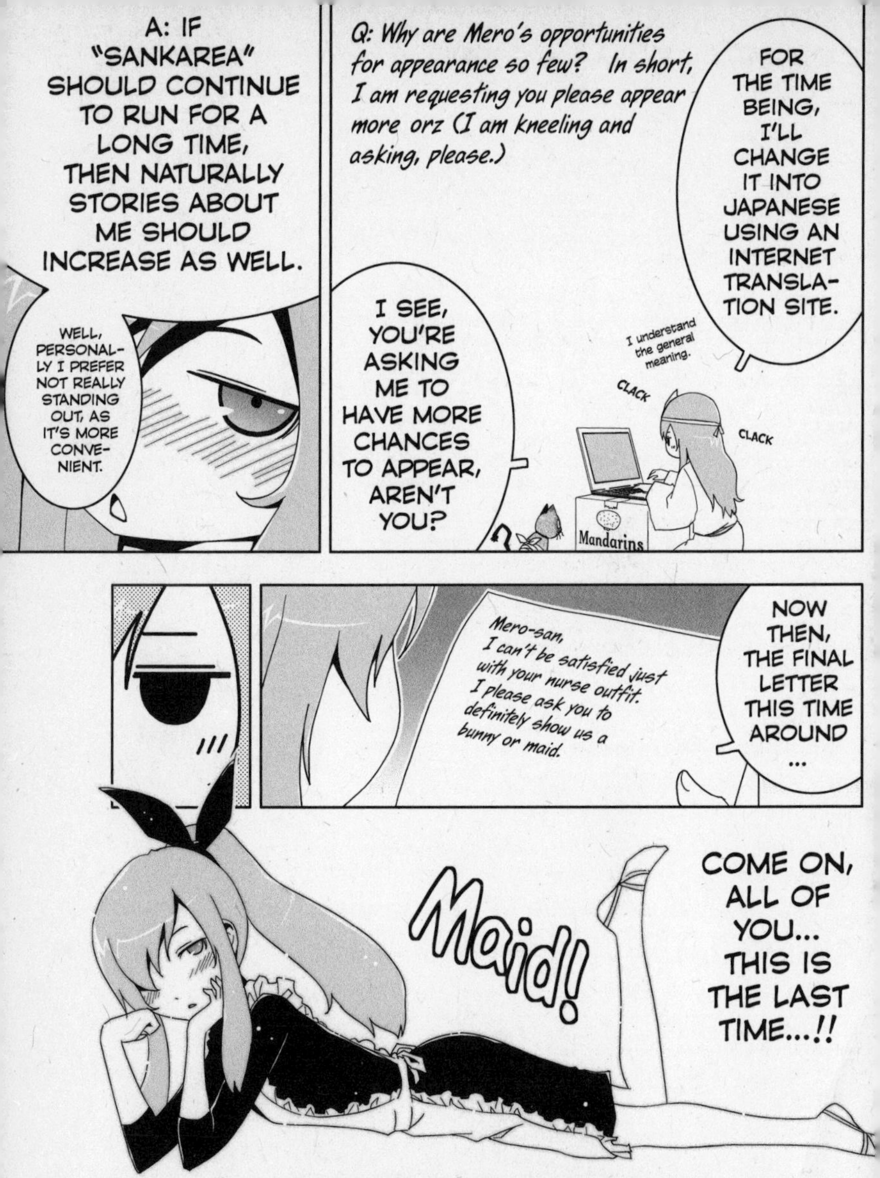
Q: Why are Mero's opportunities for appearance so few? In short, I am requesting you please appear more orz (I am kneeling and asking, please.)
FOR THE TIME BEING, I'LL CHANGE IT INTO JAPANESE USING AN INTERNET TRANSLATION SITE.
CLACK
CLACK
I understand the general meaning.
I SEE, YOU'RE ASKING ME TO HAVE MORE CHANCES TO APPEAR, AREN'T YOU?
Mandarins
A: IF "SANKAREA" SHOULD CONTINUE TO RUN FOR A LONG TIME, THEN NATURALLY STORIES ABOUT ME SHOULD INCREASE AS WELL.
WELL, PERSONALLY I PREFER NOT REALLY STANDING OUT, AS IT'S MORE CONVENIENT.
NOW THEN, THE FINAL LETTER THIS TIME AROUND ...
Mero-san, I can't be satisfied just with your nurse outfit. I please ask you to definitely show us a bunny or maid.
COME ON, ALL OF YOU... THIS IS THE LAST TIME...!!
Maid!

"Mero's Zen Riddles" e-mail address:

(Put something like "Zen Riddles" or "Questions for Mero" in the subject line.)

kodanshacomics@randomhouse.com

*Questions we couldn't answer this time may be picked up in the next volume or after, as well.

TRANSLATION NOTES

Honorifics: This series retains the Japanese honorifics. Here's a guide:
-san: Polite, equivalent to "Mr." or "Ms."
-sama: A term of great respect.
-kun: Used for boys or people in a lower position.
-chan: A sometimes cutesy term of endearment for girls.
-dono: A very respectful and now old-fashioned term.
-sempai: Refers to a student who entered school before you, or a colleague who entered the company before you. (The equivalent for your juniors is "kohai.")

p. 3, Heart Sutra: Sutras are Buddhist sermons or prayers. The Heart Sutra is probably the best known and most popular of all the Buddhist Sutras. Though they were originally written in Sanskrit, the version known in Japan has been transcribed into Chinese characters.

p. 6, Castella: A sponge-like sweet cake of Portuguese origin that is popular in Japan, not only as a snack food at festivals like this one, but also at bakeries and as gifts.

p. 18, Yakisoba: Stir-fried noodles, very similar to Chinese lo mein, which is popular as a festival snack food or take-out type food. It generally contains cabbage, pork, onions and pickled ginger, and may be topped with roasted seaweed, dried bonito shavings, and mayonnaise.

p. 8, Yukata: A yukata is a very light cotton kimono, worn by both sexes but more commonly by girls than boys, and synonymous with the summer months and in particular, summer festivals in Japan. Made in a variety of colors and patterns, both traditional and non-traditional.

p. 9, Goldfish Scooping: A popular game at Japanese summer festivals, where players try to see how many goldfish they can scoop out of a tank and into a small bowl using a thin paper wand. The paper breaks easily, making for a challenging game. The winner often gets to take a goldfish home with them.

p. 16, Sake: The most famous alcoholic beverage in Japan, it is often referred to as "rice wine" in English. There are many varieties and they range from cloudy to clear, from dry to sweet. As the name suggests, sweet sake is a very sweet drink with a relatively low alcohol content.

p. 18, Ryotei: A traditional and usually very formal Japanese restaurant. Ranko is trying to say that her parents are relatively strict and traditional due to the nature of their business.

p. 38, ume-ame: Japanese refer to the rainy season in early summer as tsuyu, which is written as the characters for "plum" and "rain". Since Kurumiya doesn't know much about Japanese cultural customs, she's reading these characters incorrectly, as "ume-ame" instead.

p. 41, Takoyaki: Another popular Japanese festival and street food. These are very hot, small, round balls made of wheat flour cooked with a piece of octopus in the very center, along with other items like chopped pickled ginger. Usually these are served in a box or take-out container with sauce, mayonnaise, roasted seaweed, shaved bonito flakes, and sometimes green onion on top.

p. 69, Sekihan: A dish made of swet red beans and sticky rice, this dish is traditionally served at celebratory occasions.

p. 129, cosplay: The Japanese hobby of dressing up in elaborate costumes, usually from some sort of manga, anime or video game.

p. 150, "I'm Also a Zombie": The title of this chapter, featuring Bub, is a play on the famous book by Japanese author Natsume Soseki, entitled "I Am a Cat."

p. 156, Umami: A word for a particular type of taste often referred to as "savory" or "meaty."

p. 168, Namu Amida Butsu: A prayer involving saying the name of the Buddha, commonly used in Pure Land Buddhism. It is often shortened to just the first word in Japanese.

Sky Zombie

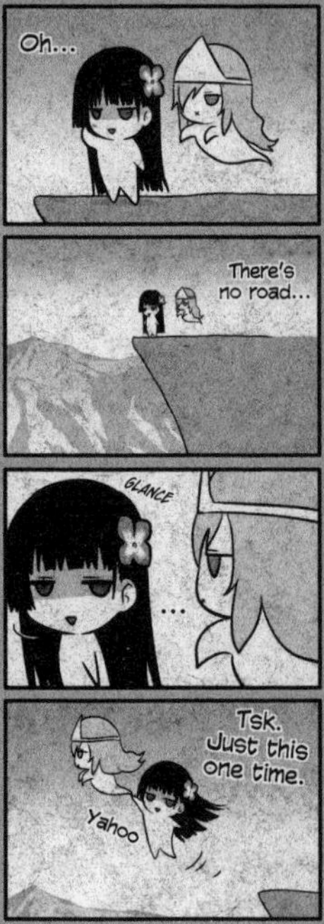
Oh...
There's no road...
GLANCE
...
Tsk. Just this one time.
Yahoo

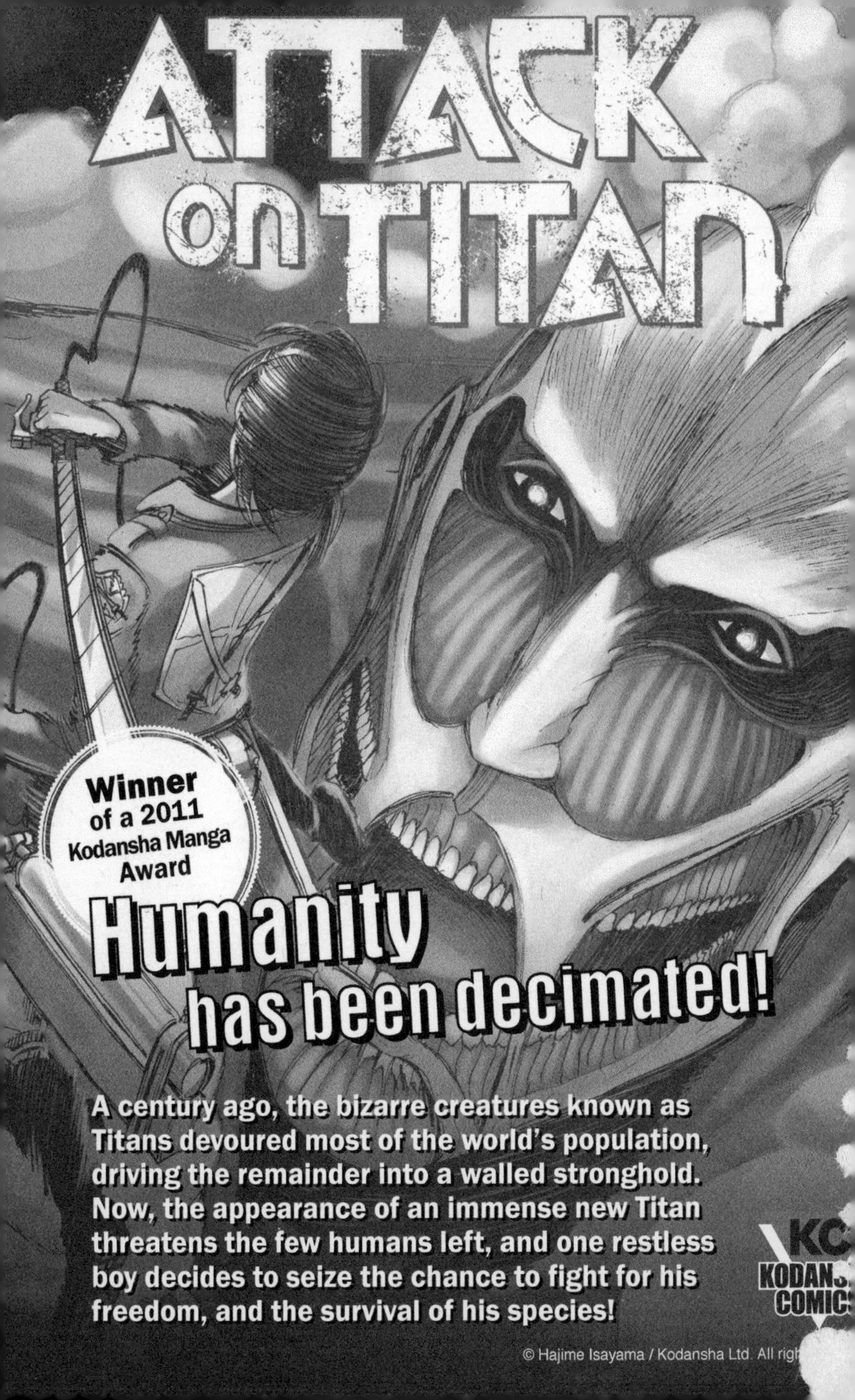
ATTACK ON TITAN
Winner of a 2011 Kodansha Manga Award
Humanity has been decimated!
A century ago, the bizarre creatures known as Titans devoured most of the world's population, driving the remainder into a walled stronghold. Now, the appearance of an immense new Titan threatens the few humans left, and one restless boy decides to seize the chance to fight for his freedom, and the survival of his species!
© Hajime Isayama / Kodansha Ltd. All righ

A Kodansha Comics Trade Paperback Original.

Sankarea volume 4 copyright © 2011 Mitsuru Hattori
English translation copyright © 2013 Mitsuru Hattori

Published in the United States by Kodansha Comics, an imprint of Kodansha USA Publishing, LLC, New York.

Publication rights for this English edition arranged through Kodansha Ltd., Tokyo.

First published in Japan in 2011 by Kodansha Ltd., Tokyo, as *Sankarea*, volume 4.

ISBN 978-1-61262-354-2

Printed in the United States of America.

www.kodanshacomics.com

9 8 7 6 5 4 3 2 1

Translation: Lindsey Akashi
Lettering: Evan Hayden
Editing: Ben Applegate